TRANSFORMING LABOUR: WOMEN AND WORK IN POST-WAR CANADA

The increased participation of women in the labour force was one of the most significant changes to Canadian social life during the quarter century after the close of the Second World War. *Transforming Labour* offers one of the first critical assessments of women's paid labour in this era, a period when more and more women, particularly those with families, were going 'out to work.'

Using case studies from across Canada, Joan Sangster explores a range of themes, including women's experiences within unions, Aboriginal women's changing patterns of work, and the challenges faced by immigrant women. By charting women's own efforts to ameliorate their work lives as well as factors that reshaped the labour force, Sangster challenges the commonplace perception of this era as one of conformity, domesticity for women, and feminist inactivity. Working women's collective grievances fuelled their desire for change, culminating in challenges to the status quo in the 1960s, when they voiced their discontent and called for a new world of work and better opportunities for themselves and their daughters.

JOAN SANGSTER is a professor in the Departments of History and Women's Studies at Trent University.

JOAN SANGSTER

Transforming Labour
Women and Work in Post-war Canada

UNIVERSITY OF TORONTO PRESS
Toronto   Buffalo   London

ISBN 978-0-8020-9711-8 (cloth)
ISBN 978-0-8020-9652-4 (paper)

Library and Archives Canada Cataloguing in Publication

Sangster, Joan, 1952–
    Transforming labour: women and work in post-war Canada / Joan Sangster.

    Includes bibliographical references and index.
    ISBN 978-0-8020-9711-8 (bound)   ISBN 978-0-8020-9652-4 (pbk.)

    1. Women – Employment – Canada – History – 20th century. 2. Women –
    Canada – Social conditions – 20th century. I. Title.

    HD6099.S25 2010   331.40971'09045   C2009-900380-2

University of Toronto Press acknowledges the financial assistance to
its publishing program of the Canada Council for the Arts and the
Ontario Arts Council.

  Canada Council   Conseil des Arts    ONTARIO ARTS COUNCIL
           for the Arts   du Canada   CONSEIL DES ARTS DE L'ONTARIO

University of Toronto Press acknowledges the financial support for
its publishing activities of the Government of Canada through the
Book Publishing Industry Development Program (BPIDP).

This book has been published with the help of a grant from the Canadian
Federation for the Humanities and Social Sciences, through the Aid
to Scholarly Publications Programme, using funds provided by the
Social Sciences and Humanities Research Council of Canada.

Contents

Acknowledgments

At the very beginning of this project, longer ago than I care to admit, Trent University provided important seed money to kick start my research through internal research funds; I am thankful for that grant, and the ongoing administrative aid of the Research office of Trent University. SSHRC funds aided this project on two fronts: first, a SSHRC standard research grant aided my archival research, and second, this book was published with the help of a grant from the Canadian Federation for the Humanities and Social Sciences, through the Aid to Scholarly Publications Program, using funds from SSHRC. Above all, I am grateful for the support of a Killam Research Fellowship which provided the essential time release that allowed me to complete this book – without the Killam, I imagine I would still be plodding through chapter 4.

A number of Trent and Carleton graduate students, Emily Arrowsmith, Will Knight, Ted McCoy, and Kelly Pineault, provided excellent research aid, and Maggie Quirt was an exceptional help with copyediting. Sanya Pleshakov, Marc Ouiment, and Aaron Berkowitz also sent me archival material gathered in Montreal and at the Wisconsin State Historical Society. I thank also the Institute for the Study of Canada at McGill University for awarding me the Seagram Visiting Chair in 2002–2003, and thus the opportunity to spend time in the HEC archives where the Dupuis Frères Fonds are held. My association with the Frost Centre at Trent University during much of the gestation of this project provided a stimulating atmosphere in which to work, pleasant teaching collaborations with colleagues at Carleton, including François Rocher, (now at Ottawa University), and contact with some wonderful graduate students. I am especially thankful to Donica Belisle, Meaghan Beaton, David Hugill, Geoffrey Korfman, Caroline Langill, Ted McCoy, Christine McLaughlin,

Brian Thorn, and Kelly Pineault for our diversionary trips to Tim Horton's, and our many discussions about history and politics. At Trent, I've also been very lucky to be part of a congenial and lively group of Canadian historians in the History Department, all of whom are a pleasure to work with: Dimitry Anastakis, Chris Dummitt, Janet Miron, and a very old friend, Keith Walden.

From the very beginning of the publishing process, Len Husband of the University of Toronto Press has been a model editor to work with, and I thank him for his unfailing backing of this project. Many wonderful academic colleagues contributed to the development of this manuscript with their support and comments. Veronica Strong-Boag provided invaluable comments on my Killam application; Leah Vosko, Bill Waiser, Andrée Lévesque, the Toronto Legal History Group, and Bryan Palmer all read and commented on chapters or pieces of chapters; and Tina Simmons offered remarks on a longer piece on beauty pageants presented at a labour history conference. Cindy Loch-Drake helped me sort out statistical information on meatpackers, Jane Arscott shared her knowledge of the Royal Commission on the Status of Women with me, and Kate Sangster-Poole attempted to teach me the mysteries of Lexis Nexis in order to search for legal decisions on grievances. Over the course of writing, my ideas on feminism and labour history have been nurtured in many good conversations with Betsy Jameson. I am indebted to many other colleagues who offered moral and intellectual encouragement, as well as important academic leads during the process of researching and writing this book: Constance Backhouse, Linda Briskin, Sarah Carter, Magda Fahrni, Alvin Finkel, Amanda Glasbeek, Linda Kealey, Greg Kealey, Valerie Korinek, June Hannam, Stephen Lee, Mark Leier, Heather Murray, Wade Matthews, John Milloy, Tamara Myers, Mary Jo Nadeau, Silke Neunsinger, Karen Teeple, and Brian Young. Carol Williams was a marvellous colleague to co-organize a workshop on Indigenous women's labour with, and I thank all the participants, especially Marlene Brant Castellano, for their comments on my writing on Aboriginal women and work. In the later stages of this book, I directed a SSHRC-funded Working Lives Research Cluster, and I am very grateful to Jeff Taylor for his unfailing work on that project.

The final revisions to the manuscript were completed while I was in the United States in 2008–9. Sue Cobble, from Rutgers University, made my stay in Princeton very enjoyable, and at Duke University, Jolie Olcott, Jane Moss, and John Thompson provided good conversation. I am particularly thankful to Alice Kessler-Harris for her kind mentoring and long-standing support of my work. My time as an associate editor of *Labor: Studies in Working Class History of the Americas* has provided me with a very rewarding opportunity to interact with Latin American and US labour historians, particularly Leon Fink, Eileen Boris, John French, Julie Greene, Susan Levine, Shel Stromquist, and Jim Barrett. Some of them may suspect I harbour some politically incorrect nationalist tendencies in these transnational times. I hope this book suggests that we can do histories based in the archives of one nation that nonetheless resonate across national borders.

While I laboured over my chapter on grievances, I became involved in a grievance issue, later a libel action, involving my own union. In this sad case of life imitating – or perhaps mocking – one's writing, the benefits and perils of trade-union politics were brought into bold relief for me. It was a depressing experience for those of us committed to the social justice unions should deliver, to the academic freedom they are supposed to protect, and to the leadership they ideally need. While few of these were in evidence, my faith in political integrity and honesty was kept alive by a few good colleagues including Peter Dawson, Bryan Palmer, Gillian Balfour, and Mary Jo Nadeau. I thank Gillian and Mary Jo especially for their friendship during trying times.

Books are written not only in an intellectual and academic context, but in a personal one as well, and without the love and support – and sometimes sceptical ribbing – of my family, I can't imagine that my work would hold as much pleasure and meaning as it does. I am extraordinarily lucky that my intellectual and personal lives overlap in my partnership with Bryan Palmer, with whom I have shared my thoughts on this book, on politics, and on history more generally, for more than a decade. This is not to say that our political perspectives are always simpatico; but intellectual differences can be enlivening and stimulating, and his support for the project at the heart of my work – creating a feminist labour history – has always been unwavering. I sometimes feel as if he writes books faster than I can read them, but I know we work to different rhythms, creating different kinds of history, while supporting each other with love and affection. I count it our good fortune that we are finally together in the same city: with him close, as Bruce says, 'these are better days it's true.' Our children, Kate, Laura, Rob, and Beth are now all away from home, following their own different intellectual and political paths, which we follow with great pride and interest. They remain a joy, even when they sigh and commiserate over their parents' outdated Left lifestyle.

As I wrote this book, I found myself sometimes reflecting on my own memories of the post-war years, on what it meant to grow up in a time of contradictory messages to girls and women, not only about education and work, but also about the family, in real life often falling short of its over-idealized popular image. I want to thank my older sisters, Carol and Wendy, for weathering those times together, for their unfailing support over the years. We grew up as baby boomers, and experienced, first hand, the promise, the opportunity, but also the disquieting contradictions of life in the post-war interregnum. This book is for them.

TRANSFORMING LABOUR: WOMEN AND WORK
IN POST-WAR CANADA

Introduction

When I first began writing labour history thirty years ago, I could never have imagined researching this book. The subject was too close to the present, too close to my own childhood. In the 1970s, I was only beginning to puzzle through what feminist politics, women's history, and socialism meant. Then, I might have perceived women's labour activism of the 1950s quite differently, perhaps as overdetermined and constrained by the prevailing ideology of femininity. After all, we were trying to escape our mothers' lives, escape the prescribed femininity and domesticity doled out in home economics classes, and escape the meek politics of respectable social democracy. We wanted to build a politics of radical transformation and new lives of possibility and equality.[1]

Those dreams of transforming women's lives have yet to be fulfilled. I am not one of those baby boomers who looks back on the 'long sixties' and tut-tuts our political naivety and foolishness in imagining radical change, but I do recognize that my scholarly and political perspectives have shifted. I may now have more empathy for women of my mother's generation, more understanding of the struggles they faced, and more awareness that they were living through significant changes in women's working lives. Of course, perhaps it is simply the knowledge that we have now become what our daughters wish to escape that has altered my perspective.

Many women, I now realize, while not self-described feminists, felt quite deeply the contradictions and inequalities in their work lives. As one homemaker wrote privately in 1968 to the Royal Commission on the Status of Women (RCSW), 'married women with children' are now at a 'crossroads ... [They] are in the unenviable position of being 'damned if they do, damned if they don't. On the one hand, we hear about the damaging effects on the family unit if the mother goes out to work,' and on the other hand, 'we are being constantly urged to make more use of our potential.'[2] Single mothers writing to the commission, who supported their children on meagre 'women's wages' did not have the luxury of this choice, but they too felt the unfairness of an economic system that did not compensate them as breadwinners, and the restrictions of a familial ideology that made their children 'third-class oddities' because they had single working mothers.[3]

The post-war period looked very different in 1974, the year I graduated from university. The first ripples of an oil price crunch had generated some government budget cuts to social services and education. These cutbacks seemed so shocking in 1973 that our radical student union, with a Trotskyist as the president, shut down the university for a day to debate the cuts. Little did we know that this 'crisis' in capitalism would become normalized and, as a result, that the state would move decisively away from a Keynesian compromise; that welfare-state principles of universality and entitlement would be whittled away; and that education costs would be placed more squarely on students' heads, making the limited democratization of education that my generation had briefly enjoyed even more limited. These 1974 cutbacks signalled what we would later call the beginning of the end of the post-war Fordist accord or 'accommodation,' the tacit agreement between capital, the state, and the established labour movement that gave labour some important legal protections, and capital the stability it needed to Taylorize production, augment productivity, and sustain profits. Always a double-edged sword offering labour very real benefits but also constraints, this accord was based on the assumption that increased consumption would ensure both rising wages and profits, that respectable organized labour would support an anti-communist offensive within the labour movement, and that North American capital would remain a dominant force in the world.[4]

Those of us who became involved in socialist and labour politics did not immediately absorb the extent of change occurring – or perhaps we did not want to see it – until the early 1980s. By then, many women who had fought their way into non-traditional work were laid off. Public-sector unions, which had only recently secured the right to strike, were fighting a rearguard state action to limit their power, and a new term, the 'feminization of poverty' had emerged, a reference to the growing income spread between 'haves' and 'have-nots' that would increase over the 1990s. The last twenty-five years of the century have been characterized, in contrast to the Fordist period, as an era of 'competitive austerity,'[5] in which the promise of permanent, full-time paid work has begun to unravel, and, in the context of intensified global competitiveness and state deregulation, more precarious, flexible employment has emerged in its place.

This narrative of decline is, however, problematic, for it assumes there was a decisive break between the post-war era and the post-1970s crumbling of the accord. Some critics, feminists among them, are not so sure that a 'virtuous circle'[6] of growth characterized the twenty-five years after the war's end, and warn that a 'golden age' perspective masks continuities in the pre- and post-1970s economy. Most important, such an outlook obscures the experiences of female, immigrant, and racialized workers. I would certainly concur. Fordism, however, remains useful as a historical label, even if the contention that post-Fordism was a 'radical break' with the past is less salient.[7] After all, the accord was not a figment of our imagination: it worked reasonably well for some powerful sectors of the economy, usually mass production work, and, as the chapter on grievances indicates, the legal changes it ushered in had a broader impact on the 'rules of the game' in the workplace. Those workers benefitting from this arrangement may have been the exception, but the security the accord seemed to promise also became an important goal and symbol for other workers. Moreover, the accord's assumption of a male breadwinner ethic structured other key elements of the welfare state, such as unemployment insurance and welfare provision, and its emphasis on consumer power became a driving force in union bargaining. As Lizabeth Cohen argues for the United States, however, such bargaining ultimately produced some negative consequences for women workers.[8]

Furthermore, the term 'accord' should not be equated with quiescence. The achievement of industrial legality (the right to bargain collectively with employers) after the Second World War was obtained after immense struggle, and was rather grudgingly offered by capital and the state.[9] Nor did it suddenly put the lid on all class conflict: tensions, disagreements, and, by the 1960s, outbursts of angry rebellion were also part of post-war labour history. Perhaps scholarship has concentrated inordinately on the death of the accord because it became a symbol of what some workers had fought for, but also lost.[10] The post-1945 period may not have been a golden age, but the more recent decline in union density, along with the concurrent intensification of work, and worldwide emphasis on the rights of capital, does indicate a depressingly successful attack on workers' rights.

Focusing too intently on the accord, however, problematically re-creates a labour history that privileges certain regions of Canada, and especially white, male workers, the main beneficiaries of post-war unionization. The accord was premised on what Leah Vosko calls the 'standard employment relation' (SER), equated with permanent, full-year, long-term jobs, often with one employer, and carrying benefits linked to the job; married women were assumed to be working in the home, supported by their husbands' wages.[11] This SER may have been a normative ideal, but it was not necessarily the norm. Fordism was also characterized by a 'second tier'[12] labour force within Canada: those workers without the security, pay, and entitlements enjoyed by the better-paid, permanent unionized workers. Many of these workers, though not all, were also more likely to be found in the 'have not' regions of the country, where multiple jobs and forms of labour were patched together for a living. Capital's search for more flexible, contingent labour, while equated with more recent times, was therefore already present in the 'af-fluent' post-war period, even if it has taken on more concerted, intense, and brutal characteristics in the latter part of the twentieth century.

As the importation of European women as contract labour, described in chapter 2, indicates, the state saw some groups of non-citizen workers as flexible and expendable, even if immigrant workers themselves had other hopes for their lives in their new country. International migration, often from poorer areas of war-torn Europe, provided a reserve of low-paid, flexible labour that was crucial for the expanding economy and a secure rate of profit.[13] The post-war accord was thus also premised on the tacit assumption that some new Canadian workers would have more cir-cumscribed work opportunities and mobility; many immigrant families relied not on a male breadwinner, but on the pooled resources of the family wage economy. This second tier of labour was also gendered fe-male. Contingent (part-time, insecure) work for women blossomed dur-ing the post-war period; employment agencies such as Drake Personnel and Kelly Girl, for instance, drew in women who could not obtain perma-nent work because of a continuing marriage bar set by employers, or because they had to combine both home and wage labour. Moreover, the labour of these 'white collar wives'[14] was premised in turn on the im-portation of immigrant women who would pick up the jobs in domestic, manufacturing, and service work that these women wished to escape, a point made in the chapter on immigration.

As the last example indicates, the Fordist period was characterized by a significant change in the gender composition of the paid labour force, and over time this transformation had consequences far beyond the workforce, shaping home, family, and reproductive labour, and raising questions about the gendered division of labour, mother work, and the heteronormative family. An increasing 'feminization' of the workforce occurred as a rising percentage of Canadian women went out to work, particularly after marriage and children.[15] As chapter 1 indicates, there were significant differences in women's labour-force participation based on class, immigrant status, ethnicity, race, and age, but the overall theme of feminization was still quite clear. Many working-class families needed a second income simply in order to reproduce themselves; women in professional occupations were staying in the workforce for longer periods; and female-typed jobs were opening up in rapidly expanding and traditional sectors of the workforce. This feminization of work, in a period when a male breadwinner ideal was still strong, reinforces the contention of many historians that the much vaunted affluence of the post-war period was more circumscribed than we often think, and that the reigning cultural ideal of home-bound wives, whether in *Playboy* or on TV sitcoms, was just that – a popular image.

Of course, women had not suddenly discovered 'work.' As many homemakers writing to the RCSW in 1968 tried to point out, they worked too, often with little 'esteem or recognition.'[16] The feminization of the workforce, then, represented a shift in the nature and place of women's labour, sometimes resulting in a difficult double or triple day for women. The dominant scholarly definitions of work, as many feminists have argued, have been saturated with masculinist biases, putting market-related labour at the top of a hierarchy of importance, and women's unpaid, voluntary, and informal labour at the bottom.[17] Feminist political economists have challenged this hierarchy with excellent research on social reproduction (defined here as 'the daily and generational maintenance of working people'), examining its pivotal role in capitalist economies, its significance to family survival, and its relationship to women's paid work.[18] While unpaid familial labour is a theme that weaves itself through some chapters, and is central to my discussion of Aboriginal women, I have focused predominantly on waged labour, and especially that of blue- and white-collar women, in order to probe women's experiences of work as wages became more and more central to their lives, in a period when the 'citizen-worker' stood at the centre of the welfare state entitlement.[19]

Questions about the nature of the Fordist accord have been less central to historical research than to political economy. Nonetheless, a growing literature on the post-war period has resulted in a proliferation of excellent work exploring the welfare state, culture, legal and moral regulation, nationalism, the Cold War, family forms, and youth revolts, to name a few areas of research.[20] As Magda Fahrni and Robert Rutherdale argue, there are some overarching themes that provide a backdrop to this era: the emergence of the welfare state, the rise of nationalism, Cold War politics, urbanization and suburbanization, increased affluence and consumption, the baby boom, and reinvigorated immigration.[21] Within these broad themes, there are some minor interpretive differences: some writing on the welfare state, for example, stresses gender as a defining influence, while other historians and political economists explore the interconnected dynamic of class and gender relations shaping welfare provision.[22] In contrast to earlier scholarship focusing on political life, many social historians are exploring the divisions, differences, and inequalities characterizing post-war Canadian society, demystifying the image of an unmitigated post-war consumer heaven and also making the point that citizenship was always defined in gendered and racialized ways, establishing a hierarchy of 'insiders and outsiders.'[23] Periodization may also be a point of difference. Nancy Christie and Michael Gauvreau, in their work on post-war citizenship, accent shifts in the economy over time, distinguishing the immediate post-war years from a period characterized by increased affluence after the mid-1950s.[24] While I agree that the post-war era was characterized by economic change, including a short depression in 1957–8, I have used Fahrni and Rutherford's more expansive chronology of 'les trente glorieuses' to frame this book, trying to balance general conclusions with some attention to change over time.

A proliferating historical literature on the sixties, including attention to youth radicalism, Red Power, the rise of feminism, and a wildcat labour rebellion, indicates the difficulties of generalizing about this decade in particular, as demands for social change seemed to escalate significantly at the very end of the decade. This was true for the labour feminists described in chapter 7 who spoke out during the RCSW, yet for the rank-and-file meat packers and telephone workers discussed in chapter 5, these movements may not have had a decisive impact until the early 1970s. For the Dupuis Frères department store workers, the 1952 strike, with its frontal challenge to Quebec's political, religious, and economic elite, might have been more of a turning point than events usually associated with the 1960s. In short, periodization is necessary, but always problematic and contestable.

While some American historians have stressed the cultural conservatism and confining gender roles promoted during this period, particularly during the Cold War, a 'revisionist' current has increasingly
challenged this interpretation, pointing to alternative images of 'achiev-
ing' women in the media, to women's continuing paid labour and political activism, and to evidence of women's refusal or negotiation of prescribed gender, sexual, and familial roles.[25] These two approaches are
seldom posed as starkly oppositional and absolute, yet historians often
lean one way or the other, notwithstanding our repeated invocations to
contestation and contradiction in our writing. As my chapter on representations suggests, idealized, popularized images of gender 'norma-
tivity' varied according to who was speaking, and are not to be confused
with reality. However, even if June Cleaver was a figment of the contemporary 'Mad Men's' imagination, the idealized, domesticated femininity
promoted in advertising, film, and magazines had an ideological influence, always existing in tension with women's actual working lives. Like
the labour-movement beauty contests described in chapter 1, an idealized, heteronormative femininity fostered class-based, racialized, and
gendered images of desirable bodies and working-class womanhood that
implied women's paid labour might be less important than their romantic and familial goals. As Joy Parr argues in a collection on Ontario post-
war women, despite ample evidence of women's activism, this was still a
period of 'fear, conformity, consensus and denial.'[26]

Canadian writing on women's paid work has contributed to this revisionist view of the post-war years with studies of women's unionization,
workplace cultures, and immigrant labour.[27] As in the American literature, there have been important attempts to decentre the prevailing historical emphasis on white working women,[28] though notions of 'race'
and race politics obviously played out quite differently in the United
States. Indeed, while there were similarities between working women's
experiences in the United States and Canada – not the least because of
international unions that spanned the border – there were also diver-
gences in our histories and historiographies. The linguistic and cultural
divide of English and French was particular to Canada, while the civil
rights movement in the United States arguably had a more powerful
influence on labour women's struggles for equality in the 1950s and
1960s.[29] Labour feminists (trade unionists promoting gender equality)
were presumably a less organized group in Canada than in the United
States during this post-war period, due to our significantly smaller labour
movement, the lack of a long-standing federal Women's Bureau able to

unify union women around one agenda, and the reality that labour women were also pouring their energies into the CCF (Co-operative Commonwealth Federation) party.[30]

Transforming Labour is meant to build on this revisionist strain of historiography, deepening our understanding of women's labour in the post-war period through case studies constructed around debates, themes, occupations, and events that typify one aspect of the changing landscape for working women in this period. Given the importance of the mass media, I begin with an examination of representations of working women in a range of print publications, showing how these images existed in tension with the daily realities of working women's lives. Another key aspect of the broader political and ideological context of the post-war years was the fear and anxiety generated by the Cold War, resulting in the persecution of any and all suspected communists in the labour movement: the result was a 'political chill' that suppressed dissent and radical ideas, creating an inhospitable climate for progressive coalitions in particular, and labour feminism more generally.

This book also contributes to a gendering of the Fordist accord by examining women workers in 'growth' areas of the post-war economy, such as service and white-collar labour. Using the example of a Montreal department store, Dupuis Frères, I explore the regulation, experiences, and protests of women in the retail sector, whose bodily labour incorporated emotional and aesthetic as well as physical exertion. While many service workers extracted few advantages from the Fordist accord, the unionized women presented in chapter 5 tended to be more direct beneficiaries of industrial legalism. This is well illustrated by their utilization of newly secured grievance systems, though even here, the legal processes involved were saturated with gendered assumptions. The limited gains of Fordism have to be balanced by a discussion of women with fewer work choices, those making up that 'second tier' of jobs and occupations in the accord. This was true of the European immigrant women recruited for contract labour, discussed in chapter 2, as well as of the Aboriginal women who attempted to sustain themselves, their families, and communities, often in the face of worsening economic conditions, with their unpaid and paid labour. Both the latter examples also raise questions about the ways in which state policies contributed to the racializing and gendering of work. Last, but not least, the second-class employment status many women endured did not go unchallenged: women's changing consciousness, their desire for equal entitlement, and their expressions of discontent were expressed quite clearly in union briefs and women's testimony before the Royal Commission on the Status of Women.

In the following chapters, there is a strong emphasis on labour-movement history, still largely unexplored for this period, yet important because unions were a key 'social space'[31] where workers addressed transformations in the workforce. Even still, I have barely scratched the surface of a diverse and complex history yet to be reclaimed. There are many topics I do not attempt to address – women in the professions, and in criminalized work, domestic labourers, public-sector unionism, and seasonal resource workers, for instance. Methodologically, I have also concentrated on the retrieval and analysis of documentary, media, and archival sources, though these range broadly from union and government-collected records to legal cases, the popular press, and ethnographic writing. Every source presents its own partialities and interpretive dilemmas, but taken together, interrogated against each other, and viewed critically in the context of their own provenance, intent, assumptions, and voice, they offer the possibility of piecing together a picture of women's paid work in post-war Canada.

Some basic questions raised by political economy, feminism, and historical materialism were useful starting points for my research: What were the social and economic conditions in which women's labouring lives were embedded? How did working people negotiate, accommodate, understand, and resist changes in social and material life, drawing on the cultural and ideological resources at hand? How did class, gender, and other social relations 'interpenetrate each other' in this changing historical context?[32] Cumulatively, these questions assume the historical significance of capitalist accumulation, colonialism, and state initiatives, while also recognizing that ideology, culture, and human agency were integral to the nature of class, gender, and race relationships.

Class, race, and gender are now almost routinely described as mutually constituted, a recognition that women's lives are not lived out as separate categories of difference, yet exactly how these 'macro systems' are linked and reproduced is sometimes left unexplored.[33] Intersectionality offers an appealing vocabulary that seems to move us beyond an 'add-on' analysis of multiple oppressions, by paying attention to the mutually constituted points of difference – and power relations – experienced by women. However, at one end of the spectrum of intersectionality writing, all categories of analysis are deconstructed, and key ontological differences between kinds of inequality – race, class, gender – are occluded. Notably, class relations are often sidelined, or erroneously portrayed as an identity, undifferentiated in nature from other identities of race, gender, or sexual orientation.[34] In order to understand women, gender, and work, suggests Joan Acker, it is still necessary to acknowledge the importance of class formation as a process that is gendered and racialized, starting with excavations of women's experiences, and developing an understanding of social interaction that is simultaneously historical, materialist, and feminist.[35]

Feminist political economy provides useful insights in this regard. It has built on political economy's assumption that material conditions are a 'starting point' for social analysis, but rather than accepting class as the (over)determining category of analysis, it insists that other hierarchies and oppressions, both within and across class relations, be addressed as well. 'Gender, race, [and] sexuality,' as Gillian Creese and Daiva Stasiulis argue, must also be seen as part of the 'material.'[36] Class formation is always mediated by gender and race relations, and while theoretically distinct, these categories are actually inseparable. One might pull out gender or 'race' as a dominant thread of analysis, but they will always be interwoven with class in our lived social relations. There may be a tendency in feminist political economy to operate at a higher level of theoretical abstraction, to emphasize structural analyses, and to provide a 'macro' view of social relations. After years of postmodern writing that doubts or derides structural relations and notions of social causality – even the term 'social determination' is now viewed as gauchely economistic – this emphasis on the 'macro' has the benefit of providing a corrective to excessively linguistic or idealist views of the past.[37] Structures do matter, not in a deterministic sense, but rather in a contextual one; moreover, structures are always undergoing processes of composition and re-composition.[38] If political economy has erred on the side of structure and theoretical abstraction, paying less attention to human agency and subjectivity, one answer is the connection of political-economy questions with feminist historical materialism. Feminist historians may place more emphasis on interpretations drawn from the accumulated evidence of women's daily lives, and on the integration of culture, belief, and tradition into the process of class formation; feminist political economists may accent macro social structures of gender, race, and class relations; however combined together, both material structure and human agency, social formations and lived experience, become part of a whole, and integral to our analysis.

Feminist historical materialists, while far from being a homogeneous group, often stress the importance of theorizing through empirically based studies of women's daily lives and labour,[39] or through the 'excavation' of gender and race from women's embodied, everyday activities.'[40] This 'Marxist method,' as Martha Gimenez argues, involves a search for the 'origins' of social phenomena, but it also entails the questioning all aspects of 'reality' that seem 'concrete and obvious,' insisting that the conditions of their possibility be the focus of investigation: empirical research and theoretical questions are thus always in critical dialogue.[41] While few materialist feminists lay claim to a 'scientific' reading of Marx, neither are they averse to all 'truth claims.' One can speak of 'kernels of truth,' suggests Hennessy, about the determining logic and inherently exploitive relations of capitalist and colonial relations, assuming that 'the cultural and political expressions of society will be marked by this kernel of human relationships.'[42] While anathema to some postmodernists, I would argue this is one element of historical materialism not to be jettisoned, nor need it mean we are unaware of our own interpretive influence, or simply assume that women's past experiences are unmediated, easily readable reflections of reality.

For materialist-feminists, class and gender formation are perceived as processes that are embedded in historically changing and specific material contexts, but that also encompass human agency, culture, and ideology. A 'dialectical dialogue'[43] between social being and social consciousness is assumed; indeed, within this nexus, there may still be tensions, contradictions, or dissonances that emerge between human subjects' being in the world, and their contemplations of it.[44] To suggest the possibility that women and workers – as well as historians – might reflect critically on these dissonances, stepping back temporarily from the dominant norms, even subverting them, does take for granted more 'traditional' (but still relevant) categories of feminist theory and Thompsonian social history: the importance of human agency and experience, and the positive possibilities of social transformation.

While the impact of post-structuralist and linguistic theories on feminist writing is undeniable, so much so that, as Barbara Foley argues, these assumptions have subtly pervaded the 'groundwater of critical theory,'[45] materialist assumptions concerning working-class experience have proved somewhat resilient, even if they have not necessarily been vigorously defended – perhaps because Marxist writers have been so clearly on the defensive over the past two decades. However, in the eyes of some feminist theorists and historians of the working class, experience is not a completely flawed or discredited concept, to be relegated to the epistemological trash heap. The postmodern critique of experience as a flawed foundational concept, a 'linguistic event that does not happen outside established meanings,'[46] has been the subject of recent challenges from scholars ranging from existential feminists to Marxists and liberals. Some, for example, dispute a history in which discourses are inescapable 'closed circuits' of meaning shaping our interpretations of the world; others point to a distressing tendency to portray historical subjects as no more than 'vectors' for ideology/discourse.[47] These recent attempts at recuperation and re-theorization suggest a more generalized disquiet or exhaustion with pessimistic denials of agency, 'historical reason,' and our ability to think outside the pressures of discursive possibilities. 'De-legitimizing a theoretical project that explores linkages between social location and identity,' post-positivist realist critiques warn, obviously has immense problems for those recuperating the history of the marginalized or subaltern. While granting that experience is always mediated through culture, they still see it as a 'cognitive process that can render relatively 'true' and objective knowledge' – recognizing that objectivity is not neutrality.[48]

Like these critics, I do not think the concept of experience has been effectively 'disposed of'[49] by postmodern critiques. 'Experience' remains useful to the writing of women's labour history if we explore it as a layered process that is both lived and construed; as both a point of origin and as discursively constructed; as a dialectic of both 'first and third person' perspectives.[50] If viewed with the reflective scepticism that is central to all historical research, it need not be 'put on a pedestal,'[51] reified, or taken as self-evident. Materialist feminist writers are quite aware of problems with a false notion of neutral objectivity, on the one hand, and the perils of complete relativism, on the other hand: 'doing' history often involves walking a tightrope between the two.[52] We can reflect critically on the way in which our methods, sources, and the interpretive frameworks available shape our writing, yet also make political-ethical judgments about our subjects' experience of oppression and exploitation. If we dismiss the complaints, voices, and actions of workers in the past as little more than rhetorical devices, discursive possibilities, or one of many contending perspectives of the time, the concepts of exploitation, oppression, and justice become rather meaningless.[53] I believe the political *sensibilities* that helped create a 'new' labour history at precisely the chronological moment this book ends, in the 1970s, remain relevant today. Our attempt to write histories that see the working class not merely as a structured abstraction from above, but also as historical subjects, that probe both changing material conditions but also the 'minds and feelings'[54] of workers, and that offer a critique of the structures of class, gender, and colonial power, but also contemplate how they might be challenged, are still of critical importance.

Chapter 1

Representations and Realities: The Shifting Boundaries of Women's Work

In the 1950s, a woman going out to work to pack sausages, empty bed-pans, type memos, or wait on tables was confronted with an array of diverse and sometimes conflicting images of herself as a 'worker.' While some union publications stressed a woman's common interests with her union brothers, many also conveyed her femininity, her role as home-maker, and her sexuality, exemplified by pictures of union-sponsored beauty queen contests. Popular magazines debated the positive and negatives consequences of married women with families working outside the home, while the business press ruminated on the role of such women in the new consumer society. A very small, emerging state bureaucracy concerned with women, such as federal and provincial women's bureaus, charted the rapid increase in the number of married women workers, and asked repeatedly: Why did they work?[1] Women who worked for wages permanently, temporarily, or intermittently might be forgiven for feeling uncertain about which part of their identity to embrace: wage worker or homemaker, beauty object or union leader?

But were women confused by this array of seemingly dichotomous images? Did their negotiation of gender, class, and cultural loyalties perhaps draw comfortably on, and integrate, multiple points of identity? For most working-class, and many middle-class, women who came of age during the Depression and the war years, work for wages at some point in their lives was taken for granted. The change in women's work that so fascinated observers in the quarter-century after the war was simply the intensification of this commitment to the labour force, especially for married women with children. Responding to federal Women's Bureau surveys, the majority of these women asserted that their wages were ne-cessary to the family economy, yet many also felt compelled to justify,

Gleason

excuse, and apologize for their labour outside the home. It is one of the seeming contradictions of this period that, even though more women were going out to work, popular culture exalted the connection between domesticity and femininity, and many psychological experts promoted women's full-time role in guarding the health of the nuclear, hetero-normative family. As Mona Gleason shows, the reigning psychological paradigms of the era designated the stay-at-home mother as the norm, and also the best way to produce healthy children, good schooling, and sound families.[2]

Revisionist historians have argued persuasively that this 'Leave It to Beaver' culture of happy patriarchal families and female domesticity was never as hegemonic as popular culture suggested, or as widespread as nostalgic reactionaries would have us believe.[3] Unlike June Cleaver, women were working outside the home, organizing, advocating, and unionizing in these years. Liberal, social democratic, and communist women continued to mobilize around women's issues, from equal pay to world peace, giving the lie to the characterization of this period as a hopeless 'trough' between two waves of feminism.[4] Still, why do middle-class and working-class women workers with families often remember this era as a time when their work outside the home was devalued? Why did the media feel a debate about working mothers was right for the times? Why did my mother, as I remember quite distinctly, keep her part-time job quiet in the neighbourhood, and why did I equate my day care with maternal abandonment, to be passively resisted by refusing to put clothes on in the morning? Perhaps we should be cautious in our re-visionism, altering, but not completely jettisoning, an interpretive em-phasis on the political conservatism and recommended domesticity of the era: even if women were encouraged to pursue work outside the home, there were always limits and boundaries placed on their work lives. Nor can we take the post-war period as an unchanging whole; there were major differences between exhortations for women to leave their war-time jobs in 1946 and discussions of women's right to work in 1966.

This chapter looks at the changing realities of women's labour-force participation, counterposed to representations of women workers in the mainstream and labour press. To what extent did they overlap, and in what ways did they diverge? Postmodern critiques of the scientific 'fact' will certainly find fault with the apparent dichotomy suggested in this juxtaposition between reality and image. Are not all things ultimately discursively constructed? Certainly, images from the mainstream and union press tell a very partial story, one created to sell magazines or get a union message across, and one also shaped by the dominant ideological proclivities of the period. Nor should we equate prescriptive literature with reality; readers negotiated and interpreted these images in different ways. While it was hardly the case that women obediently followed the advice proffered in the mass media, these images created an atmosphere and climate of opinion that laid out the parameters of what was possible, preferable, or impossible for women. Even if we concede the 'inescapability of representation,' this does not suggest 'nothing is at stake,' for these images had tangible effects on women's worlds.[5] Statistics were also collected and reported in a manner shaped by ideology and politics, but there are, nonetheless, some basic realities captured in the census returns, in Women's Bureau reports, and, indeed, in the changing economic organization of advanced capitalism after 1945. How women's material needs and economic activities were then interpreted was shaped by the dominant gender order, for gender was both implicated in, and constitutive of, class and social relations.[6]

Measuring Women's Work

The most salient fact about women's labour-force participation in the post-war period is that it increased significantly over time. While it is true that over the entire twentieth century women's participation rate, and the ratio of women to men in the labour force, was growing gradually, the increases indicated between the 1941 and 1971 censuses were far steeper. In 1941 women's labour-force participation rate was 20 per cent, by 1961 it was almost 30 per cent, and by 1971 it stood near 40 per cent.

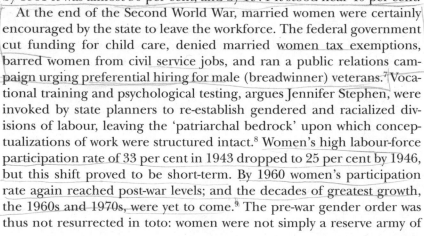

At the end of the Second World War, married women were certainly encouraged by the state to leave the workforce. The federal government cut funding for child care, denied married women tax exemptions, barred women from civil service jobs, and ran a public relations campaign urging preferential hiring for male (breadwinner) veterans.[7] Vocational training and psychological testing, argues Jennifer Stephen, were invoked by state planners to re-establish gendered and racialized divisions of labour, leaving the 'patriarchal bedrock' upon which conceptualizations of work were structured intact.[8] Women's high labour-force participation rate of 33 per cent in 1943 dropped to 25 per cent by 1946, but this shift proved to be short-term. By 1960 women's participation rate again reached post-war levels; and the decades of greatest growth, the 1960s and 1970s, were yet to come.[9] The pre-war gender order was thus not resurrected in toto: women were not simply a reserve army of labour drawn into the workforce during the war; rather, the long-term trend was for more women between thirty-five and fifty-five to return to work. Indeed, their participation rates grew even in bad times when men's rates faltered,[10] despite very clear disincentives, such as the lack of state-legislated maternity leaves and bars on women's entrance to certain professions and government jobs.

The increasing number of married women working for pay was the truly 'revolutionary' change of the post-war period: the married woman worker was becoming a permanent fixture of the labour force, albeit not as a well-paid welder but as a low-paid clerk. While the proportion of married women working for pay remained fairly stable from 1946 to 1952, in every year afterwards there was a sharp rise in the ratio of married to single women workers.[11] Just fewer than 5 per cent of married women worked outside the home in 1941, but by 1961 this figure was 21 per cent, and by 1975 it was 41 per cent.[12] A 'two phase' life cycle of wage work was emerging, as women worked until they were married or had their first child and, after a period outside of the paid labour force, they returned to wage labour when their children were older. This two-phase life cycle took shape amidst demographic changes: in the aftermath of the war, marriage rates soared for the youngest cohort of women, bringing the average age of marriage down by three years, and the 'baby boom' was evident in increased fertility rates, particularly for women under thirty. By the 1970s, and especially the 1980s, the two-phase life cycle was altered again as more women were returning to work soon after a maternity leave. By the end of the 1980s, all 'traces of the reproductive function,'[13] as economists put it rather clinically, were disappearing from women's patterns of paid work. Of course, the likelihood of a woman going out to work varied with her age, marital status, education, and the ages of her children, as well as by region and place of origin. Social class was obviously a crucial predictor in this regard. For married women, a husband's income mattered a great deal: as that rose, women were less likely to work for pay, an equation underscoring trade-union and feminist arguments that women sought wage labour in order to fulfil their own basic economic needs, as well as those of their family.

Social observers who expressed anxieties about the working wife or working mother rarely complained that women were taking away men's jobs unless, very occasionally, the career woman was the focus of their ire. Even these critics would have conceded that women's increasing integration into the labour force was shaped by a sexual division of labour that firmly structured women's work options. 'Women,' as one Women's

Bureau report admitted, 'do not, as a rule, compete in the same labour markets as men.'[14] As the Armstrongs' pivotal study of the early 1980s showed, women were 'segregated into the rapidly growing but frequently low-paid areas of work,' and they were also 'slotted into a limited number of jobs in those industries.'[15] This division of labour was justified in part by a male-breadwinner ideal that was intrinsic to the Fordist accord brokered by the state, business, and organized labour.[16] Women workers were more likely to be in part-time and interrupted employment, in lower wage brackets, and, save for teaching and nursing professionals, in jobs with fewer benefits and less security. Whether one attributed gender segregation, as mainstream economists later did, to the hierarchical power of 'gender queues,' or, following Marxists, to gendered ideologies coupled with patterns of capital accumulation,[17] the evidence that work was profoundly bifurcated by gender was quite stark and indisputable.

The post-war economic expansion encouraged the use of female labour in service jobs, while a rising standard of consumption and falling real wages by the 1960s meant that two incomes were often required in many working-class households. Moreover, in the immediate post-war years, a lower birth rate during the Depression had created a small demographic shortage of single women joining the workforce to fill jobs designated as female. By the 1960s, economic growth contracted in primary industries like mining, while it expanded in community, business, and personal services, where a multitude of pink- and white-collar jobs were filled by women. While women workers did find jobs in manufacturing, particularly in textiles, food production, and garment making, they were increasingly labouring in three large areas: finance, trade, and service, and within these areas, in a small range of sex-typed jobs. The one area of decline was personal domestic service, always a 'last choice' for many women, so much so that the federal government turned to temporary labour and immigration recruitment from the Caribbean and Europe to fill these positions.[18] More than half of all women worked in ten occupations – for example, as waitresses, typists, or store clerks – and within areas such as retail sales there was intensive sex-typing: men sold beer, women sold shoes, women were cashiers and clerks, while men had higher-paid sales positions.[19]

Clerical work provided a dramatic example of both occupational shifts and the sex-typing of jobs, indicating a persisting racialized-gendered division of labour: between 1940 and 1950, clerical work shifted from male-dominated to female-dominated, though within that sector, a gendered and racialized hierarchy was maintained.[20] Segregation was even more pronounced for those born outside Canada: one third of all immigrant women were located in service labour and in 'product fabrication' such as garment work.[21] The same division of labour was found in the rapidly growing state sector (the public service, hospitals, schools, social services, and so on), which was one of the most important areas of employment for women.

Women's work in the service sector was often designated as low in productivity by economists, and it was certainly remunerated with lower pay than for men, a fact noted again and again in statistical studies of the period. Sex-related compensation went hand-in-hand with sex-typed jobs, with the result that women's wages were, on average, 25 to 35 per cent lower than men's. During the 1950s and 1960s, women's lower wages were taken for granted by many economists as an indication of job worth, or as the rational operation of a dual-track labour market in which women were temporary sojourners in the workforce. Even feminists in the 1950s arguing for equal-pay laws put enormous faith in scientific job evaluation schemes that, as later feminist writers have shown, were saturated with socially constructed and gendered notions of skill and worth.[22]

Rationales for differing wage remuneration did vary. Owners and managers justified women's lower wages by pointing to their family responsibilities, absenteeism, inability to take on supervision, lack of technical skills, and temporary stay in the workforce. Some even referred to women's innate character traits, such as their intense emotional nature. In 1970 the Royal Commission on the Status of Women (RCSW), reflecting its liberal-feminist orientation, gave these explanations a public and critical airing, substituting their own explanations that stressed discriminatory attitudes and prejudices against women in the workplace. More conservative commentators, however, continued to put forth human-capital theories that rationalized women's secondary status in the labour force as a logical result of low skills, resources, and education. Few explanations, save within the political left, explained sex-typing with a more radical critique of capitalism, and until the explosion of feminist research after the late 1960s, the left often reiterated Marxist orthodoxies that saw a functional fit between capital and women's lower wages, and avoided a discussion of social reproduction.[23]

Management strategies did play a key role in labelling jobs as 'female' when they were being feminized for economic reasons. The wider social context for these management decisions, as Gillian Creese argues, was also important.[24] Material and ideological forces reinforced and reproduced management-designed divisions in a multitude of ways, through institutional practices of unions, and through the ingrained ideas, actions, and customs of men and women on the job, and at home. Gender segregation and pay differentials did not go entirely uncriticized: some unions decried women's lower pay and insisted this injustice was simply another indication of employers' search for profit. However, unions were more likely to move beyond incensed rhetoric in situations where gendered pay differentials threatened men's pay; if this was not the case, their opposition was less than stellar.

One significant outcome of the Fordist accord was the increased percentage of unionized women, a pattern that accelerated significantly once public-sector collective bargaining rights were granted, generally in the post-1964 period (though in Saskatchewan after 1944). The consolidation of industrial unions during and after the Second World War indisputably aided women in mass-production plants, offering them higher wages and more job security. By 1966, though, women in these international unions were slightly outnumbered by those in national and government-sector unions.[25] Occupational segregation did shape the extent of women's unionization; the high numbers of women working in smaller 'light' manufacturing, service work, and workplaces without strong union traditions – such as retail stores – affected their unionization levels negatively. Until the early 1960s, women constituted about 16 per cent of all union members, a percentage that increased dramatically with public-sector organizing; by 1980, women made up 30 per cent of union members.[26] As recent commentators have noted, increasing female membership (as women unionized more rapidly than men) has staved off some of the decline in union density associated with more recent, neo-liberal times.

Both unionization and labour-force participation also varied by province and region.[27] In the 1960s, Saskatchewan, Quebec, and Alberta claimed a higher density of unionized women workers,[28] but across all provincial borders, women were severely underrepresented in the leadership of all unions. Even at the local level, women were far less likely to occupy executive union positions. In the Canadian Union of Public Employees (CUPE), a union with a high female membership, the 1969 executive board of fifteen had only one woman.[29] The very few women who became executive members in large unions, such as Hugette Plamondon of the United Packing House Workers of America, were seen as exceptions, though they were also made into convenient public examples of the gender blindness of union democracy.

Region also shaped women's occupational and workplace attachment. Higher percentages of manufacturing jobs were located in industrialized central Canada, while more seasonal, service, or resource-linked jobs were the only option for women in the regional 'hinterlands'; and the latter tended to be overlooked in state studies and planning. In fishing communities, women's unpaid shore labour for the family economy or, later, their paid labour in fish processing plants, was often part-time or seasonal. However important their work was to family survival, the 'ideo-logical pre-eminence' of the male 'catcher of fish ... masked women's work,' and since their labour did not approximate the 'standard employ-ment'[30] norm, it was often underrepresented and undervalued by the state. State accounting might also incorporate lingering patriarchal norms into its measure of work; in the Newfoundland fishing industry, for example, male household heads collected women's share of un-employment benefits, assuming a pooled family economy of scarcity.[31]

Race and ethnicity, intertwined with class and gender, also shaped the options, patterns, and place of women's labour. Many studies, including those done for the RCSW, did not effectively integrate ethnicity and race into their analyses of job segregation, despite some emerging concerns expressed by feminists about the double 'disadvantage' of non-Anglo immigrant women in the workforce.[32] Women of colour were a small minority of the population, but racial stratification was still evident in the workforce: on the prairies, Aboriginal women were overrepresented in service work such as waitressing, while in Toronto, African-Canadian women, who constituted less than 1 per cent of the population, were nonetheless clustered in domestic and service jobs. Due to exclusionary immigration policies, there were very few women workers of Asian back-ground, and, after years of racial exclusion in areas such as nursing edu-cation, the number of 'professional' Asian women was still very small.[33]

Immigration policy was used to maintain a predominantly white work-force, at least until the partial 'de-racialization' of immigration policies in the late 1960s.[34] As the next chapter on the importation of women textile workers makes clear, the recruitment of immigrant women was shaped by the needs of employers, the state's understanding of economic development, and preconceived notions of racially and ethnically appro-priate roles for female and male immigrants. The state's goal was always to 'meet labour market needs' without importing such large numbers of people that the 'market' would be 'disrupted,'[35] or the racial complex-ion of the population dramatically altered. Although over two million immigrants arrived in Canada between 1946 and 1961,[36] they were un-evenly distributed across the country; most new job seekers gravitated towards large metropolitan centres such as Montreal, Toronto, and Van-couver, while rural areas and smaller cities were peopled predominantly with the Canadian-born. Whether the census looked at place of origin or ethnicity, these differences were significant: in 1961 83 per cent of Halifax residents designated themselves as being of British or French origin, while in Toronto only 56 per cent did.[37] Until the late 1960s, the large numbers of British, American, and northern European immigrants who arrived in Canada reflected the existing ethnic 'vertical mosaic'[38] of the Canadian power elite. At the same time, the eastern Europeans who had come before the war and the southern Europeans who arrived after the war were altering the face of some large urban centres, which were transformed yet again with increased numbers of immigrants from Asia and the Caribbean in the 1970s and 1980s.

Immigrant women, whatever their ethnic and national background, were more likely to be in the workforce than native-born women, al-though this gap began to narrow gradually after 1961.[39] Moreover, it is also likely that immigrant women were over-represented in the informal economy in areas such as child-minding. The 'two phase' life cycle, with women leaving the workforce between the ages of twenty-five and thirty-four, was also less pronounced for immigrants, whose retreat from paid labour often spelled more difficulty for the family economy.[40] The 'double negative' of being both female and foreign-born, one sociologist argued, put immigrant women in the lowest rungs of the occupational and pay ladders owing to a constellation of systemic factors that included language skills, 'employer discrimination, ethnic-immigration labour markets and sex stratification of the workforce.'[41]

Class, gender, and race/ethnicity interacted as structural and ideo-logical factors shaping immigrants' experiences of work. In the 1950s, all women working in manufacturing tended to be clustered in the lower-paid 'niches' of this category; however, immigrant women were over-represented in manufacturing (as well as consumer services) to begin with. Indeed, almost half of immigrant women laboured in the needle trades, a notoriously low-wage sector.[42] Women immigrants, of course, were not an undifferentiated group. Those who arrived immediately after the war (primarily English-speaking and northern European) had employment histories similar to Canadian-born women, while those who arrived in the mid-1950s, as new regulations encouraged more southern European immigrants, were more likely to be in manufacturing and personal services. Those from historically preferred immigrant groups, usually white and English-speaking, clearly had more employment choices, an indication of how tenacious systemic ethnic and racial hierarchies were in Canadian society.[43] Within immigrant groups, however, class, education, place of origin, and one's mother tongue shaped work options. Well-educated, presumably more middle-class immigrant women, for example, clustered in business and social services, just as did native-born women.[44]

It is perhaps no surprise that the dominant image of working women and the discussion about the 'problem' of the working mother did not reflect the diversity of the female workforce. The National Film Board (NFB) production *Women at Work* was intended to both inform women immigrants about their work prospects and also guarantee viewers that these newcomers would easily 'fit into' Canadian society – a reassurance that had much to do with race and ethnicity. The seventeen women featured are all white, and fifteen come from northern Europe. In the film, these job seekers are aided by an employment counsellor, who goes through her Rolodex of great employment opportunities for women under the categories of 'banking, service work, communications, and clerical work.' The jobs awaiting newcomers are presented in a highly idealized manner: tellers are moving ahead in the 'field of business,' meat wrappers are 'working under ideal conditions,' and clerical workers are thrilled with their company bowling alley. Some women are so well educated that their job placements are – in retrospect – ludicrous: a waitress in a Montreal restaurant, for instance, is highly valued by the management and customers since she 'speaks six languages.' While the film reinforces an image of a white Canada, the women are all still destined for 'appropriate' female jobs.[45]

film
vs
reality

Discussions of women's work by bureaucrats, unionists, and feminists before 1970 revealed other omissions as well. One of the most resounding silences was the discounting of women's unpaid labour. The collection of statistics, shaped by the ideological value put on capitalist productivity, ignored women's unpaid activities that contributed to family enterprises and economies. Some censuses collected data on the labour of women doing unpaid labour for farms and small family enterprises, leaving no mistake that women provided much of this labour. The legal ramifications of this social discounting could be disastrous for divorced women trying to lay some claim to the fruits of their labour: in the famous Irene Murdoch case, a woman whose labour had built the family ranch could not secure her share of this enterprise in her divorce, even though the case went to the Supreme Court.[46] Social reproduction – the intergenerational and daily reproduction of the workforce – was deemed a 'labour of love' with no price tag, obscuring much of women's daily work, a problem that persists today.[47] By the 1960s, the RCSW did try to put a price tag on household labour, claiming that women's housework equalled about 11 per cent of gross national product, or $8 billion.[48] More radical socialist-feminists were by this time demanding wages for housework. These calls for attention to social reproduction as a sine qua non of capitalist accumulation became far more important to feminist theory, but they were not necessarily absorbed into mainstream economic thinking on women's work.

Somewhat contradictorily, the state and policy makers avoided a discussion of social reproduction, yet it was an implicit ingredient of their construction of the standard employment relationship intrinsic to the Fordist accord. Some unions, for example, still urged management not to employ married women; women and men at BC Telephone protested the employment of married women in 1947 when management announced that mounting job vacancies made such hirings necessary.[49] The ideal of the male breadwinner was also assimilated and internalized as an integral ingredient of one's respectable masculine persona. As late as the early 1970s, one male restaurant worker filing a grievance offered a rationale for his case that equated his interests with those of a male management trainee, in opposition to his female co-workers: 'They [the female workers] think seniority is everything … [but] both Louise and Vi do not need the work – they're only supplementing their husband's earnings, working for something to do, whereas the management trainee and myself are working for a living.'[50] It is hard to imagine that Louise and Vi were cooking hamburgers in a hot kitchen for fun rather than for 'a living,' but the idea of women's wage work as equivalent to men's was for some workers still unthinkable. Yet the reality that more and more women were going 'out to work' to support themselves and their families contradicted this resilient image of the breadwinning male head of the household. The tensions inherent in this contradiction were displayed, both visually and textually, in images of women workers in the mainstream as well as the labour press.

Picturing the Woman Worker

Recent studies of post-war Canada have suggested the need for a more precise periodization of the era, distinguishing between the immediate reconstruction period, rising affluence after the mid-1950s, and a period of transition and increased radicalism in the late 1960s.[51] As Valerie Korinek's research on *Chatelaine* (the only English-language Canadian magazine for women) indicates, the 1950s were different in tone from the 1960s, when editor Doris Anderson encouraged more and more articles on social issues and gender equality.[52] A similar alteration occurred in the French *Châtelaine*, even over the course of a decade. From its inception in 1960, *Châtelaine* included discussions of politics, including a forum on Simone de Beauvoir's *The Second Sex*.[53] However, articles on women as homemakers in the early part of the decade were substantially augmented by the late 1960s with discussions of work and careers: one journalist suggested a new future was now emerging for young women, whose dreams included a combination of work and motherhood, not a choice between the two.[54] While debates in mainstream magazines and newspapers – important conduits for knowledge at this time – about the paid labour of married women and mothers shifted over time, they permeated this entire period, and were often linked to other social issues such as marriage, family stability, juvenile delinquency, sexual morality, urban decay, and the Cold War.[55]

Many Canadians also read American-produced magazines for women, in which similar debates took place, although the Cold War seemed an even more prominent anxiety in these publications.[56] While American historians have been sceptical of the extreme, class- and race based rendition of the 'feminine mystique' forwarded by Betty Friedan, some still argue that the 'white mainstream media journalism idealized the stay-at-home wife' and 'stigmatized' those with jobs.[57] After the war, a popular, authoritative Freudian 'ego psychology,' Mary Jo Buhle argues, walked 'hand in hand with popular culture'; femininity and family, psychoanalysts warned in the media, would inevitably be sacrificed on the altar of a career.[58] So too would children's healthy upbringing, according to American paediatric advice guru, Dr Benjamin Spock.[59] Other studies of US print media put more emphasis on attitude shifts over the 1950s and 1960s, or stress revisionist readings, questioning the effectiveness of expert advice and suggesting that magazines' portrayal of successful, public women contradicted the feminine mystique. Some writers also detect cultural suggestions of subterranean female frustration or anger percolating beneath the surface of prescribed images of maternal domesticity and the sexualized 'Girl-woman.'[60] Yet the point that these *were* subterranean and suppressed should not be forgotten.

Figure 1   Huguette Plamondon, an organizer for the United Packing House
Workers, and vice-president of the Canadian Labour Congress, featured in
Maclean's Magazine, December 1956, with the caption 'She's not checking the
quality of the family roast, she's a union organizer in Montreal.' (LAC,
PA3933347, Basil Zarov Fonds, R8134-0-3-F)

Debates in Canadian magazines about the 'unsolvable dilemma of
home and career'[61] did shift over this twenty-five-year period. Near the
end of the Second World War, Canadian reporters began to ask if women
war workers would exit the workforce willingly and retreat to the home.
Although discussion about, and images of, working women during the
war had often implied that women's new roles were temporary, and that
women's loyalty to homemaking would triumph after the Axis powers

were defeated, some writers nonetheless suggested that women should 'be free to choose exactly what they want to do.'[62] Those with feminist inclinations saw the opportunity to question the prevailing gender norms in employment: Why should women teachers be forced to resign on marriage, asked one female writer, since there was no evidence that she suddenly became a bad teacher 'when she donned a wedding ring.'[63] A *Maclean's* investigation reported that over half of the women surveyed wanted to 'continue working,' yet the reporter relied less on these numbers than on her own ideological assumptions. 'Most unmarried women will want to marry,' she surmised, assuming heterosexual coupling was the inevitable goal of all, and, once married, the 'average man' would want the woman to offer her housekeeping work in exchange for his paycheque. Although the article held that women were best suited to some kinds of female labour needing dexterity, many men felt 'women shouldn't earn men's wages, married women shouldn't work, and women workers were unreliable.' The solution, it was hinted, was finding appropriately sex-typed jobs for women,[64] and in one sense, this was precisely what happened.

Feminist calls for post-war employment choices for women were certainly articulated in left-leaning publications such as *The Canadian Forum*, but the more staid and influential *Saturday Night* published anxious denunciations of working wives as the war drew to a close. One such male author attempted to expose the 'fallacy of equal pay for equal work,' noting it was 'dangerous, unjust ... and a sure prelude to race suicide.' Presuming that equal pay would press all wages down, he argued that it was a threat to all but the spinster and bachelor, for it upset the family wage system, forcing a married man to exist on the wages of an unmarried person, and pressing wives to go out to work: the latter would result in juvenile delinquency and family breakdown, or even in people not having children.[65]

By the end of the 1940s, the debate had shifted from the immediate consequences of women's war work to a broader debate about women combining careers and marriage. Ideological defences of patriarchy and the male-breadwinner ideal came from women as well as men. Citing her own decision to stop working in order to salvage her marriage, one writer claimed married women's work 'gypped men ... and damaged their egos,' with disastrous consequences. Husbands should not have to come home to an empty home and have 'no one to tell their latest coup to,' and wives should be 'well turned out' for their husband's return to his domestic domain, with 'his slippers in hand,' ready to listen.[66] Like many of the writers who were hostile to married women's wage labour, this woman's primary concern was the preservation of the traditional family, always a highly subjective if not mythical entity.

Not everyone sang this patriarchal Father Knows Best tune. For other women, the memory of the war, the belief that jobs should be for veterans, and also the appeal of 'home dreams' shaped their views of work and family; they saw reciprocal benefits to a male-breadwinner model, namely, the luxury of dedicating themselves to one job, mothering, which they believed had social value.[67] For women in less than satisfying jobs, or those with memories of wartime loss, the appeal of 'home' was understandable. A Polish woman who had worked in Ludger Dionne's Quebec textile mill before moving to Toronto told a reporter that, if finances permitted, she would like to leave her job at Simpson's and become a 'housewife ... with a home of my own ... so I can see [my children] off to school.'[68]

In mass-circulation magazines, both positive and negative arguments were forwarded about the wage-earning wife and mother, with the latter a more serious concern than the former. Often, experts such as doctors or those from the 'psy' professions were called on to serve both as authors of articles and as commentators for articles written by journalists. For some experts, the wage-earning wife spelled ambivalence and anxiety. As one journalist wrote in 1949, the paid labour of wives was among the 'Seven Threats' to a healthy marriage; a woman could not handle two jobs and still provide the 'gaiety and energy' needed to keep her marriage going.[69] Other opinion pieces were so extreme that one suspects they were intentionally used to provoke reader responses. The author of 'Don't Educate Your Daughter' argued that reading 'the Brontes' was of little use to someone washing dishes and changing diapers, a thesis that engendered some strong protests from readers in letters to the editor.[70] In a confessional piece titled 'I Quit My Job to Save My Marriage,' an ex–career woman rightly identified the problems of working at two jobs inside and outside the home; however, she blamed women's overextended consumer ambitions for their predicament. Working women longed for luxury consumer items, such as 'a cottage at the lake, a television,' and selfishly refused to put the family first, a failure that produced de-masculinized men, robbed of their proper place as 'head of the household.'[71] Similarly, a Protestant minister offering advice to newlyweds stated categorically that working wives 'unmanned' men and threatened the family.[72]

For these conservative commentators, the issue of married women's work was inextricably linked to the preservation of the patriarchal family. However, some articles that lauded women's work as homemakers simultaneously celebrated their voluntary contributions outside the home to social, religious, or political causes. One woman anointed 'Madame Châtelaine' of 1965, for instance, was 'une mère moderne,' whose contributions to the community indicated that she did not 'seclude' herself in the home; on the contrary, she was active, concerned, a woman who refused 'de vivre en marge de sons temps.'[73] Some liberal expert commentators conveyed support for women's autonomy along with concern for the family. Dr Marion Hilliard, for instance, encouraged women's activities outside the home – though within certain limits. Working and raising young children simultaneously was a 'bad' thing: 'Society agrees that babies and little children need their mother ... The mother who rushes her children through a dawn breakfast, nags them to hurry with their clothes so she can deposit them somewhere on her way to work, and then returns, exhausted, in the early evening to prepare an ugly meal and send her testy children to bed is suffering a defeat on all counts.'[74] It is easy to see why some working mothers felt the need to apologize for their work: the picture conjured up of ugly food and testy children was hardly reaffirming. Indeed, even *Chatelaine* editor Doris Anderson complained that she was taken aside after a speech or at a party by other women who demanded to know 'Why aren't you home looking after your children?' The notion that women were not happy as full-time housewives was simply so 'unsettling,' she remembers in her autobiography, that a controversy about the 'right of women with children to work outside the home raged in the press all through the fifties, sixties, and even the seventies.'[75]

Married women workers also had their defenders. Some journalists argued that 'long accepted patterns' had been sundered during the war, and there was no need to return to the days when women did not 'use their talents outside the home.'[76] Work for pay might add to the family income, improve women's self-image and happiness, and thus help to sustain the nuclear family.[77] Wives and mothers who were providing for their families by working should be recognized as a 'fact not a fad,' asserted Christina McCall in an article that emphasized the exhausting 'grind' of working women's 'two conflicting jobs.'[78] Articles presenting highly satisfied working wives were also featured, though it is instructive that some of these individuals had children in school, or were involved in part-time labour scheduled around the demands of domestic labour;

arguably, these stories were meant to reassure those fearful of the nuclear family in crisis. The women held up as exemplars of the new working women could also be rather esoteric examples: in the French *Châtelaine*, a famous media personality or lawyer might be featured; the portrayal of a factory worker was a rarity, even in the 1960s.[79] A fashion designer, with a full-time housekeeper, explained to the English *Chatelaine* how she was able to balance home and work quite well, but the issue of her housekeeper's work life, wages, and choices was never mentioned, reinforcing the middle-class viewpoint that underpinned many of the articles in all mainstream magazines. Indeed, class was often an unspoken word, obscuring the unequal relationship between women workers: the freedom of the middle-class fashion designer to go out to work was premised on the economic needs and labour of working-class women tending her home. While some articles addressed ethnicity – usually in relation to immigration – profiles of non-white and non-Anglo working women were less common, and as Korinek argues, in the fifties there was no mistaking the positioning of these women as 'others,' who were fortunate to have a chance to build a new life in Canada.[80]

Concerns about the effect of women's wage work on the family persisted into the mid-1960s, but by the mid- to late 1960s, a shift had occurred in many magazines, and especially in *Chatelaine*. To be sure, there were still some writers who claimed married women were 'fools to take a job.' Doing routine work by day then housework by night was hardly a liberating life, one female author intimated, but her emphasis was on exhaustion and the 'home-work conflict' reality, not the morality of women who worked after marriage and children. The sexual division of labour within the home – the notion that wage-earning women were still primarily responsible for the domestic work – was hard to break. It was taken for granted that the female factory worker featured in *Châtelaine* would face a 'double métier,' with consequential costs in fatigue and exhaustion.[81] Even the feminist-inclined *Chatelaine* offered tips on how to juggle domestic and wage labour, an approach that reaffirmed the idea that women were responsible for two jobs, and might occasionally suggest the stereotype of the 'less reliable' female worker. One advice column, for instance, cautioned women not to become office gossips, to be well groomed, and quick off the mark to show the employer that domestic affairs would not interfere with their work.[82]

However, articles that offered advice for women re-entering the workforce were still quite different from those lamenting the demise of the patriarchal or male-breadwinner household. By the late 1960s,

Protestant ministers were no longer denouncing the unmanning of men, and some journalists, emboldened by feminism, were questioning why women's workforce contribution was downplayed, denigrated, and denied social support, indicating a new direction in the discussion of working wives and mothers.[83] In *Chatelaine*, such feminist concerns paralleled increased attention to questions of racism, and to the grinding poverty shouldered by many women.[84]

Agonized fears about the family were far less visible in the business press over this entire period; economic, not social conservatism characterized its response to married women workers. While some authors acknowledged the ongoing 'moral' debate,[85] women workers were more often seen as a useful resource and as a stimulus to consumption: 'home-stuck' mothers were literally a 'wasted resource.'[86] Because women's earnings were often geared towards raising the family's standard of living, their wages also meant 'extra buying power and extra cash for retailers.'[87] Public-opinion polls indicated that the majority of Canadians were opposed to married women working outside the home if they had small children; however, employers recognized that women were filling positions in the expanding service and trade sectors where few men laboured. They provided Ma Bell, for instance, with a needed resource in a 'tight labour market.'[88] One executive dismissed limitations on married women workers as outmoded, noting that efficiency was not related to marital status: one simply had to hire the reliable woman worker, as opposed to the slacker – the single woman who ducked out to get her hair done or the married one who left early to pick up 'little Ermintrude at nursery school.'[89] Indeed, stereotypes about women workers crossed the marital divide: office 'girls' were 'spoiled,' one male employer reported to journalist Eileen Morris. They had never had it so good, yet they could not take orders or criticism. His dismissive, superior tone would surely have rankled women whose efficient white-collar work kept offices running smoothly.[90]

For the business press, then, women workers were a human resource in the marketplace of capitalist accumulation. There was even some lament that womanpower was less effectively utilized in Canada than in European countries.[91] Although Nikita Krushchev and Richard Nixon may have argued publicly in 1959 over the 'consumer oriented modern home,'[92] with Nixon lauding woman's role as homemaker, in the *Financial Post* the competitive rhetoric of the Cold War was used to contrast Canada's underused female labour to the Soviet example: 'Russian women put their Canadian sisters to shame in the job-holding category,' observed one *Financial Post* contributor.[93] This is not to say that the business press was promoting feminism. By and large, business leaders described women as a flexible labour force, though one defined by marriage: 'It is commonly accepted that a girl will take a job at least until she finds a husband.'[94] Yet homemakers' unpaid domestic work was discounted, designated a relic of the past due to the magic of frozen peas and vacuum cleaners.[95] The dominant myths about the special problems associated with married women workers – their absenteeism, lack of job commitment, and so on – were also trotted out regularly. Nor were state efforts to enhance women's equality welcomed. Equal pay was criticized as something women did not really want, and the unemployment insurance system, it was argued, should be tightened up to prevent abuse by married women.[96]

One might assume that the woman who ran to catch the bus every morning after dropping off her child with a sitter could open a union newspaper and find a stronger endorsement of her wage labour. Not so. Granted, there were a range of views and even contradictory images presented, and the labour movement's conception of the woman worker also varied according to the time period and the union. Nonetheless, there were some recurring themes that revealed how central a masculinist, male-breadwinner perspective remained to the public face of the labour movement.

On one level, the union press offered images of working women that stood in stark contrast to those found in mainstream magazines, let alone Hollywood movies. Although women may not have been prominently featured, when they were present, we find a more realistic display of working-class occupations, from textile workers to flight attendants, rather than the career women featured in mass-circulation magazines. Second, women are portrayed positively in active, political roles, meeting, organizing, and picketing; these public, committed, confrontational women bore little resemblance to an idealized June Cleaver. In the Canadian Labour Congress's (CLC) *Canadian Labour*, founded after the merger of the Trades and Labour Congress (TLC) and Canadian Congress of Labour (CCL) in 1956, women are pictured on the picket line; in *The Canadian Packinghouse Worker*, they are leafleting at Eaton's; in *Textile Labour*, women are protesting the use of injunctions; and in *The Fur and Leather Worker* – a 'communist' paper that existed before the anti-communist purge of this union – there are pictures of international Women's Day celebrations encompassing black and white women workers.[97] Stories of strikes involving women workers, such as the 1958

Cornerbrook Hospital strike in Newfoundland, the longest in Canadian history at that time, drew attention to the heroic women 'on the picket line for 18 hour days ... in all kinds of weather.'[98]

Attention to the exploitation of women workers also set the labour press apart from mainstream magazines. In contrast to ads for lingerie in women's magazines, *Canadian Labour* urged unionists to 'declare war, on poverty in the lingerie industry,' for immigrant women garment workers were being 'exploited to the core' in factories that did not even pay the average garment wage.[99] As in *Chatelaine*, non-Anglo and non-white women were far less visible in labour reporting, but they were not completely absent. If the union portrayed itself as left-wing, it was more likely to stress women's activism and rights: communist-led unions tried to highlight women's union and class consciousness, while some social-democratic unions such as the United Packing House Workers featured articles on issues such as equal pay. Unions sometimes used their papers to address gender inequality more indirectly, with humour or anecdote. Slipping a radical cartoon into the paper was one small way of poking fun at gender norms, including that of the male-breadwinner figure. In the UTWA (United Textile Workers of America) paper, under the direction of Madeleine Parent and Kent Rowley, one cartoon presaged the sentiments of a subsequent feminist era: a young woman is consulting a male medium, who is reading a crystal ball, and the woman quips, 'Can you skip the long voyage and handsome man, and just tell me when I'm going to get a job.'[100]

Although a new political vocabulary of human rights emerged in the aftermath of the war, neither the TLC nor the CCL integrated gender into the fight against prejudice and discrimination. In cartoons, briefs to the government, and editorials, it was racial and religious 'discrimination' that was decreed the enemy. In Vancouver, a Labour Committee for Human Rights held annual institutes, but 'fair employment practices' meant discussions of discrimination based on religion, race, or Aboriginal status, not gender.[101] Within the newly formed CLC, human rights were described, revealingly, as 'a man to man affair,'[102] until a 1966 convention resolution called for an 'end to discrimination' against women workers and, finally, a 1968 addition to the CLC constitution added 'sex' to its definition of grounds for discrimination.[103] The CLC's public, promotional magazine reported that a 'predominantly male' convention showed 'overwhelming support' for the 1966 resolution, painting a picture of progressive male comrades, but convention resolutions are not necessarily a sound measure of deep political commitment. As chapter 7

shows, by the 1960s a small group of women leaders with secondary positions in the CCL/CLC bureaucracy was emerging, some of whom were
concerned about equity issues. However, *Canadian Labour* relied heavily
on International Labour Organization (ILO) and International Council
of Free Trade Unions (ICFTU) pronouncements for copy on women's
issues, which suggests that the Canadian movement was far less interested in developing its own positions on gender equality.[104]

Until the late 1960s, the typical wage earner in many union papers was
portrayed as white and male. Given its craft basis, this was not surprising
for the *Trades and Labour Congress Journal.* Its ideal woman was featured in
the regular Home Section: she was a matronly soul, sporting an apron
and a bun, serving food to a gaggle of children. A column of recipes followed in every issue, and the recipes' decidedly bland nature and Anglo
origin said much about the dominant ethnic identities of many craft
unionists. Unless it reprinted an article from another union central, or
invited the federal Women's Bureau (after 1954) to offer a piece, discussion of women as workers was almost non-existent. Gender was apparent,
to be sure, in the images of workers as male breadwinners, fathers, and
crusaders against communism. Advertisers also presumed to know who
the TLC worker was: someone interested in electric shavers, hockey, fishing, and beer.

Given the new opportunities to organize women through industrial
unions, and its own 1952 retail union drive, it is especially surprising that
the CCL's organ, the *Canadian Unionist,* did not take up the challenge of
appealing to women workers more assertively. It might report on Eileen
Talman's trip to the ICFTU's women's school in Paris, or reprint an article by the soundly middle-class National Council of Women, but it rarely
addressed gender-based workforce inequalities. Cartoons in the labour
press also replayed misogynist images from mainstream culture, including the nagging housewife lecturing her husband, the buxom female
office worker interested in sex, or the politically naive woman worker
who knew nothing about unions. Masculinity might be portrayed with
wry or critical humour (after all, the nagging housewife is lecturing an
uncouth couch-potato husband), but it was, more often, linked to assert-
iveness and action. The archetypal worker in union-sponsored cartoons
may not have been macho or aggressive, but he was certainly muscular
and masculine.[105]

These images not only reflected the dominant gender norms, they also
made real the 'accommodationist' side of the Fordist accord. Newspapers
of the union centrals were, in general, politically unadventuresome, often

Figure 2   Ad from *The Canadian Unionist*, September 1954.

parroting mainstream politicians;[106] trade unions were articulating their respectability, whether that meant supporting charity drives, battling communists, or holding beauty contests. Using the female body to appeal to male readers was standard fare in the advertising industry, but many unions were happy to use it too. Ironically, just as increasing numbers of women were claiming a wage, the female body was featured more, not less, perhaps a reflection of masculine anxieties about shifting gender norms. Although women were not taking 'men's' jobs, they had been welding iron and wielding butcher knives only a few years before during the war. Even if women had dutifully returned to female-typed jobs, they were still becoming more visible in the workplace. Recent American studies of blue-collar work suggest that women's and African Americans' increasing incursions into white male work spaces in the 1950s elicited defensive, and sometimes hostile, responses, especially from those workers versed in a 'rough culture' of masculinity.[107]

In the *Canadian Unionist* the lithographers promoted their union in a full-page ad, adorned with a sultry, pouty pin-up in a frilly two-piece bathing suit: the caption, 'nice job,'[108] offered a clear double entendre that was apparent in many other sexualized images of women's bodies. Pin-up images were not entirely new in union papers; however, they proliferated in the post-war period, mirroring changes in popular culture, as men's skin magazines such as *Playboy* became big business, and fashion revealed more of the female body.[109] Nonetheless, by the late 1960s, unions were well aware of an emerging critique of mainstream culture's depiction of women, so some pictures seem out of place. Under the ironic title 'They're Your Brothers,' the *CUPE Journal* displayed a posed picture of three union women in Hugh Hefner–inspired bunny costumes, leaning forward into the camera for ample breast and leg visibility. This appeared in 1968, the same year the union told the RCSW that women workers were badly in need of a 'new deal' from their own unions.[110]

The labour movement's visual and textual equation of work for pay with masculinity was perhaps less understandable in *Textile Labour*, which had to appeal to a mix of male and female workers, yet more understandable in a United Auto Workers publication, *The Oshaworker*, which spoke to a decidedly male-dominated workplace. It was not that women were entirely absent in *The Oshaworker*, but rather that the reigning 'gender order' assumed women and men occupied different cultural spaces, despite their overriding, common class interests: women were addressed as auxiliary activists, while men were hailed as plant workers and participants in the masculine culture of the 'Rod and Gun' club.[111]

Given that there were workplace, union, and political differences distinguishing many of the union papers, are any general conclusions about labour-movement representations of women possible? One constant was the acceptance of the prevailing gendered division of labour. Most editorials and articles on women (when they appeared) argued for better compensation for women's occupations, better minimum wages, or equal-pay provisions. They did not call for the abolition of sex-typing of jobs. At one extreme, some articles assumed innate physiological and mental differences between women and men; as one exploration of office automation pointed out, women were more likely to have a 'comparatively high incidence of nervous troubles'[112] when adapting themselves to new techniques. Female bodies were more fragile, female minds more prone to nervous exhaustion. The *Canadian Unionist* occasionally tried to address women workers' distinct needs, but in the process endorsed the notion of a more vulnerable female workforce. 'Tired women,' one article declared, were rarely the product of 'physical labour alone,' but rather the result of the 'nervous tensions of work' and perhaps their 'unsatisfactory *personal* adjustment at work or in the home.'[113] The gendered division of labour was also a form of unspoken reassurance to many male trade unionists: as long as women did not do men's jobs, they were not seen as threatening or overstepping their bounds. At best, male workers claimed the division of labour indicated that women worked with 'brains not brawn'; thus, it would be 'foolish to have women digging ditches.' At worst, they saw women as 'emotional' or repeated fears that women's femininity was endangered in male work spaces and places. 'Have you ever noticed the hands of a woman worker are not feminine,' one blue-collar worker told two investigators for the RCSW.[114]

A second commonality was the lack of an acrimonious debate within and between unions over protective legislation like the one that had divided American trade-union feminists in the post-war period. Although some female trade unionists called for an equal-rights approach to women's equality, health and minimum-wage protections went largely unchallenged within the labour movement in the post-war period, until they were abandoned after the 1960s. The overwhelmingly social-democratic orientation of the labour movement probably shaped its sympathy for protective legislation; moreover, the CLC took many of its cues from the International Labour Organization (ILO), which still accepted protective measures for women. Nor did Canada have a National Woman's Party lobby, as in the United States, advocating militantly for individualist, liberal-feminist positions.[115]

Third, and perhaps most important, the male-breadwinner family wage, though not as adamantly promoted as in earlier eras, still underpinned most labour analyses of social-policy issues.[116] 'Do women cause unemployment?' asked one union staffer writing about unemployment insurance in *Canadian Labour* – a provocative headline that would not have been displayed in the more radical *UE News*. Written by a National Union of Public Sector Employees (NUPSE) officer, the article reassured men that the 'gloomy statistics' showing women had lower unemployment rates did not indicate that women were taking men's jobs; rather, there was growth in the female service sector and a decline in heavier, manual male work. In an attempt to reassure its male readers, the article reproduced many of the prevailing myths about women workers. Sure, most women are working 'because they have to,' the author conceded, but everyone knew a few married women who worked for 'extra conveniences ... where the motive seemed to be greed.' Women's household labour was fast disappearing due to new technology, so 'increased idleness at home' would likely encourage bored women to set their sights on the workforce. 'Unless something drastic is done to retain a large part of our male labour force, women will steadily replace men as the chief breadwinners,'[117] the author concluded. While the article never directly attacked women's right to work, the myths of the idle homemaker and the married wife working for luxuries were reproduced, and nothing was done to discourage men's fears of losing their patriarchal status within the household. The author could not shed the heavy ideological baggage of the male-breadwinner ideal, and in that sense, his article captured much about labour-movement thinking that prevailed until the late 1960s, and which in turn reflected broader ideals. When *Châtelaine* surveyed Quebec men and women at the time of the Royal Commission on the Status of Women, a gender gap was clear: only 15 per cent of men wanted their wives to work, yet overwhelming majorities of women endorsed a combination of work outside the home and raising children, as well as day nurseries, and maternity benefits.[118]

The family-wage ideal was not limited to a few articles in the labour press, but was articulated in countless other examples of trade-union thinking, from union organizing and strike pamphlets to many unions' rationales for contract negotiations. It was a core finding of one study of union men's attitudes done in the late 1960s. Not only did 85 per cent of the blue-collar men interviewed say that women should not work if they had young children (one claiming it was 'a little less than criminal ... leaving permanent scars'), but 56 per cent even disagreed with married women working at all. Men emphasized that their masculinity and sense of pride would be hurt if their own wives worked outside the home, and they resorted to transhistorical, 'scientific' claims to justify their views: 'throughout human history, man's task has always been to be the bread-winner ... with women in the home.'[119]

The implicit acceptance of this 'gender contract' was also displayed in women's columns in the labour press. While glimpses of women as workers were visible, it was often assumed that married women primarily worked within the home.[120] These columns did vigorously promote social-justice issues and women's political activism. The home was not seen as a private retreat; rather, columnists argued that women's dedication to family welfare and their identification with working-class interests should be channelled into political causes. Many women's columns, for instance, urged women to build up trade-union auxiliaries that linked the family, community, and their husband's work. As Christine McLaughlin points out, the family-wage ideal also made it important for unions to foster solidaristic links between home life and the workplace.[121] Despite some differences between social-democratic and communist-identified union auxiliaries, they shared a strong conviction that women's domestic and maternal roles could, and should, be harnessed to support social-justice causes, in a manner not unlike earlier versions of left-wing 'militant mothering.'[122]

The *Canadian Packinghouse Worker*, to take only one example, had a lively women's column written by Peg Stewart (a prominent CCFer), and later Eileen Robins. Sewing patterns and household hints were offered on the women's page, assuming they would appeal to women readers, who were 'in the home, stuck with young children,' as Stewart bluntly put it. The solution for these women, Stewart said, was to get a bit of time away from their domestic 'cage,' so that they could cope better   advice not unlike that given by Dr Marion Hilliard in *Chatelaine*.[123] Housewives were urged to support the union label campaign, and during strikes they were celebrated as the 'backbone' of the struggle, since 'they know that their families will benefit from higher wages' won by male breadwinners.[124] Offering a pep talk about women's auxiliary work, Stewart noted that all the wives had one thing in common: the welfare of the union that is the 'backbone of their [husbands'] job.'[125] The *Canadian Packinghouse Worker* women columnists sometimes lauded women workers' activism, reminding readers that some women were breadwinners too, or protesting discrimination against married women in unemployment-benefit rules, but they were primarily interested in appeals to the married homemaker.

Finally, women workers were portrayed in many papers as problems, exceptions, or anomalies, not as the norm. As Alice Kessler-Harris pointed out, instead of asking 'where are the organized women?' unionists lamented the 'double difficulty'[126] of organizing women because they were concentrated in difficult-to-organize occupations or because they were presumed to lack the political initiative necessary for unionization. Even labour feminists publicly lamented that women were 'not playing their full roles in unions.'[127] They needed that extra political push, as they were 'shy about voicing their ideas.'[128] Women may well have been less forthright about speaking out in a movement that was so male-dominated, though once involved, they rejected the assumption that they were less able unionists; when the Ontario Federation of Labour convened a women's conference in 1966, delegates spoke critically of the 'low confidence' that 'male unionists' had in women's abilities.[129]

The absence of women from union leadership positions, apparent in so many photos of the labour movement, from summer schools to conventions, was occasionally noted as a problem needing attention, though rarely was a plan of action discussed. To be sure, the movement celebrated its very few female leaders; however, they were also designated as superwoman anomalies. In the CLC, for instance, much was made of Hugette Plamondon, who had emerged from the Quebec United Packing House Workers Union, and was the *only* woman on the CLC executive for many years until the 1970s. The story of Plamondon's rise from secretary to union official was offered repeatedly, including in *Maclean's* magazine, as an example of what women might accomplish if they were truly committed to their jobs. In the 1950s, at least, Plamondon downplayed her gender: the 'era of spectacular demands in favour of women's rights is over,' she told *Canadian Labour*, 'all that a woman [has] to do is assert herself through work and ability, as any man would.'[130] Plamondon was likely uneasy about claiming a feminist mantle, as this would not have sat well with her male comrades in the inner circle.[131] She fought vigorously on behalf of women and men because, she stressed, 'to look out only for the former would amount to discrimination ... The men accept me and respect me for that.' In some interviews she went so far as to say, 'Women are our own biggest enemy ... We have nothing to fear from men.'[132] Every article on Plamondon, inside and outside of the labour press, also stressed her femininity and her attractive, well-dressed persona. One of *Maclean's* magazine's stable of female reporters referred to her as an 'exotic,' an unlikely labour leader in 'four inch heels and heavy costume jewellery.'[133]

Plamondon's reassurances probably reflected her attempt to calm anxieties about women assuming male roles. Rank-and-file union members, for instance, admitted that women were seen as 'unfeminine' and 'tomboys' if they assumed leadership positions.[134] Studies for the RCSW uncovered a moral and social double standard plaguing women activists. 'There is a great pressure on women union delegates to behave at conventions,' admitted one interviewee. 'The guys may laugh as they tuck some drunk into bed, but if it's a woman they tend to raise their eyebrows.'[135] As I have argued elsewhere, some blue-collar women workers, well aware of the prevailing class prejudices, stressed an image of themselves as respectable working women in order to challenge derogatory images of 'rough' working-class women.[136] Even if women were happy to abandon this decorous persona on a picket line, the mainstream CCL, and later CLC, union press were not about to throw respectability to the winds.

Union Beauty Queens

The search for respectability was one reason that the labour movement embraced the beauty-queen contest as cultural practice in post-war Canada. Similar events had been sponsored by employers or integrated into labour festivals before the war,[137] but they became more widespread in the post-war era, in both unionized and non-unionized workplaces.[138] To judge these events only through post–women's liberation eyes would be a mistake, for working women at the time may have perceived these displays not as insulting or demeaning, but rather as validation and entertainment, while unions used them to celebrate working-class community, women's work cultures, and labour-movement causes. Still, some retrospective critical analysis is in order, especially since recent post-structuralist analyses of beauty contests have downplayed issues of class and commodification, stressing instead women's agency and their search for a positive identity through beauty-contest rituals. Perhaps more troubling, 'third wave' feminist writing has almost entirely ignored the structures of class and gender power involved, stressing instead the 'varied cultural meanings,' personal empowerment, and 'sexual self determination' of beauty culture.[139] Second-wave feminist hostility to beauty contests, these critics claim, was a reflection of misguided socialists 'elevating the shabby over the chic,' their politics amounting to judgmental, simplistic, and condescending portrayals of women suffering from false consciousness.[140] While this is something of a caricature, feminists in the

1970s did link beauty pageants to patriarchal ideologies, racism, and capitalist commodification: contests for the title of 'fairest of them all' were critiqued for defining women by their looks, creating unrealistic Cinderella fantasies, promoting an image of heterosexual, white femininity as the norm, fostering competition between women, and encouraging neurosis about weight and appearance – among other things.[141] These are precisely the reasons that the labour movement stopped supporting beauty contests in the 1970s.

Beauty contests in post-war North America were 'flexible displays' that could be 'molded to different agendas,'[142] and even within the trade-union movement, they were not uniform, crossing the spectrum from the crowning of a 'queen of the picket line' to exact replicas of mainstream contests. Beauty contests are often linked to notions of nation and identity; 'outsider' groups – usually defined by race or ethnicity – established separate beauty contests, such as Miss Indian Princess, as a means of validating their own cultural notions of beauty, and to counter the hegemonic, white European 'look' that was equated with beauty in popular culture.[143] Some labour-movement contests were conceived in a similar vein: if Miss Canada was meant to symbolize the virtues of the Canadian nation, Miss Labour Day contests were a public articulation of community pride and labour's 'civic virtue,'[144] as daughters of labour (sometimes literally, as they were daughters of trade unionists) were featured on stages and in parades. If the photos in labour archives are any indication, however, union contests largely reproduced the idealization of white, European beauty.

Beauty culture events and contests were also used as a recruiting or fundraising tool: women packing-house workers in Winnipeg, for instance, organized their own fundraiser fashion show that featured members modelling the latest clothes for union and other supporters.[145] The women were not competing beauty queens, and the show reflected both the dominant post-war emphasis on consumption, as well as a long-standing interest of women workers in fashion. No doubt part of the rationale was to draw unpoliticized women into the union, making the latter appear feminine and friendly. However, union fashion shows closely replicated similar department-store events, designed primarily to encourage consumption; these fashion spectacles, as Donica Belisle argues, also subtly commodified women workers' bodies in the service of corporate ends.[146]

Parades, special events, and political campaigns were also advertised with beauty contests; the annual Labour Day parade was often inaugurated

*the Cinderelle
       myth*

with the crowning of a queen drawn from a bevy of 'union maids.'[147] Pictures of pin-up girls (in bathing suits or languishing invitingly on new cars), beauty-queen contests, and fashion shows were all used to advertise the union label. The International Ladies Garment Workers Union (ILGWU), especially reliant on the union label to secure good working conditions, frequently sponsored these events, securing garments for its models from employers, and inviting local Liberal and Conservative politicians and their wives as a means of securing their political endorsement. A broader quest for respectability underpinned other beauty contests: the Miss Okanagan Trades and Labour Council contest, cosponsored with employers, was initiated in 1949 as part of the council's wider strategy of 'integrating' unions in the community. Posing demurely for the camera with an International Brotherhood of Electrical Workers' banner adorning her bathing suit, Miss Okanagan was portrayed very much like contestants in the Miss Canada contest.[148]

Perhaps the best example of the contradictions characterizing postwar beauty contests was 'Le Bal des Midinettes,' sponsored annually by the Montreal ILGWU after 1946. These elaborate fancy-dress balls, combining a beauty contest with an employer-sponsored fashion show and French Canadian artistic performances, reflected the union's long tradition of integrating cultural events into union life. However, they were also attempts to sink roots into the French Canadian community, perceived to be a more uncertain and tenuous constituency, as the union encountered tremendous opposition from both the Catholic Church and local employers during its 1930s organizing campaigns. Contestants were almost always French Canadian 'daughters of the nation,' suggesting the contest was a statement of both working-class and cultural pride. There was, in contrast to a Miss Canada contest, some element of democracy involved in the selection process: garment shops nominated their own contestants, then played fairy godmother by creating elaborate white gowns for the fancy dress ball where the queen was crowned. Many aspects of Le Bal des Midinettes mimicked mainstream beauty contests: the build-up in the union paper stressed the competitive and prestigious nature of the event; praise was heaped on the 'petite, beautiful vivacious' contestant and her 'ladies in waiting'; and it was intimated that the queen would have a happy life of romance and marriage awaiting her in the future.[149] However, the ceremony was not entirely devoid of working-class content as the queen's crown was a thimble and her sceptre a long needle, a playful use of artisanal symbolism.[150] Indeed, the union consciously used the ball as a means of advertising union organizing, and to celebrate garment workers' skill, hard work, and the dignity of their labour.[151]

The event, however, also celebrated, if implicitly, the tripartite accommodation at the heart of the Fordist accord. These balls were used by the male union leadership to cement ties with employers, union leader 'celebrities'[152] from the United States, and notable provincial and federal politicians (all of whom shared the ILGWU's anti-communism), who came as honoured guests. Workers, the union publicity emphasized, had helped to make Montreal a centre of couture, yet the sweatshop conditions and low wages that still existed in some shops, and the difficulties of the double day that married women endured, were never mentioned. Moreover, much of the publicity reaffirmed the gendered division of labour as well as an image of married female domesticity: in *Pins and Needles*, an NFB film on Le Bal des Midinettes, women were praised for their 'inborn' female talent for needle work.[153] Le Bal des Midinettes thus offered women a respite from the shop floor and a sense of pride in their work, but it simultaneously promoted consumption, decorative femininity, a gendered division of labour, heterosexual romance, and the patriarchal symbols associated with beauty contests.[154] Ironically, while validating working-class femininity, Le Bal also carried an illusory message about class: contestants were told that they might 'dance the night away' on the arms of a cabinet minister or judge, suggesting that class might be escaped through individual 'self-improvement' or by 'marrying up.'[155] This was hardly a call to solidarity; encouraging young women to play the role of Cinderella kept their sights firmly fixed on the goals of beauty and marriage, and left men the undisputed leaders of the union.

The beauty-queen title could be used for more subversive ends. During a strike of factory workers at Rogers Electric in Toronto, the *UE News* designated a 'pin-up' girl for the union, showing a photo of a striker who was dressed normally while on the picket line. Her claim to fame was not her legs but the fact that she had faced down a line of hundreds of police outside the plant: the beauty-queen title could thus be used to challenge the notion of decorative beauty in favour of advertising the beauty of courage and militancy.[156] Other beauty contests held during strikes were employed as a recognizable cultural ritual used to sustain social solidarity during the struggle. Yet the images offered of these picket-line queens could be frustratingly contradictory. Women were celebrated as strikers, yet portrayed as passive objects: a UTWA 'queen of the picket line' was photographed in a bathing suit, sitting and gazing into the camera lens.

Figure 3   Bernard Shane congratulates Denise Martineau, la Reine des Midinettes, adorned with thimble crown and needle sceptre. (Kheel Center for Labor Management Documentation and Archives, Cornell University, Ithaca, NY, Box 3, ff6, #5780PB3F6A400, UNITE HERE papers)

Could women really be believed as militant unionists when they were inert and unclothed, while men were active and clothed?[157]

By the late 1960s, there were changes in labour beauty contests; some rules required women to answer a question or compose an essay relating to labour in an effort to counteract the cheesecake image of these contests. Moreover, not all women workers were adverse to using their bodies for public display. Some did so intentionally to shock audiences for political purposes: during an outside CUPE municipal strike in Windsor, unionist Faye Lunday walked the picket line wearing only a green garbage bag to show her solidarity with the garbage collectors.[158] For younger women, influenced by a youth rebellion that crossed class lines, there was a certain pleasure in challenging authority through one's dress – or undress. As Susan Douglas indicates, in the 1960s, the mass media's emphasis on sexual 'respectability' for teenage girls was accompanied by contradictory images of sexual rebellion and experimentation.[159] Femininity, style, and appearance, Beverly Skeggs also points out, are forms of investment for young working-class women, 'one form of cultural capital they have access to.'[160] Inevitably caught up in the popular culture of the time, working-class women were eager to claim their share of its prizes and pleasures, especially if they felt their femininity was challenged by class-based stereotypes of the rough working class.

While labour beauty contests did validate working-class women's identity and promote trade-union causes, they must also be viewed as a troubling reflection of women's subordinate role in the labour movement, and as one of the symbolic means by which their subordination was reproduced. The labour movement may have seen these contests as a means of portraying the archetypal, wholesome 'good labour gal,' but this image stood in contrast to the more valued, serious representation of labour masculinity: men were not judged by handsomeness and dress, but rather by intelligence, political acumen, and activism. Ironically, just as women, such as the retail clerks described in chapter 4, were flooding into service jobs that demanded attractiveness, deference, and politeness, they were confronted with powerful representations of the body, promoted by their own union movement, that valorized the dominant social norms of femininity. These were precisely the norms that kept women ideologically marginalized on the sidelines of the union movement. To offer this critique is not to denigrate the so-called 'false consciousness' of the contestants; rather, I am suggesting that we need to understand the seductive, class-based appeal of the Cinderella myth, the pervasive capitalist commodification of female bodies, and the structural power relations of gender and race that underlined beauty contests, both within and outside the union movement.

Moreover, criticisms of the sexualization of women in the union press are not simply the overly judgmental hindsight of contemporary feminists. Some women workers at the time suspected that pictures of women in skimpy bathing suits were used to appeal to male unionists, reinforcing their own outsider status in the labour movement. When the *Canadian Packinghouse Worker* featured a front-page bikini shot in 1963, a furor erupted in the next issue. Some male workers offered their approval. 'Send me her phone number,' joked one, while a high-ranking CLC staffer smugly complimented the paper on its facelift. Some women approved of this purported fashion news, but more complained. 'Stop wasting space on alleged news about clothes,' wrote one woman; 'we can't afford them and can read about them in women's magazines.' There was, to be sure, moralism at work: women denounced this 'immoral, dirty, sexy trash' or claimed only a 'low and sexy' character would display her body like this.[161] Yet another female correspondent complained that she was sick of the media's portrayal of sex scandals; in her view, the labour press should provide an alternative to this obsession with 'sex, sex, sex'[162] – and surely, she had a point.

The 'New' Working Woman

Representations of women's wage labour were never entirely value free, no matter who initiated them or how many experts, statistics, surveys, or polls they cited. This was true for the mainstream and labour press, as it was for the federal Women's Bureau, set up in 1954 in response to liberal-feminist lobbying to guide government research and policy relating to the expanding female labour force.[163] Justified by the reigning Liberals with business-friendly language stressing the need for efficient use of female labour power, the bureau nonetheless began to document the barriers to women's paid labour, and to advocate some equal-opportunity initiatives, though its sights remained fixed on gender inequalities, ignoring the importance of race, ethnicity, and language. The bureau's many reports were used to justify married women's increasing role in the labour force, as its surveys repeatedly stressed the link between women's wages and the fulfilment of basic family needs. Who could argue with these unselfish goals at a time when the nuclear family was celebrated as a cornerstone of the nation and a bulwark against communism? Whether the bureau was investigating equal pay, maternity leave, or child care, its conclusions often reinforced a liberal-feminist perspective, stressing the value of very limited state intervention to provide 'equality of opportunity' for women workers and enhanced health protection for women and children.[164] Similarly, newly established provincial women's bureaus studied where and why women worked, attempting to substitute moralizing judgments about bad mothers with seemingly neutral, social-science conclusions showing women's wage labour was a familial necessity and a boon to sectors of the economy needing 'female' labour. While some state sectors still assumed a male-breadwinner model, these Women's Bureaus, though mere outposts in state bureaucracies, were far more attuned to the new realities regarding the modern family-wage economy.

State-sponsored investigations of women's labour may have revealed implicit political agendas, just as censuses, with their emphasis on the formal economy and paid work, masked the extent of women's daily unpaid work, but both spoke to an undeniable reality: the labour force was in transformation as the proportion of adult women working for wages increased dramatically, and as their age profile and relationship to the family shifted. Higher percentages of women were going out to work, albeit in a highly sex-segregated labour market, and the most significant new woman worker was one with family attachments who was returning to the labour force after a period of mothering work in the home. The tempo of these economic changes did shift over time; what began as a gradual upward swing in the 1950s accelerated significantly into an irreversible trend by the 1960s and 1970s. The push-and-pull that impelled women's wage labour was unmistakable: individual and family needs, new consumer standards, and employers' search for a flexible labour force for the burgeoning service, trade, and public sectors were all important. However, women were not simply an inert economic factor in this process; material need was always intertwined with their decisions, choices, and desires: going out to work held out some promise, however fleeting or illusory, of enhanced economic security, independence, and respect – from one's family, employers, or co-workers.

This new economic reality did not always match the prevailing representations of gender and work that both men and women encountered in their everyday lives. While granting the period from 1945 to 1965 was not simply a Leave It to Beaver story of suburban retreat, feminine domesticity, and familial retrenchment, we cannot ignore the idealization of the nuclear, heteronormative, male-breadwinner family that pervaded much popular culture and advice literature. This social conservatism constituted an ideological backdrop to women's work outside the home, creating contradictions between cultural ideals and material realities, between an idealization of female domesticity and women's difficult double day. Despite the recognition that women were far from a marginal or reserve army of labour, there were always constraining ideological limits put on their paid work. The 'new' married woman worker, for example, was the focus of considerable debate, ambivalence, and anxiety. While these women had a few vocal defenders, particularly if they were cast as worthy (i.e., poor or widowed) working mothers, one would be hard pressed to argue that, in the fifteen to twenty years following the war, there was a widespread endorsement of married women's work for pay. No wonder these women felt that apologies and justifications were the order of the day.

Women's subordination in a sex- and race-segregated workforce also went largely unquestioned, even by a newly invigorated trade-union movement. Labour activists accepted the gendered division of labour as natural and inevitable, and in the labour press a concern with gender equality was muted despite new interest in human-rights issues. Beauty contests symbolized the double-sided and gendered nature of labour's Fordist accord. Conscious of an expanding female workforce, many unions made efforts to validate women's work and draw female workers into the labour movement – but generally on terms that replicated prevailing gender norms and a highly sexualized image of women. Anxious to integrate into the community, the ILGWU leaders who created Le Bal des Midinettes embraced the prevailing popular culture, made temporary peace with employers, and, in the process, endorsed a shared vision of women as temporary, secondary, and decorative workers. The language of individual empowerment and improvement that characterized these contests – ironically, not unlike post-feminist, agnostic 'third wave' writing on beauty culture – contradicted a union politics of solidarity and collectivity.

In contrast to the labour press, mainstream magazines paid scant attention to working-class women on strike and were far more preoccupied with the 'problem' of the married woman worker, though the business press was concerned with pragmatic questions about women as a flexible labour supply, and as a welcome stimulus to consumption. Married women workers were a new resource to be managed and trained, part of a complex business equation, rather than a deeply troubling moral issue. Popular English-language magazines, in contrast, consulted psychological, medical, and social-science experts, asking if married women's work would produce latchkey children languishing on street corners. It is possible that this popular debate was shaped, in part, by the inclination of the press to pose stark questions and oppositions in order to increase sales, but the issue of married women's work clearly had some resonance for readers who responded, pro and con, with letters to the editor. This popular debate also had very clear class, ethnic, and racial biases; although most women laboured on assembly lines or waited on customers, the professional or 'career' woman was more often the example used of the new woman worker. Racialized women, who had higher labour-force participation rates, were also less visible: though many African-Canadians laboured in service and domestic occupations, their work travails were rarely discussed in *Chatelaine*, and despite the ongoing concern with the integration of southern and eastern European immigrants into the community, realistic articles on their working conditions were also fairly rare.[165]

The contradictions between representation and reality that had been brewing for some time after the war were becoming more visible and contentious by the late 1960s. Women's work for pay was at the centre of new social debates and political organizing: a Royal Commission on the Status of Women was appointed, some women were pressing from within unions for change, and the feminist movement outside unions was assuming a new face and political profile. In letters penned to the RCSW – discussed in chapter 7 – women demanded to know why women struggling to be both good mothers and workers were not 'given their due' by society. The following chapters offer a number of examples of women's work as it was transformed, and as women were transformed in the process, in the quarter-century after the war's end.

Chapter 2

Gender, Ethnicity, and Immigrant Women in Post-war Canada: The Dionne Textile Workers

In the aftermath of the Second World War, the labour press and mainstream magazines were less concerned with women's post-war status than with emerging debates about the relationship between immigration and labour. This was an old issue, but it assumed a new form as Canada faced an international refugee crisis, a humanitarian tragedy of unprecedented scale in modern Europe. Hundreds of thousands of displaced persons in temporary camps could not or did not want to be repatriated; the Canadian government could not turn its back, as it did on pre-war Jewish refugees, and it was impelled by both domestic and international pressures to admit some of the refugees needing a new home. By the early 1950s, the door was also opened to 'voluntary' European immigrants who came by the hundreds of thousands to escape war-damaged countries, to seek economic opportunity, and also to join their families. This post-war influx of immigrants had a significant impact on the cultural, economic, and political character of Canadian working-class life, particularly in very large urban centres and in southern Ontario, where most immigrants settled.[1]

This chapter explores the themes of immigration, gender, and ethnicity in Fordist Canada through the lens of one controversy, concerning the importation of a group of displaced persons, sometimes referred to as the 'Dionne girls,' brought to work in Ludger Dionne's Quebec spinning mill as 'unfree immigrants,' as they were bound by contract to their employer for two years.[2] While the initial controversy centred on whether Dionne had misused his power as a Liberal Member of Parliament (MP) to secure workers for his family's mill, this small group of refugees, largely of Polish background, quickly became a compelling symbol for broader debates concerning Canada's responsibility for refugees, the politics of immigration, and women's place in the labour force during post–Second World War reconstruction.

Political debates about the Dionne workers revealed both continuities with and discontinuities from earlier debates about immigration and labour. State policies, as well as the process and experience of immigration, were shaped by perceived labour needs and relations of class, ethnicity, 'race,' and gender, as they had been before the Second World War.[3] Yet the post-war context was decidedly different. While it is probably not surprising that many of these women faced an entrenched sexual division of labour and limited job opportunities, their eastern European background was not viewed with the same alarm that it would have been before the First World War: they were not racialized as problematic 'peasant stock,' but were portrayed as modern, cultured immigrants. In part, this reflected their symbolic status as refugees from the horrors of communism, a theme that was to become more and more important as the Cold War heated up. It also spoke to altered state, expert, and popular discourses concerning ethnicity and immigration. In the aftermath of a war ostensibly waged against fascism and racism, there was a new awareness of human rights and conscious attempts to represent the Canadian nation as more tolerant, open, and humanitarian in its approach to new Canadians.[4] Social workers and journalists alike spoke less about the need for assimilation, and more about the successful 'integration' of immigrants; some tried to claim a new agenda promoting Canadian 'diversity.'[5]

In one sense, the Dionne labour scheme signalled changing notions of ethnicity and 'whiteness' in Canadian society, reflecting much longer-term post-war shifts in the cultural and political approval of continental European immigration.[6] This was a process, however, that simultaneously maintained rigid lines of exclusion for other less acceptable immigrants of colour.[7] Moreover, all prejudices concerning southern and eastern European immigrants did not suddenly evaporate; they were all too evident in the persisting hierarchy of preferred immigrants, in continuing anti-Semitism,[8] and in the assumption that refugee and immigrant women from Europe were most likely candidates for service, domestic, and factory jobs. Debates about the Dionne refugees thus indicated both contradiction and change. Despite the labour movement's antipathy to their role as 'unfree' or contract labour, they were portrayed as deserving immigrants who would be a benefit to Canadian society; despite insulting questions about their morality, the government and reformers insisted they were welcomed as equals; and despite attempts by politicians to cast them as pitiable victims, they rejected paternalism, attempting instead to make new lives in Canada on their own terms.

Figure 4   Displaced person at Dionne Spinning Mill. (LAC, Montreal Gazette Fonds, PA115767)

Setting the Context: Debating Immigration and Labour

The Dionne affair was but one example of debates taking place in political, bureaucratic, and public circles about refugees and immigration policy in the post-war period.[9] Even after many refugees were resettled, questions about immigration policy persisted through the 1950s and 1960s: How important should family reunification be? Who should be excluded and included? How should labour needs be assessed and met? How should 'security' concerns be addressed? How could immigrants be remade as 'Canadian' (usually denoting Anglo, English-speaking) citizens?[10] These debates shifted over time, moulded primarily by the economic and employment context, extra-parliamentary lobbies, contending visions of immigration policy (even within the state), dominant ideologies of ethnicity, culture, and 'race,' and Canadian foreign relations. Even though it sometimes went unnamed, gender was also a critical factor in these deliberations, not to mention in the day-to-day experiences of new Canadians.

When Dionne was on his way to Europe in 1947 to recruit women refugees as workers, Mackenzie King's cabinet was discussing a selection policy on displaced persons.[11] As the scandal unfolded, deliberations on a long-term immigration and refugee policy were taking place within the federal bureaucracy, the House of Commons, and the Senate Standing Committee on Immigration and Labour. Internally, government policy-makers mused about how the existing 'character' of the country could be maintained, offering preference to Anglo (British and American) immigration, while also enhancing European numbers, and barring most Asian entrants or British colonials of colour.[12]

Mackenzie King's famous 1947 pronouncement on immigration, articulated with his trademark politically acute vagueness, reflected these priorities: population growth through immigration was to be 'encouraged,' but with an eye to careful 'selection' of those who could be 'absorbed' into the national economy. The fact that immigrants from 'the Orient' were to be discouraged from immigrating indicated that 'absorption' referred both to labour and racial considerations.[13] While sounding a note of openness, the government sidestepped the persisting racial discrimination in its policies. Although the *Chinese Exclusion Act* was repealed (probably reluctantly), for example, the door was hardly wide open to Chinese immigrants, for regulations still prevented significant numbers of them from entering Canada.[14] Aside from a few limited labour emigration schemes in the 1950s, recruiting women of colour for domestic and nursing jobs, informal racial prohibitions remained integral to official immigration policy until 1967.[15] The limited schemes that existed for domestics and nurses were responses to employer demands for 'scarce' labour, and they were designed to discourage a larger family migration; the numbers of African-Canadian women workers thus remained very small, and they were concentrated geographically in a few key areas.

Similar considerations of 'absorption' and labour needs were factors shaping refugee policies immediately after the war. In response to international pressures, Canada had to open its doors to some refugees, but the state wanted tight control over the selection process. King spoke publicly of Canada's 'moral' duty to welcome 'thousands' of refugees, but no actual numbers were given, likely to calm any opponents, and Orders-in-Council first allowed close relatives to sponsor European refugees to offset public fears that these newcomers might become dependent on the state. A policy was worked out by bureaucrats in the Department of Labour, and those responsible for immigration, paying attention to opposing views from the private sector and trade unions, as well as pressures from ethnic and refugee support groups. The refugee compromise might be seen as yet another ingredient of the post-war Fordist accord. Many refugees without relatives had to agree to work for a period of time in jobs shunned by Canadians; this would please employers and silence negative public opinion,[16] including the voices of some labour organizations that feared rising unemployment. Even if the labour movement voiced its opposition to 'unfree'[17] immigrant labour, involuntary labour placement was, in some senses, part of the negotiated accord that it accepted in the immediate post-war period.

Dealing with the public's ethnocentric fears about displaced persons was also a concern for the government. As Irving Abella and Harold Troper have shown, many Canadian officials who first visited the camps in Europe recommended a hierarchy of ethnic desirables, with northern European Balts at the top, Jews always at the bottom, and Poles somewhere in between. In a 1946 public-opinion poll, Canadian reaction to Polish immigration was somewhat more positive, as long as these immigrants were separated out from the category 'Jewish.'[18] However, by late 1947 the state was becoming more sympathetic to increased immigration from all European groups as an economic-development perspective prevailed within the cabinet. Reassured by high levels of employment, and buttressed by many employers clamouring for labour, pro-immigration arguments took precedence, though the association of certain ethnic groups with specific occupations, and the desire to control the numbers of each national or ethnic group admitted, never disappeared from the state's agenda.

During debates in the House of Commons concerning the importation of the Dionne women, there was some evidence of both persisting ethnocentric concerns about eastern Europeans and support for the facilitation of refugee immigration. Representing the former impulse, one Toronto MP urged the government not to forget those 'suffering' in the 'Mother Country' of Britain, some of whom would be only too happy to emigrate and work in textiles. Minister of Labour Humphrey Mitchell also alluded to ethnocentric concerns voiced about undesirable groups, as opposed to 'British stock.' However, he then stressed that Canada now had an 'open door' as never before, and he emphatically urged against restrictive views, insisting that Canada should not 'throw cold water' on any group, be 'they English, Jewish, Ukrainian or Polish.'[19] Though this was partly a well-crafted defence of Dionne's scheme, it was a view repeated by many other MPs from different parties. These politicians tried to emphasize (in public at least) their sympathy for the suffering in Europe and support for European immigration, as well as the contribution of different 'racial' groups such as the Poles and Ukrainians to the war effort[20] – even though a lingering Anglo paternalism was also apparent in some speeches.

Public presentations to the Senate Standing Committee on Immigration and Labour revealed shifting and divergent views on ethnicity, 'race,' and immigration within the labour movement. The more conservative Trades and Labour Congress (TLC) favoured economically selective immigration, as well as the 'exclusion of races that cannot be assimilated into Canadian life,'[21] invariably a reference to Blacks and Asians. The more liberal Canadian Congress of Labour (CCL), whose ties to the CCF (Co-operative Commonwealth Federation) and campaigns against anti-Semitism had likely led to more enlightened views, spoke to the need for a de-racialized immigration policy.[22] Over the ensuing decade, the position of these organizations did not vary significantly.[23] The language of 'race,' however, varied considerably, depending on who was speaking: civil servants presented statistics that included skin colour, religion, and nationality, calling all these categories 'race,' while French Canadian commentators used the term 'racism' to describe anti-French feeling. Journalists used 'race' interchangeably with 'nation' or 'skin colour,' and European ethnic leaders addressing the Senate used it to denote different historical-cultural groups.[24]

Quebec-based Catholic unions were even more suspicious than the TLC of immigration. Like some French Canadian politicians and intellectuals, they feared that immigration would 'swamp' the French-speaking population, and to some extent this anxiety was borne out as post-war European immigrants favoured English schools.[25] The Confédération des Travailleurs Catholiques du Canada's (CTCC) opposition was unmistakeable: in a document prepared for the government in 1947, it denounced federal immigration policy as 'illogique, ridicule and révoltante.'[26] The CTCC's paper, Le Travail, published numerous anti-immigration articles in the late 1940s and 1950s, regularly sending resolutions of protest to the federal government.[27] Fears of cultural dilution and political contamination[28] were at the core of their opposition in

1947: Canada was already taking many immigrants; there were still many unemployed workers; the birth rate was not in need of external augmentation when it could be aided internally; workers were still leaving for the United States; and, finally, immigration was a dangerous 'réservoir du communisme.' What was 'rotting Europe' could taint Canada, said *Le Travail*, as indicated by the likes of (communist) immigrants 'Tim Buck, Fred Rose, and Sam Carr.'[29]

The standing committee also heard from members of the Canadian Jewish Congress, who were concerned about persisting anti-Semitism in government policy. Alluding to the Dionne workers, they noted perceptively that the importation of these women (all Catholic) who were brought to work in textiles revealed an implicit 'religious qualification' that excluded Jews.[30] Other groups who appeared before the standing committee ignored anti-Semitism, but insisted that the past denigration and screening of Europeans based on their racial origins had to end. In an effort to sell the idea of more refugees, a Polish representative also claimed that the hopeful newcomers, in contrast to the primarily rural peasants of the past, represented a 'cross section of skills.' . These newcomers, he noted, should be considered in light of the 'nobler values of western civilization' they represented; moreover, with the 'white races in decline,' and some countries under communist control, this might be Canada's 'last chance' to take in so many 'Old World Europeans.' Tolerance obviously did not extend to all potential immigrants. After the representative of the Canadian Polish Congress had decried exclusions of the past, he was asked 'What about the coloured races?' The answer was quite clear: he was only thinking of 'the European races' immigrating; Asian immigration was not an issue at this time, though this might change in the future, as Asians 'were progressing.'[31]While the privilege of whiteness was perhaps being slowly and grudgingly extended to European immigrants, many Canadians in turn distanced themselves from the non-preferred immigrants of colour.

Although some commentators suggested that educated and professional women fleeing Europe should be allowed similar opportunities in North America, it was assumed that most new immigrants would fill working-class occupations. The 1947 standing committee presumed immigrant women would fill 'shortages' in service occupations that Canadian women had abandoned as soon as they could during the war, though some were also to be placed in manufacturing.[32] These occupations were nonetheless portrayed as a step up for many refugees. Women such as the Polish displaced persons were fortunate to come to Canada, the minister of labour claimed, because they would be relieved of 'pulling a plough' by hand, as they did in Europe; in a similar vein, Senator Carinne Wilson chided Ukrainian men appearing before the standing committee for 'working your women too hard.'[33] A simultaneously ethnocentric and class-based image of eastern European women workers was obviously difficult to dislodge.

Concerns about displaced women's work prospects were also voiced by women's reform and charitable organizations. Prominent social reformer Dr Olive Russell told an Ottawa meeting that Canadians should be guided by their moral obligation to aid these women, rather than 'thinking of our [labour] needs,' but other speakers automatically assumed the displaced women would 'fit [into] service jobs' in the economy.[34] If Canadian women reformers thought refugees were escaping arduous 'peasant' labour, they had no problem imagining them in arduous Canadian service jobs. Similarly, the Catholic Women's League, echoing generations of middle-class women, pointed to the need for domestic servants who could be 'trained, supervised, and educated in English,'[35] and indeed, the largest group of displaced women signed domestic service contracts.[36] Working-class women immigrants had long been associated with domestic service, and this was even true for the Dionne women. After they arrived in Canada, Ludger Dionne began to receive letters, including from the United States, asking if he knew where one could find a good 'Polish maid.'[37] No wonder – he had already publicly told his fellow MPs that Polish women would make wonderful 'maids.'[38]

Women's employment was not the only concern of women's groups. At the time of the Dionne affair, the Ottawa YWCA presented a brief to the government that began by decrying religious and racial profiling, then insisted that female refugees be examined for mental and physical problems, including venereal disease; the latter reflected concerns that the moral character of newcomers may have been compromised.[39] Countering such fears, their sponsors insisted that the women had taken Wasserman tests, and that their 'intelligence, politics and work habits' had been rigorously assessed: they had 'unusually high standards of cleanliness and neatness,' insisted one federal official in an interview.[40]

Another litmus test for immigrants concerned their political ideology. Potential immigrants from communist countries, and especially those suspected of communist sympathies, were denied entry, yet increasingly this did not apply to some European fascists, now potential allies in the war on communism.[41] During parliamentary debates about the Dionne workers, all parties agreed on the need to 'screen communists'[42] from entering Canada, though the CCF saw some merit in maintaining diplomatic ties with new communist states such as Poland. MPs sympathetic to Ludger Dionne's scheme urged the government to save the Polish women from the terrible fate of repatriation to a dictatorial Red Poland. Like many subsequent refugees during the Cold War, the Dionne women became symbols of brave opposition to eastern European communist states.[43] For French Canadian newspapers, Ludger Dionne's efforts to save these Polish women from repatriation was evidence of Quebec's special contribution to the crusade against international communism.

This explains, in part, why the Quebec press criticized immigration policy in general, though not the Dionne scheme. When the standing committee publicly endorsed a pro-immigration policy, Le Devoir denounced its recommendation, claiming it reflected 'des intérêts sordides et du racisme chevroné.'[44] Quebec public and political opinion towards immigration may have been generally 'negative'[45] in this period, but support could be rallied for Catholic 'néo-Canadiens' who might be integrated into Quebec society as fellow combatants for 'l'ordre social Chrétien'[46] and against communism.[47] The support for Dionne's labour-importation scheme in Quebec, however, was not universal. The opposition of the union movement to this group of 'unfree' workers indicated that class, as well as ideology, gender, and ethnicity, was an important factor shaping this complex controversy.

The Dionne Labour Importation Scheme

The Dionne story is simultaneously one of political patronage, bureaucratic infighting, shaky international relations, and widespread public commentary on, and disagreement about, the scheme. In October of 1946, Ludger Dionne, the Liberal MP for Beauce County, south-east of Quebec City, wrote to a number of cabinet ministers complaining that he could not secure labour for his rayon spinning mill, and asking permission to recruit displaced persons as workers. 'I know that this permission can be given to me if you care to talk [about] the matter with the minister ... I know Mr. [Humphrey] Mitchell and I am positive he will do everything he can to help me,' Dionne wrote to a civil servant, suggesting to the ministerial underling that he had some political capital with the minister of labour.[48] The Department of Labour grudgingly conceded that there was a shortage of labour at the mill, particularly because wages were better elsewhere;[49] however, it was John Glen, the minister responsible for immigration, who secured an Order-in-council from the cabinet

(PC 1193) that granted Dionne permission to bring over about one hundred women from refugee camps.[50]

Louis St Laurent, the newly minted minister of external affairs, intervened to secure Dionne's passport in record time, and Dionne left almost immediately for American-controlled 'DP' camps in Germany. With the aid of the International Catholic Welfare Association (specifically two Polish-American priests), and the Intergovernmental Committee on Refugees (IGCR), he selected his prospective workers.[51] Before leaving, they signed a labour contract that bound them to work for Dionne for two years, unless by mutual agreement they were terminated. They were to receive the legal minimum wage in Quebec, but piece-rate earnings above the minimum were to be held back by Dionne until they had finished their two-year stint. Newspaper accounts also quoted Dionne as saying that the women would pay back 25 per cent of their fares. The women, in short, were trapped in an 'in between' category of 'unfree immigrants': although the state saw them as 'permanent settlers and citizens,' they initially faced 'political and legal restrictions on their ability to circulate freely in the Canadian labour market.'[52] Unlike some Polish military men who came as farm labourers, these women were not initially funded and monitored by the state, but by their employer, a fact that only fanned the flames of opposition to the scheme.

Even in Europe, Dionne admitted, some IGCR officers were worried that he was looking for 'contract' labourers who would be 'slaves until they paid back their transportation.'[53] Later, when External Affairs (EA) was trying to patch up the bad international relations he had created, Dionne could scarcely recall which organizations he had worked with: he was interested in the results, not the process. Three air charters, paid for by the IGCR and Dionne, then ferried the women to North America. Their arrival was covered in Quebec newspapers with positive fanfare. *La Presse* photographs showed Dionne and the smiling women descending from the plane, and also the happy women consuming a good meal – their first in a long time, we are told – in the airport cafeteria, with Mme Dionne serving them in a charming if somewhat unrealistic reversal of social roles. Another photo showed a happy Polish woman ready to strike up a folk tune on her cherished accordion; she and her singing companion were dressed respectably in their old girl scout uniforms. On arrival in Saint-Georges-de-Beauce, the women were to be immediately housed in the convent house, built with Dionne's aid, run by 'Les Soeurs du Bon Pasteur,' who often cared for criminalized girls and women.[54]

La Presse also declared indignantly that 'les réfugiées polonaises ne sont plus des esclaves.'[55] By the time the women landed, a political controversy over Dionne's scheme had already erupted. There were three epicentres of debate: one was played out in the House of Commons, another in the press, while a third zone of conflict was the diplomatic nightmare Dionne had created for EA. Opposition MPs pressed for a special debate on the Dionne scheme, initiated by CCF leader J.S. Coldwell's motion that censured the importation of indentured labour on behalf of 'select industrialists' and called for the immigration of refugees only as 'free human beings.'[56] MPs focused their criticisms on the violation of the *Alien Labour Law*, which prohibited assistance to and the importation of workers who had signed contracts prior to their arrival;[57] on the use of 'unfree' workers who were bound by contract to one employer; and on the political favouritism shown Dionne – all juxtaposed to the lack of a comprehensive refugee policy designed to aid displaced Europeans.

Opposition critics were incensed at Dionne's use of political connections to jump the immigration queue, adding that many of their constituents were overwhelmed with frustrating government bureaucracy as they attempted to bring destitute relatives from Europe. While some historians have noted that opposition members from the West took the lead in the debate, it was party politics and pro-labour sympathies, not regional concerns, that animated the discussion. CCFer Angus McInnis lambasted Dionne's scheme as one dressed up by the Liberals in the guise of humanitarian aid, but really 'done on the basis of pure, cold business,' a point exemplified in Dionne's admission that he faced a rapid turnover of 550 girls a year in his family-owned mill. Dionne had also stated that he needed to meet the Polish girls in person in order to 'make sure that they are fit for work,' a statement that conjured up images of a new slave trade for CCFer Gladys Strum: 'I do not think it improves our standing in the united nations [to have] ... scenes from 'Uncle Tom's Cabin' which remind one of the old slave markets where girls were put up for auction with someone looking at their muscles and someone else looking at their teeth.'[58] Communist groups and newspapers adopted the same theme in more hyperbolic language. The *Canadian Tribune* compared Humphrey Mitchell to 'Simon Legree, importer of slave labour,' while the left-wing Polish Democratic Association decried entrepreneurs such as Dionne who picked up the 'choice pieces [of humanity] from the bargain counters of human misery.'[59] The repeated rhetorical use of this language of slavery by many commentators summoned up older metaphors of 'wage slavery,' a term that some later

criticized for diminishing chattel slavery and racial power. Given underlying concerns about the women's moral vulnerability, resemblance to
the terminology of 'white slavery' may have been implied as well. [60]

Coldwell's claim that the *Alien Labour Law* was violated lost some of its
bite when Liberal cabinet minister C.D. Howe, now speaking for the
immigration portfolio in the debate, produced a contract that did not
include worker repayment of transportation costs. It appears the original contract had been modified in the face of public outrage. The
CCF was at pains to condemn not the immigration of refugees, but
rather the preferential treatment of Dionne and contracts that 'indentured' women to one employer. Some politicians also repeated sensational and inaccurate newspaper accounts alleging that Dionne had
forbidden the women to marry for two years, wear lipstick, or visit with
other Poles, save for their priest. America's *Time* magazine offered a
more lurid report, claiming Dionne had originally ordered up 'virgins'
from the camps, though he was dissuaded from making this stipulation
by one of the American officers.[61] The story may have contained a small
grain of truth, as the Polish women later told reporter Mavis Gallant
they resented having their moral characters scrutinized, giving the example of Dionne's initial interview, in which he asked each one: 'Are
you a good girl?'[62]

Dionne was defended by three influential cabinet ministers, all of
whom championed his humanitarian motives, creating, in the process,
a piteous picture of the 'starving girls' whom Dionne had rescued.[63]
Dionne was simply a 'realist,' C.D. Howe claimed, aiding the few people
he could, while Humphrey Mitchell maintained that these women
should be grateful, as they were far better off in Canada – a standard
rationale used then and now in the case of non-citizen workers. 'Every-
body knows these people do not want to go back to the [communist]
place they came from, asserted Mitchell. 'They want to live here in an
atmosphere of freedom – freedom of religion, freedom of the press ...
those great freedoms which have made this a great country.' St Laurent,
undoubtedly speaking for the benefit of Quebec, noted the importance
of Dionne aiding Catholic refugees who would be the 'only ones happy
in the surroundings of Beauce.'[64]

Both opponents and defenders of the scheme, therefore, positioned
themselves as protectors of defenceless women, a view that left little
room for the women's own agency in their decision to sign the contract.
While the Polish refugees were undoubtedly extremely vulnerable in the
camps, even desperate to leave, they had also managed to survive horrific

conditions, and some of the Polish women later reminded critics that they were quite capable of making their own decisions about immigrating.

Pressed to justify the scheme, Dionne presented himself as a model French Canadian entrepreneur, concerned with providing good jobs in Canada so that French workers would not leave Quebec for the United States. His language reflected lingering corporatist ideals, and his self-image was paternal. It was not the pursuit of profit, he said, but rather his commitment to a French Canadian, rural, Catholic way of life in Beauce that had animated his decision. While he recognized that many local families had to combine wages and agricultural work to make a living, he tended to trivialize women's waged contribution to the family economy. Most women, he claimed, only worked for pin money 'until marriage, or [until they could] enjoy the beautiful summer sun at ... home.'[65]

It was not a stretch, then, for Dionne to portray himself as a paternal 'guardian' to the refugees he had imported, whom he described as 'his little Polish girls.' Casting himself as a saviour, he told his fellow MPs that he had been moved by the 'tears and pleas' of female refugees who 'got down on their knees' in the camps, begging him to take them.[66] Dionne, like his Liberal defenders, also attempted to shift the debate from his misuse of political influence to the larger need for refugee aid, particularly as the spectre of European communism loomed. While the Polish women were again often rendered dependent and vulnerable in this picture, it was also in Dionne's interest to give them some historical agency: he reminded his political foes that the women were able to make their own decisions about coming to Canada.

If Liberal solidarity characterized the government's response, the press reaction was more complex. While some English Canadian papers were critical of Dionne, French-language papers in Quebec assumed a more laudatory, defensive, and nationalist tone. The influential *Globe and Mail* condemned the importation of the refugees 'under conditions of semi-servitude' as 'shocking to the public conscience.' The scheme 'clearly violates the Alien Labour Law' and begged the need for a fair, transparent immigration policy, asserted the *Globe* editorialist, declaring it 'intolerable' that the 'importation of human beings' into 'semi servitude' was granted to a 'private firm.'[67]

Many Quebec papers took exception to this portrayal of Dionne, and of Quebec society more generally; they were understandably suspicious that the partisan, Conservative *Globe* was adopting the same language as the labour movement simply as a means to criticize a French Canadian Liberal MP.[68] *La Presse* claimed Dionne had undergone a moral metamorphosis;

his road to Damascus occurred in the camps in Germany, for he went there as 'entrepreneur,' but his eyes were opened by the misery and despair he witnessed and he became a 'humanitarian.' There was nothing reprehensible about Dionne's scheme, agreed an editorial in *Le Soleil*, in contrast to the nasty Congress of Industrial Organizations (CIO), which the paper claimed was stirring up trouble, 'preaching violence and demagoguery.' Dionne was simply a victim of an unfair political attack, 'la cible de toutes les attaques imaginables.' Some articles shifted the debate to a moral defence of the women, whom they suggested were maligned by English politicians as docile, pathetic, even sexually immoral – categories that had never actually been invoked by Dionne's critics.[69]

Le Devoir journalist Pierre Vigeant, a well-known defender of the French language in Montreal,[70] reiterated the suspicions of many Quebec commentators when he argued that anti-French sentiments lay behind the controversy. 'L'immigration est bonne quand elle est britannique,' he wrote, yet when a 'humanitarian' French Canadian tried to aid immigration, his efforts were maligned unfairly. Dionne's project, he concluded, 'est condamnable parce qu'il a été mis à exécution par un industriel de langue française et parce que les immigrants se trouvent dans une atmosphère française, dans un foyer dirigé par des religieuses.'[71] *Le Devoir* did convey some of Coldwell's concerns about unfree labour, but many Quebec papers, in their haste to counter a perceived portrayal of Quebec as a backwater of corruption and exploitation, adopted a tone of nationalist defensiveness that simply echoed Dionne's statements uncritically.

Understandably, the local paper in Saint-Georges, *L'Éclaireur*, defended Dionne, the town's own home-grown industrial magnate, philanthropist, and influential citizen. Its reporting did capture some of the 'Hollywood'[72] feeling of the events, as the international press, fascinated by the story of young female 'DPs' 'saved' by an industrialist from the clutches of a communist country, descended en masse on the small town. Critics of Dionne, such as the two CIO union organizers who began to distribute leaflets at the factory, were quickly branded 'agents de l'extérieur' by *L'Éclaireur*, and the local elite immediately mobilized against this unionization effort. When another TLC trade unionist, Madeleine Parent, dared to suggest in her union paper that housing the women in a Catholic foyer might not encourage unionization, she was accused by the paper of fostering 'hatred' of the church.[73]

L'Éclaireur also interviewed some of the Polish women, who indicated how 'happy' they were to be in Canada. Over the ensuing months, it

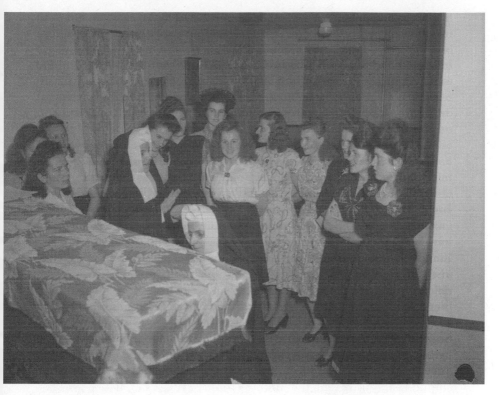

Figure 5 The 'Dionne girls' at the convent. (LAC, Montreal Gazette Fonds)

consciously fostered a positive view of these newcomers, stressing they were cultured and sometimes multilingual 'modern' Europeans, as well, of course, as being fellow Catholics. A special performance of ethnic dancing in costume was organized by the village, an attempt to use familiar symbols of folk culture to create a positive – and non-threatening – picture of the Polish women. Their youth and vulnerability were also stressed by *L'Éclaireur*. Local residents were warned not to harass and stare at them, but to treat them as they would their own 'jeunes [filles]'; 'les Polonaises' were cast as 'pauvres, petites orphelines' who appreciated the 'maternal' care of 'Les Soeurs du Bon Pasteur.'[74]

Public commentary, however, was divided not only according to partisan politics and language, but also along lines of ideology and class allegiance. *Le Devoir* took issue with the fact that English politicians were making comments 'méprisantes aux lois ouvrières de la province de Québec,'[75] but some Quebec labour activists were also affronted by these laws. *Le Travail* printed its resolution condemning the 'grand scandale' of Dionne's scheme in May of 1947, challenging his claim that labour was impossible to find by pointing out that there were '141,000 chômeurs, 2,000 jeunes filles ouvrières dans la seule région de Québec [qui] sont en quête d'emploi.'[76] In an editorial on 'le traitement des Polonaises' the following month, the paper used the same language of 'slavery' employed by English newspapers to describe the scheme, though it then turned to a more general condemnation of the low wages and long hours that prevented working-class 'chefs de famille' from supporting their children and enjoying family life.[77] By and large, Quebec and English Canadian labour shared a common view of the Dionne scheme. Like *Le Travail*, the CCL's organ, *The Canadian Unionist*, condemned Dionne's 'one-sided binding contract at scandalously low wages,' and it too drew comparisons to the slave trade: 'The only missing features in the government approved policy are the galleys and auction blocks which formed part and parcel of the slave trade.'[78]

Le Travail's response was shaped in part by the changes taking place in Quebec's Catholic union movement, which was now distancing itself from its earlier corporatist sympathies and embracing a more militant call for a new 'humanisme démocratique.'[79] While the CTCC, the union that later tried to organize Dionne's workers, embraced 'le nationalisme autonomiste,'[80] stressing the unique ethnic heritage of Quebec workers, it was not ready to jump on a press bandwagon defending the politician. Dionne's nationalist rhetoric did not sway these unionists, who remained suspicious that the importation scheme had more to do with low wage rates than with essential French Canadian values.

The fall-out for the Liberal government was also international; bureaucrats at the Department of External Affairs had to clear up a diplomatic mess in the wake of Dionne's labour-importation scheme. As Escott Reid quipped to Lester Pearson in private, civil servants were extremely upset with having to 'pull other peoples' chestnuts out of the fire' when they had 'never been adequately informed about the Dionne plan as the arrangements did not come within ordinary immigration regulations.'[81] While bureaucrats at the Department of Labour were no happier, claiming they had never really been 'consulted' about the project, it was EA that bore the brunt of the diplomatic work, trying to mend tattered relations with the Polish government.

Many memos concerning the Dionne scheme flew back and forth between EA personnel Lester Pearson, John Rae, Escott Reid, and Leslie Chance for months. Despite their growing concerns about eastern bloc communism, they felt it important to respond tactfully to the Polish government.[82] Their treatment of the Dionne situation also reflected Canada's emerging refugee policy. Immediately after the war, there was some support for repatriation, but by 1947, along with the United Nations, the United States, and its allies, Canada added protective provisos to repatriation to prevent coercive relocation for those fearing 'persecution'[83] at home.

The Polish ambassador to Canada sent his official protest on 3 June 1947. The girls and women, he claimed, were Polish citizens, some mere children deprived of their families. They had been lured to Canada improperly and prevented from returning to Poland, where they were needed to rebuild a devastated country. They were treated, inhumanely, like a 'human reservoir upon which foreign governments could draw,'[84] and their repatriation was essential. Ken Kirkwood, the new chargé d'affaires in the Canadian embassy in Poland, had barely unpacked his bags when he was summoned by a hostile foreign ministry to explain the Dionne scheme, which was being denounced in a virulent campaign in the Polish press, as well as by a Polish representative at the United Nations. Kirkwood sent home translations of denunciations of Canadian inhumanity from Polish newspapers, trying to impress on his colleagues the seriousness of the problem. The Polish women were designated as both 'tragic war victims' and 'white slaves.' Sarcastic headlines like 'piety, Canadian style' were used to highlight the hypocrisy of the Catholic Church's role in the scheme. The press reprinted pitiful letters, reportedly penned by the Dionne women, claiming they were depressed, their health was deteriorating, and their hearts were aching for home. Making a connection to Nazi labour camps, one letter lamented the fact that 'at least we knew the Germans were our enemies ... Now we are supposed to have liberty but we are locked up in something worse ... We are simply white negroes.'[85]

Hoping to both calm the international waters and reassure labour critics at home, the federal government sent Victor Podoski, a former Polish diplomat in exile (and thus no friend of the Polish communist government), to Saint-Georges to study the women's working and living conditions. Podoski was to investigate charges, including some from non-communist organizations, that the women were subject to Dionne's authoritarian control. Claims were made that their mail was opened and read, that their social life was monitored, and that they were kept away from Polish visitors, who were portrayed by Dionne as potential criminals. Deportation was supposedly used as a threat if the women did not live up to these rules.

Podoski met with local police, religious leaders, and company representatives as well as the women, who now constituted about one-fifth of the mill's payroll. His report, filed in September of 1947, vindicated the company in almost all respects. Like other eastern European émigrés who opposed communism in their own country, he was quick to condemn Canadian communists as instigators of mistruths. It was Polish communists in Canada, Podoski insisted, who were fomenting many of the stories of the women's exploitation at the Dionne mill – even though the mainstream press had been far more influential in this regard. The women, Podoski wrote, were not indentured since they could quit their two-year contract by mutual agreement, and even though the company was putting aside the 'extra' monies earned on piece work, some funds were released to help pay for items such as winter coats. Girls who were 'hysterical, unbalanced,' or unable to fit in had been released for domestic jobs (a telling view of such work), but by and large, the girls liked their employment and did not find it onerous. Their accommodations were 'nice and clean,' their meals 'plentiful,' and their social life was only monitored to protect the girls from marauding men with base instincts. Language and cultural barriers, Podoski insisted, were at the bottom of many misunderstandings, and now that a Polish priest was visiting, things would improve. Describing Dionne's treatment of the women as fair and 'Christian,' he pointed to evidence of their filial affection for Dionne, who took them on picnics. 'Why we even call him 'Daddy,' he quoted them as saying, legitimating Dionne's paternal self-image.[86]

While Podoski was undoubtedly correct in disputing the more sensational claims of women's slavery and incarceration, his report was also shaped by his patrician identification with the owners, a salient reminder that class differences within ethnic groups shaped very different immigrant experiences and allegiances. He was known to be hostile to the Polish government, and though he clearly wanted to hear the women's own voices, he was insensitive to the fact that they may have feared deportation if they complained. Yet this kind of public scrutiny did push Dionne to modify the much-criticized contract and give the women more freedom than he had originally planned to do.

High-ranking civil servants spent months crafting a reply to the Polish government, attempting to avoid controversial issues that might reignite the controversy. Every Polish accusation about the Dionne scheme was perused with fine toothcomb, down to the claim that the women received weekly wages equal to a pair of stockings. After testy communications with Department of Labour bureaucrats who made clear their lack of 'joy' with the Dionne contract, and their despair with 'utterly confusing' replies from Dionne about what the actual wages were, EA ultimately left out any reference to this charge. After all, quipped Chance, 'if anyone is to become involved in a discussion of what is an exorbitant price for nylons, I'd rather it was not our department.'[87] His acerbic comment was the tip of the iceberg, as there was clearly distaste among the External Affairs bureaucrats for the entire Dionne file. The final official reply to the Polish government made a few key points: the Canadians believed in voluntary repatriation; the women came to Canada of their own free will; they were selected by reputable international and Catholic agencies; they received the Quebec minimum wage; and their living conditions were quite respectable and decent.[88] EA civil servants just wanted the Dionne affair to go away, and it is revealing that Dionne's attempts to get special treatment for his next trip abroad were rebuffed by the minister.[89]

During the heated parliamentary debate about his Polish workers, Dionne was quoted as saying that all unions were free to organize his plant, 'though the Catholic union' was the 'proper' union for the area, as 'we are all Roman Catholics.'[90] If Dionne thought the Catholic union would be appropriately deferential, however, he was proved wrong when a strike broke out a year later at his family's mill. The determination of the strikers was emblematic of labour's post-war militancy across the country, as well as of the more assertive brand of Catholic unionism emerging in Quebec, a theme explored in more detail in chapter 4.[91] The presence of women on the Dionne picket line, where they outnumbered men, along with their visibility at other strikes at Dominion Textiles, also suggested the changing gendered face of the labour movement. Though under-represented in the union leadership, women were gaining experience and visibility as rank-and-file actors in the labour movement.[92]

In 1947 Dionne's workers organized a local of the Fédération Nationale Catholique de Textile, affiliated with the CTCC. After a year of frustrating dealings with Dionne, a resolute anti-unionist, the union called a strike on 19 July 1948. Many Polish women (between 61 and 75 in reports) still laboured at the mill. It was very difficult for them to leave the town, let alone picket with fellow workers, because their board at the convent was still paid by Dionne. Moreover, he held on to their passports and documents – until the CTCC put pressure on him to give the documents back. Contractually, Dionne did not have to pay the women their 'extra' piecework earnings if they were dismissed, which resulted in a strong fear of displeasing him. The Polish women visited the picket line, but they were reluctant to speak to any reporters or give their names, though one ventured that 'everyone in the mill' knew a strike was coming.[93]

After a long, hostile strike, the workers were ultimately outmatched by an unsympathetic Quebec state, a judiciary ready to issue injunctions against the union, and, as the union put it, by a trio of 'patrons au point de vue industriel' who controlled the Beauce region.[94] Union wage demands were never met, and the promise of a long-lasting collective agreement did not materialize.[95] Although the Polish women were some of the first to return to work, the union avoided placing any xenophobic blame on these workers. According to the CTCC, the women had communicated their wish not to break a legitimate strike and confided their disillusionment with the disjuncture between the promises Dionne had made them and the reality they encountered in Saint-Georges-de-Beauce.[96] Moreover, in September, a group of the Polish women left for Toronto in search of work; by the strike's finish, the majority of the displaced persons had abandoned Saint-Georges.[97] Dionne's paternalism, it appears, had worn thin for the Polish women, just as it had for the Québécois workers who had called the strike. At the CTCC's September convention, Dionne was publicly denounced for his 'anti-labour, anti-social and anti-union' views, and even though only eighteen Polish women were left at the mill, the union insisted they should be allowed their 'freedom,' released from 'forced' conditions, receiving low wages and paying for food that was 'worse than that in the camps.'[98]

Le Devoir's fears about the nature of Canadian immigration – with English, not French, benefiting – seemed to have been proved correct, as many of the women sought out work in Ontario or the United States as soon as they could. By May 1949, only eight of the original one hundred were left.[99] The women were well aware, claimed reporter Mavis Gallant, that English was the 'managerial language' in Canada and their key to economic mobility, so they scattered to English-speaking areas. Moreover, the structural conditions of the women's lives precluded their easy integration into mill life and the union. From the very beginning, Dionne had 'cloistered' the women in the walls of the convent, thus discouraging their integration into social groups such as local families or

Polish visitors (the latter were always feared as potential communist spies). Within the town, the new arrivals felt they were curiosities, greeted with 'stares ... pity ... and a slight hostility,' in part because workers feared they had been brought to the mill to keep wages low. The women's lack of French language skills also prevented their integration into work culture and strike events, though strikers claimed the women became sympathetic to their cause, recognizing that any increase in wages would benefit them.

Everything done for the Polish women, as Gallant pointed out, was justified by Dionne's phrase 'for their own good,' but this heavy-handed surveillance isolated the women from the community. Even Dionne grew tired of justifying his paternal role: during the strike he grumbled that the Polish women 'morally ... owed him something ... for he wanted a return on his investment.'[100] Ironically, by the end of the strike, other workers had come to accept the immigrants they initially feared, while the employer who fervently promoted their immigration had come to resent their lack of deference.

Conclusion

How the Dionne workers themselves perceived their experiences is difficult to surmise, since reports of their responses vary wildly. When Mavis Gallant gained entry to the Catholic convent where the women lived, she heard complaints about the bad food (Gallant agreed after a taste test), restrictions on the women's liberty, worries about money, and also the Podoski report, which was in the women's view a whitewash of their situation. Their responses hinted that they too realized that Podoski's upper-class background precluded him from seeing the difficult conditions under which they laboured. The women's employment strategies – leaving Saint-Georges to seek out other Polish-speakers or to search for better-paying jobs, security, and upward mobility – repeated the tactics utilized by earlier generations of immigrant women, who saw their move to a new country as an invitation to strive for better lives, not as an obligation to be eternally indebted to those who aided their passage.

Dionne may well have perceived his efforts as being charitable and protective, but as an entrepreneur he also saw these new immigrants as a resource, part of the equation of production.[101] This is hardly surprising: many employers and industries facing perceived labour shortages lobbied for refugee, and later immigrant, workers using similar terminology. It is possible that the main reason for Dionne's importation scheme was not simply to secure employees willing to work for low wages, but also to establish a stable, loyal labour force in a rural area where the rhythms of seasonal agricultural labour competed with mill work. These hopes were shattered when, only a year after the Polish refugees arrived, the mill workers rejected old-style paternalism in favour of modern unionization, their rebellion symbolizing the emergence of more militant confessional unions, and also marking the increased rank-and-file participation of women within the labour movement. Without even mentioning Dionne, *Le Travail* assessed paternalism as an industrial strategy in 1947 and found it wanting: it led some employers to treat workers like 'children,' and as far as the union was concerned, employees had now 'reached the age of majority.'[102] It was a telling metaphor for a wave of labour organizing that engulfed the country immediately after the war.

Given what we know of new immigrants' job prospects in the post-war years, it is unlikely that many of the Dionne women found an easy path into the affluence of the Fordist accord. Although it is difficult to generalize about immigrant women's labour prospects over the two decades following the Second World War, only a minority of new Canadians, usually those who came with educational qualifications, made their way into the professions. Far more coped with lower-paid, female-typed jobs in the manufacturing and service sectors. The importation of refugees and immigrants such as the Dionne women as contract workers, bound or relegated to lower-paid or less appealing jobs, is a reminder that contingent, marginalized labour is not only part of our 'new economy': it was part and parcel of the process of capital accumulation that shaped the Fordist accord.

Despite their status as contract labourers, these Polish women were not racialized as undesirable immigrants in the same manner as eastern European newcomers had been thirty years before. In Quebec, this was due in part to the fact they were Catholic. The strong and growing influence of anti-communism also undoubtedly helped to make the Dionne women, and refugees that followed from Eastern Europe, more acceptable and desirable immigrants. This, in turn, contributed to the process of 'whitening' eastern and southern European immigrants, as some non-Anglo ethnic groups were slowly accorded grudging acceptance in the aftermath of the war – though other immigrants of colour were certainly not. The Dionne women may have been the focus of immense paternalism, viewed as potential domestics and described as helpless slaves by politicians and labour, but their own actions in deserting Dionne's mill as soon as they could indicate that they did not internalize this version of the helpless and dependent immigrant. Rather, they actively sought to create new lives of labour and dignity in their adopted country.

Chapter 3

Women and the Canadian Labour Movement during the Cold War

At seventeen, I applied for a civil-service job in Ottawa as a means of finding temporary employment. After a security clearance, I was hired by the Royal Canadian Mounted Police (RCMP) in the Vanier unit, where the organization's archives were located. Each day, a group of about four to six clericals staffed a table where we waited patiently until orders came to fetch a numbered file folder for the bosses. In these pre-politicized days, I did not think of reading any files (I would have been fired instantly), but I did try to imagine the rationale for the numbering system, as rows and rows of French or eastern European names suggested that dangers to the state were laid out in geographical/thematic rather than alphabetical order. As a new file fetcher, I was called into a 'higher up's' office for an interview. A pleasant RCMP officer, in uniform, and vaguely resembling actor Tony Randall, asked that I read a statement and sign it. The paper in question warned me that, as a young woman, I had to be aware that I might be approached by 'suave' and charming men, probably foreign agents, who might try to insinuate themselves into my life, tempting me to do something untoward with those rows of files. I thought Tony was playing a practical joke: it must be part of an office initiation scheme. Seeing the look on his face, I realized a humorous repartée was not in order, and I dutifully signed. I was actually intrigued by the thought of 'suave' agents in hot pursuit of me. To my disappointment, none (that I know of) ever approached me. That was 1969.

As this incident suggests, the Cold War, though often associated with the 1950s, had a longer reign in North America. Some scholars estimate that its chronological sweep ranged from the 1940s until the fall of Soviet hegemony in eastern Europe in the late 1980s; others point to its early origins in the development of a Canadian security state after the First

World War. My experience in Corporal Tony Randall's office suggests the longevity of Cold War fears of communist agents and the 'enemy within,' well into an era we assume was more liberal and open. It also underscores the connection between sexual dereliction and disloyalty common to Cold War thinking by the state.

The fear that communist spies might use sexual encounters as entrapment, and the notion that the heterosexual, nuclear family and stalwart men were the bedrock of democracy's strength were all part of the ideological and cultural trappings of the Cold War that pitted the capitalist West against the communist Soviet Union. Canada had its share of high-profile 'spy' scandals and Cold War persecutions, from diplomat E.H. Norman's suicide after he was pursued relentlessly by McCarthyist forces to the later exposé of Tory cabinet ministers' sexual dalliances with German immigrant, sometime model, and 'party girl' Gerda Munsinger. Munsinger's role as a spy was highly questionable, but as Bryan Palmer has recently argued, she fit the RCMP's sexual and cultural 'Mata Hari' stereotype so well that they could not believe she was *not* a security risk.[1]

From the time of the 1945 'official' kickoff of the Canadian Cold War, with Russian cipher clerk Igor Gouzenko's defection and his sensational stories of Canadian spy rings, the majority of women affected by the Cold War were not involved in espionage. Women whose experience of the Cold War was most direct and vicious were those fired from jobs at such agencies as the National Film Board (NFB) or the Red Cross, whose communist or Marxist politics, sympathies, past associations, or even family members' associations, made them the target of employer or state suspicion and harassment.[2] Their public outing might involve the loss of employment, blacklisting, or the silent retreat of friends. Some of those targeted were Communist Party members; others were sympathetic leftists caught in a rather indiscriminate state dragnet. There was also a larger group of women, more uncertain in numbers, whose experiences are more difficult to assess: those who were affected by the communist purges that engulfed their unions. Comprehending their experience of the Cold War, however, is a vital piece of the larger picture of the postwar situation for women workers, for their understanding of politics, union activism, resistance, and appropriate gender roles were all affected by the anti-communist cloud of anxiety that hung over Canadian society. Using three areas of union organizing – fur, electrical, and textiles – as case studies, this chapter explores the consequences of the Cold War for these women workers, and for the labour movement's commitment to gender-equity issues.

For women workers watching the Cold War unfold in their unions, an important lesson was not just what happened to communist men and women, criticized for their 'treasonous' politics, but what might happen to any woman whose expression of dissent appeared to be too communist in tone. Given how central the coercion emanating from the state, the law, and policing was to the Cold War, we have understandably focused our historical attention on these forms of regulation; however, we cannot lose sight of the more diffuse and subtle means by which anti-communism was sustained. Foucauldian insights into the *process* of social and self govern- ance are useful here: discipline does not simply go to work on the promin- ent communist being ostracized; it circulates far more broadly and insidi- ously, reminding other workers what might happen to them if they cross the line from 'loyal' to 'disloyal' citizen, thus encouraging their own pol- itical self-disciplining. The effects of these anti-communist discourses, however, might be better described as ideological, for the latter were dif- fused through education, the media, and daily life, creating a seemingly 'common sense' fear of communism that both shaped self-governance and bolstered the power of the state and capital to deal with the commun- ist 'menace.'[3] The dominant ideology of anti-communism that suffused Canadian society offered employers, the state, and anti-communist union leaders a potent tool in their efforts to rid the union movement of a per- ceived political menace. More generally, though, the mere knowledge of the Cold War's power to ostracize was a powerful weapon stifling left-wing dissent for many years after Gouzenko's defection.

Canada's Cold War: Less Cold than Others?

Faced with the spectacle of Joe McCarthy and, most horrific, the execu- tion of Julius and Ethel Rosenberg, some Canadian journalists argued that Canada's 'Peaceable Kingdom' experienced a kinder, gentler version of the Cold War than the one in the United States. Such self- congratulation was misplaced. Canadian magazines and newspapers purveyed similar fears of communism, equating it with hostile invasion from outside the country or insidious takeover from within. Numerous articles told readers they were vulnerable not only to nuclear war, sabo- teurs, invading armies, or nearby 'Russian subs' on our coastline,[4] but also to the internal threat of the fanatical, all-consuming poison of ideol- ogy 'possessing'[5] our minds. Liberal journalists discussed whether they should ostracize communist friends, no matter how old or dear,[6] while conservative writers called for draconian measures, banning communists from all areas of public life.[7] If a 'grey'[8] area existed, it was in the debate over how best to combat communism: with existing laws, good foreign policy, or anti-communist education.

While it is true that the Canadian state never used the electric chair to make its point, many purges were effected away from public view, but nonetheless with severe consequences for the people involved. Reginald Whitaker and Gary Marcuse's extensive study traces state surveillance and purges within the National Film Board; the civil service; peace, educational, and reform organizations; and unions.[9] As the previous chapter on the Dionne workers indicated, the Cold War also shaped immigration policy, and thus the post-war workforce. Potential immigrants from countries with strong communist parties were strictly inspected and those suspected of communist tendencies were denied entry, yet leniency was granted to some European fascists, now potential allies in the war on Canadian communism.[10] These state policies still have some contemporary defenders who claim that communism posed a serious danger to Canadian society, though a more critical approach favours the view that the 'insecurity' state manufactured scares, ignored civil rights, and used anti-communism as a means of crushing anti-capitalist and anti-NATO dissent.[11] Finding a middle ground, Reginald Whitaker and Steve Hewitt conclude that there was indeed some security risk, but that the state purposely exaggerated this as a means of silencing dissent, and in the process rode roughshod over the lives of those targeted.[12]

Trade unions were central to the Cold War, and indeed, the Cold War was one element of the post-war Fordist accord between capital and the mainstream labour movement.[13] Since communists associated with the Communist Party (after 1943, the Labour Progressive Party), and social democrats and their allies (the former linked to the CCF) both saw influence within the house of labour as a sine qua non of their political success, unions became the site of intense internal political struggles. Few labour historians argue that the anti-communist purges that resulted were a 'necessity'; more often, they contend that anti-communists sacrificed 'truth and justice' in their misguided crusade, and that the long-term consequences of internecine warfare were negative for the entire labour movement.[14] Ironically, they point out, the CCF-led campaign also backfired, as it too suffered fallout from anti-socialist campaigns waged in the name of anti-communism.[15] Attempts to rewrite labour history without the blinders of Cold War ideology led to a profusion of less 'leadership-focused' histories of communism in North America, centring on local, single-issue, and rank-and-file organizing.[16] While these

New Left–inspired analyses of the local, on-the-ground permutations of communism have contributed valuable perspectives, there is a simultaneous tendency, as Bryan Palmer points out, to sidestep unpleasant questions about decisions from the 'centre,' Party leadership, and Stalinism.[17]

Perhaps all these contending positions can agree on one thing: all three trade-union centrals – the TLC, CCL, and CTCC – were adamant supporters of a Cold War in labour.[18] Editorials and news items in the TLC paper presented communism as a dangerous revolutionary and conspiratorial plan to overthrow democratic institutions. Campaigns associated with communists, such as the Stockholm peace pledge, were ridiculed, and a direct link between communists, espionage, and betrayal of one's country was often asserted. Lines were firmly drawn: as for the Rosenbergs, a TLC editorial sneered unsympathetically before their execution that 'at least they had a trial' [unlike in the USSR].[19] Similarly, the CCL paper warned that communism threatened 'Christianity and civilization ... It [was] godless, materialistic, opposed to every form of worship,' as well as guilty of 'suffocating the human spirit and preaching eternal war.'[20] Democracy versus dictatorship, patriotism versus disloyalty, were the stark political choices offered in this battle.

At the beginning of the Cold War, some union centrals also defined the 'free world' in terms of its defence of the traditional family. After the World Federation of Trade Unions (WFTU) meeting in Rome – before the CCL quit the WFTU claiming it was communist – the *Canadian Unionist* reported that equal pay became a contentious political point of difference for the delegates. Eastern European 'iron curtain' unions reported that the work of married women was increasing, and was 'promoted as national policy.' The CCL responded that 'abolishing' the exploitation of married women was its historic goal: 'Every working family should have a home and the mother should be required to stay home and look after it.'[21] The association of communism with the evils of working mothers and state-sponsored day nurseries was also used as an ideological weapon by politicians intent on eliminating day nurseries set up during the war. With day care labelled a 'Red' demand, the issue was sidelined, and its supporters cast as adversaries of the traditional family.[22] While a defence of the male breadwinning family may have been part of the CCL's anti-communist pitch, it was a less overt theme in their political arsenal than fears of Soviet world dominance, undoubtedly heightened in a nuclear world only recently recovering from war. Still, fears of subversion and war could not be completely severed from a defence of the family, since Cold War rhetoric often equated the stable, happy

Figure 6   Canadair ad, *Canadian Congress Journal*, April 1955.

family with protection against the communist menace. Unions were also quite content to join with the private sector in this ideological campaign. Some allowed companies to use union papers as a vehicle to promote anti-communism and sell their product at the same time, although only Canadair's ad warning that Canadian men might be becoming too 'soft' to fight the Soviet menace used a clearly gendered approach. Another Canadair ad, featuring a female school teacher and young student, urged parents to beware of the infiltration of 'godless' communist ideas into the educational system: otherwise, communism might 'take the citadel from within' by corrupting the minds of youth.[23]

Trade unionists who refused to join the anti-communist crusade were deemed suspect; consequently, independent socialist and even civil-libertarian positions were difficult to sustain in this highly polarized atmosphere.[24] When communists and their 'sympathizers' were barred as delegates from TLC meetings, concern about their 'democratic rights' was dismissed as naive support for revolutionaries who wished to 'destroy democratic rights.' In an ironically authoritarian statement, local labour councils were told to 'obey' the new rule of banning communist members. The TLC assured these locals it was not engaging in a US-style 'witch hunt,' since it knew for a fact that communists were evil destroyers of democracy and freedom, and 'saboteurs' to boot.[25] The state was not a neutral bystander in labour's Cold War. While some appointed bodies such as labour-relations boards had to appear neutral, the state also offered its ideological support to unions' anti-communist program. In specific cases, such as the Canadian Seamen's Union, or Maurice Duplessis's Quebec government, it actively intervened to facilitate the removal of communists from the union movement.[26]

Imagined enemies of the state were not simply trade unionists but, like the homosexuals fired from the Canadian civil service, they might be sexually non-conformist 'deviants,' supposedly more likely to succumb to the insidious blackmail of the 'suave' agents circulating in Ottawa. The connections between the containment of the nuclear, heteronormative family and Cold War politics, between domestic conformity and foreign threats, were suggested initially by American writers Elaine Tyler May and John D'Emilio, and despite subsequent critiques of their work, their insights have sparked important new debates concerning gender, sexuality, and the Cold War.[27] Exploring the gendered impact of anti-communism is also important because American feminist historians have argued that we previously exaggerated the negative impact of the conservative Cold War period on women's labour activism, arguing that this era saw an increase in unions' equality-seeking campaigns.[28] Another point of view, however, still faults the Cold War for suppressing the unionization of women (and, in the United States, African-American) workers, and stifling discussion of equity issues.[29] Of course, the Canadian Cold War in labour was not an exact replica of the American one: we did not contend with the same 'race' questions in southern organizing; a few communist-led unions survived here without the terror of the US Taft-Hartley law, which required union leaders to sign statements swearing they were not communists;[30] and the communist issue was linked to nationalist debates about Canadian union autonomy *from* the US union leadership. Nevertheless, we cannot extricate our history from that of the United States too neatly, since anti-communist battles were played out within the intricate politics of international unions that were essentially under American control. This was precisely the case for women fur workers, whose union, the International Fur and Leather Workers Union (IFLWU),[31] was destroyed by the Cold War.

The Cold War in Fur

Just as the 'insecurity state' was rooted in a pre–Cold War past, so too was the intra-union conflict that characterized the Cold War struggles in fur unions. Long before Igor Gouzenko and the Iron Curtain, there were antagonistic divisions in labour organizations, reflecting opposing social-democratic and communist perspectives.[32] To understand the vehemence of the Cold War in fur, and its impact on women, it is necessary to look briefly at union political strife in the 1930s and 1940s.[33]

Women workers had an established, if secondary, status in the Canadian fur industry, a business geared almost entirely to the production of coats for women consumers. Fur production was characterized by a high number of small workplaces: in 1949 there were 642 manufacturers in the country, concentrated in Winnipeg, Toronto, and Montreal, with the latter emerging as the post-war capital of fur production.[34] The workforce in these three large cities had historically had a large number of European Jewish workers; in the 1930s, some union meetings were conducted in Yiddish, and the few remaining membership lists for Winnipeg indicate the geographical and social clustering of a strong Jewish union membership.[35] This ethnic pattern was somewhat different in Montreal, where French Canadians also worked in the shops, and in Toronto, where non-Jewish and Jewish workers actually had different locals at one point, causing some tensions, particularly since the Jewish workers saw their non-Jewish comrades as more conservative.[36]

The work process within the industry was segregated more by gender than ethnicity, as the skills required to create coats from pelts were primarily the preserve of men, apprenticed to learn the techniques of sorting, wetting and stretching, blocking, then cutting the skins. Women, in contrast, worked as sewing-machine operators, making linings, and finishing the coat; some also worked with men in the fur-dressing business, preparing the raw pelts for manufacturing. Women's work was generally designated as less skilled (even when they shared the same operator jobs with men), and in Canada, their share, even of operating jobs, decreased in the post–Second World War period, in part due to the influx of many displaced male fur workers from Europe.[37] Despite the gendered division of labour in the industry, women shared common concerns with male fur workers about the industry's low wages, seasonally long hours, and unhealthy working conditions (tuberculosis and respiratory problems were prevalent). The industry was still very difficult for unions to tackle, not only because of the profusion of small workplaces, but also because anti-union employers, also often European immigrants, were ready to use injunctions, dismissals, yellow-dog contracts, and strikebreakers to maintain control of their factories.[38] As if that were not enough, organizing was characterized by divisive, ongoing struggles between social-democratic and communist fur workers. In some cities, a modicum of unity prevailed;[39] however, in general, rival groups competed for members and territory, and over union property.[40] The conflict in Toronto became particularly personal, violent, and extreme, with 'hot battles in the streets'[41] between communists and their opponents, each group claiming its opponents employed gangsters as enforcers.

Unionization in the industry was aided by the presence of the politicized, left-wing Jewish immigrants working in fur, including women who were prominent on IFLWU picket lines in the Depression. In Winnipeg, activists Freda Coodin and Pearl Wedro – both communists – were arrested for their activities, with Coodin spending a year in jail.[42] While activist female fur workers were not shy about blocking workplace doors and intimidating scabs during strikes, they were not found leading the violent intra-union skirmishes, an indication that such Cold War bullying might have marginalized them within the union. Hiring local thugs, doing business in pool halls, and trashing cars with baseball bats were not gender-neutral activities: this was a masculine and sometimes macho environment that was not welcoming to female leadership.

A brief attempt at unity during the Popular Front broke down when the social-democratic leaders in Toronto, Max Federman and Harry Simon (both associated with labour Zionism), were charged in 1938 with misappropriating workers' unemployment benefits. While their self-appointed committee cleared them, the international office of the IFLWU and the Toronto District Labour Council found evidence of guilt.[43] Dual unions then materialized, with the IFLWU staying within the CIO, and the AFL chartering an autonomous fur local in Toronto under Max Federman's leadership. The social democrats were not disgraced for long: they enjoyed a comeback when the Hitler-Stalin pact put the communists on the moral defensive; indeed, the Federman leadership instructed employers not even to recognize the rival CIO union, now denounced as 'fifth column Nazi agents of Stalin.'[44]

As the Cold War heated up considerably after the end of the Second World War II, cooking the books seemed a lesser evil than the Soviets to both the CIO-CCL and the American AFL leadership. This intensification of anti-communism left the larger Canadian IFLWU at the mercy of the American state and the American trade-union leadership. Expelled from the CCL in 1950 on the flimsy pretext that it had criticized the leadership on the issue of wage and price controls,[45] the IFLWU struggled on independently, trying to organize new leather and shoe locals. However, in the United States, court cases launched against the international president, Ben Gold (an open party member), severely crippled the international, and in Canada, the AFL fur union was trying to raid IFLWU locals in Montreal, whose existence was also threatened by a 1954 Quebec law barring communists from union office.[46] Ironically, though, it was ultimately Communist Party advice to its own union members to find refuge in the 'mainstream' of the labour movement that resulted in an IFLWU decision in 1954 to merge with the AFL's Amalgamated Meat Cutters and Butcher Workmen (AMCBW). Since a few key fur-union leaders in Canada, particularly President Robert Haddow, were essentially party appointments, they were unlikely to ignore this advice.[47]

The Canadian IFLWU initially embraced the merger plan, even though the lack of a Taft-Hartley law in Canada made the situation somewhat different for their locals. During extensive merger negotiations over 1954 and 1955, Canadian fur workers were reassured by the new, non-communist American IFWLU that their national 'autonomy and sovereignty'[48] within the AMCBW would be assured. In fact, exactly the opposite was true. A blacklist of all the suspected Canadian communists to be fired was given to the AFL by Harry Simon and Max Federman, who would only join the merger if their old communist enemies were vanquished. They had their way. When Canadian IFWLU locals objected to the extent of the blacklist, resisting what they saw as both colonial treatment and the beheading of their own leadership, they were put into receivership by the American leaders. A movement for an 'autonomous'[49] Canadian IFLWU emerged, but this was soon put to rest, not simply because of American pressure but, ironically, because the Canadian Communist Party – for all its anti-American rhetoric – insisted that the party line of 'mainstreaming' came first.[50] The Canadian IFLWU agreed to humiliating terms and a purge of its leaders that even the opponents admitted was 'ruthless.'[51] Dismissed communist organizers such as Muni Taub and Pearl Wedro found themselves unemployed and blacklisted, and they were forbidden by the merger agreement even to run for office.[52]

Nor was the Cold War in fur over. Until the late 1960s, anti-communist fur workers continued to lobby vigilantly for the 'cleansing' of any and all communists from their midst.[53] You 'can't get rid of an octopus by just cutting off the arms, but the head,'[54] they argued, linking communists with Soviet espionage, treason, and dictatorship.[55] When Federman wrote the history of the Toronto union, not only did he blame communists for the 'ruination'[56] of the union, but he airbrushed out female activists such as Coodin and Wedro. Pearl Wedro, the union's most prominent female organizer, had long been berated publicly in pamphlets by the Federman group as a 'Stalinist fish wife,'[57] an anti-communist designation also meant to elicit a picture of an overbearing, ugly, nagging old woman. Like other women on the left, Wedro found that her body and sexuality were as much fair game for ridicule as her politics.[58]

During this long Cold War in fur, the contending fur unions were united only once, in a joint effort to rescue five hundred furriers from 'Displaced Persons' (DP) camps in Europe, though unionists disagreed afterwards on whether to expose the government's hidden quota on Jewish fur workers. The DP rescue effort purposely sought single male workers, a reflection of the long-standing endorsement of a male skilled/breadwinner model, and it is true that neither the social-democratic nor the communist union fundamentally challenged the gendered division of labour and differential wages within the industry. Did the Cold War really matter, then, to women fur workers?

An examination of new organizing, equity issues, and the union leadership suggests it certainly did. First, these unions were also those with the potential to reach out to women, immigrants, and non-Anglo/

workers. After the Second World War, the IFLWU tried to maintain its base in Canada with new organizing in tanneries, shoemaking, and leather goods, unionizing small workplaces where women were a significant part of the labour force. In Vancouver, Pearl Wedro organized a string of shoemakers so small in size that she astutely secured a common agreement to protect all of them.[59] In another leather-goods workplace in southern Ontario, Wedro also tried to raise the issue of equal pay for women workers during the organizing effort.[60] After 1946, locals of tannery, pocket-book, and shoe workers were also founded in Quebec, in the face of the provincial government's intense antipathy to the IFLWU. Although faced with repeated raids, the IFLWU was able to hold on to workplaces it had organized, many of which had used the state machinery of the War Labour Board to substantially improve conditions, securing a 44-hour week, overtime, and increases across the board that aided women workers in particular.[61]

In concert with attempts to organize new workplaces, there was renewed discussion after war's end within the IFLWU of separate women's committees, designed to train female union leaders and address issues of equal pay, maternity leave, retention of seniority rights on maternity leave, and special health protections for women's work.[62] Women's committees (for workers) and women's auxiliaries (for wives of workers) were originally to be organized jointly, but by 1950 it was suggested they work separately, sharing some projects such as International Women's Day.[63] Canadian organizers Pearl Wedro and Montrealer Charlotte Gauthier were involved in the organization of the international women's committee, with Gauthier serving as secretary.[64] In Canada, with a smaller membership base, the union had more success setting up auxiliaries, designed, as one such group announced, 'to help our men fight for better working conditions and better lives for our families.'[65] Some auxiliaries were involved in respectable philanthropy,[66] but others addressed political issues, including the specific problems of women workers. The Winnipeg auxiliary passed resolutions supporting married women workers' right to collect unemployment insurance, while the Toronto one addressed issues such as women's need for day nurseries.[67]

The IFLWU's efforts to address the specific needs of women workers may have been, in part, an attempt to secure the loyalty of a minority constituency in difficult, anti-communist times, though the union agenda also mirrored a long-standing communist political platform on women's equality. One should not overemphasize a heartfelt commitment to women's equal integration into a union that had been built on masculinist power structures. On hearing a resolution for more action on equality issues from the women's committee in 1946, Gold paternalistically acknowledged this little 'spanking,' from the women, and he asked that they add words of praise for the union's good track record on women's wages and status.[68] His letters to Canadian organizer Charlotte Gauthier were also coloured by a peculiar paternalism.[69] Gender equality may have been more 'convention talk' than action – a problem echoed in the union's own self-criticism – but the rival AFL union was even less vocal on women's issues, and when the union merged in 1955 with the AMCBW, the situation became even more dismal.

There were no women organizers in the new amalgamated union, though Gauthier retained her business-agent position in Quebec. The 1962 pamphlet celebrating the union's history made no reference to gender equality, and featured pictures of its all-male executive board. Nor were the specific needs of women workers discussed in the new AMCBW paper, *The Butcher Workman*. In the column reserved for fur workers' news, Abe Fineglass penned an article on women in 1955 that was symbolic and revealing: it discussed women only as potential consumers of fur coats. Women as fur workers were now absent from view.[70]

Finally, we cannot discount the fact that fending off Cold War attacks took up inordinate union time and energy that might have been spent on both internal and external organizing.[71] It was a critical economic moment, for after 1949 the fur industry was contracting: as the union lamented, fur had become a 'sick business.'[72] Yet the IFLWU spent its time fending off annihilation and the AFL fur union spent its time attacking the IFLWU. The IFLWU's efforts to lobby parliament to stem the tide of job losses of men and women were undoubtedly weaker due to the anti-communist climate.[73] Communist Party practices of following the advice of their international leaders, inserting party appointees as union leaders, and endorsing 'mainstreaming' at all costs only worsened the situation. Indeed, an all-Canadian IFLWU might have survived.[74] Ironically, a long-standing communist commitment to women's equality opened up space for innovative organizing, while at the same time Communist Party Stalinism limited and constrained those efforts.[75]

Assessing the impact of the Cold War on unionized women inevitably involves conjecture about such 'mights.' It is clear, however, that the outcome for women fur and leather workers was placement in a union without a strong tradition of concern about women workers, with a leadership in Canada that disdained democratic process in favour of political control. However important leadership decisions were to these Cold War battles, they were buttressed by the more widespread acceptance

Figure 7   May Day Parade, 1954. (York University Libraries, Clara Thomas Archives and Special Collections, Toronto Telegram Fonds, F0433, Image no. ASC05328)

of anti-communism that had become 'common sense' by the mid-1950s. Moreover, the prevailing Cold War Manichean rhetoric juxtaposing a 'fifth column of traitors'[76] to anti-communist 'patriots' had a dampening effect, not only on official communism, but on a wider swath of radical dissent, and since communists made gender equality part of their rhetoric, raising these issues within a union might only mark one as an unwanted dissenter.

The Cold War in Electrical

The small IFLWU may have been considered an insignificant loss by some union leaders, but this was likely not the case for a large industrial union such as the United Electrical, Radio and Machine Workers of America (UE), given the central role of the electrical industry – making everything from refrigerators to turbines – in post-war North America. While some authors have discussed the history of the UE in the post-war years, it is worth assessing the Cold War's impact on its female members by comparing its policies to those of its anti-communist rival, the IUE.[77]

The CIO/CCL expelled the UE in 1949 and within hours of the purge the larger body had chartered the International Union of Electrical Workers (IUE) to take over the UE's territory. For a number of reasons, including Taft-Hartley, the American UE suffered significant losses to the IUE, while the Canadian UE managed to exist outside the mainstream labour movement as a viable independent. Debates about the reasons for the Canadian UE's survival have been shaped by lingering Cold War feelings. According to the IUE's official historians, the UE leadership was dictatorial and overbearing, though effective in its strategies,[78] while UE leaders, as well as sympathetic labour historians, have attributed their survival to the union's encouragement of rank-and-file militancy, and its ability to 'deliver the goods' on workplace issues.[79] Also, when the IUE began to raid the UE, workers were likely loyal to those who originally organized them, and they were often well aware that the IUE was the company's favoured union. It is also true, however, that the UE leadership was at times manipulative and controlling in intra-union battles, and even though only some members of the leadership were communist, the union's public stance on foreign-policy issues invariably stood in close proximity to that of the Labour Progressive Party.

These sympathies for the Soviet Union were often the key focus of IUE attacks on the UE leadership. The association of the union with subversion gave the state the excuse to become involved. In Quebec, the IUE was aided by the Duplessis government, which simply decertified rival UE locals, some of which were organized by a dynamic female organizer/business agent and communist, Leah Roback. Without the right-wing Duplessis government, the official IUE historians admit, this breakthrough in Quebec 'could not have happened.'[80] Anti-communist labour battles across North America were shaped by these kinds of local factors, including the particular blend of religion, ethnicity, gender, and politics in the union's locale.[81] Still, there were some recurring patterns of anti-communist persuasion, and some American historians have recently stressed anti-communist (and sometimes communist) deployment of gendered appeals in this battle, with both sides claiming they would protect traditional gender and family norms.[82]

Securing family support was one tactic used by both sides in Cold War battles. In the IUE/UE battle for union recognition at the massive General Electric (GE) factory in Peterborough – the largest plant in Canada and therefore a key fulcrum of the Cold War battle in electrical – workers were visited in their homes by IUE organizers in the hopes of bringing wives, often assumed to be fearful of radicalism, on board. Appeals were made by the local bishop of the Catholic church to vote against the UE as well, using arguments that one assumes referred to the anti-family perspectives of communists, given the Catholic press's preoccupation with this issue.[83] On the opposite side, communists organized workers' wives to assert the superiority of UE contracts in a time of rising prices.

Yet, the primary code words used repeatedly by the IUE were democracy, freedom, and patriotism, counterposed to communist treason, destruction, conspiracy, and dictatorship. Communists' cynical disregard for workers' real needs was another theme. For instance, when one woman worker supporting the IUE wrote to the local Peterborough newspaper, she warned that communists wanted to 'confiscate' private property, including homes, abolish inheritance, and charge large taxes.[84] A testimonial read on the radio by another IUE rank-and-file woman stressed the bad contract that the UE had negotiated for the 'girls' in the plant.[85] During four attempted raids by the IUE in Peterborough, the political propaganda machines on both sides dealt primarily with issues of loyalty versus subversion, and good or bad contracts. Anti-communists charged that the UE was 'actually serving the Soviet Union' and that 'the vote in Peterborough [would] be a symbol of decency or a vote of betrayal.'[86] UE vets, in response, reassured the public that they were loyal Canadians, and would be in the 'forefront in fighting any aggression or invasion' of Canada.[87] If patriotism is considered a masculine value, then the battle might be construed in gendered terms. By and large, though, this war of words dealt – at least on the surface – more with charges of disloyalty and dictatorship than with fears of gender subversion.[88]

Whatever the political justification for anti-communism, women, because they were a significant percentage of the electrical workforce, could not help but be affected by these Cold War contests. Women's work in the electrical plants varied considerably between the production of lighter products such as radio tubes, in which more women worked, and heavier equipment such as transformers, dominated by men and the skilled trades.[89] By and large, the industry was shaped by a firmly-entrenched sexual division of labour that was intertwined with a heavy emphasis on piecework in the sectors of the industry where women were concentrated. Although these patterns were slightly disrupted during the Second World War, management insisted on the reconstitution of the gendered division of labour and differential wage rates after the war. The UE protested but did not push the issue to open conflict, which is hardly surprising given the union's overall preponderance of male members and the dominant ideology of the era.[90]

How, then, might we assess the Cold War's effects on women on the job? As Maurice Zeitlin and Judith Stepan-Norris point out in their US study, there are some concrete measurements that one can use, including women's participation in the leadership, and union commitment to contract issues such as equal pay. After quantifying a series of such measures, these authors concur with more impressionistic accounts that claim communist unions had a better track record in fostering female leadership and addressing women's equality.[91] Similar conclusions can be drawn about the Canadian UE, although this was less apparent in the actual numbers of women in the leadership. The UE had a small number of exceptional women on its national staff, including a dynamic research director, Idele Wilson, and long-time organizer, Jean Leslie Vatour; the IUE, in turn, had a woman organizer in its Quebec section, Jeanine Theoret, and a long-serving secretary treasurer, Evelyn McGarr, who was also on the international board. Women were generally more active at the local level; in the UE, they were prominent as shop stewards in sections of the workplace with a high number of women workers. Although women still constituted a minority of local executives, by the mid-1960s four locals were led by women.[92] As Julie Guard documents, though women made up 25 per cent of the UE membership, they formed about 13.5 per cent of the District Council and, on average, 11 per cent of the delegates to annual conventions.[93] The IUE leadership was similarly imbalanced, but more dramatically so. Women made up about one-third of the membership, but held one or, at the most, two positions on the district board.[94] Even union locals that boasted a 70 per cent female membership sent a male president to the annual convention,[95] where as little as 4 per cent of those identified were women.[96]

Quantitative measures of office holders, however, offer a very partial picture. If we examine union newspapers, contract language, convention resolutions, political lobbying, and special efforts to organize women, there emerges a pattern of stronger UE advocacy for women workers, though by the late 1960s the IUE too was aware of the need to address gender issues. The UE's strong record of advocacy on behalf of its women members was always part of its public defence against anti-communist raiders from the IUE; it advertised important grievance victories and improved wages it had secured for women.[97] Indeed, tension over women's contractual rights was a defining division in the initial skirmish between anti-communists and communists in the 1949 battle for the Peterborough local. The IUE faction, led by a prominent CCFer, supported single women in the factory, who maintained that they should have preferential seniority rights over married women. The communist leadership intervened forcefully, chastising them for abandoning union policy on equal seniority.[98] To abandon married women's rights would have contradicted the UE's post-war 'Win the Peace' program, which included a call for full employment for those who needed it, a principled position that explicitly allowed women to lay claim to wage work whether they were married or single. This platform diverged sharply from the approach of other industrial unions that quickly accepted the re-imposition of pre-war barriers to married women workers. The UE publicly urged the provincial government to take legal steps to protect women's right to jobs and backed up this demand for full employment with calls for day care and equal pay.[99]

The UE's attempt to organize special women's conferences and its consistent invocation of equity issues at conventions also made this union distinct from the IUE in the 1950s. Though one could argue that the UE was astutely working to secure the loyalty of a constituency that, in the United States, had been considered key to defections to the IUE,[100] there was also a minority group of radical UE women, in the politicized leadership and at the grassroots level, committed to this agenda. The union's approach to gender equality bore a strong similarity to the communist tradition's treatment of the 'woman question.'[101] Leadership speeches, newspaper articles, and special pamphlets stressed that women's equality should be part and parcel of union demands; however, it should not overshadow class concerns. According to the top UE leadership, including Vatour, primary attention should centre on wresting better conditions from employers and the state, not on coalitions with middle-class feminists or critiques of the masculine prejudice of fellow workers.

The UE's stance on gender equality was not without contradictions. It sometimes reflected the dominant ideology of femininity, equating women with family and domesticity, but it also incorporated more radical equality impulses. It constantly stressed class solidarity, but also recognized acute gender differences in the workplace. Women's 'special abilities' to do 'fine work' were invoked as justifications for the worth of their labour, but men were also reminded that they should support women's fight for better pay or else men's work might be 'degraded' into female jobs.[102] The union struggled to come to terms with both women's difference and their right to equality, a difficult balancing act in an era when the former tended to dominate in popular culture. Astutely, the union drew on the dominant cultural equation of women with the home to make political connections between social reproduction and production. One radio broadcast used a dramatic skit to point out that manufacturers claimed they wanted to make women's home labour 'easier' and 'drudgery free' with labour-saving devices, yet these were built with the exploited and fast-paced labour of women workers: 'Yes, the General Electric Company puts women on a pedestal in the home – But it puts them through the wringer in the plant.'[103]

As women's conferences and committees unfolded, the special needs of women members could not help but come to the fore despite the president's claim that these were not women's conference but 'union conferences.'[104] The first UE women's conference after the war was held in 1949, with organizer Idele Wilson insisting on female-only attendance, in order to give women a comfortable space to speak openly. Future conferences included men, and by the late 1950s some local executives were appointing, not electing, delegates, a sign the union was less democratic than it boasted. Part of the program was definitely shaped, top-down, by union staff.[105] However, delegates were urged to bring their own concerns to the table, and women often ended up discussing their double burden of work and family care, as well as the lack of support from some union men on equity issues. The seemingly intractable problems women faced in the workplace were discussed repeatedly: how, they asked, could the union break the discriminatory wage differentials between men's and women's jobs and also challenge the draining incentive pay system that many women laboured under? The need for better health, safety, and 'welfare' conditions – rest periods and washrooms, for instance – was continually raised, as was the women's opposition to gender discrimination in federal and provincial labour legislation.[106]

These equity issues were not confined to women's conferences, but were raised too at annual conventions, in the union press, and in circulars to district representatives. In 1952, for example, organizer Ross Russell spoke to the convention about the inadequacies of the recent Ontario equal-pay bill that measured only identical jobs, a rather easy law to circumvent. The union's own brief on equal pay advocated for a definition of 'comparable worth' instead, using concrete examples from the electrical industry to show why the equal-pay bill was toothless.[107] Not all locals were invested in this struggle; the leadership publicly chastised these foot draggers for 'not raising the issue of job opportunities and equal pay'[108] and for not even ensuring that the 'highest paid female rate in their plant equals the lowest male rate.'[109]

Political commitment had to amount to more than letters to the government, and there is some evidence that the UE followed through with its members. It lobbied publicly against the unemployment insurance regulations that discriminated against married women, but also took up women's individual grievances against the Unemployment Insurance Commission (UIC). In some bargaining rounds, UE locals did try to push the envelope on gendered wage differentials, and it is important to note that employers always forcefully opposed these equity measures. In 1949, for instance, a UE local argued that the war had proved that it was simply a 'fiction that women are unable to do many [male] jobs,' and that continuing wage differentials were unjust. Indicating management's firm determination to maintain sex-typing of jobs, General Electric mustered a long list of reasons why women were inferior workers, ranging from supposed absenteeism to women needing more training and aid setting up their work. Invoking reigning community standards of (unequal) pay, and pointing out that past union contracts had accepted differentials, management adamantly rejected the case for similar pay rates.[110] Admittedly, the commitment to women's equality varied substantially from one local to the next, in some cases, there was little interest on the part of men in disrupting the gendered division of labour or existing power relations, a fact that a small cadre of UE women began to criticize at annual conventions, in letters to the union, or at district council meetings.[111] Indeed, as Guard points out, it was the union's *claim* to take equality seriously that gave women the opening to speak up, the space to develop politically, and, eventually, the impetus to develop cross-union alliances with other women's rights groups.[112]

An examination of the Canadian *UE News* during the 1950s reinforces the differences between the UE and the IUE. Like many of the union papers described in chapter 1, the *UE News* often assumed the archetypal worker to be the white male breadwinner, and many articles addressed women as wives and auxiliary members, central to the domestic but not the industrial sphere. While wives were encouraged to take up political issues ranging from peace to prices, the female homemaker was addressed as someone who should back up 'hubby,' who went to work worrying about the mortgage.[113] However, a parallel theme – the attempt to validate women, whether single or married, as workers and activists – provided a corrective to negative public images of female radicals, particularly in the midst of the Cold War. This stereotype was well summed up by one of the RCMP spies in the union's midst. UE leader Evelyn Armstrong, the informer reported to his superiors, had been known in past years as a communist 'agitator,' but her politics had now 'mellowed,' as indicated by the fact that she had 'spruced herself up,' and was 'dressing attractively' and acting 'pleasantly.'[114] RCMP inanities to the side, the UE News attempted to create an image of working-class women that blended working-class femininity with activism. Photos, for instance, portrayed women in action, on picket lines, at meetings, and also suffering from the same things men did, such as lost fingers.[115] Articles quoted women rank-and-filers who said they had to 'fight aggressively'[116] for their rights, and stressed the need to oppose lay-offs of women. They also emphasized the importance of closing the wage gap between men and women, and pursuing women's grievances on pay-rate discrimination. Pictures of smiling women showing off their settlement cheques after winning such grievances made this point forcefully. Whether the paper exaggerated the UE's commitment to women workers or not, there was a deliberate attempt to foster female militancy in the workplace.

Contrasting this record to the IUE News is difficult, since the IUE had a smaller base and used an American-based paper throughout much of this period, sporting little Canadian news. When a Canadian newsletter did exist in the 1950s, it seldom featured women as workplace militants but, like the TLC, sponsored a traditional women's page. Titled 'What a Woman,' the IUE column offered household hints (on decorating and diets, for instance) rather than calls for the political mobilization of housewives. Indeed, the consumer message in the IUE News was far more accommodating, telling housewives how their 'wise shopping' could cut the family's food bills in half.[117] During the 1950s, a 'food and flair' section also existed in the IUE News; though not named a woman's page as such, the consumer hints on the same page often stressed the connection between (attractive) women models and their consumer purchases. Beyond the union press, the IUE did not mobilize its female constituents in the same manner as the UE: it did not sponsor women's conferences in Canada in the 1950s, and there is no evidence that the union aggressively took up social-policy issues such as gender discrimination in UIC regulations. IUE conventions are remarkable for their silences on gender equality. The first convention in 1952 had resolutions on combating racism and on setting up auxiliaries, but no mention of women workers.[118] The issues raised within the UE, particularly relating to physical conditions in the plant, closing the gendered wage gap, or establishing day nurseries, were not the subject of ongoing IUE convention debate. Even its discussions about how to organize white-collar clericals often assumed a male-breadwinner worker.[119]

By the time a bilingual IUE paper, *Circuit*, emerged in Canada in the late 1960s, the politics of gender had shifted, with women's issues now far more prominent. This shift reflected established practices in the far larger and arguably more politically diverse American IUE, as civil rights, equal pay, and other equity issues had been on their agenda for some time, promoted by a few dynamic white and African-American women leaders in the union.[120] In 1969, a special conference for women was organized by the Canadian IUE; guests included American IUE women who had longer and more extensive experience in equity organizing. Evelyn McGarr, the only woman on the Canadian executive for fifteen years, urged the assembled women to use the existing contract to fight for their rights.[121] McGarr's subsequent discussion of women's conferences before the entire union indicated that IUE women shared some of the same problems UE women did, though both groups would have been loath to admit this. Both had to reassure their union brothers that they were not separatist feminists, 'trying to separate from the men in the union.' They did not ask their president to 'wear a skirt,' quipped McGarr in order to calm her male comrades with humour; 'we just want women to take a more active part in the union.'[122] There were other similarities too: both unions were influenced by the dominant cultural constructions of gender difference and both faced employer hostility to any alteration in the gendered workplace. By necessity, union battles were often waged to increase control over the work process or augment the worth of women's jobs – but without challenging the gendered division of labour.

Notwithstanding these similarities, the distinctions between the communist and anti-communist union were striking. The UE's promotion of female union militancy, separate organizing of women, full employment, and equity 'talk' were unusual during the Cold War, distinct from the platforms of other industrial unions such as the IUE. Anti-communist purges, then, removed a union from the CCL that might have pushed the envelope on women's equality, competing with, or challenging, other unions to take up similar issues. Instead, two electrical unions spent their energies in battles ranging from the ridiculous (competing Labour Day picnics) to the tragic, as the IUE used an anti-union state in Quebec to force out a dynamic female organizer and destroy its rivals. While a few politicized women, such as Leah Roback or Jean Vatour, were just as involved as their brothers in these Cold War politics, it is possible some rank-and-file women were alienated by these battles. Characterized by divisive meetings, such infighting could end with members engaged in raucous shouting matches and physical fights.[123] Indeed, Guard concludes that some UE women resented a style of male leadership – including that of the charismatic but stubborn President Jackson – that was dogmatic, macho, and condescending.[124] Still, many women workers remained loyal to the UE during the Cold War, not because they endorsed the *UE News*' defence of the Soviet Union, but because they paid close attention to the bread-and-butter gains the union promised, along with its claim to defend the special interests of oppressed women workers such as themselves.

Textiles: Nationalism and the Cold War

During the Cold War battle for the loyalty of electrical workers in Peterborough, the IUE brought Sam Baron, president of the Textile Workers Union of America (TWUA) in to speak at a Labour Day picnic. His anti-communist tirade, urging UE workers to 'cease ... financing the program of the agents of Stalin,' said the local paper, was the 'strongest anti-communist speech heard in the city since the Korean war began.'[125] Baron, a well-known anti-communist crusader, had been imported to Canada from the United States in 1946 by the CCL to organize an alternative to the existing AFL textile union, the United Textile Workers of America (UTWA),[126] presumed by social-democratic unionists to be under communist control. The ensuing battles between the anti-communist TWUA and the more left-leaning UTWA directed union funds and immense energies into intra-union struggles in an industry with notoriously low wages and a high participation rate by women workers. Anti-communism also became intertwined with battles over union democracy, and national or 'international' (i.e., American) control of Canadian-based workers. Although these political struggles rarely addressed women's equality explicitly, the Cold War did affect both unions' organization of women workers, and their ability to take up issues of central concern to women.

The CCL's fear of the UTWA was based largely on the presence of a few prominent communist organizers, including Val Bjarnason, Charles Lipton, and, later, William Stewart in the Ontario section.[127] Yet there is no evidence that executives of union locals were communist-dominated. In Quebec, UTWA leaders Kent Rowley and Madeleine Parent were also viewed with suspicion: Rowley had been interned with communists at the beginning of the war, while Parent's earlier marriage to Bjarnason led to the conclusion that she too must be a Red. While both Parent and Rowley were Marxists and leftists who were willing to cooperate with Communist Party trade unionists, they were not, at this point, party members.[128] Their persecution, though, illustrates the polarized climate of suspicion in the Cold War union movement, and the impossibility of any collaboration with communists on issues of common concern.

Textiles had historically relied heavily on cheap female labour in jobs designated semi- or unskilled, though this pattern varied between cotton, synthetic, and wool manufacturing, and also by plant size and location. Until the Second World War, the majority of these women were young, single workers, though some textile plants that drew on kin-based networks also employed married women with families, a pattern that increased after the war. Other characteristics of textile work remained constant: as the 1937 Royal Commission on the Textile Industry documented, it was a highly competitive industry, with lower wage rates and more physically exhausting conditions than many other mass-production industries.[129]

The industry thus appeared to be ripe for unionization in the more propitious wartime and post-war context, though the task was still exceptionally difficult in Quebec, where the UTWA faced the combined hostility of the Roman Catholic Church, the mainstream press, a powerful company (Dominion Textiles), and the Duplessis government. Indeed, even the laws that did exist were simply flouted by Duplessis and his labour minister in their campaign against the UTWA. Despite the use of police, arrests, scabs, and widespread intimidation, Parent and Rowley had major successes at Dominion Textiles in Montreal and Valleyfield in 1946, and at a Lachute woolen mill in 1947, where they also faced a TWUA raid. It was Parent and Rowley's unique ability to mobilize the rank-and-file, including women, that lay behind their success, rather than backroom advice from the Communist Party. Every success simply led to more persecution; in 1947 Duplessis had Parent and Rowley arrested for seditious conspiracy, and their subsequent trials were used to try to convince the public that these individuals were dangerous communists bent on destroying the social order. Well into the 1950s, the mainstream press kept up this anti-communist crusade: while admitting a recent inquiry had found 'no conclusive proof' that Parent and Rowley were communists, *Saturday Night* magazine proceeded to claim the contrary, claiming their dangerous 'red-line' union slavishly followed the 'twists and turns' of communist policies.[130]

This anti-communist campaign was not without gendered connotations. During the Dominion Textile strikes, a rumour was leaked to the press that Parent was a Russian spy who had been dropped off on the Gaspé Peninsula by a submarine. To further buttress this myth, her arrest writ for seditious conspiracy at Lachute then appropriated a version of her first husband's birth name to make her 'Dame Vladimir Bjarnason.' Although tales of submarines may appear ludicrous today, in the wake of Gouzenko's claims and Communist MP Fred Rose's conviction for spying, such claims had a palpable 'fear factor' in Quebec.[131] Moreover, as Parent pointed out to Denyse Baillargeon, her opponents also 'wanted to show that there was something unnatural or strange about a woman fighting for the workers.'[132] A woman doing dangerous organizing work, mixing with men, travelling alone, speaking in public, and holding radical views was obviously a communist, and in the words of *Saturday Night* a 'fire-eating' one at that![133] Anxiety about gender and familial roles, along with the fear that left-wing ideas would turn workers into atheists, animated the Catholic Church's adamant opposition to the UTWA. In contests over the Cornwall mill and others nearby, the TWUA issued pamphlets claiming the UTWA had sold out the workers, parroted the (communist) line, and was opposed by the Catholic Church.[134] In the wake of the war, the church feared the disruption of the patriarchal family and opposed married women's labour outside the home; because communism was associated with these evils, it was important to urge parishioners to abandon 'communist' unions such as the UTWA.[135]

Cold War contests for certification between the UTWA and TWUA involved many bargaining units with a substantial number of women workers. Their experience of conflict, factionalism, and sometimes violence, and their exposure to red-baiting as a tactic of denigration could not but colour their experience of unions and their understanding of the 'Left' more generally.[136] During the war and the immediate post-war years, the

UTWA was able to organize mills previously considered unorganizable, including some in small-town Ontario. That the union could keep organizing after 1946, when the rival CIO union was painting it red, *and* as front-page newspaper headlines about Rose and Gouzenko created fearful pictures of communists, speaks to the UTWA's tenacity. The TWUA sometimes responded not only with anti-communist denunciations, but also by attempting to sign up the same locals. Since certification gave the union exclusive bargaining rights, fights over initial certification were especially hard fought. In contests in 1948 for small textile plants in the Ottawa Valley, where a large number of strikers were women, the two unions clashed repeatedly. The CIO union refused any cooperation with existing UTWA locals, even if it might mean better wages for its female members. Getting one's anti-communist foot in the employer's door and being certified first was considered more important than anything else. In one confrontation over the TWUA's attempt to raid a UTWA local, violence occurred, and three UTWA representatives were convicted of assault.[137]

Rank-and-file women workers negotiated these intra-union battles amidst an increasingly hegemonic anti-communism, promoted in the mass media as well as in other union publications. Women simply could not ignore the issue of communism: when the TWUA tried to take over Toronto's large Silknit mill from the UTWA, a rank-and-file worker sympathetic to the UTWA went to (TWUA leader) Ed Cluny's office to confront him about the negative conflict, only to receive a long lecture: 'He red baited me and gave me a history of all the AFL and CIO years ago [but] I tried to tell him that it's the workers of today I'm interested in,' Doris Barless countered. Taking such a strong, oppositional stance with a union leader was difficult, and rare, in the political climate of the Cold War.[138]

Issues of democratic control and Canadian autonomy became closely intertwined with anti-communism. While unions such as the UE shared similar political perspectives across the Canadian-American border, the UTWA leadership in the United States was anti-communist and conservative. During a 1952 strike in Quebec, Rowley and Parent did not want to accept a lacklustre agreement being foisted upon them by the American leadership. The UTWA promptly removed them illegally, locked them out, removed their files, and replaced them with its own appointment, a disgruntled former UTWA official fired earlier for embezzling union funds. This putsch in the UTWA had been concocted together with the TWUA's Sam Baron as an anti-communist measure. In a confidential memo two years before, Baron had lamented that removing the Canadian UTWA leadership 'legally' had not been possible, so he set out plans for a joint AFL-CIO purge: '1. Discharge the whole Canadian staff. 2. Clear Beaucage [the fired official] and rehire him ... Make public all this at a conference attended by Valente [American head of the UTWA], TLC, CCL heads.' The American UTWA carefully waited until after the Canadian convention,[139] then it enacted the plan. Later that year, Baron became embroiled in a power struggle within his own union. He held on to his leadership position by playing the nationalist card of Canadian autonomy, and when that failed, he absconded to the rival UTWA, having paved the way for a leadership change with his earlier intrigue. Two American UTWA omit leaders involved in the purge were later indicted on criminal charges of fraud. All in all, it was not a pretty picture.

This experience convinced Rowley and Parent that Canadians had to control their own unions, as American-based ones were more likely to be tied to conservative, anti-communist politics, corruption, and American imperialism. They founded a new Canadian union, the Canadian Textile and Chemical Workers Union (CTCU), that was quickly disparaged by the CCF (later the NDP) and international unions as a communist front. This equation of nationalism and communism by anti-communist trade-union leaders simply exacerbated opposition to any calls for a measure of Canadian autonomy from American head offices, as well as suspicions about campaigns for more democratic, rank-and-file controlled unions. The latter, as many studies have confirmed, directly facilitated women's participation in unions.[140]

Moreover, the track record of the new CTCU with women workers was strong: it made a commitment to organize the unorganized, including marginalized immigrant women workers, it encouraged women's participation in their locals, and it also supported women's equality issues, such as equal access to jobs and seniority rights. Even before its ousting of Rowley and Parent, the UTWA had tried to raise equality issues, such as the discrimination in UIC regulations against married women. In contrast, there was little in the rival TWUA paper in the 1950s discussing these issues; its 'Mostly for Women' column discussed how to organize picnics, not workplaces. By the late 1960s, the CTCU also supported a range of women's equality rights, before other unions were doing so, and it attracted a cadre of New Left feminists as organizers and supporters, thus reaffirming its commitment to the mobilization of women workers.

Well into the 1970s, many TWUA leaders in Canada promoted a virulent, if not irrational, Cold War crusade, so much so that younger staffers were sometimes embarrassed by this Cold War rhetoric.[141] All staff appointments had to be cleared for political approval through the American office, as new hires were informed (wrongly) that Taft-Hartley provisions applied to Canada.[142] The long-lasting impact of the Cold War, and the way in which it potentially hurt the organization of women workers, was evident in many battles for small textile plants in southwestern Ontario. Anti-communist propaganda written in the 1950s, taken from stories in the mainstream press the TWUA knew to be wrong, was reprinted in pamphlets distributed during attempts to raid CTCU locals in the 1970s. The TWUA claimed that association with the CTCU would lead to ostracism from other unions, violent strikes, and direct support for a Moscow-linked Communist Party. Ill informed on international differences, these union leaders tied Parent to both Moscow and Peking, claiming her communist connections had been exposed when she joined a delegation to 'Red China' (which included Pierre Trudeau). It was also fond of ridiculing the communist 'husband and wife' team of 'Mrs Kent Rowley.'[143] Communism apparently masculinized women and feminized men. Perhaps the more male-dominated TWUA leadership was also threatened by Parent, who was effective on the public platform, had a formidable intellect, and was becoming associated with feminist causes.

Support for the CTCU by New Left and Waffle adherents also irritated the TWUA, an indication of the way in which anti-communism was transformed into a more general anti-left perspective. Some of the TWUA hostility, however, was simply generated by the New Left's criticisms of international unions. When the CTCU was fighting a difficult battle in 1971 to secure a new contract at Texpack, a small Brantford company with a majority of women workers, the TWUA and the OFL forbade other unions from offering any aid. Moreover, the TWUA seemingly colluded with the company in an attempt to raid the CTCU local when the company tried to shift its operations to a new location.[144] Even in the 1970s, Cold War fears thus led to desperate and damaging strategies. During the Texpack struggle, two female strikers remember, the TWUA broadcasted claims that Parent and Rowley were communists; this initially scared them, fostering some doubts that these dedicated CTCU leaders had the workers' interests at heart.[145] Similar scare tactics were attempted in other strikes.[146]

When either the UTWA or the TWUA led struggles of women workers without any raiding, they often fought hard for their constituency, risking or taking jail sentences.[147] Nonetheless, each union did interpret the world of labour–capital relations somewhat differently. For Parent and Rowley, class conflict was an inevitable characteristic of capitalism, and the working class could not count on the state to act as an advocate or impartial empire. This 'class struggle' approach to labour organizing was ridiculed not only by the conservative *Globe and Mail*, but also by some leaders in the TWUA, which equated this militancy with Parent and Rowley's supposed communism. In the long Cold War, Marxist and left-wing thought, outside of a more accommodating social democracy, remained suspect, silenced, and ostracized, an indication of the effects of Cold War ideology, as it stifled radical dissent within the labour movement. At this point in time, when the Canadian textile industry was heading into economic crisis, it might have been preferable to act collaboratively, and to think collectively, perhaps even daring a radical analysis, without fear that those espousing a radical approach would be labelled seditious spies, communists, and thus the enemies of labour.

Better Unorganized than Red?

The Cold War, as American historian Lizabeth Cohen has recently warned, was not 'everything' about the post-war era.[148] True enough, but neither should the Cold War become a mere ghost in our labour histories: those leftists who burned their books, sent their children away, and feared imprisonment were not irrational given the intensity of anti-communist feeling. Nor should we underestimate the destructive and conservatizing impact of the Cold War on the labour movement, and on the broader intellectual climate of the times: we need to take this repressive atmosphere into account in our assessments of popular and political representations of gender relations in the post-war period, including the prototype of the strong, male-led, 'traditional' family as the bulwark against communism. McCarthyism may have been fostered by anti-communist unionists as a means to oust their communist enemies, but once this genie was out of the bottle, it became a much broader assault on radical thinking, labour militancy, and critiques of American imperialism.

This is not to say that critical assessments of communist trade-union strategies are not in order. Clinging to Soviet advice, impervious to any critique of Stalinism, and advocating tired tactics of union manoeuvring, the Communist Party could lead workers into a political cul-de-sac. Encouraging communist fur workers to merge with the AMCBW led to the destruction of a small union, control from American head offices, and a ruthless blacklist of communist fur workers. In the case of the IFLWU, it was not local activists but rather party directives and decisions from the 'centre' that prevailed. However, other unions labelled communist did not follow party advice: the UE did not agree to 'mainstream,' and the left-led UTWA was punished more for its refusal to denounce the communists than for any loyalty to them. Social democrats, of course, honestly undertook this fight believing that they were the *right* left, but one might ask if leftists should use undemocratic means to purge unions, cooperate with the security arm of the state, or prevent other radicals from cooperating with communists.

At the time, the victorious side of the union movement did not consider whether the Cold War had a differential impact on women workers: it assumed women were better off without communist unions – in fact, better off with no union at all rather than a communist one. Historical hindsight suggests otherwise. Some anti-communist unionists used fears of gender subversion and a defence of the existing 'traditional' male breadwinning family in their ideological assault against communism; however, this was not the dominant strain of anti-communist union rhetoric in these three unions: rather, the emphasis was on disloyalty, subversion, treason, and bad contracts. It is true that the unions ostracized and purged were often vocal about issues of women's equality, and however limited their approach to the 'woman question,' they at least thought there was one. Banishing these unions from the house of labour simply removed the possibility that these issues would be raised regularly at conventions, and that unions might actually compete for political stature on gender-equality issues. While Sue Cobble argues that, in the United States, many AFL-CIO labour feminists pushed an equality agenda forward, in Canada, similar efforts were somewhat weaker, and not as well coordinated. The purging of left unions, led by dynamic feminist organizers such as Parent and Roback, who often held anti-racist views as well, simply marginalized equity issues all the more.

Many of the unions isolated through anti-communist purges were precisely the ones that had the political zeal to organize the unorganized, and they represented workplaces where many women, including immigrant women, worked for relatively low pay. Ironically, some of these union constituencies would prove to be an important part of the labour movement's future. In Vancouver, for example, leaders of the fledging Restaurant Workers were purged by the International; the subsequent decline of the union left women in the service industry with inadequate or no contracts.[149] In 1950, CCFer Barbara Cass-Beggs wrote to the head of the CCL to inquire about the Office and Professional Workers Union (OPWU), another suspect union expelled soon afterwards. Cass-Beggs wanted to help organize the largely female support staff at the University Settlement House; she was told, however, not to bother, as the OPWU was 'communist dominated.'[150]

Fear of being tainted with the communist label kept Canadian unions tied to American head offices of unions that did not always have the best interests of Canadian locals at heart. In many respects, this hurt female and male workers alike. The 1952 Dominion Textile settlement imposed from Washington is a good case in point, as is the assumption that the anti-communist sections of Taft-Hartley should simply apply to Canadian unions. It is difficult to measure if, and how, the issue of Canadian autonomy affected women. However, organizing in the 1960s and early 1970s by independent Canadian unions committed to rank-and-file activism and women workers suggests that being free of the bureaucracy and political constraints of the large internationals opened up some space for new innovative organizing. Moreover, links to gangsterism that discredited the labour movement in the 1950s were not only absent in communist unions; in fact, gangster leaders such as Hal Banks often secured their leadership positions based on their anti-communist credentials.[151]

Anti-communism led not only to pacts with gangsters, but also to the subtle endorsement of more accommodationist language and strategies within the labour movement. This shift was part and parcel of the larger Fordist accord, which anti-communism played a part in cementing.[152] Working with the state to inform on communists, and reassuring employers that non-communist unions would be more respectful of the legal and social order, did not generate militancy in working-class politics. Disparaging 'communist' unionists such as Parent and Rowley for their outdated class politics or criticizing them for being too confrontational created an image of dutiful citizen workers as opposed to unwanted radical outsiders. While unions of all political stripes understandably wanted the protections offered by industrial legality – which they had all fought for – more radical unionists also understood, like Rowley and Parent, that within capitalism there were always limits to the recognitions offered by the state and capital.[153] Practical alliances with communists were also decried as conspiratorial at best and naive at worst, given the propensity of communism to invade and 'possess' one's mind. The result was an ideological chill that abnegated left positions outside of the accepted CCF and NDP ones. Fighting communism was also equated repeatedly with patriotism and loyalty to the nation, values associated with militarism and masculinity.

Finally, anti-communist efforts to destroy existing unions and set up dual unions wasted immense time and energy that might have been focused on new organizing. Not only is there evidence that women avoided the more violent of these confrontations, but we also know that such competition focused energy inwards in internecine warfare rather than outwards, towards marginalized, under-represented workers. Adapting the 'better dead than red' maxim of right-wingers, anti-communists thought it better to leave women workers unorganized than in a communist union. On the contrary, the evidence suggests that women were well represented in communist unions, and that the Cold War did them no good, and more than a little harm.

Chapter 4

'Souriez pour les Clients': Retail Work, Dupuis Frères, and Union Protest

Anti-communism was also a potent force in union struggles far removed from fur, textiles, and electrical unions throughout the 1950s. During a 1952 strike of retail workers at Montreal's Dupuis Frères department store, the employer claimed the union had been infiltrated by 'outsider' communists, much to the indignation of the anti-communist Catholic union leading the strike, the Confédération des Travailleurs Catholiques du Canada (CTCC).[1] Since the 1930s, the Dupuis family, along with its allies in the clergy and the store's union, had prided itself on providing a bulwark against communism in Quebec.[2] Management's endorsement of a Catholic union, the owners believed, inoculated its workers against the evils of communism, a view repeated in the store publication, *Le Duprex*, when it reprinted a CTCC convention speech decrying the attack of communist 'subversive' agents on all Canadian democratic institutions.[3]

The suggestion that communist agitators were behind the strike was simply the imagination or fabrication of an employer intent on discrediting the union in the midst of a confrontational labour conflict, one of the most significant examples of retail worker resistance in Canadian history. This chapter ends with a discussion of the 1952 strike as a symbol of the significant political and social changes in the post-war Quebec labour movement; however, it is useful, first, to explore the nature of women's retail work. What was the gendered division of labour in department stores, how did employers try to regulate their workers, and what were women's own experiences of this work? Using the Dupuis Frères archival records, we can make some comparisons between retail work in this quintessentially French Canadian enterprise and women's work in the major English Canadian store, Eaton's, which underwent a massive organizing campaign at precisely the same time, with very different results. While there are strong similarities in the gendered culture of work, the commodification of women's femininity, and management's deliberate attempts to create paternalist workplaces, culture, religion, language, and nation also shaped the lives of Quebec retail workers in ways distinct from their English-speaking sisters.

Post-war Consumption and Service Labour

In popular culture, the post-war period is often represented by symbols of consumption – TVs, washing machines, finned cars, and saddle shoes. A new consumer culture was certainly one characteristic of post-war social life, though Canadian historians have argued that economic prosperity and the enhanced means to consume did not really emerge until the mid-1950s.[1] Moreover, images of exuberant consumerism should not obscure the very different levels of purchasing power, determined by social class and the persistence of poverty that existed in tandem with economic growth.[5] Feminist scholars have also challenged the notion that the profusion of domestic labour-saving consumer goods after the Second World War suddenly emancipated women from long hours of housework, as commentators at the time so confidently claimed.[6]

Consumption may not have been a progressive, unmediated, undifferentiated characteristic of post-war society, but economic indicators did demonstrate the expansion of consumer-oriented production, and new patterns of family buying. For the first time, it has been argued, one could talk of mass consumption: working and middle-class families with secure incomes had enough disposable income to purchase goods that went beyond the basic essentials of food, clothing, and housing. Consumption was fuelled by Cold War military spending, some welfare-state measures, the growing desire of families for home ownership, and the advertising industry's clever cultivation of new consumer needs. It was also an integral part of the post-war Fordist accord: as economies reconverted from military to consumer production, it was assumed that economic growth would be sustained by offering steady wages to unionized workers, who in turn would be able to purchase the products of their labour. Consumption was sold to the post-war labour movement as Fordism's economic reward, and as Lizabeth Cohen argues, it became an integral part of labour's new claims to citizenship and entitlement.[7]

Department stores were not the immediate major beneficiaries of expanding consumption. During the Depression, the 1934 Royal Commission on Price Spreads relayed public suspicions that the department-store sector was dominated by a few giants who could 'call the shots'; in Quebec, the Dupuis Frères store, along with its catalogue business, was one of the largest players. Yet, only 10 per cent of the retail market was actually controlled by department stores. Even if department stores were taking in a record amount in sales after the war – $781 million in 1951 – their share of total retail sales fell to as low as 6 to 8 per cent. Department-store market share, noted the federal government, was 'in a rut' for a range of reasons: shoppers abandoned downtown stores for shopping plazas, cars were capturing more consumer dollars while a decreasing percentage of spending when to basics such as shoes, and a high capital outlay was needed by stores to counteract the exodus to the suburbs.[8] These patterns were reversed by the mid-1960s; however, Dupuis Frères' concerns about market share were undoubtedly a key factor shaping its massive modernization program that exacerbated workplace relations before the 1952 strike.[9]

Even if department stores were fretting about their declining market share, the overall impact of mass consumption was to open up new jobs for women. The long-term trend in retail since the 1920s, argues Nona Glazer, had been the gradual replacement of male with female labour as the work was de-skilled, made part-time, and altered by the introduction of self-service.[10] In Canada, retail work in general expanded from the 1930s onward, but women's share of those retail jobs also grew significantly, especially after the 1940s.[11] Retail was also part of a much larger expansion of service-sector work for women in these years, with women serving customers everything from hamburgers to haircuts. By the latter part of the twentieth century, service labour, with its large youth, female, and 'visible minority' workforce, had become the archetypal symbol of post-industrial society: products were not made, but rather services delivered, with the worker sometimes recast as part of the 'product.'[12]

In the 1950s, however, economic planners in the Bank of Montreal were not particularly enthusiastic about retail expansion, recognizing that it did not produce a large wage bill, and, according to their formula, was very 'low in productivity.'[13] Their study for the Royal Commission on Canada's Economic Prospects also took the prevailing gendered division of labour for granted: retail work employed many unskilled (female) workers who looked after 'simple' operations as they bided their time in the 'few years of work between school and marriage,'[14] and more career-oriented (male) workers whose incomes were commensurate with other white-collar sectors. Just over a decade later, a female economist writing for the Royal Commission on the Status of Women (RCSW) offered a completely different view of work in the retail sector. Rather than taking the gendered division of retail work for granted, Marianne Bossen asked why it existed, and if women stood any chance of promotion within department stores. Her conclusions, echoing the liberal-feminist tenor of the RCSW, were disapproving of the 'inefficient use of [female] talent' in department stores. Using a sample of 38 department stores, she found that over 50 per cent of all full-time employees and 79 per cent of part-timers were women, though the number of women on the selling floor was higher, with women making up 67 per cent of full-time and 87 per cent of part-time regular employees.[15] She concluded that stores in some areas of the country, like Quebec, were more tradition-bound in their rigid adherence to a gendered division of labour, but patterns of male advancement and female clustering at the bottom of the store hierarchy were universal. Her findings, from our vantage point, were hardly surprising: women were paid less than men even at the same rank, kept out of high ticket commission areas, and actively dissuaded from applying for management training. In addition, women who worked part-time lacked many benefits and job security. Even still, a government lawyer considered Bossen's language and conclusions too extreme for some employers, and she was pressured to censor her commissioned report to make it more palatable.[16]

Bossen had put her finger on a contradiction in retail work: women might be the majority of workers in a store, yet a highly masculinist culture of individual advancement prevailed. At Dupuis Frères, men moved around the store as floor walkers – and proceeded up the employment ladder – while women were more likely to be stuck in lower-level sales and clerical jobs, even if they were 'career' workers. Women were perceived less as workers than as young women waiting for marriage, or married women with other (family) priorities. The store managers responding to Bossen's survey justified the division of labour by labelling women as 'timid' and 'emotional,' less likely to commit to work due to family responsibilities, and more likely to be absent or to quit. Yet Bossen's study found that young men, due to job mobility, were even more likely to leave, and it is hardly surprising that those workers with little autonomy or control over their jobs were bored, sick, and absent, even without taking women's added family responsibilities into account. Many managers also claimed that job designations were simply reflections of customer preferences; after all, who would want to buy an electrical appliance from a woman? When one woman at Dupuis Frères asked to work in household appliances, and seemed to do well, her supervisor still could not believe her success; he insisted that 'a man would probably be appreciated by the customers' because he could secure their confidence by commenting on 'mechanical subjects' relating to the appliances.[17]

The Dupuis Frères' annual 'Journées des Femmes' of the 1950s, in which women temporarily took over the management of the store, reversing the usual gender order, reveals much about what the natural gender order was perceived to be. In these playful inversions of gender roles, 'Mme Albert Dupuis' became the head of the store, with other women occupying the top management roles. It was the first time in Canada, claimed Dupuis Frères proudly, that 'a department store will be administered by women.'[18] The employee newspaper suggested that the Journées des Femmes offered women an opportunity to show that they were actually superior to men in the retail business, more practical and courageous, with a broader vision.[19] But the compliments were fleeting, for the exercise was one in which women were 'on top' only temporarily. Like the peasants who might take over the manor for a day during annual festivals, these workers eventually had to return to their proper place.[20]

One of the final admonishments in Bossen's study was for female retail workers to unionize: 'Improve your status through collective bargaining. Press for better promotion opportunities,' she concluded.[21] The two were not necessarily linked. During the 1950s, retail unions were seldom concerned with breaking down the gendered division of labour – and sometimes even reinforced this distinction.[22] Moreover, very few retail workers were organized. Nationally, only 5 per cent of retail workers came under collective agreements; Dupuis Frères was the only unionized store in Montreal.[23] Department stores proved to be difficult nuts for the new industrial unions to crack, in part because of intense employer opposition, but also because unions could not convince all white-collar workers that it was in their interest to unionize. The structure and nature of retail labour militated against organization: high turnover, seasonal work, large numbers of part-time workers, and workers' fears of losing existing benefits were all problems, but so too was management's successful cultivation of workers' sense of status and loyalty, and indeed workers' self-regulation as agreeable service workers.[24]

The explosion of service-based work in our times, along with feminist theoretical preoccupations with the body, has generated new scholarly writing about the organizational attributes, self-regulation, and embodied experience of women's service labour. The body has long been an 'absent presence' in labour-history paradigms, including Marx's theories of alienation,[25] and earlier studies of retail work were often concerned, implicitly at least, with questions of women's embodiment.[26] Nonetheless, contemporary ruminations on the body, in conjunction with sociological studies of the work process, offer new insights into women's retail work.

Service labour may seem 'intangible' in one sense, for it is both produced and consumed simultaneously, with customer service being the very essence of the work process.[27] Sociologists argue that 'interactive service labour,'[28] with face-to-face communication, often involves 'emotional labour,' a term coined by Arlie Hochschild to denote the work of projecting or displaying emotions, or manipulating the customers' feelings.[29] Working as part of the 'emotional service proletariat,' with little control within the workplace and limited monetary rewards, is very different from the emotional labour required of professionals such as doctors or social workers, just as it is distinct from work on a production line. Service workers, as Cameron Macdonald and Carmen Sirianni have put it, are expected to 'inhabit the job'[30] differently: on the shop floor a worker may curse at the line, but the woman behind a store counter must pretend to love her job. In service work, the worker also figuratively becomes the product sold. Selling is based on a presentation of the self that involves appropriate displays of deference, good humour, sympathy, advice, commiseration, or many other emotions performed as work. Though retail work, like production labour, may suffer de-skilling efforts by management, the worker's self-presentation remains at the core of the work process, and should the range of tasks or skills be narrowed in any way, emotional labour then becomes more and more the very essence of customer service.[31]

The management of such interactive service labour as retail work also takes on distinct forms. Surveillance, routinization, and appropriation of all 'thinking tasks' to management constitute one strategy, but there are also models of control that encourage workers' self-regulation and 'voluntary' identification with management – perhaps a more insidious form of control.[32] These employers select workers who are more likely to be transformed through training into the ideal service provider; the goal is to 'create the kind of worker who makes decisions that management will approve of.'[33] This management style was far more in keeping with Dupuis Frères' paternalist strategies.

Whatever the management model followed, the 'deep acting' required of workers, Hochschild argues, eventually leads to burnout, as employees

Figure 8   Dupuis Frères employees and their float at the St-Jean-Baptiste Day parade, 1954. (HEC, Montréal, P049X990001, Dupuis Frères Fonds)

are alienated from their own feelings, a process that parallels the alienation from one's corporeal body delineated by Marx. Postmodern writers have taken issue with Hochschild's presumption of a core 'inner self' of authentic feeling, juxtaposed to a corporeal bodily 'surface' and suggest, instead, the term 'aesthetic labour' to denote the completely embodied character of service work. Drawing in part on Bourdieu, they argue that employers make use of existing bodily 'dispositions,' shaped by social and gender relations,[34] which are then selected, developed, commodified, and transformed through persuasion and training into essential requirements for the job. In interactive service work, distinct 'modes of worker embodiment' are corporeally produced, creating new regimes of the body and the inner self.[35] If emotional labour suggests the alienation of 'real' feelings, aesthetic labour stresses the bodily performance of style, femininity, and heterosexuality that comes to shape the worker's own identity.

Hochschild's insight into emotional alienation is, I believe, still relevant for retail labour, though the notion of aesthetic labour is also valuable, highlighting how appearance and femininity are required attributes, created and fostered on the job, and commodified by the employer in order to promote its business and products. Although retail employees at Dupuis Frères would not have employed the contemporary term 'branded,' they were certainly aware at the time of the 1952 strike that they were a constructed image – the Dupuis family – that was an advertisement for the store, fostered deliberately by the company to justify and legitimize its pursuit of profit.

Souriez pour les clients[36]

A jarring disjuncture unfolded before my eyes as I sat in the archives, reading employee files, on the one hand, and the store's in-house employee magazine, *Le Duprex* (*LD*), on the other. While *LD* offered idealized pictures of contented workers often striving to be even better workers, the personnel files suggested instead the unhappiness and discontent associated with the emotional labour of retail work. It was hard to imagine that these two sets of documents were referring to the same workers.

Le Duprex was founded by the Dupuis Frères management in 1926 in collaboration with its independent Catholic union, established in 1919 as Le Syndicat Catholique et National des Employés de Magasin. A self-described 'périodique de famille,'[37] *LD* was similar in tone and content to many other company newspapers, providing tidbits of personal and workplace information, lively gossip, letters to the editor, news about the store, advice columns, union news (mainly social activities), and even some poetry and fiction. Management was largely in control of its production, though workers contributed as well, reinforcing the image of reciprocity so integral to paternalist workplaces.[38] While it is true that many employers, particularly in retail, attempted to portray their workplaces as a family, Dupuis Frères was more insistently and intensely paternalist than most, using both welfare benefits and discretionary paternalism[39] to consolidate an almost mythical reputation that was inter-woven with appeals to French Canadian nationalism and Catholicism.

Passed down through the Dupuis family since it was founded in 1882, Dupuis Frères developed innovative welfare programs that included annual paid vacations, days off for birthdays and Catholic holidays, and sick/death benefits, with contributions and payment determined by gender, reinforcing a male breadwinner model. Payments could also be rescinded if the illness was caused by 'intemperance' or 'mauvaise con-duite.'[40] There were many store-sponsored social and athletic activities, involving hockey teams (with uniforms paid for), bowling, choirs, annual trips, lavish dances, and banquets for special occasions, to name only a few. Rituals and celebrations were used repeatedly, always saturated with paternal metaphors and speeches stressing the familial ties binding store workers and managers. Ties of gratitude and recognition were consoli-dated with gifts, prizes, plaques, donations, and other material symbols. When the store president, Albert Dupuis, was made Chevalier (Knight) in the Catholic order of St-Grégoire-le-Grand, a nomination supported by the union, a massive banquet was held for employees to advertise this honour. Dupuis then used the event to announce a large donation to the union on its tenth anniversary.[41] When the same honour was bestowed on the long-time 'chef d'enterprise' and vice-president, A.G. Dugal, a similar celebration was held, and 'Saint Dugal's' birthday was commem-orated regularly.[42] The founding family was described using not only pa-ternal, but also religious allusions; one employee equated Albert Dupuis with the patriarchs of the Old Testament, and thanked the Dupuis family profusely on behalf of all the workers: 'Quoique votre grand coeur nous ait habitués à vos paternelles bontés.'[43]

Dupuis family members were something akin to modern royalty. They were portrayed as compassionate, generous, and charitable, yet there was a fascination too with their wealth, dress, and vacations – in other words, their conspicuous consumption. They mingled with employees at the annual dress ball and sports awards dinner and toasted workers' long service at the twenty-five-years club (established in 1944), and the Dupuis men, in top hat and formal dress, walked beside the store's float (adorned with women salesclerks in formal dress) every year in the St Jean Baptiste day parade. The Dupuis family used its financial largesse and social pos-ition to promote Quebec history within the province, marketing nation-alist pride, along with its merchandise, to the public and its employees.[44] Québécois history was equated with the store's mission in everything from window displays celebrating Quebec's 'first teacher,' Marguerite de

Bourgeoys, to *LD* articles extolling early heroines such as Madeleine de Verchères.[45] Other ethnic or cultural groups, such as First Nations or the Inuit, made symbolic trips to Montreal or tributes for store celebrations, but they were clearly exotic outsiders on display, not family insiders.[46]

While tradition and history – of both the Dupuis family and the Quebec nation as a whole – were venerated, modernity and progress, equated with successful businesses and consumption, were also admired. As an enterprise serving a French clientele, in both Montreal and rural areas via its catalogue, Dupuis Frères was praised publicly by Catholic and political elites; it became commercial proof that Quebec need not be dominated economically by 'les Anglais.' *Le Duprex*, as Mary Jane Matthews states, employed metaphors of battle to describe the store's efforts to valiantly defend its precarious position in the hostile, English-dominated market: 'Chaque jour est pour nous, vendeurs and vendeuses, un jour de bataille.' Just as 'faith in God was necessary to religion,' so too was 'faith in the sale' necessary to the store's material success and existence – and thus, that of the nation too.[47] *Le Duprex* claimed Dupuis Frères had to regularly dispel evil rumours that such a successful store could not possibly be francophone-owned. Because French Canadian business was threatened by immigration, American capital, and English and Jewish competitors, Dupuis Frères clerks were urged to be superlative sellers, their sales protecting Dupuis Frères against hostile 'outsiders.' In the 1930s especially, appeals were made to defend the French Canadian 'race' against English and Jewish competitors in a tone that took on xenophobic overtones.[48]

Protecting the French language and culture was one of the founding family's civic mandates. The store favoured French Canadian job applicants (who did not need to be bilingual), and promised French clients respectful service in their own language, instead of the condescension they were likely to encounter further west on St Catherine Street at Eaton's or Morgan's. Since most francophones could not secure employment in these 'Anglo' enterprises, the promise of secure employment at DF was obviously a significant factor shaping employees' loyalty to the Dupuis. The Dupuis family donated monetary prizes to school students for French-language accomplishment, advertising these contests through the radio and in its own publications.[49] A close, mutually symbiotic relationship with the clergy was also fostered over the years. The Catholic clergy (both English- and French-speaking) had its own department (for religious clothing) and dining area within the store, which also sold Catholic school uniforms. Masses commemorated special Dupuis Frères occasions, clerical leaders visited the store to endorse the enterprise and praise the Dupuis, and reportage on clergy activities was given a prominent place in *LD*. To both potential customers and employees, therefore, Dupuis Frères was portrayed as a defender of language, nation, and faith, as well as the familial patron of its employees' economic welfare.

Le Duprex never tired of equating the workers' welfare with the economic health of the store, printing many articles on how to become the ideal salesperson, a category that, for women, often revealed employer attempts to transform raw labour power into aesthetic and emotional labour. Character, morality, and religion were essential attributes of a good employee; it was not simply how much you sold, but whether you embraced the store's mission as an upstanding member of its Catholic, French Canadian family. Nor was good character simply expressed with the right turn of a selling phrase; rather, character had to be built over time in a process that suggested self-regulation and one's inner empowerment.

Like other employee magazines, *LD* incorporated many contributions from employees, including the occasional debate about gender roles. When the paper was established, some female employees lamented the paucity of material on women, though they were not pleased when an author, whom they designated the store 'Don Juan,'[50] wrote a column portraying women as frivolous, consumed by romantic dreams and other trifles. One female respondent chided him for failing to recognize their intelligence and the important contributions women made to the family economy.[51] In subsequent years, a women's column was added, incorporating advice to women on romance, etiquette, and appearance. A fictional novella about a young female Dupuis Frères employee was also serialized, with a Cinderella plot common to romance novels: the young Dupuis Frères saleswoman who is in love with a visiting salesclerk from the United States discovers that the man of her dreams is the wealthy son of an American department store owner when he returns to claim her hand in marriage.[52]

By the 1950s, there are more articles in *LD* documenting female achievement and upward mobility within the store, an important reflection of the expanding and aging female workforce, as well as new attention to wage labour as an integral part of women's identity. Still, much of the advice on how to become an excellent seller bears strong similarities to advice offered in the thirties. Too many girls think they can become saleswomen overnight, lectured one article, but they have to learn the many ingredients of good selling: 'If she [the seller] doesn't advance as much as she would like, this is perhaps because she is not engaging, she doesn't know how to smile, she doesn't know enough about the merchandise, she neglects her personal appearance, she isn't always polite, she often breaks regulations of the store, [or] she doesn't always speak in praise of the store and her superiors.' The article cleverly laid out an ideal method of interacting with clients, while also telling saleswomen that if they did not do well, it was their own fault. Women could help themselves become ideal saleswomen, it was suggested, by seeking out the wisdom of their superiors.[53]

Advice on interacting with customers always urged a careful balance between knowledge and deference, authority and servility. One had to assess the exact emotion to project with each client, sometimes knowing who to flatter: little boys, claimed one article, ruin [their] clothes more than girls but they are 'coquets' just like girls, so the best seller must 'flatter the mother [and] the son.'[54] Class dispositions, described so well in Bourdieu's work, were replicated in the subtle inflection of the seller's role as adviser not dictator, servant not master of the encounter over the counter. Both appearance and demeanour were important: saleswomen were advised to be correctly dressed always, with 'not a hair out of place,' but to 'never be more elegant than your customer.' Be extremely nice with the snobbish woman, a bit friendly with the woman with a baby, and 'strictly proper with the distant woman.' 'The customer is always right' was the motto continually pressed upon the salesperson. 'Never lecture, do not use technical words, never rejoice that you have 'taken [customers] for a ride' as nine times out of ten, they won't return.' Sellers also had to be observant without being observed: 'If the client is browsing, don't let on that you know.'[55]

Those offering advice, convinced of essential differences between the sexes, suggested sellers learn how to manage the different shopping styles of men and women, since men think only of 'their basic needs, shop faster, don't exchange items, are less demanding and don't look for bargains,' while women, described in stereotyped and less flattering terms, 'shop just to keep up with the Jones or to show off their wealth.'[56] The view of rural 'bumpkins' was also somewhat unflattering: 'when speaking to people from the country, speak clearly and simply.'[57] Discussions about exactly how to smile were incessant, a telling indication of how deeply the women were expected to internalize their roles, so that they were no longer acting, but feeling their role: 'Smile and learn …, even if you are sad or suffering, to have a natural smile.'[58]

Women praised for their long service in the pages of *LD* were often described in terms that reflected this ideal saleslady. During a dinner for the twenty-five-years club, one woman was lauded for being an 'expert' in her area of sales (in this case shoes); she was elegant, 'always smiling' and in 'good humour.'[59] Management also tried to offer training in good selling in the guise of recreation; women were encouraged to embrace self-improvement by participating in the many women's associations, music and athletic groups, or charitable efforts promoted by the store. Not only did bowling offer excellent exercise, said *LD*, but girls who bowl always 'seem to be in a good mood.'[60] A women's section of the APEM (Association Professionnelle des Employées du Magasin) was founded at *DF* before the First World War to 'train young girls to be devoted, courageous, serious women who want to elevate their own social, moral, even material status.' By the 1930s it was begging for members, a sign that moral admonishments were less appealing to young workers than store dances, which, in contrast, were well subscribed to.[61] Some of the activities recommended to female workers, such as night classes in domestic training, were run by 'ladies who occupy a high rank in Montreal society,' including those associated with the prominent women's reform organization, the Fédération Nationale Saint-Jean-Baptiste (FNSJB). The role of middle-class reformers in imparting good morals to working-class girls, in other words, was integrated directly into the store rather than promoted outside of it.[62]

In the interwar years, store amusements were promoted as positive alternatives to the dangers of the movie theatre; by the 1950s, this particular bugaboo was gone, but there was still a strong desire to involve saleswomen in character-building activities that would produce moral, healthy young workers and, eventually, model, Catholic mothers. The Dupuis women at the head of the family empire were cast as role models in this regard, with many references to their humility and good works, particularly their involvement in Catholic charities such as l'Association des Dames Patronnesses de l'Institution des Sourdes-Muettes. Women workers were encouraged to do their own charitable work, such as knitting for poor children,[63] an undertaking that inculcated the values of compassion and generosity, and also reminded employees that there were always others far worse off than them.[64] The significance of Madame Dupuis as a social reformer and maternal role model cannot be underestimated. While historians have often focused our attention on the patriarchs directing paternalist businesses, the wives of such men, through their charitable and reform work in the larger community and in the workplace, played a crucial part in advertising, justifying, and sustaining paternalism.[65]

Embracing one's womanly duty was a theme that extended beyond the store to one's future familial role. Unlike other employee publications of the period, LD put an extraordinary emphasis on religion, on women's familial role in reproducing the nation,[66] and on creating ideal families. This fit well with the store's promotion of paternalism, extending the familial metaphor deep into the personal lives of workers. In one long article, two different voices spoke about what they looked for in an ideal husband and an ideal wife. From a man's point of view, the ideal wife did not nag or speak about her daily problems when he arrived home from work, but would bear with him the burdens of life. She would 'send him off in the morning with good wishes and welcome him home at night with a kiss … The children would do the same … with [a] smiling baby in the cradle.' She 'would not compare herself to her neighbour' (envy clearly being a feminine vice), and she would align her authority 'in perfect harmony' with his, rewarding him daily with 'thriftiness, prayers and tender affection.'[67]Although external changes in women's habits or appearance were recognized over time – as one article after the Second World War noted, women did not smoke or wear make-up in the past as they did now[68] – their devotion to God's will and to their families remained unchanged.[69]

This emphasis on woman's role as wife, and her innermost qualities of loyalty, devotion, humility, and deference, created a persona that fit well with the emotional work expected of saleswomen, while also promoting the patriarchal, male-breadwinner familial model. Even single women were admonished to sacrifice for the family; one young woman was praised for giving up her job to a needy widow with children. At Dupuis Frères, saleswomen were also encouraged to emulate popular standards of beauty, promoted through in-store photographic beauty contests, LD's advice columns on beauty culture, and various public displays of feminine beauty – such as 'nos fleurs,'[70] the formally dressed women workers on the St Jean Baptiste Day float. Dupuis Frères, like other department stores in this period, encouraged saleswomen to work on their bodies and appearance as 'mirroring objects'[71] that would encourage, attract, entice, or reassure potential consumers. Fashion shows were sponsored regularly, sometimes with female employees as models. In 1947, members of the Dupuis Frères women's sewing circle presented their own creations on a 'fashion runway' in an event presided over by the store matriarch, Mme Dupuis. Her speech stressed women's fleeting role as temporary but attractive workers at the store: 'Unfortunately these young women won't always be with the company, however the memory of their charm ... will continue.'[72]

Beyond beauty contests, Dupuis Frères also promoted employee consumption in countless other ways, such as in-store employee contests using merchandise as prizes. Department store employees, Donica Belisle argues, were both courted as potential consumers and commodified as advertisements for consumption.[73] While the devoted saleswoman who equated her interests with those of the employer also appeared as a key archetype in the English Canadian store newsletters studied by Belisle, *Le Duprex* offered somewhat different prescriptions about appearance and beauty. Dupuis Frères workers, for example, were not sexualized to the same extent they were in the Hudson's Bay Company or Eaton's publicity – and this applied to the respective English and French trade-union papers as well. While *LD* often published in-store gossip promising young women the possibility of romance or marriage, allusions to sexuality were almost non-existent. Unlike in other stores in the 1940s and 1950s, bathing suits and the display of partially undressed bodies were not part of fashion shows or beauty contests. After one fashion or 'elegance' contest for the employees, which involved the modelling of new clothing, *LD* proudly reproduced a letter from La Ligue de Décence congratulating the women on the 'modest clothing' and the lack of swimwear in this exhibition.[74]

Le Duprex did encourage and include employee voices, but this publication was primarily prescriptive in nature, an instrument to create a collaborative, paternalist workplace modelled after the patriarchal family, and to promote a vision linking the nation, religion, and the business of selling. Such prescriptions nonetheless indicate the training, transformation, and commodification of labour that service work required, and the ways in which the performance of emotion and the cultivation of appearance were both considered necessities for a woman saleslady. That these prescriptions were sometimes too difficult to follow becomes much clearer when one turns to managers' evaluations of their own employees.

'My miserable knees'[75]

According to historical gossip, Dupuis Frères was known for its employment of the 'elderly, disabled and widows.'[76] While employee files do indicate some commitment to keeping widows, in contrast to married

women, on the payroll, there is no other evidence to support this claim
from a sample of eighty-seven employees who worked at the store in the
1950s.[77] Although the women sellers at Dupuis Frères are not easily
categorized, there are a few generalizations about their background one
can make. Women came from working-class and petit bourgeois backgrounds, and had fathers who were engaged in a range of jobs from
machinist to journalist. Their formal education was rather minimal;
many completed the eighth grade (8e), though by the 1950s more
women had some high-school education. A minority claimed to be bilingual, a skill that is remarked on positively in the 1950s as the store begins
to talk about attracting an English clientele. At least half of the women
in this small sample came to the store from other jobs in retail, clerical,
or factory work, either because they were laid off, or because they were
searching for more secure, enjoyable white-collar work. Retail work did
offer the appearance of enhanced respectability and upward mobility for
blue-collar workers, even if the wages and long hours did not necessarily
substantiate this image. Moreover, young women's interest in beauty and
fashion culture was also an enticement. An investment in fashion and
adornment had long been part of working-class women's sense of feminine identity, and discussion about appearance and clothes then became
part of their work culture. Nor was it insignificant that young working-
class women were encouraged to see attractiveness as one kind of 'cultural
capital' they could lay claim to, a possible benefit to their own futures.[78]

Given the claims of many observers that women workers were mere
sojourners at work before marriage, the longevity of women's work lives
is noteworthy. Even if women left paid employment for temporary periods, they often returned, putting in as much as twenty years in the store.
For the burgeoning group of women workers with families, whose wages
were especially critical at particular moments in the family life cycle, or
when other family earners were off work, this option of recurring full or
part-time work was particularly advantageous. Employment at Dupuis
Frères also had other appeals: its benefits, recreational offerings, and the
promise of internal promotion (however small for women) were enticing
prospects compared to conditions in other blue- and white-collar jobs.
Applicants clearly knew, too, that Dupuis Frères promoted an image of its
'better class' of female workers; would-be employees sought out letters of
reference from clerics, friends, or neighbours who could speak to their
good character and morality, as well as their skills and diligence.

Evaluations of women's work as retail clerks by their managers reveal
the same attempts to train and transform workers into the ideal worker

promoted in *Le Duprex*.[79] Saleswomen who were most easily 'managed' were described as polite but assertive sellers; they were never impatient with clients; they understood the rules of etiquette, never becoming too personal with customers; and they were always devoted to their jobs. 'Devotée' was the key word for both good and bad sellers: the first had ample devotion, the latter never enough. What is remarkable is how many women had trouble living up to the store's standards. No matter how intensely they were surveyed and regulated, there was a discrepancy between the ideal saleswoman and the reality of selling, evidenced in countless tensions, corrections, orders, and also patterns of noncompliance and resistance on the sales floor.

Employees were evaluated repeatedly during the year, usually with standard forms that judged and ranked employees from good to bad on appearance, language, initiative, quality of work, attitude, and collaboration. Surveillance was particularly intense in certain periods, such as during sales, so much so that a special form was developed to judge employees' work during a sale. Evaluation categories were extremely subjective; a seller who was judged to be very good by one boss could then suffer intense critique in the next evaluation by another manager. Assessments in one file ranged from 'she is good at helping others' to 'she has a persecution complex.'[80] Surveillance of male employees was also intense; however, more men laboured in jobs offering some mobility, distance, and autonomy from managers: men managed to escape their overseers on the loading dock, in the parking lot, or in behind-the-scenes packing rooms. Men clearly used their spatial freedom in an attempt to carve out a few minutes for talking, smoking, or having lunch off the property; this was simply not possible if one worked behind a counter. Moreover, sellers had to contend with double surveillance from both their superiors and from customers; phone calls or letters of complaint from the latter could endanger their employment or crush the possibility of promotion.

And complain customers did. When aggrieved customers took the time to write to the store, their letters were noted in a worker's employment file, and there was no evidence of any opportunity for rebuttal. Mistakes, impoliteness, and failure to pay attention were some of the main sins that sellers committed in the eyes of irate customers. One aggrieved 'regular customer' wrote complaining that 'H' had given her the wrong information about her account, which resulted in the customer taking an unnecessary trip to the store with her three young children. She was not amused. The same employee, who had moved from selling to accounts, enraged another customer who complained that she had been treated 'rudely' on the phone. Apparently, H grew tired of calling about the customer's unpaid bill and scolded her for her immoral life, asking, 'Why is it that we can't get a hold of you? ... We know that you are separated from your husband but live in concubinage with [your] boss.' She also called the boss and asked him to pay. While Dupuis Frères' moral code might have frowned on common-law relationships, the employer was undoubtedly more interested in keeping customers happy and paying than in denouncing their marital status.[81]

Customers' most effective complaints were those that provided tangible proof that an impatient or incompetent seller had cost the store a sale. One woman wrote to the president of Dupuis Frères, saying she had come to buy her wedding dress but, faced with the seller's lack of 'comportement,' went instead to Eaton's to make her purchase. We lost a $100 sale, lamented the seller's supervisor, and after another complaint the employee was suspended.[82] Another salesperson was faulted for failing to accept a return, a pair of leaky boots; the customer surmised that the seller was simply anxious to 'go home' at the end of the day, but perhaps the seller also suspected the return was not a legitimate one. In order to alter her selling style, the worker was warned that she had to be more 'flexible and gentle' with customers.[83]

Customer complaints were harmful, but not as plentiful as the long list of faults recorded by management. Women were continually criticized for not being attentive or devoted enough: 'she lacks enthusiasm about building sales,' 'she does not preoccupy herself with the business,' 'she is undisciplined when responding to clients,' 'she is mediocre during sales,' and 'she does not seem to care if her sales are good or not' were just a few examples of employee appraisals.[84] Women's tardiness (every late arrival was counted) and absences were also censured. So was women's 'time theft' from the business, an accusation often made in other service jobs such as telephone operating.[85] Women were chastised for talking to family on the phone, gossiping, or 'occupying themselves too much with the affairs of other employees.'[86] Even though the latter was clearly a significant part of the work culture, and Le Duprex traded on gossip in its columns, managers had their own individual notions of how much talk was allowable in their respective departments.

A seller also had to negotiate the fine line between cooperating with other employees and pursuing one's own sales aggressively; she had to be independently assertive, but not too competitive with her fellow clerks. Given that commission sales existed in some departments, this put sellers in a no-win situation: they needed to make sales but could not be too forceful in doing so. 'No one can work with her; she is an impossible character … She does not cooperate with others,' claimed one manager in furs. Another manager complained that women fought over the number and type of tables each would look after during a sale, while the workers in turn kvetched that they had to tolerate terrible injustices and 'des bêtises' from their fellow sellers.[87] Indeed, a few women became informers, sending letters to management that damned fellow workers' bad behaviour or exposed their cheating on the health insurance plan.

The most serious flaw of a seller was almost always her failure to act appropriately with customers. Risking sales by being rude to a customer was extremely egregious. 'How many clients have we lost with her bad behaviour,' asked the fur manager about the difficult employee above, noting that he had to rescue one sale when the employee was tactlessly demanding the client buy a 'brown rather than black fur.'[88] Being too intimate with customers ('talking to customers about things she should not speak about'), or too loud or vulgar with other employees, were also blunders of significance.[89] One woman who was accused of sitting down too much was doubly damned, first for failing to attend properly to clients (sitting was not respectful service) and second for failing to be appropriately deferential to her managers. Women were also criticized for clumsiness when they blocked the pneumatic tube with their invoices, or dropped dinner plates in housewares, but it was the 'deference deficit' that usually raised management's ire. If service was the essence of the work process, if servers were part of the product being offered, it is easy to see why managers gritted their teeth when faced with indifferent sellers. Their attempts to remould their employees into more accommodating workers simply underlines the key importance of emotional labour to the retail process.

Similar complaints about unenthusiastic service and low sales were found in male salespersons' files, especially if they worked behind the counter. Men in jobs such as delivery also faced customers' complaints, particularly when they took no gaff from clients; one delivery man dismissed a woman customer by telling her she was 'crazy in the head.'[90] Needless to say, she complained. Mistakes, lateness, and absences were noted, though one is struck by some tolerance for mistakes, as with the man who had five delivery-truck accidents, including one knocking a woman down, and yet was not fired.[91] Still, the prevailing gender ideology mattered in the store's disciplinary strategies: women, for instance, received more criticism for their bad humour than did men. Expectations clearly were that women should be innately more obsequious and polite; when they were not, their transgressions were viewed with particular impatience. The sexual division of labour in the store exacerbated this. Men who moved up through the store hierarchy escaped the intense surveillance associated with selling, yet many women sellers might work in the same position for years, and could be transferred at management's whim. One woman whose long years at Dupuis Frères were publicized positively when she retired, admitted that she had wanted to leave when management transferred her to the 'basement with little air like a cellar.'[92]

No wonder, then, that women complained of fatigue and ill health, or appeared tired and bored. Women had doctors' notes excusing them for illnesses such as asthma, hypertension, depression, and arthritis; often these problems were aggravated by long hours of standing and the pressures of emotional labour. At the most extreme, managers criticized women for severe physical problems, such as deafness or memory loss. Given the longevity of many employees, it is not surprising that ill health is noted in their files, but there was no recognition of the ways in which service work actually caused or exacerbated women's ailments, except for the occasional comment that age made a woman 'slower and slower, with her sore feet.'[93] This was well illustrated by a woman who worked at the store, off and on, for over thirty years. By the time she was fifty-eight, there were many doctors' notes in her file, when she asked, at one point, for another week off, she wrote plaintively to her superior, 'when I saw you earlier … I gave you lots of 'precision' on the details … It [the leave] is to give my miserable knees which are causing me suffering for 20 years [a rest] … The hospital said to me, nothing will do, walk less and this is why I am absent.'[94]

Women may have suffered from physical problems, but managers tended to psychologize their female employees all the same. Women, they wrote, had persecution complexes, 'childlike personalities,' and 'strange personalities,' and more than one female was labelled a 'nervous personality,' a designation that likely had gendered connotations.[95] 'This employee has bouts of humour that are incomprehensible,' wrote one manager, noting that he had warned the worker in question to 'leave her personal troubles at home.'[96] One can only surmise what those troubles were. No matter how 'authentic' an employee's unhappiness, it had to be suppressed at work, replaced by the Dupuis Frères smile.

White-collar labour may have been perceived as less physically strenuous than factory work, but it carried its own perils. Petty accidents were part of the territory. Women tripped on uneven carpets, fell down stairs, cut open fingers, were hit and injured by falling stands, and got caught in elevator doors. A survey of negligence cases in the courts during the 1950s indicates that small accidents in department stores sometimes turned into painful injuries and lawsuits. Truly disgruntled employees might look for reprieve in the courts, but this was not a propitious way to secure compensation, and ironically, workers might be held accountable by their employer for any mishaps and accidents suffered by customers. Employees could be held responsible for these lawsuits, surely an added stress for the workers.[97]

Attempts to alter women's physical appearance reinforced the importance of body work as well as emotional work in retail. To some extent, women were placed in the departments that they looked the part for, even if they did not want to be there. An older woman, for instance, was removed from children's clothing and sent to the basement, as she was told she was too old to serve in an area for young people,[98] while women who were considered fashionable were put in the Petit Salon. The concern with women's appearance was replicated in many files, as the management tried to reshape bodies and appearance into more appealing commodities for the customer gaze. Women were told outright to correct their bad breath, attend to their weight, or improve their appearance, though one suspects that part of the hiring process was meant to screen applicants, and search for a particular physical look. But women found themselves falling from grace with age, over time, or with different supervisors. One employee originally described as a 'feminine soul … well brought up, [with a] good appearance,' was criticized later for not being able to 'do better in her appearance,' then finally was condemned for having 'no taste for her appearance.' While there was clearly a recognition that this woman knew the department well and taught new employees about it, an obsession with her appearance continued, with more and more comments of disgust: 'Her appearance is horrible and people are talking about it … I can't see her as a buyer.' The final critique that she was 'slow' and needed to buy a corset suggests it was her weight that bothered her fellow employees and her manager, who seemed unmoved by a customer letter praising her 'kindness' and care. A single, lifetime worker, the woman did manage to move into an assistant department-head position due to her honesty and competence, but her looks clearly disqualified her for other jobs, such as that of buyer.[99] Appearance was not unimportant for men, though there were more concerns about their sobriety than their weight; men were also more likely to be disciplined for smoking in the back hallways or stealing time away from their position than for their looks.

For both men and women, however, it is difficult to ascertain whether non-compliance with the rules was conscious or accidental. Did women consciously ignore beauty tips? Was the woman dropping plates in housewares clumsy or just fed up with her job? Was the woman who blocked the pneumatic tube consciously cavalier? Certainly, some women were careless, broke the rules, pilfered occasionally, or refused to do certain jobs. They also talked back to supervisors, earning them disciplinary letters. Money sometimes disappeared, with women chastised for being even four dollars short on their cash. For losing $10, one woman was suspended for a month.[100] Another seller seemed mysteriously to lose more than one dress in the delivery process: was this pattern really an accident? One woman who looked after orders to fix sewing machines did not write any dates or details on her orders and stashed them away until over eighty were discovered, much to the horror of her manager. It could have been forgetfulness, but it might also have been wilful disregard.[101] While these small rebellions were individual in nature, women's work culture in retail provided ample opportunities for information sharing and the concoction of collective strategies that might ease the burden of work or resist management control, by sharing insider knowledge about customers, manoeuvring around difficult managers, moderating the pace of work, or ostracizing difficult felllow workers.[102] Women sellers, in other words, were not always successfully transformed into deferential workers. Critical letters, suspensions, and, very rarely, dismissals were used to discipline women, but the dominant method of control was more gentle, subtle, and absolutely incessant, involving attempts to persuade them to act differently. The ideal worker was one who was 'empowered' to self-regulate, entreated to embrace the service ideal as her own, concerned that her smile be 'natural,' and last, but not least, convinced that she should be grateful for the benefits of a paternalist workplace.

On Strike

Paternalism at Dupuis Frères seemed to suddenly unravel when a strike was called by the employees in 1952. The Dupuis Frères strike was quite a remarkable event in a period when retail workers were extremely difficult to organize; only a year before, a three-year organizing campaign at Eaton's in Toronto had failed to secure a union. Yet the Dupuis Frères strike becomes intelligible when viewed in relation to two overlapping contexts: the political changes in the Canadian and Quebec labour movement after the war and the tensions and discontents already developing in the paternalist accord at Dupuis Frères.

The union at Dupuis Frères was established in 1919 at the encouragement of store patriarch Narcisse Dupuis, a fact the family never tired of reminding its employees about. Founded as Le Syndicat Catholique et National des Employés de Magasin,[103] the union intended to follow the advice of Pope Leo XIII's 1891 encyclical on labour and capital, advocating the cooperation of workers and management, and the promotion of religious values; the union even forbade 'discussions politiques'[104] in its meetings. During the interwar period, both managers and workers attended meetings that were largely consumed with social, religious, and cultural activities, though also with the administration of sick benefits and *Le Duprex*. Despite the fact that many employees were women, union executives were almost entirely formed of men, with only one exception.[105]

A significant shift took place in the post–Second World War period as the union, officially a part of the CTCC since 1935, shared in that organization's transformation. Abandoning its earlier corporatism, now tainted by its fascist associations, the CTCC embraced a liberal-humanist politics, symbolized by the ascendancy of the more militant Gérard Picard to the CTCC presidency in 1946. In the immediate aftermath of the war, Quebec witnessed the same outburst of union protest as occurred in the rest of the country, as workers fought for democratic and collective bargaining rights, precisely the demands of the Dionne textile workers. By the time of the Dupuis Frères strike, the CTCC represented almost a third of unionized workers in Quebec, and, in contrast to the interwar period, participated in as many strikes as the international unions.

A parallel shift in political tone took place in the Dupuis Frères union, now called Le Syndicat National des Employés de Commerce de Montréal (Le Syndicat). The union's transformation was symbolized by two events seven years apart. In 1943, the Dupuis Frères union was in arrears to the CTCC, as it was not paying the full per capita dues owed. A series of letters back and forth over the next year indicated attempts to work out a compromise, including one revealing the patriarchal suggestion from the Dupuis Frères union that 'men will continue to pay but not women who will not be a part of the union.' The CTCC head, Alfred Charpentier, asked Albert Dupuis very deferentially to intervene and press the union to pay up; in the end, the store gave about a thousand dollars to the

CTCC to clear up the matter, a gift that most craft or industrial unions would never have countenanced.[106]

By 1950 the situation was different: the union moved its meetings and books from the store to the CTCC office, and it announced in October that it was seeking permission from the Commission on Labour Relations to become the sole bargaining agent for employees, in order to negotiate a collective agreement. As one female union activist who signed up employees with new union cards remembered, the union was quickly transformed from a company to a real union, with the employer no longer deciding one's union status: 'Nous avions un syndicat de boutique … dont le président était toujours un gérant, plus soucieux des intérêts du patron que des travailleurs. C'est le patron qui décidait de ton entrée dans le syndicat.'[107]

What had changed? The transformation in the CTCC was one factor, but the store's traditional paternalism was also faltering under the pressure of contradictions. Raymond Dupuis, who assumed the store's family mantle in 1945, had embarked on an expensive and ambitious modernization program after 1947. This encompassed a multi-million-dollar physical facelift and the importation of new management, including accountant Roland Chagnon, a 'modernizer' who replaced Émile Boucher, a well-liked individual who personified traditional paternal management.[108] Chagnon soon unveiled plans for a cost-cutting Taylorist reorganization of the store; on the eve of the strike, the union was protesting to provincial authorities about dismissals and 'unjustified' transfers within the store.[109] According to Michel Chartrand, who became Le Syndicat's business agent after the strike, Chagnon had announced that there were '300 filles de trop dans le magasin' who had to be laid off, a threat that fanned the fires of union protest.[110] Workers' discontent with their wages, lower on average than other department store workers in the city, was also a mobilizing factor. After all, they worked in a business premised on the promise of consumption, yet their take-home pay, the union argued, was far below that of other stores: contrary to the promise of the Fordist accord, these workers could not consume the products they handled every day on the job.

Workers may have been disillusioned with Dupuis Frères, but they bent over backwards to give their employer the opportunity to bargain and come to an agreement. One reason may have been lingering loyalties to the store's owners. Even in the post-war period, francophone workers found themselves barred from the same economic opportunities as anglophone workers; as a result, the ethnic and linguistic divisions in the province were embedded in the class structure, with francophones relegated to the lower rungs of the economic ladder. At the end of the 1950s, francophones still controlled less than 20 per cent of the Quebec economy, and in Montreal, francophone speakers, though 65 per cent of the workforce, occupied only 17 per cent of administrative positions.[111] As one radical of the 1960s put it quite succinctly, 'In Quebec, Capital speaks English; Labour, French.'[112] Given this persisting 'colonial' political economy, French-speaking workers understandably appreciated employers for whom language was not a barrier to employment and promotion – indeed, quite the contrary.

The infinite patience of the strikers was one reason they were later able to garner strong public support, since it was clear they had given the store every chance over a year and a half to negotiate a contract.[113] The union had received its legal go-ahead to bargain in January of 1951, and by May the store was still playing politics, attempting to divide the union by demanding separate bargaining units for the store and the mail-order workers. The Labour Relations Board supported the union's adamant rejection of that tactic. When the union proposed a contract with wage increases in the spring, the store suddenly posted its own increases, while also reducing the number of employee hours and re-organizing commission sales to the detriment of workers. Workers saw Dupuis Frères make much of wage increases, yet when they opened their paychecks, they found their pay unaltered, a further cause of disillusion. Still, conciliation continued, and when that failed, arbitration followed, with another eight-month delay. Despite a detailed arbitrators' report calling for the Rand formula, a grievance procedure, and pay raises, Dupuis Frères would not even agree to the amounts suggested by its own nominated arbitrator.[114] Even after Dupuis Frères rejected the arbitration report, the union tried to negotiate through April 1952. These countless delays, along with the stubborn refusal of Dupuis Frères to budge on the major issues, were later offered as proof of the employer's arrogance and intransigence in a pamphlet, endorsed by public figures at l'Université de Montréal, entitled 'Pourquoi ils sont en grève.'[115] On May Day, 1952, 1000 workers, by secret ballot, voted 97 per cent to strike. Few strike votes are ever so overwhelming.

The strike of 1200–1300 store employees,[116] about 57 per cent of whom were women, lasted 13 weeks.[117] One reason the Dupuis Frères strike captured the interest of the public and the media was the militancy of the strikers, particularly their willingness to use disobedient and disruptive tactics against an employer who had long claimed the mantle of

Figure 9 'La grève, 1952.' (HEC, Montreal, P049X99001, Dupuis Frères Fonds)

paternal concern, and who was esteemed by sections of the Quebec elite. A group of strikers thronged through the doors on the first days of the strike to disrupt Dupuis Frères sales, after the company had advertised a 20 per cent discount to shoppers crossing the picket line. Strikers continued to try to block the St Catherine Street entrance until police – with no real legal right – ordered a reduction in the number of picketers to ten people. A pattern of indifferent disregard for authority on the part of strikers set in very early. Two teenagers pasted walls in the vicinity of Dupuis Frères with stickers supporting the strike; another striker created a large picket sign using a picture of police horses' rumps accompanied by a caption: 'les arguments de Dupuis Frères.' When the police tried to ban the sign, the union published the picture in *Le Travail*.[118]

Rebelliousness was combined with parody and humour: one man paraded down St Catharine Street on his horse, imitating the local mounted police, nicknamed the 'gestapo' by some strikers because of their strong-arm tactics. As if to mimic Dupuis Frères' cultural nationalism, a group of female picketers composed a song, putting lyrics mocking Dupuis Frères to the tune of the traditional folk song *Frères Jacques*: Dupuis Frères, Dupuis Frères / Dormez-vous, Dormez-vous. / Sortez-donc vos piastres, Sortez-donc vos piastres. / Payez-nous, Payez-nous.[119] A regular Friday evening demonstration of hundreds greeted the scab buses (this was symbolic, since Friday evening work was a sore spot for workers);[120] crowds sang, laughed, and shouted at police and strikebreakers. It could be a time of revelry, but also anger: one bus of strikebreakers had one of its windows broken by a rock. By June, there were also incidents of vandalism, as store windows were smashed. CTCC leader Michel Chartrand concocted the tactic most associated with the strike: many white mice were released in the women's lingerie section of the store, resulting in 'near chaos.'[121] The rodent tactic was later followed by stink bombs, frogs, and bees let loose in the store, as well as firecrackers strategically set off.

Confrontational tactics, particularly at the picket line, where protesters tried to prevent scabs and customers from entering the St Catharine Street store, also resulted in at least seventy arrests of both women and men. Women's militancy took the union and the employer by surprise. On the first day of picketing, they were in the majority, according to union lawyer Pierre Vadboncoeur, and though completely unaccustomed to the intimidating police presence, 'les petites employées' simply laughed at their threatening, 'scowling faces.'[122] Raymond Dupuis's sister, though critical of her brother's bad management, also registered her shock that 'their' women employees could be so ungrateful, and so terribly angry.[123] Despite the many court appearances of those arrested, only one person served prison time for throwing rotten eggs at Montreal's mayor Camilien Houde, a supporter of the Dupuis family, during the St Jean Baptiste Day parade.[124]

The tone of rebellion, in other words, was unusually disrespectful: for women it was doubly 'rude.'[125] As white-collar workers, the Dupuis Frères women may have perceived themselves to be respectable and modest, yet in the strike they were thrown into completely opposite roles, highly visible in public, picketing, parading, and yelling at customers, including some clergy; one was even arrested for spitting at those crossing the picket line. The disjuncture between the emotional labour of service work, premised always on deference, politeness, smiling, and serving, and the physical, emotive rebellion of the workers, especially the women, was very significant.[126] Perhaps the strike provided the opportunity for strikers to unleash their long-submerged unhappiness and tensions lingering below the surface smile of service work. Even women who continued in serving roles during the strike became politicized in its wake. One woman who ran the canteen for strikers on a nearby corner, serving them coffee and sandwiches day and night, later became very active in the CTCC. This cashier threw herself into strike organizing, joined the union executive, and left Dupuis Frères five years later to help run Les Presses Sociales with Chartrand. Some interviews with women on the picket line stressed the novelty of public picketing for women long accustomed to a regulatory regime of demure service: one sixty-two-year-old female picketer said she would never have imagined herself on a picket line at her age, while a younger 'debutante,' full of 'pep,' as she led a chant, assured the reporter that she was quite happy on the line, supported not only by her family, but by her fiancé as well, who was also out on strike.[127]

The union leadership knew that the strike would be a 'war of nerves' and 'une guerre de propagande,' especially since it was taking on a revered institution.[128] In general, strikes in service work rely heavily on public support, since absent customers and organized boycotts can bring a business back to the bargaining table. Both the union and the store understood the importance of capturing the hearts of the public, an uphill battle for the CTCC, since many Montreal newspapers were unsympathetic to the strike, repeating outlandish rumours initiated by the police anti-subversive unit that communists were secretly involved in the strike.[129] Even Le Devoir's editor, Gérald Filion, who was eventually called in to mediate, bemoaned the calamity of two great French Canadian institutions in combat; he was long on lamentations for the tragedy of the strike, but did not offer strong editorial support for the strikers.[130]

The union's disruptive actions were accompanied by tactics of mobilization that kept the strikers in the public eye. Mass meetings were called that the press could not avoid, and radio addresses were used by Picard to persuade listeners that Dupuis Frères was flush enough to raise its wages. The union reminded listeners that the company endorsed Christian values, but practised a very un-Christian exploitation of workers. The CTCC sought the support of other non-CTCC unions, especially those allied with the CCL, gaining endorsements and promises of boycotts. Even before the strike, the CTCC had gently reminded Dupuis

Frères that Montreal trade unionists had always been encouraged to shop at the store: what would happen now? CTCC leaders travelled to secure the support of textile strikers in Louiseville, and the CCL-affiliated unionists on strike at the Simmons mattress factory in Montreal exchanged picketing duty with Dupuis Frères strikers.[131] The CTCC scored a public-relations coup when it persuaded American boxer Joe Louis not to cross the picket line for a scheduled store appearance; 'born into the working class,' Louis did not dishonour his roots, said a triumphant *Le Travail* on its front page.[132]

Dupuis Frères used the press as well, not only to advertise its discounts, but also to (mis)inform the public that the majority of strikers had returned to work. It also promoted its introduction of self-service, a management innovation that had much to do with its opposition to the union. Self-service, a direct threat to workers' jobs, had long been used as a strike-breaking and efficiency tactic by retailers.[133] The business press applauded Dupuis Frères for embracing the wave of the future, pointing out that strikers should beware of losing their jobs.[134] Yet Dupuis Frères' tactics were also clumsy: Raymond Dupuis's escape on a European vacation in early May, to note one example, was seen as rather cavalier in the midst of a strike. By July his new modernizing manager had consulted a public-relations firm. They warned that the union was winning the public-relations battle, with the store, in contrast, seen as 'ungenerous,' assuming 'les traits du vainqueur piétinant le vaincu.' Their advice: make some concessions and, in the long run, improve human relations at the store. This may have helped push Dupuis Frères back to the table.[135]

Moreover, despite its hallowed reputation, Dupuis Frères also did not have the support of the entire Quebec social elite, leaving the store vulnerable to critical publicity. Prominent Université de Montréal academics signed 'Pourquoi ils sont en grève,' and also decried the use of student strikebreakers from the Hautes Études Commerciales (HEC). Some Catholic clergy crossed the picket line, but a few defended the strikers. Henri Pichette, the chaplain of the CTCC, chastised Dupuis Frères for abandoning the tenets of social Christianity and lauded the strikers as 'révolutionnaires chrétiens' in the struggle for a better society.[136] 'Neo-nationalist' intellectuals such as Filion may have urged cooperation between worker and employer, seeing foreign ownership as more of a threat to the nation;[137] however, Citélibrists such as Vadboncoeur and CTCC staffer Jean Marchand were critical of Dupuis Frères' brand of nationalism, used, in their view, to excuse the exploitation of workers. Strikers clearly responded positively to Gérard Picard's admonition that Dupuis Frères could no longer 'exploit nationalist and religious sentiments' as a way of avoiding a collective agreement. Chartrand put it more bluntly: Dupuis Frères was offering an 'opium [for] the people,' a false nationalism that allowed the employer to 'defend the French language while starving those who spoke it.'[138]

Social and intellectual upheavals particular to Quebec society were thus mirrored in the strike, though the struggle also had parallels with labour disputes in English Canada. Other service-worker strikes, such as the Toronto Royal York one in 1952, counted on public support and a customer boycott to succeed, though that union's lack of militancy led to a defeat.[139] Second, as in other long strikes, the police and the courts became part of the battle. As Vadboncoeur quipped, when an employer starts to fail, it turns to the courts.[110] Dupuis Frères initiated two legal actions in court, one for damages against union leaders for publishing a pamphlet that claimed that the store had hypocritically raised prices by 20 per cent before reducing them by 20 per cent during its strike sale. While the store succeeded in arguing that this damaged its reputation, its second attempt to use the courts to shut down the strike was not entirely successful. Dupuis Frères did obtain an interlocutory injunction for a week in May, arguing that the union and its officials had pursued a campaign of lies, harassment, and destruction: '[Ils] sont systématiquement et illégalement concertés pour conduire une campagne d'injures de dénigrement, de mensonges et de calomnies dans le but bien arrêté d'éloigner sa clientèle.'[141] The store's list of affronts perpetrated by the union was unending, as were its demands for restitution: no more pamphlets, demonstrations, phone calls, or incursions into the store, to name only a few.[142] On 13 June, however, Judge Brossard terminated the injunction, as there was no clear proof in the affidavits of illegal activities.[143] Given the propensity of the courts to continue ex parte injunctions in unruly strikes, the decision was noteworthy. Of course, the injunction was only one law-and-order tactic used by Dupuis Frères; it also requested public police protection and placed over a hundred private security guards inside the store. These guards even tried to remove journalists' notes until the latter protested the illegality of such seizures. As the strike unfolded, then, it stimulated new social and legal battles, encouraging others, as Vadboncoeur argues, to stand up for their civil rights as well.

On 26 July, after renewed negotiations and the mediation of Filion and Archbishop Paul-Émile Léger, a contract was secured with substantial wage increases, the Rand formula, and grievance and transfer procedures. Boucher was hired back to replace the unpopular Chagnon, and legal procedures against the union were halted. The settlement represented a rare victory in the retail sector. At a union rally that day, Raymond Dupuis spoke to the strikers, welcoming them back as a parent would an errant child: 'La vielle maison canadienne-française se sera bien heureuse lundi matin d'accueillir ses enfants. Elle les recevra avec le même coeur qu'autrefois, avec un amour maternel.' Even CTCC staffer Philippe Girard could not resist a marital metaphor: 'C'est comme une femme qui revient à son homme.'[144] Dupuis's use of familial allegories suggested his continuing investment in the ideal of a paternalist workplace, but the strike had permanently unsettled this negotiated bargain. The workers' decision to opt for collective bargaining over paternalism was not entirely peculiar to Dupuis Frères, or even to French Canada. The unionization attempt at Eaton's in Toronto, though it closely missed securing collective-bargaining rights, represented precisely the same challenge to paternalism, as did other successful unionization efforts in the 1940s and 1950s.[145] In the light of the Fordist accord, some workers preferred the certainty of industrial legality over the uncertainty of discretionary favours from the boss.

The 'Woman Question' Emerges in Catholic Unions

Le Syndicat's success reflected the CTCC's change of political tune, as well as a rapprochement with international unions, both demonstrations of Quebec historians' admonitions not to see the 1950s simply as a period of stasis before the sudden awakening of the Quiet Revolution. Rather, the decade represented 'un terrain fertile pour les luttes sociales,'[146] and for workers' mobilization around new demands for economic citizenship. This more radical and expansive union mentality would also create the ideological space necessary for the integration of more women workers into union activity. Before the strike, women were almost entirely absent from the union leadership, and the CTCC avidly supported the male breadwinner ideology, seeing women as 'temporary or exceptional'[147] workers, just as some craft unions did. However, women's active participation in the strike, particularly in the theatre of public events, showed their resolve in a new light, and drew attention to their abilities and their commitment to unionism. Madelaine Brosseau, an office worker who helped with the new sign-up campaign, was persuaded to join the union executive in January of 1952 by union leader Marcel Lanouette, who told her they needed someone like her, with the courage to speak back to the boss. After the strike Brosseau became vice-president of the union, and later became one of the vice-presidents of the CTCC.[148] The incorporation of women into the union, as she remembers, remained somewhat tokenistic and 'marginal' in the fifties. Due to reigning prejudices, no woman could be president of Le Syndicat, as that position was 'reserved' only for men, though within the CTCC, optics required at least one woman among seven vice-presidents when almost a third of the members were women.[149]

From its inception in the 1920s, the CTCC had called for the limitation of women's wage labour so that they might return to 'hearth' and home, an ideological position strongly encouraged by the Catholic Church: the consequence was that women were not 'accepted into the heart of the CTCC.'[150] This 'traditionalist' ideology, centering on women's roles as homemakers and denying their role as workers, suggests Mona-Josée Gagnon, remained fundamentally unchallenged until initial questions were raised in the 1950s, and it left its ideological imprint on the CSN (Confédération des Syndicats Nationaux) until the early 1960s, when it was finally revised.[151]

In the aftermath of the Second World War, and through the 1950s, the union was wrestling with the contradiction of women's changing role in the workforce. Le Travail acknowledged that the influx of married wives and mothers into the workforce during the war had sparked women's new taste for independent wages and lives outside the home, yet it feared this irreversible trend would have potentially 'disastrous' consequences for the family, including the decline of paternal authority.[152] Contradictory efforts to come to terms with an expanding female workforce were reflected in countless Le Travail articles. On one hand, women's primarily maternal role was taken for granted, and articles discussed 'proof' of women's essential, psychological differences from men: women were subjective, suggestible, romantic, and adaptable, while men were more objective and cerebral.[153] On the other hand, articles, often reprinted from the Bureau International de Travail (ILO), paid new attention to woman workers as unionists, if also 'problems' to be addressed. And in contrast to some articles decrying the 'conséquences désastreuses' of more women workers, other writers acknowledged the legitimacy of women's paid work, particularly in occupations such as the social services, which suited women's 'nature.'[154]

Moreover, some advocates of women cleverly argued that it was precisely because women were more timid, adaptable, and in need of protection that their participation in the workers' movement should be encouraged. A special course on unionism, for example, was offered to some CTCC women employed in the commercial and hospital sectors under the direction of a local chaplain. Readings for the course, prepared by Laure Gaudreault, a well-known unionist and founder of the Fédération catholique des institutrices rurale, captured this double emphasis on female difference and trade-union mobilization extremely well.[155] Capitalism, she wrote, definitely benefited economically from women's labour, not the least because of women's feminine attributes – adaptability, endurance, patience, and so on. Women's participation in unions must follow their expanded role in production, though the author also suggested 'un syndicat féminin' where women could share their concerns without fear of prejudice or discomfort. Like many authors, Gaudreault used religious arguments to support egalitarianism: the right to equal pay, she reminded others, was supported by a papal statement. Perhaps most interesting was her equation of women's work with a positive, evolving identity: 'La femme doit donc entrer avec confiance dans les sphères nouvelles d'activité [que] notre siècle de vitesse et de progrès ouvre chaque jour. Elle doit y entrer non seulement avec le souci de pourvoir à sa propre subsistence ... mais pour y exercer son influence, y remplir la tâche qui demeurera toujours le plus bel apanage de son sexe: une mission de collaboratrice et d'éducatrice.'[156] Catholicism, Michael Gauvreau contends, was being recast in this period; a 'personalist feminist' tradition, inherited from Catholic Action, emphasized women's personal and spiritual fulfilment as well as more egalitarian, rather than biologically determined, maternal roles. As a result, women's work for pay could be reinterpreted 'as a pole of stability in a period of bewildering social and cultural change,' or as an means – in some feminized professions – to express women's distinct character and their 'aptitude for spiritual maternity.'[157]

In 1952 the CTCC created 'le Comité de la condition féminine' to review the special problems faced by women workers within its ranks.[158] Finding only one woman on a union executive associated with the CTCC, and only one at the CTCC executive level, the female authors of the report timidly asked that there be an effort to secure better representation of women in the future. Far being from a critique of patriarchy, the report mildly reproached men who did not think of women as equals, but also chastised women for not taking sufficient interest in their own union. Although this new attention to women may have been prompted largely by the lobbying of a few individual women, in particular Vice-President Jeanne Duval, it marked the beginning of new efforts to consider women's issues. A decade later, a far more decisive shift was apparent. Instead of proffering advice (and recipes) for the wives of workers, the union paper addressed the female third of its membership who were in the workforce, and it sponsored a convention resolution reaffirming 'la liberté de choix' for all women who wished to work. Although the women's committee was officially dissolved in 1960, the union, now the CSN, produced a brief for the Royal Commission on the Status of Women, issuing a list of extensive demands, including better education, training, equal pay, and state-funded child care so that married women would not have to sacrifice family well-being if they worked outside the home.[159]

The presence of a legal union at Dupuis Frères, buttressed by the Rand formula, and now dedicated to union, not paternalist, practices, also propelled women into new roles by offering them a new vocabulary, ideas, and principles that could facilitate their struggles within the workplace. Trade-union rhetoric extolled fairness, justice, and collective rights, as well as democracy and the 'rule of the contract.' Even if Dupuis Frères women accepted the dominant gendered division of labour in retail, they could use union tools, such as the grievance procedure, to bring increased job security and rights into their own sphere of gendered labour. After the strike ended, Filion acted as a mediator, settling outstanding grievances. It is revealing that women used this process just as men did, often challenging the store over classification issues and how their positions would be remunerated. One woman even claimed her rights as a 'breadwinner-mother.' Under the contract, she argued, the store offered an educational benefit to heads of families with children over sixteen who were attending an accredited educational institution. When denied her stipend for her two children, she grieved the matter and won her case.[160] This willingness to stand up for one's entitlements and, in this case, one's due as a working mother, was to become more and more prevalent within the next generation of female union activists.

Conclusion

If one consulted only *Le Duprex*, the 1952 strike might appear to be a sharp rupture in the smooth functioning of a paternalist workplace. Reading the unhappiness, fatigue, and small disobediences that emerge in workers' personnel files, however, makes the strike far more understandable. Still, the Dupuis Frères strike remains a unique and all-too-rare instance of successful department-store organizing in the post-war period.[161] The post-war accord offered retail workers the promise of union check-off and industrial legality, along with the certitude of grievance procedures in place of the pleasures of parties and bowling teams, yet few unions were able to successfully overcome the structural and ideological barriers to effective organizing in retail. Ironically, the Dupuis family unwittingly laid the groundwork for the union's later success. Though it encouraged a highly deferential, meek, cooperative, Catholic union, the mere fact of the union's presence, and the networks of communication and sociability it had fostered, allowed it to move expeditiously to more forthright demands for a contract and the Rand formula in the post-war period. Unlike in the Eaton's case, half the battle – that is, simply organizing a union – was already won.

The brand of paternalism cultivated by Dupuis Frères was shaped by distinctive Quebec social conditions and culture. Not only did the Catholic union, fostered by the state and the clergy as an alternative to secular – or, more horrific, 'communist' – unions provide a valuable jumping-off point for more militant union organizing, but the course of the strike itself was shaped by debates within the Quebec elite about the value of French Canadian–owned businesses, the promotion of the French culture, and the appropriate alliances (cross-class and national, or class-based) for the Quebec working class. The Dupuis family's long-standing equation of its business with the French Canadian nation and its linkage of paternalism with Catholicism and nationalism was also unique. Certainly, both Eaton's and the Hudson's Bay Company promoted themselves as historic institutions, their evolution equated with the progress of 'the nation,' a category that was constructed in English Canada as white, Protestant, and Anglo-Saxon.[162] However, the intensity and determination of Dupuis Frères' use of nationalist ideology was quite remarkable, and there is every reason to believe that the Dupuis family itself was deeply invested in this project, seeing its enterprise as both a model for Catholic benevolence and a bulwark against Anglo business domination within the city.[163]

The strike also symbolized a transitional moment for women workers. Even if maternal duty remained at the core of women's perceived social role, wage labour was becoming a more prominent concern and a measure of women's identity: changing labour-force patterns and culture interacted dynamically, shifting ever so slightly both women's experiences, and their understandings, of work. While the store's particular brand of paternalism bore the distinctive marks of Quebec culture, the gendered work process at the heart of selling, as well as the alienation and commodification of workers, bore striking similarities to retail work elsewhere and, indeed, to other female-typed service work. Retail labour had long been sold to women as a more respectable, genteel, even fashionable prospect than factory work, but the intense surveillance, pacing, measurement of sales, and even physical tedium, bore some similarity to blue-collar work. To be sure, women clerks and cashiers tried to use the more flexible work environment – for there was no assembly line – to create a culture with a certain degree of sociability, gossip, and mutual support on the selling floor. The benefits, holidays, awards, social events, and praise associated with the negotiated bargain of paternalism at Dupuis Frères also made these retail jobs attractive. At Dupuis Frères, women with long employment records might also hope for some upward mobility to supervisory or buyer positions, and women tried to transfer out of departments where they were unhappy, from mail order to the store, or from selling to office work. The latter promised not only improved pay, but relief from the critical gaze and demands of customers, and long hours on one's feet.

Retail labour clearly took its toll on workers' bodies. Women's complaints of depression, exhaustion, fatigue, and 'bad knees,' along with their antipathy to customers' complaints and management's surveillance, speak to the tensions of sales work. Women sellers were selected for certain jobs based on existing gendered and class 'dispositions,' but they were also constantly encouraged to 'inhabit' their work roles with emotional enthusiasm, and to dedicate themselves to projecting an aesthetically pleasing appearance. If supervisors' reports are to be believed, saleswomen were always a 'work in progress' for the store; they needed constantly to be regulated, re-fashioned, and also encouraged to make over their own image, abilities, character, and bodies. The hope of Dupuis Frères was that women's innately more agreeable and generous personalities would make an ideal fit with the emotional labour of selling, and even after women abandoned wage labour, their modest, charitable, and Catholic character would continue to fit well with their role as mothers of the nation.

Service labour, argues Chris Schilling, involves two overlapping expenditures of effort: the official labour performed by the body and the necessity of women going to work on their bodies in order to create an appropriate image and persona for consumers.[164] The Dupuis Frères store fostered the latter brand of labour by encouraging its women workers to see themselves as fashionable consumers, but also simply by telling them what to wear, and how to look on the job. The perpetual smile advocated for retail work was more than bodily image, it was also emotional labour, a form of acting that has to be taken into account when describing the daily strains of work. Just as Marx understood that workers became alienated from their sensual bodies when their labour was appropriated by capital, so too materialist-feminists have delineated the way in which emotional labour appropriates one's feelings and emotions. Both forms of labour, integral to selling, become subtly embodied as part of the retail work process and work culture.

While feminist insights on embodiment open up new ways of seeing service work, materialist understandings of bodily labour, alienation, and commodification are also important. The performance of women's labour in the public eye of the department store, and the performance of strike activity in the theatre of the streets, cannot be simply interpreted as instances of Butleresque 'performativity.'[165] Performance may help to constitute the labouring body, but there are important differences between Bourdieu's concept of performance as part of habitus, with his emphasis on the conditioning power of social norms and institutions, and postmodernist conceptions of performance as inscribed on the body, but with far less consideration of the material circumstances and social structures circumscribing women's choices. Women retail workers were expected to put on a classed and gendered performance, but they did so within conditions not of their own choosing. When they rudely 'acted out' during the strike in unruly contradiction to their normal service labour, this was not a mere reflex reaction to power, but a form of active, conscious rebellion against a form of paternal management that increasing numbers of women at Dupuis Frères found wanting.

Chapter 5

Discipline and Grieve:
Gendering the Fordist Accord

In 1949, a young woman working in a blue-collar factory job in Niagara Falls was discharged from her job when she gave birth to a child. She left work only two days before she delivered, but when she called her foreman a week later to say she could return to work, she was fired over the phone. Management admitted she was a reliable worker, and her crime was not taking time off to have a baby: rather, it was her status as an unmarried mother. According to her employer, this was her second illegitimate child and she had agreed not to do it again or face dismissal. Her grievance over discharge, taken up by her union, the United Electrical, Radio and Machine Workers of America (UE), was dismissed by the majority of the arbitration board, which decided that the company had just cause for discharge, since it was trying to maintain a certain 'respectable moral standard' among its female workforce.[1] This case of the unmarried mother speaks to the way in which the dominant middle-class sexual prescriptions were normalized through workplace discipline, just as they were in the criminal-justice and welfare systems. Yet the arbitration also points to women's new means of resisting employer discipline. Had this dismissal happened in the 1930s, it was unlikely the woman would have had any legal means of redress. Now, a codified grievance system gave her the opportunity to object to her employer's moralistic retribution, and also the right to demand that her union defend her.

Grievance arbitration was one of the three pillars of the post-war Fordist accord. Unions secured collective-bargaining rights and state-sponsored tribunals to help settle disputes within the terms of a contract; in return, they gave up the right to strike or walk out during the contract's term. Even employees without unions encountered comparable committees and tribunals in their workplaces, as management

imitated grievance systems in efforts to stave off unions and to benefit
from the discipline that such codified rules provided. Indeed, grievance
systems were not the creation of unions alone; historically, they had been
an integral part of companies' efforts to create employee associations
in the place of unions.[2] Grievances thus provide an interesting window
into women's workplace lives in this period, particularly the tensions,
disputes, discipline, minor rebellions, and resistance that characterized
women's daily wage labour. By looking at both discipline and grievances
filed, we can ask a number of questions: What were the tensions and
pressure points for women at work, and did these differ from men's?
What did employers discipline women for, and were there similarities in
women's experiences across blue- and white-collar jobs? Were women
able to use the grievance system to challenge unfair discipline and to
secure better conditions, wages, benefits, or dignity on the job? And does
gendering the Fordist accord provide us with a fundamentally different
view of labour, capital, and the state in the post-war years?

Discipline and grievances were intricately entangled in workplace
relations: many grievances were objections to employer discipline, yet
some scholars have suggested that grievance systems merely reconstituted employers' disciplinary tactics. Modern work discipline, in some
senses the essence of capitalist work relations,[3] has been the subject of
countless studies, from industrial-relations experts searching for the
most efficacious means to maintain workplace rules to Marxists critical
of the role of discipline in strengthening capitalist control over the
workplace.[4] Grievances, associated primarily with post–Second World
War industrial legality, have been usefully examined through case studies of particular unions or locals, analyses of the evolution of legal precedents over time, and examinations of broader theoretical debates
concerning labour–capital relations, though few studies have explored
gender, women, and grievances.[5]

Following a brief discussion of grievances and the Fordist accord, I
turn to women and men in unionized meat-packing plants across
Canada, examining women's shop-floor gripes and grievances that, by in
large, never made it to formal arbitration. The discipline and grievance
files for white-collar women telephone operators, designated 'the voice
with the smile' by their employer Bell Telephone, provide a point of
comparison and contrast to women slicing bacon. Finally, I explore
grievance arbitrations contesting women's dismissals in order to ask if,
and how, unions challenged discharges that women perceived to be unfair and discriminatory.

Grievances and the Fordist Accord

First articulated during the Second World War through PC 1003 – the federal order-in-council endorsing workers' right to organize and bargain collectively – the rights/responsibilities principle of grievance arbitration was later integrated into provincial statutes regulating labour relations. In industrialized Ontario, where the most arbitrations took place, unions and management opted for either one arbitrator or a tripartite board, which often divided predictably between the union and management appointees, with the government-appointed chair casting the deciding vote.[6] Legal regimes did vary by province, with some incorporating more ministerial discretion (British Columbia), some opting for fewer restrictions on unions (CCF Saskatchewan), and Quebec integrating some 'continental' (French) precepts into its state machinery.[7] The relationship between grievance arbitration and Labour Relations Boards differed federally, and across the provinces, and this also changed over time. Over the course of twenty years, critical issues, including compensation to injured parties, the 'reserve rights' of management, and whether the courts could second-guess tribunals, were the stuff of ongoing arbitral decisions, debates, and court challenges across the country.

The key point, however, is that a new labour regime was emerging, though primarily for unionized workers. Scholars generally agree that in the Fordist bargain, workers surrendered spontaneous forms of protest in return for mandated arbitration of their grievances by 'neutral' labour tribunals legislated into being by the federal and provincial governments. New 'recognition of [unions'] legal status' engendered new 'responsibilities' to embrace mandatory dispute resolution so that production would not be disrupted by work stoppages. Legislated rights arbitration (over the nature of the contract once signed) was a particularly Canadian dimension to the Fordist accord: situated in between 'formal and informal law, the state and civil society,' arbitrators became akin to 'local law makers in a particular trade or industry.'[8] Scholarly disagreement emerges, however, over whether, or to what degree, grievance systems enhanced workers' ability to transform the labour–capital relation by tempering unfair discipline and creating more humane workplaces.

Many women in white-collar, public-sector, and especially more marginalized service jobs did not benefit from legal grievance arbitration until they unionized in greater numbers after the 1970s,[9] though they were not unaffected by the overall trends in labour–capital relations.

Even unionized women and men found formal grievance systems were a mixed blessing. Complex grievance systems led to larger union bureaucracies and also the legalization, and eventually judicialization, of workplace conflicts, a process early on recognized by one trade-union leader as an emerging 'picnic for lawyers.'[10] Moreover, underlying the very real gains of collective bargaining, secured with immense working-class struggle, lay an inescapable relationship: capital did not look at labour as a partner, but rather as a commodity. The new industrial legality, or 'industrial pluralism,' argue Judy Fudge and Eric Tucker, masked the underlying persistence of industrial 'voluntarism' – that is, with employer control ascendant – as capital ultimately made the 'most important decisions about employment and industrial policy.'[11] No matter how strong a few unions became, they did not wield the same power as capital, and if labour wanted to secure its new place at the bargaining table as a 'junior partner,' it knew it had to behave responsibly.[12]

The new industrial legality – also dubbed 'worker contractualism'[13] – and grievance systems that were a part of it were also created with mass industrial unions in mind. The latter were largely male-dominated. So too were formal grievance arbitrations, as few women ever took part in hearings, save occasionally as the aggrieved worker.[14] While 'left' critics have developed incisive analyses of the shortcomings of liberal pluralist faith in grievance arbitration, with the exception of Judy Fudge, they have seldom made gender central to their critiques.[15] These critics are certainly not 'impossibilists' denying any use for arbitration, but rather self-named 'realists' offering critical theoretical overviews of the system.[16] In the 1980s, for example, Katherine Stone suggested that grievance arbitration had legitimized a liberal ideology that encouraged workers to give their consent to industrial pluralism, 'contributing to the illusion that there is no class conflict in the U.S.'[17] Canadians have been no less critical. Labour lawyer John Stanton used statistics to show that workers lost as many cases as they won and faced an uphill battle with arbitrators who lived in the same 'mental world' as employers.[18] Using a comparative analysis of national grievance systems, Larry Haiven offers an incisive litany of problems with Canadian arbitration: it obscures the workplace as an arena of coercion, individualizes worker complaints, offers distracting 'busywork' over minor legal issues, gets lost in questions of procedural fairness, and delivers a mere fraction of economic improvement to workers.[19] Critics have certainly recognized that grievances have contradictory outcomes, perhaps piquing worker dissatisfaction with the limits of industrial legality, but the primary raison d'être of grievance arbitration is nonetheless to find 'an entente between the [two] parties,' never to question the nature of workplace discipline at its core.[20]

Daniel Drache and Harry Glasbeek put the dilemma succinctly: grievance arbitration was a 'paradox' that offered both 'empowerment but also disempowerment.' The initial hope for empowerment 'grew organically' out of workers' efforts to challenge the power and arbitrariness of management control – unfair transfers, dismissals, denial of seniority, and safety issues. From its inception, liberal legal experts equated grievance arbitration with the possibility of improved conditions, dignity, and decision making for workers.'[21] Unencumbered by common law and the courts, they also hoped to work out practical solutions that were more 'sensitive' to the industrial and social context of the workplace.[22] Bora Laskin, undoubtedly the most influential legal advocate and architect of the new system, saw arbitration as a crucial antidote to industrial strife; while he believed in 'balancing the interests of the parties,' he also saw grievance arbitration as a path to enhanced worker dignity in the workplace.[23] Subsequent liberal pluralist writing, building on this foundation, has defended the system with rationales ranging from its role as 'an outlet for festering discontent' to its use as 'an instrument of employment justice.'[24] Some have even advocated its enhancement.[25] Those immersed in the system understandably press home its usefulness and flexibility, and the range of negotiating possibilities still available in decisions.[26]

Any romantic notion of the unqualified benefits of liberal pluralism, critical legal scholars nonetheless contend, must recognize the reality that it operates within a system in which property rights are sacrosanct, workers' interests are more difficult to defend, and absolute victories difficult to secure. Statistical studies seem to bear out their scepticism.[27] This debate, however, is focused primarily on the contemporary period. Did workers initially reap more benefit from the system in what Harry Arthurs dubs the 'golden age' of grievance arbitration, before the meaner and leaner 'New Legality' led to a denigration of both collective bargaining and state intervention? Or was legal redress always 'more promise than reality'?[28] And does gender matter in this equation?

Grievance arbitration may have developed into a confining 'web of legalism,' reinventing workplace discipline, but grievance files from meat-packing plants in the 1950s and 1960s attest to another layer of the story. Workers initially experimented with the grievance system quite enthusiastically, asserting their customary rights and challenging discipline, working conditions, and rules perceived to be unfair or intolerable. By examining the range and rationale of women's grievances, we can see how women used the system to try to make their lives just a little better, as well as the encouragement and roadblocks they encountered from their union, and the limitations that characterized this pillar of industrial legality.

Women Meatpackers, Grievances, and the UPWA[29]

Since the time of Upton Sinclair's *The Jungle*, meat-packing plants have been equated with inhuman conditions, particularly on the killing floor, where men did heavy, smelly, and exhausting work. A sexual division of labour emerged by the First World War that persisted for decades, interrupted briefly during the Second World War by women's temporary presence on the killing floor in some plants. Men, some the 'butcher aristocrats'[30] of the industry, predominated in the killing, dismembering, skinning, and cutting processes; wielding and sharpening knives were designated masculine skills. Women's jobs were spatially segregated from men's work, closer to the finished product: they worked in processed meats, canning, sausage making, packaging, and especially bacon production. Rarely were women introduced into 'men's' jobs unless there was a technological conversion from skilled to unskilled tasks taking place.[31] The gendered division of labour meant that women were a minority of the workforce, constituting about 19 per cent in the post–Second World War years, until technological changes after the mid-1960s reduced that to about 16 per cent nationally, or as low as 11 per cent in Alberta.[32]

While the sexual division of labour was similar in US and Canadian plants, the presence of African American workers in US meat packing created different racial tensions and union battles, including a growing commitment to civil rights by the United Packing House Workers of America (UPWA). Meat-packing plants have also been historically associated with eastern and southern European immigrant labour, though 'new' European workers were not in the majority in all Canadian plants in these years, as the ethnic composition of the workforce differed by region and province. In New Brunswick, for instance, Canadian-born French and British identified workers predominated, while in Alberta, European immigrants were more visible. Labour-force statistics suggest that the majority of meat-packing workers across the country in the immediate post-war period were Canadian-born, with slighter lower levels of female compared to male immigrants. By 1971, however, there were clearly increased numbers of immigrant workers, with eastern and southern European workers closely following the British and French in numbers.[33]

Unionization of mass-production meat packing was given a boost in 1937 with the establishment of a vigorous new Congress of Industrial Organization (CIO) union, eventually named the UPWA. It soon garnered a reputation for militancy, consistently charting a course as a 'centre left,' social-democratic union, guided in Canada by Co-operative Commonwealth Federation (CCF) activists.[34] The UPWA had to first eliminate its union competition in Canada's directly chartered Trades and Labour Congress (TLC) unions,[35] and it existed in tandem with the established and more conservative American Federation of Labour (AFL) union, the Amalgamated Meat Cutters and Butcher Workmen. The UPWA's power was consolidated during the Second World War, when the need for meat, low unemployment, and government intervention in labour matters all aided the fledgling union in securing collective-bargaining rights and better working conditions. By 1947, after a militant national strike, pattern bargaining was also secured, a practice that arguably aided both the union and employers in a field dominated by the Big Three: Burns, Swift, and Canada Packers. Dominated by social democrats, without a strong communist opposition, the Canadian UPWA also managed to escape some of the more vicious and debilitating purges of the Cold War.[36] Its troubles came later. After the industry began a downward spiral in the 1960s, it merged with the Amalgamated Meat Cutters in 1968, later becoming the United Food and Commercial Workers.

The larger and more racially diverse American UPWA developed a core of working-class feminists who eventually mounted inter-union and legal challenges to the discriminatory sexual division of labour and seniority provisions in meat packing.[37] Women in the Canadian union did not mobilize on the same scale, even though they recognized the need for equal pay,[38] an issue the union was especially concerned with when it feared female substitution might put downward pressure on male breadwinner wages.[39] Indeed, international conventions repeatedly proclaimed the need for equal pay, but conceded the lack of progress on the issue.[40] The sexual division of labour and investment in the male-breadwinner ideology were also reflected in women's lower strike pay, even for those breadwinners 'supporting families,' and in the scarcity of women in union staff or leadership positions.[41] According to activist May Fingler, a few 'free thinkers,' such as western organizer Adam Borsk, urged women to become involved in the union,[42] and some women found their political feet as shop stewards and in local executives. Yet there is ample evidence that women were not always welcome in union halls. Dissension about the right of married women to

Figure 10   'A woman employee in an Alberta packing plant uses a ribbon brand to stamp 'Canada' on hog sides.' (LAC, NFB, Still photography division, 1943, PA108157)

even hold jobs was vigorously voiced by one Calgary local,[43] while men in Medicine Hat adamantly rejected the notion that women's issues needed attention: this executive wanted reference to the women's and civil-rights committees removed from the constitution because these politics were 'irrelevant to their union.'[44]

In addition to being characterized by separate jobs, seniority lists, and differential wages, meat packing maintained a discourse of masculinity stressing physicality, toughness, bravado, and sometimes roughness and violence.[45] As Steven Meyer argues for auto plants, the 'rough' masculinity of male workers emerged in response to the degradations of work and a mass-production, Taylorist assembly line, though men might also articulate a 'respectable' masculinity that was more protective towards women.[46] Women meat packers had to negotiate this public image of a tough workplace and confront working conditions that affected their physical and mental well-being. Knowing what was involved, few longed to be on the killing floor; as one woman reasoned, 'I didn't want to work like a man [on the killing floor], therefore I would not get his wages.'[47]

A Winnipeg woman who became a shop steward remembered being surprised that women were not the 'rough and tough' bunch she expected when she started in a meat-packing plant during the war: 'Whether you worked there ... depended on how desperate' you were. She quickly discovered that, despite women's cleaner jobs away from the killing floor, they too faced physical stress and risks: women lost 'fingers in wiener machines' and many were worn down by the cold and damp, developing chronic knee and back problems from standing on cold, wet floors for ten gruelling hours a day. May Finkler started in a Winnipeg plant because the pay was far better than office work, but soon found that working with raw product left one 'chilled' to the bone.[48] Moreover, the seasonal nature of the work plagued wage earners who counted on their paychecks. 'It took me ten years,' remembered Winnipeger Vera Slobodian, 'until I was not laid off after the Christmas rush.'[49] Another woman who worked in baby food, canning, and skinning wieners, recalled that the majority of women's complaints were always 'made in the dressing room, not to the union,'[50] but some women saw the grievance system as a major benefit of unionization: before that, recalled May Finkler, 'you could complain to the foreman, but that [was] as far as it ever [went].'[51]

Many grievances in the UWPA's five-step procedure dealt with time, money, and conditions of work, the triad of issues that symbolized management's panoptic control over workers' lives on the shop floor – and off. No issue was too small for protest, and even when workers knowingly

transgressed the rules, or had a weak case, they might pursue a grievance. This was not mere frivolousness; rather, their own notions of justice and fairness, or sometimes outrage, animated them. As early as 1949,
the union was grumbling to the state about the confining trade-off they
had made between grievance rights and their inability to strike.[52] Nonetheless, worker contractualism still held out tantalizing hope for newly
organized women workers in mass-production industries. With considerable enthusiasm, and sometimes immensely stubborn determination,
they tried to use the grievance system to 'get their due' (and sometimes
more) in the workplace.

It should be no surprise that workers producing food engaged in
guerilla skirmishes with employers over the tasting or taking of food.
Grievance files suggest that workers had a sense of customary right (as
did brewery workers)[53] regarding the culinary product of their labour.
Taking a small bit of food at work was not really 'theft' but a tiny slice
of surplus value they could claw back on the job. When one man was
caught taking some corned beef, he reasoned that it was 'his dinner' as
he had been asked to work late; besides, this hardly amounted to a 'luxury' product, like nuts, that he *could* have stolen.[54] When a female member was fired for food pilfering, the local union rose to her defence as
they did with pilfering men. Mrs P. was caught with four wieners in her
pocket when leaving the factory, the police having been called in to
search her. The union suspected she had been unfairly scapegoated for
what was a widespread practice. Head office of the UPWA was inclined
to drop her grievance, since 'it was [usually] difficult to win' theft cases.
True, theft was treated harshly by arbitrators, even if what was pilfered
amounted to a mere 35 cents,[55] but it was possible to secure mercy, and
the local union was willing to go all the way to arbitration with Mrs P's
case. The company not only fired Mrs P., it rather vindictively charged
her in police court, where the accused won acquittal with the help of a
lawyer. In Mrs P.'s grievance, the union insisted that food sampling was
routine, with women often taking 'some wieners for lunch.' Mrs P. had
simply forgotten hers in her coat pocket. The union also claimed
that this European immigrant was the target of ethnic hostility by rival
'German girls' in her department, and certainly the victim of management intimidation, as her co-workers were strong-armed into signing
witness complaints about her. As in many cases, the local was more
adamant about the grievance than was the national office; it wanted to
hire the smart lawyer who had secured Mrs P.'s acquittal and fight to
the finish.[56]

Skirmishes over time – time off, how jobs were timed, time for dinner, the timing of illnesses – were also prevalent for both women and men. Since the time discipline of an assembly line was measured to the last second, time was inevitably contested, with women on closely supervised, subdivided jobs particularly vulnerable to the time police. When employees 'steal time, they steal money,'[57] declared one meat-packing firm emphatically when pursuing a culprit who had someone else punch in for him. Time mattered in terms of dignity as well: when management hid the time clock in one factory under a metal case, the workers threatened to walk out en masse unless this insult to their honesty was removed.[58] The timing of piecework jobs was an obvious source of grievances, but so too were other issues, including forced overtime. Perishable food production needed high-volume turnaround and was susceptible to rush jobs, seasonal work, and overtime, but workers' family lives were not taken into account when they were ordered back to the factory (or risk suspension) at the drop of a hat. Many contracts said overtime could only be refused with reasonable cause, resulting in grievances over what 'reasonable' actually meant. Overtime might be a problem for men because they were exhausted or had other plans or responsibilities, but forced overtime was a particular problem for married women, who carried a much heavier share of domestic labour and child care.

Taking unscheduled time off, for either hours or days, was one form of 'time rebellion' that women commonly participated in – then were disciplined for. Two women grieved when they were suspended for two days after they failed to appear for work on Boxing Day. Required to come up with 'reasonable' explanations in such cases, women often offered up complex or convoluted stories, not unlike pardon tales. One of these two women, however, pretty well admitted that her holiday travel schedule got in the way of work, though the other claimed she was 'ill' with a problem 'not to be talked about' (rather conveniently) and for which she admitted she did not have a doctor's certificate.[59] Women, especially those with families, also wanted to avoid night work and used grievances to move into, or protect, their daytime jobs. This often meant displacing more junior women, an indication of how the grievance system also individualized problems, pitting workers against one another.[60]

Sick time was also contested, since it depended on providing due notice to the company. In the same Moncton plant, two women (perhaps assuming that there was safety and solidarity in numbers) grieved after being punished for not appearing at work one day. Their stories were exactly the same: they had called in sick to the 'boiler room' as required, but no one answered. In response to the suspensions imposed, they produced doctors' certificates at the third step of the grievance procedure. The company doctor declared these to be 'phoney,' which infuriated the local union representative, who warned the national office when it became involved that the women were being targeted for 'past absenteeism,' which was highly unfair as they had yet to receive an official warning. The national office was dubious about winning this battle, accepting the interpretation offered by Tom Danes, the Canada Packers human-resources man responsible for grievances. Danes was adamant that there had been an engineer in the boiler room who could not be absent for more than five minutes. 'So who is going to be believed ... the engineer or the women?' asked (seemingly rhetorically) John Lenglet, the UPWA staffer dealing with grievances. While Lenglet believed the company's version, the local union kept pressing the women's case. Eventually, a compromise was reached.[61]

Since illness was one of the only contractual means of securing time off, women had to use this even when it seemed a cover for something else. When a woman in a Quebec plant was forbidden a leave of absence to get married, and subsequently fired, she declared herself sick, producing a prescription written by a doctor on 21 August and a marriage certificate dated the next day. She returned a week later wanting her job back and the union supported her belief that the dismissal was 'unfair,' as she had 'good reason' to ask for a leave.[62] Local unions sometimes knew their contractual case to be weak but pressed on nonetheless, articulating their own notion of fairness, and also believing in the 'thin edge of the wedge': 'If we fight these grievances, even if we have little chance of winning, it will give us a chance to make [more] arguments in the future,' argued one union representative.[63]

Women were also more likely to grieve over washroom relief time, which equated in their minds with issues of autonomy, dignity, even harassment. Washrooms were a welcome space to escape time discipline and surveillance, and find a little human contact.[64] Two men sitting in Toronto head offices able to go to the washroom when they wanted – union staffer John Lenglet and Canada Packers manager Tom Danes – exchanged letters about the grievance of Ruby, who was suspended for three days for protesting relief time in her unit. Management had put an extra woman in the Moncton bacon room as a 'relief' person, on the condition that no woman could use the washroom unless the new worker was able to step into the line. A rebellious Ruby announced that she 'had to have personal relief and if the relief woman was busy, she was going anyway.' When the foreman suspended her and demanded she promise better behaviour in the future, Ruby refused, only to face a longer suspension for her insubordination. Tussles over washroom time were very much about who had the 'upper hand' of disciplinary shop-floor control, and management seemed especially perturbed in this plant that the 'girls were making a fool' of them by escaping to the washroom. The manager even warned the union that every second counted if the company's financial woes were to solved, implying jobs were about to be lost – with less women's washroom time presumably the answer to keeping the company afloat. National-office union staffer Sam Hughes recommended that Ruby's case be dropped, though he at least understood what was at stake in this capitulation: 'It boils down to who is going to tell who what to do, and when.'[65]

Management's disciplinary power was exactly what the grievance process was intended to temper, protecting workers against arbitrary and excessive punishments. Individual women did win their grievances outright in a few discipline cases, but more often a compromise or 'lesser sentence' resulted. In the process, discipline became better defined, advertised, and thus internalized by workers themselves. Instead of being automatically suspended for a transgression, for instance, women came to demand the right to a warning first. Countless tribunals puzzled over whether discipline was reasonable, but management's prerogative to punish was never fundamentally questioned; instead, it was given more precision. An unchanging theme in all the grievances files over this twenty-year period was the imposition of rules that replicated (or were worse than) those of elementary school. Women had to get the plant nurse's approval to go home sick; they needed to ask to use the bathroom; they needed permission to leave early or take time off for family emergencies; and they could not be 'saucy' to their superiors. Less often, but no less degradingly, men too were portrayed as 'naughty, disgruntled schoolboys' (even by their own unions) needing paternal forgiveness if they were rash in their actions.[66]

Men and women alike were punished for insubordination, especially refusing orders, talking back, or leaving without permission, but women's shop-floor misbehaviour was more indirect, quieter, and far less physical and profane than men's. It was also easier for some men, with more physical mobility in the plant, to escape disciplinary detection. Moreover, women were expected to be more polite, so that their small rebellions were less likely to be countenanced. Most serious were women's insubordinations on the line that threatened the pace of production.

One woman tried to fight a long grievance with the aid of her local after she was sent home simply for turning her back on her foreman when she was chastised for her slow production. Usually a wiener packer, she was temporarily put on a wiener-skinning machine and was told to speed up, keeping 'two skinning heads not one going.' In response, she turned her back on the foreman and was promptly sent home, losing four-and-a-half hours. Again imitating elementary school protocols, she was called back to personnel to assess her level of penitence. Far from contrite, she insisted vehemently that the machine made her back sore, so she was sent home again, for a longer twelve hours, and ordered to 'get a doctor's certificate.' Management's claim, relayed through UPWA's Lenglet, was that she was purposely slowing down since she did not want to be on this job. 'You are not going to get volume from me' the company claimed she said to co-workers, who management often tried to enlist as informers. The local continued to fight to get eight hours pay back, saying discipline had been too 'punitive,' while the head office shrugged this off as a losing battle.[67]

Both men and women complained about foremen who were abusive when meting out discipline. One Winnipeg UPWA local launched a group protest over the behaviour of a foreman who was 'unbecoming to his position, creating chaos, with no respect for human dignity, making sarcastic remarks, unwarranted speed up, preventing relief time, violating the contract, criticizing before he knows the job, intimidating workers.'[68] Four years earlier in 1958, a similar UPWA case went to arbitration, and Bora Laskin's judgment revealed the promise, but also the limitations, of grievances as a pathway to enhanced workplace dignity. A group of workers claimed a sub-foreman was abusive, subjecting them to profanity and 'belligerently' criticizing them for unwarranted reasons. They wanted him removed or demoted, decisions the company guarded fiercely as management rights. The union case was built, in part, on the claim that the contract preamble, calling for 'cooperation, good will and respect,' was legally binding. Laskin disagreed: the preamble might be a guide to interpretation, but it did not lay out workers' rights. The 'silence of the agreement,' and the limitations of narrow legal contractualism mitigated against the labour board's intervention, even though Laskin was clearly very critical of the foreman's 'ill advised and provocative' actions.[69] One of Laskin's parting comments in this arbitration also revealed how gendered cultural assumptions crept into arbitral judgments. 'A meatpacking plant is not a formal drawing room,' he wrote, but there should be mutual respect '*even* in a meatpacking plant,' with some 'elasticity' and allowance for 'exuberant language'[70] (one assumes a euphemism for swearing). The image of blue-collar work as inherently masculine and 'rough around the edges' was apparent in other grievances too.

Men's and women's transgressions, and the resulting discipline, did differ, in part due to their position within the work process. Male workers were more likely to stop work on the line to protest conditions such as intense heat and cold, or the unfair distribution of work, precisely because they had cornered the skills that gave them more power on the shop floor. Deeply ingrained cultural assumptions and behaviours also shaped these gender differences. Only men were disciplined for alcohol-related offences in these files, and they were invariably the focus of discipline for verbal and physical assaults, with attacks on foremen always seen as more serious. Men might lose their cool over a mere insult to their name: when a foreman continually and publicly reminded a male worker about a previous criminal charge, a shouting match of obscenities erupted, and disciplinary procedures followed. Violent fights between male workers also became the subject of discipline and grievances, with men sometimes extending their workplace fistfights into wedding parties, houses, and other non-workplace social spaces. Since meatpacking men worked with knives, these physical altercations could be dangerous. During a minor disagreement over clean-up, one man grabbed a co-worker around the neck from behind, and the person assaulted fought back by stabbing him. Only the second man was fired, and the arbitrators' report was suspiciously ethnocentric, referring to both men with European names as very 'temperamental.'[71] In other cases, however, fighting was seen as just inherently masculine.

Women were unlikely to be violent, although one grievance does suggest that they too might lose their cool under stressful work conditions and turn on each other. These battles then became the vector for other smoldering tensions. Margaret, warned by her supervisor not to leave her place on the production line, did so anyway, incurring the wrath of a fellow worker, Lea, who sprayed her with hot water. Margaret threw her knife either on the floor or at her adversary, depending on the witness interrogated. She was promptly fired. The union did protest her discharge, losing the case but securing some severance pay. It was clear that management wanted to get rid of Margaret, as she 'was short tempered and had problems with her supervisor,' and they pressured other workers to give the statements they needed to fire her. No wonder other women were reluctant to file grievances: they feared intimidation, interference, or retaliation from supervisors or fellow workers.[72]

Grievances that were the outcome of worker-worker conflicts placed shop stewards in unenviable situations; as one remembered, a good part of her job was listening and trying to be 'fair' in her understanding of these conflicts.[73] Personality clashes might be involved, but reading between the lines in some cases, one also suspects ethnic tensions. In one Quebec plant, the union representative said workers were ready to 'walk out' if a woman working in the canteen was not dismissed for 'unsanitary, unhealthy' practices. Workers claimed that she had used a dishcloth as a sanitary pad, then when she secured a real one from the nurse's station, washed the dishcloth out and used it again in the kitchen. The company claimed it had contrary evidence. One wonders if these rumours – and they were that – spread about 'Mrs Fagin' could really be true.[74]

However, a worker's unpopularity could be turned to advantage in grievances if the union argued that the disciplined worker was the target of either management or worker discrimination, or the collusion of both. Jean, a woman meat packer who refused to do overtime and walked out before her overtime shift was done, lost her discharge grievance in an Ontario hearing, with the union appointee dissenting. The narrow legal issue at hand was whether the company could take into account Jean's 'longer record' of causing disharmony in the workplace, or if it had to focus on simply the one instance in question. Testimony revealed how nasty worker-worker conflict could become, with some workers claiming they would 'quit' if Jean came back. In concert, the company charged that the disciplined worker was overbearingly 'bossy,' thinking she could run the plant and causing continual commotion and friction on the shop floor. Jean had also been shop steward and was adamant about her right to refuse overtime.[75] It is possible Jean was unpleasant and uncooperative to work with, but it is also just as possible she was too 'assertive' for a woman, and a union thorn in the company's side.

The willingness of other workers to support the company's case against Jean illustrates how chameleon-like the grievance system was, offering workers a possible second chance, but also buttressing employers' more powerful monopoly, not just over discipline but, crucially, over its *discursive definition* as well. Workers might well come to 'see' their interests as one and the same with the company's ideological and economic imperative for quick and smooth production, especially since a bedrock of worker contractualism was management's right to make production efficient. This mitigated against collective, solidaristic behaviour among workers. The evolving grievance system also dictated that what was considered 'fair' treatment was judged only within the narrow realm of contract language: other alternative customary understandings of justice might be dangerously forgotten or marginalized in the process. The one bright light in Jean's case was the union's determination to defend her to the bitter legal end, which suggests that its commitment to the shop-floor grievances of women members was strong – as long as the principle did not upset the gender contract in the workplace.

Not surprisingly, grievances over money – piece rates, vacation pay, transfers to different jobs, and seniority in order to keep a certain job – were common, and if monetary issues were precisely described in the contract, women had a slightly better chance of success. Even if the amount was small, women did not want well-heeled corporations to get the better of them monetarily. In one case, a local union got very angry with head office for not supporting a woman's grievance when she was denied thirty-six hours' vacation pay.[76] Grieving over job rates was also common. Many locals were keen to launch a grievance if women were put on men's jobs but not paid at the same rate. When two women in a Calgary plant were sawing off protruding ham bones and being paid at bracket 2, the grievance insisted that the women be raised to bracket 5 (the pay level enjoyed by the men who usually performed this work). They were disappointed to discover that the contract fine print offered the employer an escape clause if the job was changed to approximate other women's jobs. A Maritime local was more successful in securing the male machine-tending rate for two women assigned to the new Frank-o-matic machine, introduced in the sixties to streamline production (and which ultimately cut out women's jobs). The victory was short-lived, since the company promptly gave notice that it was not going to make the same 'mistake' and place women on this job again. Protesting the hiring of women only as part-timers was also a grievance priority; local unions clearly worried that the plant would increasingly hire both men and women part-time, at considerable savings to the wage bill.[77]

These last grievances point to the essence of male–female relations within the union: when women fought to improve working conditions surrounding their own female-typed jobs, or for a general union principle, the union was supportive. Shop stewards were almost always sympathetic when laid-off women with seniority wanted to bump into other female-typed positions. Due to bureaucratic red tape, one such arbitration took a year to decide if a group of women could learn new jobs in a 'reasonable' amount of time. Did wrapping meat resemble wrapping soap? The company claimed only it knew; the judge wanted to hear from the women.[78] The delay indicates how cumbersome, even useless, grievances were for workers who needed paychecks in the here-and-now. The principle of 'obey now, grieve later'[79] was particularly difficult for unskilled workers and those facing seasonal layoffs (not to mention those who did not speak English well); this may be another reason why women were reluctant to use the formal grievance process.

If a grievance threatened the status-quo sexual division of labour, the union was more likely to be ambivalent. When the union saw women substituting for men, engendering a fear of male displacement, it was opposed. However, when men took over women's jobs, the UPWA threw up its hands and said nothing could be done.[80] Women meat packers had good reason to be sceptical about the union in this regard: when automation led to female jobs disproportionately disappearing in the 1960s, a grievance system was of little help.[81] The UPWA made some attempt to raise women's job losses as a political issue: 'Is this the kind of automation we want?' a UPWA pamphlet asked, showing a man doing bacon slice work, and women workers with six arms, designated management's 'ideal' worker. 'Where are the women who used to do this work? What benefits are they getting from automation?' queried the pamphlet.[82] Taking steps to protect women's jobs, however, was not a top priority, and the sanctity of The Contract proved a stumbling block. In letter after letter about grievances, union officials agreed that, contractually, Canada Packers could 'put men on women's jobs, as long as the man's rate was paid.' Another strategy used by employers to replace women was to alter the job very slightly so that it included an aspect of heavy lifting – then the job went to a man.[83] In the formal arbitration system, argue legal scholars, grievance tribunals generally did not interfere with employers' right to 'set qualifications' for a job or assess workers' 'ability to do the job.'[84] These management rights, it should be emphasized, had gendered consequences, allowing employers to maintain or alter the established sexual division of labour as they saw fit.

In US packing houses, women faced the same devastating situation; however, American UPWA women organized politically against job loss, using Title VII to challenge both the state and their own union.[85] A similar campaign did not emerge in Canada. When two Calgary women tried to grieve a man taking over a women's job, arguing that separate seniority lists existed, the local was warned by head office not to even bother with the separate seniority argument. Head office further warned that even if female wage rates were brought up to men's, the company would just fire women – as it had in United States – and hire men, since the latter were 'easier to move around' the plant.[86] The union did propose a contract amendment to one company that would have protected a percentage of women's jobs, but the company refused and the union let the matter drop.

Not all male union activists were quite so sanguine about women's job losses. Just as they were willing to fight for women's rights within the bounds of a sexually segregated workplace, they were willing to concede their female co-workers had a right to a job. When the superintendent in one Maritime plant wanted to give a woman's job to a man who had been ill and needed an 'easier' position, the union intervened in defence of the woman affected, though once again, the voice of doom – the national office – prophesied defeat, declaring 'in arbitration we would be murdered.'[87] Tension erupted in another Maritime plant between an assistant and chief shop steward over the same issue, with the latter asserting that women's job loss should be stopped 'before our female seniority list drops any further.' He opposed a lower-level steward, easily 'taken in' by an intimidating foreman, who was pressing for union acquiescence to the displacement of women. The foreman posed a seemingly rhetorical question to the steward: 'After all, did he not believe it was better to have a girl on the street unemployed than a man?' The chief steward disagreed.[88]

The local-national dynamic in many of these files illustrates vividly how, by the late 1960s, women and men alike were facing the growing legalization and bureaucratization of the grievance process, which separated workers, with their stubborn determination to use the system to the fullest, from leaders cognizant of cost, time, and what could be pragmatically won. What appeared fair or even a customary right to workers might simply involve a losing battle for those at head office, well aware of the narrow legal parameters of the grievance process. Idealist militancy could only be dampened by this pragmatism. Correspondence between some UPWA paid staff and Canada Packers' Danes sometimes seemed like two old boys settling the fights of children beneath them. Their back and forth conversations turned into informal bargaining sessions as they tried to work out grievances to avoid costly arbitrations. UPWA staffers even came to identify with Danes. He [Danes] has 'headaches' with a plant shutdown in Toronto right now, Sam Hughes wrote to a Maritime local in the midst of a grievance, so don't expect him to have time to deal with your problems.[89] 'Mr Danes is in no mood to make any concessions,' another letter warned a local grieving a woman's unfair payment rate.[90] True to the Fordist 'accord,' a certain common interest was being articulated at the top, to the detriment of women at the very bottom of the industrial hierarchy.

At times, this old-boy mentality pervaded the local union. A grievance file in the UPWA collection illustrates this well.[91] Women working at a large cleaners in the 1950s collectively launched a grievance about terrible working conditions, including 'dirty, stinky, unbearable' toilets, broken windows, and violations of both the check-off and their reporting allowance (when they did not get a full three hours of work). When they set up a meeting at the local union hall, the local's business agent, Jack Brierly, did not show up. They protested to the union, asking for a 'different organizer as they feel he is much too friendly to the company and spends too much time alone in the office without the grievance committee.'[92] Six months later, with grievances still unsolved, Jack shrugged off their importance by suggesting a local plant committee work 'cooperatively' with the company to solve them. He even agreed to have lunch with the employer alone to chew over the grievance of a woman who was fired for absenteeism and illness, and there was little indication he was going to fight for her job while he ate his sandwich. Is it any wonder that the 'girls' working at the company complained? Their payoff from the Fordist accord and a grievance system was meagre indeed, not only because of the structural limitations of the grievance system, but because it was administered in this case within a masculinist and bureaucratic mindset that did not see fighting for women at the bottom of the accord as a priority.

Calling Home: Disciplining White-Collar Women

White-collar work was often presented as a social step up from physical and 'tough' conditions such as those in meat-packing plants. For men and women alike, white-collar work retained a 'patina' of middle-class respectability that workers themselves might embrace as an appealing identity.[93] As Gillian Creese's study of one British Columbia union emphasizes, office hierarchies were not only predictably gendered, but also racialized, as white-collar work was literally the preserve of whites until the 1970s. Moreover, beneath the superficial image of a more pleasant work culture lay pressures on female workers to perform in appropriately deferential and feminine ways. In a fairly rare grievance arbitration for a discharged female stenographer, Miss Allen, the majority report made no bones about the fact her discharge should be judged differently from that of a blue-collar worker who 'works at his machine ... and whose co-operation with fellow employees and whose personality have very little bearing on his ability to perform his job.' The female office worker, in contrast, had to prove her 'general course of conduct and acceptability' to her supervisor, and she had to pitch in, as any good family member would, 'filling in for others' when needed.

Miss Allen's supervisor claimed that she did not 'fit in with the rest of the staff,' was too often absent in the washroom, and did not carry her full load. Such accusations, she responded, indicated that he 'picked on her' needlessly, and indeed, there was no written evidence that her work was unsatisfactory. The Chair and management appointee relied heavily on the supervisor's evidence, including hearsay complaints supposedly voiced about Miss Allen by fellow office workers. Here was a case in which the 'common mental world' of male supervisors and arbitrators appeared to coalesce. The United Steel Workers representative, Lynn Williams, dissented, pointing to the lack of objective proof of bad work, concluding that a 'clash of temperaments' had led to the supervisor's desire to remove Miss Allen. He went to the heart of the matter when he criticized the arbitration tribunal for sanctioning different standards for white-collar cases. 'Protection against discharge for such vague complaints as 'not fitting in' is one reason white-collar workers are organizing,' he claimed (rather too optimistically). Calls for 'teamwork' and 'cooperation' were just code words for maintaining old-fashioned authoritarian rule, and 'sometimes a way to 'ride' a particular employee.'[94] His interpretation did not mention gender, but this was nonetheless key to the hierarchical expectations in most offices.

By examining the discipline and grievance files of white-collar workers from Bell Telephone and from unionized public-sector workplaces, we can highlight some similarities and differences with mass-production work.[95] Since a 1943 ruling of the federal War Labour Board, Bell operators had been legally represented in collective bargaining by the Traffic Employees Association (TEA), distinctive for its entirely female membership and leadership.[96] The TEA remained independent from other unions, inside and outside the Bell, leading some critics to dismiss it as a 'company union.' This was not entirely without truth. During the 1950s and 1960s, the TEA was quite conciliatory with management, and it lacked a strong grievance system – indeed, operators sometimes complained that the TEA was not defending them adequately.

By having a conciliatory association in place to monitor workers' 'rights,' management could discipline with wider latitude; but perhaps even more insidious, the TEA sometimes became an unwitting collaborative partner in this disciplinary project by constantly reiterating Bell's priorities, rules, and punishments to its membership. This was illustrated well in one joint management-union discussion about discipline. Women, the meeting recorded, often ran to the TEA asking for 'redress,' with their 'one-sided, distorted' versions of the story. The TEA recognized management's 'sole right' to fire, but it requested notice of impending dismissals, not necessarily to protest but rather to *help discipline* the worker to avoid discharge: 'It has happened that after management made the decision to dismiss, the TEA has succeeded where they failed, ie impressing upon the employee that management does intend to fire them and the union will not give her any backing if she persists in her unsatisfactory performance.'[97] This conciliatory attitude was also symbolized by the TEA's moniker, 'We are the voice of the voice with a smile,' which mimicked Bell's advertisement of its service product, namely, feminine politeness. Significantly, however, the TEA letterhead changed its tune by the early 1970s, erasing any reference to polite smiles and substituting its claim to be an independent union.

However strict Bell's discipline was, women wanted to hang on to these jobs, which offered some security, benefits, the possibility of work after marriage, and average white-collar wages. Operating was, without a doubt, a thoroughly feminized occupation,[98] and the TEA's discipline files also indicate a high percentage of married women operators, many with service beyond five years. It is unlikely Bell could have imposed a marriage bar even if it wanted to, as it relied so heavily on a flexible, temporary female labour pool willing to do shift work. After the war, management even admitted it could barely 'fill jobs fast enough,' as earlier marriages, a low Depression birth rate, and a booming economy created a never-ending demand for white-collar workers.[99]

Operators, management never tired of saying, were perhaps the most 'essential' of all its workers, providing front-line service, 24/7, to the public. Yet female operators faced far more rigid disciplinary regimes than did male outside workers, whose autonomy and mobility allowed them to stay under the surveillance radar. In a company known for its 'close control' of all its female white-collar employees,[100] operators may have experienced the stiffest surveillance of all workers. Despite some company reforms in work organization in the mid 1960s to increase white-collar worker satisfaction, the operators remained subject to

Figure 11   'Telephone operator connecting a caller to a French operator,' 1963. (LAC, Malak Photographs Ltd., PA185898)

'paternalist and authoritarian' supervision, in part because of the very nature of the work process[101] and also because they were situated quite low in the workplace hierarchy. Most of the telephone operators in the TEA across Ontario and Quebec still worked a switchboard that they were tied to for their entire shift, doing repetitive, exacting work; yet they were also Bell's primary link to the public, and thus monitored for their delivery of service 'with a smile.' Operators had to interact with customers, for example, arranging long-distance calls or giving information while conforming to strict time limits, and they were monitored by supervisors listening in, undetected, at any time. Operators also worked with a system of computer 'tickets' that recorded the calls they arranged: these too could be traced, a form of time surveillance that was always hanging over their heads.

Bell's white-collar office personnel, suggests Joan Kuyek, were conditioned less with direct coercion than with calls for teamwork, incentives, invocations of paternalism, and one-on-one counselling about one's mistakes – all forms of corrective regulation no less intense than factory discipline. The same was true of operators. Workplace prohibitions, telephone etiquette, and performance targets were reiterated constantly, with the hope that these would translate into employee's self-governance – which in many cases they did. In a flash of militant anger, the TEA criticized Bell management for this heavy-handed surveillance during some technological changes in 1960. Explaining the 'low morale' of operators, the TEA described the constant pressure of higher loads always expected, and the way weaker women were callously 'weeded out with labels like 'not fitting in with the office average." We are 'guinea pigs to be experimented on,' they charged, treated 'like robots.'[102]

Bell's disciplinary procedures bore some similarity to those in mass production; workers were given escalating warnings or suspensions, which the worker might attempt to counter with her own defence. Disciplinary letters were copied to the TEA, which supposedly mediated with management on behalf of the worker, but it was likely Bell's need for employees rather than the TEA's militancy that saved some women from dismissal. Given management's tight control of the work process, what were women's transgressions, the resulting discipline, and women's responses?

Operators' rebellions were more individual and sporadic than collective, though women undoubtedly learned some tactics from each other. Stealing time, being absent, and failing to live up to required standards of speed, accuracy, and politeness were the most common disciplinary infractions, though the nature of disciplinary letters (which often included a litany of problems) makes it difficult to quantify and prioritize these.[103] One company study of dismissals listed work performance, attendance, and various forms of time theft and insubordination – in that order – as the main causes of this most extreme form of discipline.

Disciplinary letters were sent out for 'time crimes' ranging from women's unscheduled days off to slow downs on the switchboard. These letters also vividly illustrate women's difficulties coping with a double day, especially their worries about children while they were at work. Women were caught 'calling home' while at the switchboard and were punished, usually with a suspension of a few days, though repeated infractions could result in dismissal. Understandably, operators were checking up on children home alone, or minded by others. One woman was disciplined for listening in on a call from her sister's, where her son was staying, while another forty-four- year-old employee was caught 'red handed' by her supervisor in the act of calling home to talk to her daughter. 'I knew it was wrong,' she replied in her defence, but 'I just did not think about it.'[104] Admitting an error and being contrite was a good strategy if women wished to keep their jobs or reduce the suspension, yet it is instructive that women often offered straightforward excuses about their need to call home.

Home responsibilities were also blamed by Ma Bell for female absenteeism, which was treated with repeated lectures about women's 'lack of dependability.' Some offices also suspected duplicity, calling employers to see if they were really sick.[105] After six years of good service, a woman was still chastised for eleven absences in one year, even though she always provided reasons: 'she had problems at home, the flu, no babysitter, laryngitis,' and so on. If the woman had young children who were ill, she probably had trouble keeping herself well. A final warning of imminent dismissal came for another operator who called in an 'emergency' when she could not get a babysitter and her 'husband could not be late for work.' To management, this was no emergency at all. She had other infractions on her record, including 'misuse of sickness benefit' (which again could relate to child care), and she was perceived to be recalcitrant as she refused Bell's offer of 'medical aid.'[106] An interview with a doctor would probably not have altered the fact that her job was seen as secondary in the family and she carried the responsibility for child care, hardly an individual illness.

Like the meat-packing women, operators also performed minor rebellions against time discipline, not just on the job, but also to compensate for their lack of time off the job. When one woman, working in Overseas Traffic, tried to give away her weekend shift and could not, she simply left town Saturday night and did not report in. For this insubordination, she received a light one-day suspension.[107] Another woman, denied vacation time to drive to the United States, arranged a compromise of a long weekend, then simply added on her own two days of extra holiday by not returning. When these time renegades were disciplined with dismissal, their grievances were not always successful: one employee who refused to work New Year's Eve lost her battle for reinstatement, though there were other complicating factors tied up with this grievance.[108]

Stealing time on the company's time was particularly heinous. Cheating Bell of labour by falling asleep on the job 'will not be tolerated,' warned one disciplinary letter sternly, though the woman in question was not suspended.[109] Some women started at Bell as young as sixteen and seventeen, so it is little wonder that one new operator tried to avoid her punishment by explaining she had just 'been out late the night before.'[110] Just as production workers encountered elementary-school rules, these women faced a regulatory regime that cast them as children, needing excuses for angry parents. One griever complained about the irritation of Bell's 'juvenile' workplace bells, like those in schools, adding that her complaining had made her the 'bad egg' of the office, where she was already known for her mischievous habit of 'throwing pencils.'[111]

Most egregious in terms of time theft, however, was the use of Bell lines for personal calls that cost the company profit, no matter how little the amount. When a woman was discovered linking up friends in New York City and Jamaica, she received a serious warning; a second infraction led to her dismissal. The temptation to use Bell lines, which were there for the taking, must have been difficult to resist in some circumstances. Two very new, young workers, on loan from their home to another Bell office in Quebec, worked in tandem to arrange a joint long-distance call to chat with a roommate at home, claiming the ticket was an 'information' call. Discovered by a co-worker, they were given a second chance, as the company 'did not want to lose' these new workers.[112]

Hiding, falsifying, or tearing up a ticket surreptitiously was also seen as grounds for suspension or dismissal. In disciplinary letters, the company referred to these offences as 'fraud' in order to impress upon women the criminal nature of their wrongdoing. One woman could not avoid a suspension after she was 'ratted out' by a co-worker who taped together her discarded ticket from the garbage pail. The informant's dedication to protecting Bell's time and profit, at the expense of a co-worker's job, indicated that worker compliance was often far more firmly ingrained than rebellion. The ideological justification of rules and discipline was internalized by some workers not just as necessary, but as *desirable* for one and all.

The only infraction as unacceptable as stealing time was offending customers. Despite its monopoly, Bell prided itself on its service, and like the Dupuis Frères employees, operators' relationship with their customers was an essential part of their work process. Any infraction, from 'unplugging a customer' too soon to failing to provide proper information, was a potential disciplinary issue. Multiple offences led to a 'bad performance' designation, the most common term used in disciplinary and discharge letters. Bad performance took in many sins: a high error rate, not working fast enough, and especially being rude or sarcastic, or correcting customers. Responding with insubordination to supervisors correcting the offensive behaviour only compounded the bad-performance label.

In a job that demanded an unfailing good temper, even in the face of mistreatment, it is hardly surprising that some women suddenly came to a breaking point, then paid dearly with discipline. One woman who did not give a hotel guest the amount of tax for his call was not only reprimanded by her supervisor, but was also insulted by the customer; when the supervisor called the man to apologize, the operator listened in and was incensed when the customer was very pejorative about her. She tore off her headset and burst out sarcastically: 'The customer is always right.'[113] In fact, this was exactly the motto Bell wanted its operators to internalize. Talking back to a customer who was harassing her and demanding her employee number was the 'straw that broke the camels [sic] back' for one twenty-one-year veteran; her grievance form detailed not only this minor blow-up but also a long litany of unhappiness and complaints, undoubtedly bottled up for decades.[114] Certainly, customers were sometimes mistreated by operators. One operator was suspended for shouting to a customer with an accent: 'Speak English, speak Spanish, speak French, or something so I can understand you.' But operators were also worn down by demanding and complaining customers, who, as one politically aware employee put it in her exposé of life at the Bell, 'feel personally persecuted by the Company' but could only extract their vengeful satisfaction from lowly workers, leaving the management untouched.[115] Operators also learned how to enact small tactics of subtle revenge, such as refusing to release the line so the customer could make another call. Such acts, however, ran the risk of discipline if the woman was caught.

It was not simply relations with customers, but office demeanour as well that was judged fastidiously by Bell. Attitude, politeness, personality, and appearance could all be the subject of criticism and discipline. Telling 'crude jokes,' being 'loud,' and disrupting other operators' work was enough to earn one woman the disapprobation of her supervisor and dismissal.[116] Even one's physical appearance could be the stuff of critique. In one case, a woman's weight problems led to her suspension. The company claimed there were 'safety problems' because she could not use the stairs, but the explanatory letter contained many details of the woman's weight and body odour. As well, the letter claimed others refused to work with the woman, suggesting safety was not really the issue. If she did not accept medical and psychological help, she faced dismissal.[117]

Negative judgments of women's appearance and attitude, or the less-than-penitent responses of some women to discipline, were often coupled with psychological assumptions about a worker's particular 'personality problem.' Miss N. used to be a good employee, but now has a 'personality problem' wrote one supervisor, noting that because of a facial disfigurement, the woman 'has a problem with people looking at her face, but she should not carry this into her telephone work.' Another woman's 'I don't care' attitude was analysed as the byproduct of her 'bitterness' with her husband's demand that she give up a promotion to 'keep better hours' (and probably cook him dinner).[118] Perhaps one can sympathize with her unhappiness. Company-sponsored medical and/or psychological aid was often prescribed for these women, and some benefit files do suggest a high number of leaves for 'nervous conditions' and 'fatigue,' surely a direct product of the work process or women's double day.

Women's problems, however, were presented as individual deviations from the norm. Disciplinary letters repeatedly recommended that 'troubled' or 'problem' women be 'rehabilitated,' language that incorporated metaphors of medicine, care, and rejuvenation. Medical aid was presented as a paternalist benefit, part of the company's welfare plan. No doubt for some women it was. However, the provision of this expert aid did not remove you from the orbit of company surveillance – quite the contrary. Rehabilitation could become 'corrective discipline' by another name. The company doctor's job was to help you recover your ability to work, not necessarily to change the circumstances causing your problems. If you declined aid, as one 'poorly motivated' woman did, this only reinforced Bell's perception that you were an unsalvageable problem.[119]

The case of a married woman worker in small-town Ontario suggests the limitations of medical aid as 'rehabilitation.' Until her marriage, she was a 'good' worker; she subsequently became a 'problem' needing 'rehabilitation.' She saw the company doctor, who she reported was 'kind and thoughtful,' for he understood she had 'emotional and physical problems' emanating from the 'home environment.' He gave her a 'nerve tonic' and sleeping pills to calm her down. Reading between the lines, one suspects disharmony at home or, at worst, domestic violence. If so, sleeping pills would not have alleviated the problem. These attempts to press non-performing workers into the embrace of medical experts were not necessarily experienced as insidious efforts at control, but they were still strategies of correction, however kinder and rehabilitative in nature, and it would seem they were shaped by prevailing notions of female and male psychology.[120]

In another 'rehabilitation' case, a veteran of five years on the job, Miss A., was warned that her performance was 'deteriorating.' In response to a disciplinary letter she offered her own counter-narrative: 'She was fed up with the job, with herself, she can't get motivated, can't concentrate on the job, [is] depressed.' Management set up an appointment with a psychologist on her day off and was most unhappy when she cancelled it. Perhaps, given the direct link she saw between her job and depression, this was simply no way to spend a day off. Perhaps Miss A. did not need psychological 'rehabilitation' as much as she needed a new job. She might have also benefited from a shop steward to counsel her on what the employer could demand of her, and to grieve the disciplinary action taken against her.

TEA women did have a rudimentary grievance procedure that was improved on over time. Initially, the multi-step process started with informal mediation, proceeded to a company grievance committee, and ended with an appeal to the company president – hardly a neutral player. The TEA's incredibly weak contract was exposed in a 1970 grievance, and a particularly sad one, of a thirty-seven-year veteran in rural Ontario. A self-supporting worker, she had been a popular union representative, and when she was discharged just years short of her full pension, she was living on a mere $124 a month. Without a contract clause protecting workers against unfair discharge, her case was not even arbitrable. Arbitrator Earl Palmer wrote to the TEA apologetically, chagrined that he had no choice but to rule for the company. The union was incensed that this 'popular, aggressive, well informed' worker who only committed the 'cardinal sin of protecting the rights of others' was treated so shabbily by the authors of this 'devious discrimination.'[121]

This was new, fighting language for the TEA. Its original grievance handbook was more polite, asking representatives to ponder if grievances were *really* grievances or if they were simply women's 'grouches.' The long list of dos and don'ts advised TEA reps to try to mediate, decline weak cases, recognize the other person's point of view, avoid empty threats of arbitration, and 'not simply go along with a grievance but find a just solution.'[122] The conciliatory tone was conditioned not by the nature of white-collar work, but by the union's overall emphasis on conciliation. Yet grieve women did, and increasingly so. Precisely because the TEA looked 'beyond the contract' and defined grievances very liberally as 'anything that relates to a member's job that irritates her,' women used grievances to vocalize their desire for dignity and respect, citing issues that were not even covered in their contract. Some grievances articulated women's unhappiness that Ma Bell was far from a caring, maternal employer, especially when women faced family crises. One incensed woman wanted to grieve her bad treatment by a supervisor who initially harangued her when she left to rush her son with pneumonia to a clinic and then the hospital. An apology and reassurance this would never happen in the office again was all she really wanted.[123] Group grievances about intolerable working conditions were not uncommon; women from a northern Ontario office were outraged that their office, not cleaned in years, was so 'filthy' that they came home looking like 'coal miners.'[124] A long, repellant list of the types of bugs, bites, and dirt in the office, even spiders on the switchboard, made their point forcefully.

As in meat packing, grievances also focused on time, especially holiday and shift schedules, seniority/promotions, and money, though the latter was more likely to involve issues such as women's right to pay for familial funeral leave. The high number of grievances over non-TEA people doing TEA unit work was significant; operators got tired of management telling them they were irreplaceable, then substituting other workers at the switchboard. Perhaps most interesting were the changes in grievances that evolved between the 1950s and the early 1970s. The TEA toughened up as it learned the hard way that Bell's paternalist claims were just that. After the 1970 non-arbitrable grievance, TEA president Mary Lennox announced that the contract had to be strengthened. The TEA was also under pressure, as the other Bell white-collar workers (in the CTEA) abandoned their 'association' for a CLC-affiliated union in 1974. Similarly, the TEA's own membership was becoming increasingly demanding, unwilling to suffer discipline silently. One Quebec member turned her grievance over to the Confédération des Syndicats Nationaux (CSN) lawyer to handle, probably expecting a more militant approach; another long-time veteran grieving Bell's refusal to give her a pension exploded in anger, stating 'I've been exploited.'[125] This was new language indeed. When a young 'new left' militant grieving her dismissal launched a public, political campaign to support her case in 1974, the older TEA executive did not know what hit them: they seemed bemused, irritated, and worried, though they still supported her grievance. This was new terrain for them.[126]

That the operators' association was forced to change over time is apparent in its views on pregnancy. In the 1950s the TEA did not target pregnancy leave as an important grievance issue. In fact, in a joint union-management committee, Bell stressed that leaves were 'a privilege, not guaranteed' and that 'pregnancy furloughs' (a puzzling military term) were an irritating 'problem' for them, even if they were granted – at the company's discretion.[127] Nor did the TEA forcefully challenge the company's subjective, moralistic take on maternity leave, articulated in 1962: 'Re-hiring is up to management [which] does not know what future conditions will be ... Health conditions or home responsibilities may make it inadvisable for [us] to offer further employment.'[128] Within a decade, the company had to eat its words: association reps were now recommending grievances when women were not reinstated after pregnancy at their previous level of pay, or when the company did not give women their unemployment insurance forms when they left to have a baby.[129] This shift had much to do with broader political changes – a renewed feminist movement, the Royal Commission on the Status of Women, new laws offering maternity leave – but it also indicated a changed mentality within the union. In the early 1970s, the TEA grievance process was brought into line with those of other unions as its own political self-definition changed: in 1974 it cast aside its 'association' label, assuming the more militant title of Communications Union of Canada. Members also began to question the value of staying separate from the larger union movement, and in 1979 the TEA finally succumbed to a raid by the more powerful mixed-gender Communication Workers of Canada (CWC). This novel experiment with an independent women's union then came to an end.

Grievance files from two mixed-gender white-collar unions, the OTEU and CUPE Local 881, suggest similarities both with mass-production women workers and with Bell's female-dominated workforce.[130] First, the grievance system was not generally used to unsettle the well-established racialized-gendered division of labour in the workplace; like women bacon packers, stenographers were generally grieving for better treatment within the parameters of female-typed job categories. When general union principles of fair treatment were involved – for example, opposing unfair discipline, unrealistic output expectations, or supervisors who vigilantly followed and tracked sick employees in order to catch them playing hooky – the union defended women quite adamantly.[131] Likewise, when a group of women demanded a better rating for 'female' jobs, the union might also be very sympathetic.[132] But many individual grievances involved women grieving their job classification, promotions that did not happen, or positions that went to other women, simply exacerbating tensions between workers. As one disgruntled woman put it to the union president when arguing for an increase for her job category, 'We are the lowest paid employees in the whole building. We do more work, [have] more responsibility. Why, I have seen girls in here who are paid more, have more time to polish their fingernails, write [personal] letters ... We have enough work in here without doing such things.'[133] Second, a common masculine mental map and assumptions about appropriate female behaviour might draw male union leaders and supervisors together in their assessment of women's grievances. When one female office worker wanted to grieve her failure to be promoted, the union president met alone with management, then suggested she back down, simply adopting the supervisor's assessment as truth and dismissing her claims that she was singled out for capricious treatment by this particular man.[134]

Discipline and grievances were inevitably shaped by the nature of the work process and work culture, so that many white-collar workers, like the Bell operators, faced subjective estimations about demeanour that were distinct from the question of whether a woman met her production quota making wieners. Despite what Lynn Williams wrote, unionized workplaces were no paradise for white-collar women: even with union protection, they were assessed on vague terms such as deportment and relationships with others. The concept of a quintessentially nice female white-collar worker, with a particular 'look' – white, polite, and decently dressed – was quite unshakeable. In one white-collar union file, women were criticized for their lack of teamwork, poor attitude, lack of tact, and even their snobby 'British' tone (although whiteness was preferred, British imperialists were not). Certainly, gendered social norms pervaded all workplaces, but white-collar women were especially vulnerable to criticism about appearance, and only the most militant or radical unions managed to avoid mimicking management's outlook on this issue. In one instance, a woman who was praised for her work was given a bad evaluation, criticized for her 'deportment and dress.' She grieved. She was then put on an eight-week warning and suddenly provided with a list of problems with her 'work' (really her demeanour): she was too loud, not polite enough, did not dress well, and had body odour. The union defending her asked whether she had been given advance warning of all her problems, but, significantly, it never challenged any of the criteria used to condemn her.[135]

However inadequate this woman's union was, she at least had a grievance procedure that might help her stave off dismissal. Most women workers did not. 'Managerial,' white-collar, public-sector, and especially contingent, marginalized workers without collective agreements – the latter more likely to be immigrant and racialized workers – were initially omitted from the Fordist accord and the legal protections it offered. Until public-sector unionization began to change the face of the labour movement in the late 1960s, more women were outside than inside the accord.[136] When faced with the most serious form of workplace discipline, getting fired, only a minority of women could seek legal redress using the ultimate adjudication for grievances: arbitration.

Fighting Dismissal

Getting fired, as labour arbitrators pointed out, was the 'capital punishment' of workplace discipline. Discharge was the threat that made discipline possible: the fear of discharge, as Glasbeek points out, was crucial to the creation of a 'compliant' workforce and to the 'extra productivity the employer is able to extract' from workers simply with the recognition of his right to dismiss.[137] If there was one form of discipline that workers needed a fair defence for, it was surely discharge. Discharge grievances expose not only conflict and tensions in the workplace, but also what unions were willing to fight *for*, since they ultimately made decisions about which grievances to take forward. Since so few grievances made it to arbitration, the process is hardly a true statistical measure of all grievances; moreover, the fact that women invariably had to deal with male-dominated union bureaucracies may have inhibited their use of the process. Nonetheless, tracing arbitral decisions offers some sense of emerging union concerns and legal outcomes. Because arbitrations were the penultimate, published legal decisions about discipline, they were also important as public statements, setting the discursive terrain for broader understandings of gender in the workplace.

Discipline and discharge grievances were some of the most commonly arbitrated, about 37 per cent of the total in one study completed in the 1970s, and although formal arbitration was the tip of the iceberg – approximately 2 per cent of all grievances – the process had an impact on the whole system since it set out principles that were then were applied downward into the workplace.[138] In their analysis of the efficacy of disciplinary techniques, industrial-relations experts perceptively pointed to the role of self-governance in deterring workers' wrongdoings. In one such study, the author argued that internalized 'voluntary compliance' to rules perceived by workers themselves to be 'fair'[139] lay at the heart of successful discipline – thus presaging what scholars might later call either the hegemonic ideology of the workplace or a Foucauldian process of self-governance. He also recognized the effect of public punishments as deterrence (also an interest of Foucault): these 'dramatizations' of the law of the workplace reminded other workers of the costs of not conforming. Instead of 'coercive discipline,' this expert advocated for 'corrective discipline,' a process whereby workers learned from their mistakes as they were 'served notice'[140] to reform – *or else*. This saved workers their jobs, and the employer the expense of new staff recruitment. In this expert's view, corrective discipline, indicated by a two-thirds 'success' rate of workers' reintegration into the workplace, was precisely what Canadian grievance arbitration did well.

Nowhere in this study was gender mentioned. A survey of arbitrations cited in *Labour Arbitration Cases* in a twenty-year period suggests that women were under-represented in discharge cases, even taking into account their numbers in the workforce.[141] This mirrored their smaller numbers in mass-production unionized workplaces, but even here their jobs were considered unskilled, their seniority more precarious. Men with better pay and more seniority may have felt there was more at stake in fighting for their position. There were also few women shop stewards or union office holders cognizant of contract language and the complex procedures involved in grievances. Aggrieved women may have simply quit, not wanting to be known as troublemakers. The delays of arbitration were also a deterrent for women whose paychecks were essential to the family economy; in Ontario, decisions could take six months, even longer, and rarely was back pay granted. The impact on a worker's yearly income was 'staggering,' especially in comparison to the relatively small financial impact of arbitration on employers.[142] Women's very marginal chances at full success (reinstatement with back pay) in this small sample lends weight to scholars' scepticism about grievance arbitration; 43 per cent lost their cases, and another 22 per cent were only reinstated with a lesser penalty of some kind.[143] Finally, the individual nature of grievances did not necessarily lead to wider, collective knowledge and protest: as one arbitrator pointed out, even if women heard by word of mouth about a successful grievance, the legal rationale was rarely explained widely in the workplace.[144]

For historians with the luxury of hindsight, however, these arbitrations, however partial as historical sources, are still illuminating. There appears to have been a slight increase in women's cases in the 1960s, including those launched by workers in smaller workplaces and service-sector jobs; as more women engaged in full-time work for pay and were integrated into unions, they became more adept at using the contract, and more courageous about asserting their rights. There were some common disciplinary charges leading to dismissal for both men and women, such as absenteeism: this was hardly a 'woman's problem,' as so many commentators claimed at the time. However, the gendered nature of conflict in the workplace indicated a crucial reason for the paucity of women's discharge arbitrations. None of these arbitrations concerned the transgressions that commonly led to men's discharges, such as alcohol abuse and fighting. Even dishonesty/theft, one of the three most serious charges leading to dismissal, was found predominately in male cases.[145] Women were also less likely to be fired for participating in illegal production shutdowns, for reasons suggested earlier. Perhaps most important, the largest number of these discharge cases cited were fought over issues of marriage and pregnancy. It appears women were not accepting employers' established rules on these issues, but rather contesting them, literally from the shop floor upwards, as few unions took a leadership role on these as policy issues. Women's grievances thus mirrored the reality of married women's increasing labour-force participation rate, but they also suggested that women were challenging the image of the working 'girl' with affirmations of their right to be working mothers.

Discharge grievances laid bare employers' unsuccessful inculcation of time discipline. Both men and women were enmeshed in work regimes with little flexibility or time off; when they self-designated time off, dismissal might follow. Women's minor time rebellions might catch up with them. Like the Bell Telephone worker who simply disappeared for a few extra days, one woman took a self-assigned one-week leave of absence. She had requested a two-week leave following the normal one-week plant shutdown in order to go overseas, but was denied the extra week. When she returned a week late, she pleaded 'inability to make travel arrangements,' a rationale that attempted to fit the contract language of a 'justifiable excuse.' The arbitrator had no time for this excuse and added a further layer of discipline by emphasizing that if the woman was re-hired, her seniority would also be lost. In a similar case in which the union tried to argue that an employer was 'unreasonable' in denying a woman a one-week leave, the arbitrator, Magistrate J.A. Hanrahan, not always sympathetic to labour, ruled that it was entirely 'reasonable,' since the company was doing inventory that week and was 'short handed' without her. If the employer could effectively argue that its ability to carry on an efficient and profitable business was at stake, the union might well lose.[146]

Not all women were pushing the envelope with self-designed absences. Some were coping with illnesses or family problems, but they desperately wanted to hang on to their jobs. However, once foremen or supervisors were set on discharging a worker for absenteeism, they might go to great lengths – phoning family members, following workers and checking up on their whereabouts – to make sure they were sick, sometimes causing personal and familial upheaval in the process. Management knew it needed concrete evidence if it came to arbitration, but this attention to 'due process,' ironically, may have resulted in more invasive surveillance of workers' private lives.[147]

How strict the arbitrators were on absenteeism varied tremendously: the context for the absences, the employee's previous record, and the hope for rehabilitation might become important variables for consideration. It was simply presumed, however, that women *were* absenteeism 'problems.' As Magistrate Hanrahan warned a hospital trying to fire a laundry worker, 'it is not uncommon for companies hiring female help to have to deal with the problem of them being ill *for certain days each month.*' Since it came with the territory, he implied, it was not especially 'blameworthy' in this woman's case.[148] Even union appointees trying to argue for women's reinstatement adopted similar arguments about women's inevitable absence for 'certain periods [of time].'[149] The problem was that the very same argument, stressing women's absenteeism, was used by management to justify differential pay in arbitrations over unequal pay.[150]

There is no denying, however, that working mothers found the restrictive rules about attendance difficult to negotiate. When Mrs Wood, the sole support of three children, grieved her discharge from General Electric, she was forced to admit that she had many absences, usually a few hours or days spread over the year, though she always gave the employer notice. After a mere five-hour absence without notice she was suddenly dismissed; following a final warning, she was away twice, though her foreman admitted he had to send her home in one instance as she was vomiting. Even the majority report rejecting her grievance attempted to appear understanding, given that she fit a sympathetic image: the honest, struggling sole-support mother. But the fact that Mrs Wood did not play that role and plead her case as a single mother was then inadvertently used against her: 'One sympathizes with her,' said the men who voted to fire her, 'but she should have taken management into her confidence.'[151]

The modest benefits of grievance systems were nonetheless clear in women's absenteeism discharge cases. Employers found it more difficult to fire a woman protected by contract language that permitted absences with 'notice,' though grievers could be impelled to produce medical documentation (begging the question of whether the women had the time and money to go to doctors repeatedly). If there was a 'verifiable health issue,' arbitrators could be quite sympathetic, urging employers to take into account factors such as overall record, work performance, and improvement over time. As arbitrator Horace Krever told a super-market when he ruled in favour of a woman's reinstatement, what counted was not her long absence (267 days in 3 years) in the past when she was ill, but her more recent, improved record of only 9 days in 2 months.[152] Liberal arbitrators might interpret the contract leniently in cases of involuntary absence, but then the problem was that a woman's fate depended on which arbitrator she drew.

Women's health and family responsibilities cycled through difficult and good periods, but employers sometimes reached an exasperation point that led to dismissals – just as in insubordination cases there might be a 'culminating incident'[153] leading to discharge. In one grievance, Ruby H. had many more years of good attendance than bad; she probably felt her employer owed her some consideration for the former when her life began to go downhill. Ruby started at a Brantford paper company in 1950 when she was twenty, first full-time, then for a number of years part-time. It was not until she started again full-time in 1965 that she had problems, now because of stresses relating to her son, as well as physical ailments emerging from that stress. This company, like Bell, used its own medical personnel to investigate who was 'really chronically ill,' but did not compel Ruby to be examined despite her long absences. Then in 1968 it suddenly fired her right after a strike, claiming her ill health were excessive over a three-year period.

The arbitrator could not but agree in principle that employers had the 'ultimate power to ensure that employees will attend work regularly,' but he nonetheless saved Ruby's job. By the time the strike was over, he argued, there was evidence that her health and attendance had, and would, improve: the company was obliged to look at the 'circumstances actually then existing.' Ruby was reinstated, but without back pay since she could not show she had actively sought work to 'mitigate' her losses, and, throwing a bone to the employer, the arbitrator assured the company Ruby could be demoted after a three-month trial period if absences persisted. Compromises in which the arbitrators recommended a lesser

penalty transpired in about a third of all discharge cases, though the favoured discipline, suspension, had a more onerous impact on workers
than employers.[154]

Ruby's case provides other clues as to why so few women persisted
with grievances through to arbitration. Ruby had only been able to go to
a doctor once in the few years she was ill, so she lacked medical documentation. More important, her arbitration was delayed because the
company lawyer first claimed that there was no collective agreement in
effect when she was fired (largely due to the complexity of ongoing
contract negotiations), and thus her grievance was not arbitrable. It was
fancy but shaky legal footwork that the arbitrator rejected after a separate hearing. Ironically, legal stonewalling did not necessarily enhance
employers' chances of winning, but the delays certainly dampened
unions' faith in the process and dissuaded employees worried more
about a paycheck than vindication with one employer. 'Acres of paper
have been consumed on the subject of arbitrability,' admitted a legal
expert in the 1970s,[155] though the labour movement put it more bluntly:
using 'legal mumbo jumbo' to delay arbitrations did not offer the worker
speedy justice.[156]

While grievance arbitration gave unionized women who could prove
illness new protections against dismissal, capricious decisions still seemed
to be made, an indication of how 'industrial voluntarism' lurked beneath
the surface of the new industrial legality. A woman who was away on two
consecutive days, and asked the person who drove her to work to report
her absence, was fired after her fellow worker forgot to follow through.
She had 'failed to follow' the required procedures of reporting, and the
company had cracked down on lackadaisical practices with recent written directives. With the union appointee dissenting, she lost her grievance by the luck of the draw since she had an unsympathetic chair who
sided with the employer. Her chances with a single arbitrator might have
been marginally better.[157]

Insubordination, a direct threat to work discipline, was probably the
most common transgression leading to a discharge grievance for both
men and women,[158] though women's insubordinations could be disturb-
ingly minor. Men, it is true, could be fired for something as petty as refusing to sweep the floor (not in their job description), but their dismissals
generally did not rest on one-time 'flare ups.'[159] Men were also presumed
to be more assertive, less polite, and more prone to 'horseplay' (a whole
category, and a completely gendered one, in grievance nomenclature)
than women. Yet 'insubordinate' women were often simply attempting,

in some small way, to assert control over their work space or work pace. One woman working in the laundry of an old-age home objected to a resident being assigned to do 'therapeutic' work folding the laundry outside her door as she said his presence in the corridor compromised safety. It also compromised her bargaining-sector work. She lost her grievance.[160] Not all charges of insubordination rested on a single issue; arbitrators were often looking for the 'culminating incident' in a long line of problems.

'Long service and quality of [past] work' could be examined when women were deemed insubordinate,[161] leading to a lesser penalty.[162] The disciplinary price of reinstatement for a pharmacy clerk was the loss of two weeks' pay and a lecture from the arbitrators on her 'thoughtlessness' because on one day only she decided to take the phone off the hook for twenty minutes so she could go to another section of the store to perform another task required of her.[163] Arguably, her reprieve was also her warning: it was 'corrective discipline' in action. In another woman's 'reinstatement with loss of pay' arbitration in 1966, a new term entered the lexicon of arbitration: rehabilitation. First used in the case of Miss Laanamae, a white-collar worker at De Havilland Aircraft, rehabilitation was defined by the arbitrator as a question of *probability*: if warned, would the worker positively conduct herself in the future? Miss Laanamae had a good record until she was transferred from the office to the laboratory, at which point management documented six incidences of misconduct. Nonetheless, she won reinstatement. It was not just her past good record that impressed arbitrator Harry Arthurs but also her future capability to be a 'useful citizen in this industrial community.'[164] As proof, he noted that she had been asked to stay late and do some typing not in her job description and she did so 'satisfactorily.' Nor was she a 'willful, malicious or hostile' employee – someone with a personality problem in Bell's terminology. Her amenable assumption of extra duties stood in direct contrast to the clerical worker defended by Lynn Williams, whose failure in this regard contributed to her discharge. 'Industrial rehabilitation' was supposedly distinct from both therapeutic and penal practices,[165] but this gentler nomenclature could not disguise what was essentially a disciplinary process of self-governance – just as Bell's medical 'rehabilitation' was.

There were some predictors for women's success in these arbitrations. If there was incontrovertible contract language or precedent offering the woman an out, and a sympathetic single arbitrator, her chances were better, though it is not clear if having 'professional' arbitrators rather than local magistrates made a difference.[166] One UAW production worker was given a new job that required wearing shackles and bending metal strips. Finding it too painful for her hands, she requested other work, but was told to 'do the work or go home.' She chose the latter, but first headed straight to the union office to file a grievance against discharge. Arbitrator Earl Palmer supported her refusal to do work that was a 'danger to her health,' one of the few allowable exceptions to disobeying orders.[167] But health issues did not always excuse women's insubordination. When a group of women poultry workers were threatened with dismissal if they did not don painful goggles distributed by management, they chose to leave the plant rather than wear goggles 'injurious to their health,' losing a week's pay. They lost a grievance for compensatory wages, since the company claimed they were simply AWOL, without formal discharge letters. Given arbitrators' general antipathy to collective insubordination, and the women's subsequent capitulation to the goggle rules, the board's unanimous ruling was not surprising.[168]

Seldom in these arbitrations was a woman completely vindicated. In a very rare case, the personal animus of a supervisor towards one woman was so crystal clear to arbitrator Hanrahan that he suggested the supervisor offer the griever an 'apology.' An activist in her UAW local, the woman was fired by her female superior for the most minor of comments, one made in response to provocation about her union involvement. Other workers protested in writing, and even the woman's foreman denied she was generally 'insolent.'[169] To actually receive back pay after reinstatement, however, was rare. In one of only three such cases discovered in this sample, a store cashier was fired on the spot by a manager who claimed the worker had broken a workplace rule that 'employees could not shop at the store.' In fact, a section manager had offered to buy her an item she needed and did so. Because of the clear lack of due and 'just' process, or perhaps secretly sensing this was a ridiculous, petty rule, the arbitrators awarded the woman back pay.[170] These victories were undoubtedly very sweet, but the more common outcome of 'job back but no back pay' sent a clear and corrective disciplinary message: workers were lucky to have a job and should follow rules carefully in the future.

Women who worked in service- and public-sector jobs had to monitor themselves particularly carefully, since they could be judged more harshly by arbitrators based on their interactions with customers or the public. Precisely because there were customers involved, a waitress who used 'loud, vulgar language' one day was fired and lost her grievance, even though she asked for mercy since she was plagued by 'personal problems' at the time.[171] Although fewer men performed service work, they very occasionally faced a similar test of public disapprobation. An arbitrator rejected the discharge grievance of a man employed by a municipal community centre after his conviction for an alcohol offence and for assaulting his wife. Since the municipal employer had given previous warnings concerning alcohol, and wished to employ only men of 'reputable character' for 'public relations' reasons, the arbitrator had no qualms endorsing dismissal. He also mused that similar standards would not apply to 'industrial employment,' where one's conduct outside of the workplace mattered less.[172] Was this a subtle reiteration of Laskin's view that the factory shop floor was not a 'drawing room'? If the dominant arbitral image of blue-collar masculinity accepted a 'rougher' demeanour, how did this affect blue-collar women on the job? The discharge case of one man for sexual assault illustrates well the negative consequences of this image, and how dominant sexual/gender norms saturated grievance hearings.

In 1949 Magistrate Hanrahan heard a man's discharge grievance concerning indecent assault against a female co-worker. The UAW defended Mr A., sixty years old, who everyone admitted had been the 'butt of some horseplay' and 'good natured ridicule' in the workplace by male co-workers. The fact that 'he did not speak English very well' was passed over quickly, but suggests that the supposedly jovial 'horseplay' could have xenophobic connotations. One day, two men were tilting a heavy drum so Mr A. had trouble lifting it onto his two-wheel truck; they then called out to a sixteen-year-old female employee working nearby, telling her to try to operate the truck. As she sat on the truck, Mr A. rushed back, seized her from behind with his hands around her breasts, and pulled her away from the truck to himself. The scene was cause for great laughter for the men, though one, seeing how upset the young woman was afterwards, offered her his sympathy and 'indignation.' In the arbitration hearing, UAW staffer John Elton claimed the young woman eagerly 'joined in the horseplay,' implying it was her own fault, and he insinuated that her feminine, youthful tears had resulted in inordinate sympathy from other workers, leading her to make a frivolous complaint.

Hanrahan described the incident in terms of traditional physical stereotypes and sexual scripts, including the rape myth of 'asking for it.' The young woman was 'slender, youthful and rather sober in appearance' and it was 'generally agreed [she was] not the type to invite familiarity such as is alleged.' The man, by contrast, had an 'inclination to lewdness,' indicated through his previous sexual remarks and actions, though the arbitrator also sympathized with him, given the public assault on his masculinity (no mention was made of ethnicity). After all, this was 'his truck' being taken over by a young woman who was going to undertake work 'he had failed to do.' Finding his masculinity challenged, the arbitrator noted sympathetically, was too much for him, and his response could be excused as mere 'anger' not the more insidious 'lustful' conduct. Hanrahan offered the young woman some consoling words, precisely because she appeared to be a model 'victim' – attractive, young, and innocent. Naturally, he commented, she felt 'revulsion' when she found herself in the arms of a 'not very attractive old man, to the obvious merriment of onlookers.'

The union, of course, argued that dismissal could only occur if this charge could be proved in a court of law, a difficult standard to meet, and not something arbitrators had yet agreed on. Hanrahan ruled to reinstate Mr A., for he did not see evidence of 'evil intent' in his actions. Mr A.'s actions were excused within the context of a rough workplace, masculinity under assault, and an overly excitable young woman who should have accepted sexualized horseplay as normal. Her acknowledged distress and the fact that at least one man broke ranks with his co-workers and supported her complaint did not sway the arbitrator.[173] Mr A., therefore, could be reinstated after physically grabbing a woman's breasts, but the waitress above lost her job for using bad language. Hanrahan's decision encapsulates how proscribed gender roles became part of grievance discourse and rulings, in turn reinforcing the ideological precepts of gender difference and moral regulation in the workplace.

The young woman who complained about Mr A.'s assault found a sympathetic audience from co-workers when she headed to the lunch room that day. Such support attests to the fact that although unions often feared that women lacked a taste for militance, women did risk their jobs with collective protests. Two such group dismissal cases involving Bora Laskin resulted in very different outcomes: one group was fired, while another received more 'chivalric' sympathy. Context, as well as gender, mattered: the first dispute involved pre-meditated worker challenges to efficient production, the second appeared to be the spontaneous outcome of management duplicity and union negligence.

When six women were discharged by Canada General Electric (CGE) for 'restriction of production,' Laskin ruled in favour of the company, with his friend and veteran labour arbitrator Drummond Wren dissenting. At stake was the company's decision to reorder the production process for increased efficiency, a management right that was difficult to challenge. The women's protests began when CGE re-timed and re-organized their jobs: instead of seven women at a table, there were now six, with new quotas required. All the women protested that the quota was impossible to meet; management replied that those who failed would be disciplined. After twelve women were warned about their low output, they were all suspended on 14 November for eight days. On 15 November, however, they showed up for work but protested by sitting at the tables, playing cards and knitting. They were ordered to get off the premises or face discharge. By their return on 22 November, six of the women made the quota, but the six who did not were promptly fired. It appears that some were willing to continue with 'ca'canny,' purposely slowing down, but others were frightened into a pace of work that they said significantly reduced the standard of what they produced.

Although the foreman claimed the women simply took too much time away from their machines, Wren produced a mountain of statistics to show this was essentially a speed up, with the company pushing for increased production at the workers' expense. He tried to recast the women as less rebellious, pointing out that they tried to bring the production problem to the foreman's attention but he refused to listen. However, women who seemed to conspire to disobey orders or who interfered with management's right to reorder work did not have a strong legal or moral case. The union knew better than to publicly support this collective protest, but the disgruntled women likely knew that the UE was aggressive in supporting formal grievances, taking them as far as arbitration. As Jeff Taylor argues, by the 1950s, the UE recognized the legal and ideological limits of grievance arbitration, but it was still an integral part of a larger radical political strategy of encouraging workers' vigilance and militancy on the shop floor and, undoubtedly, also of fostering their identification with the union. When women did win a grievance arbitration with compensation, they were shown prominently in the *UE News*, brandishing their cheques.[174]

In the second case of collective protest, forty-six women were fired after a wildcat strike at a small aerosol-can factory. Although the women were protesting employer decisions, they were also unhappy with their union, the United Steelworkers of America (USWA), as it had been less than vigilant in taking up their complaints. More than one grievance emerged from the wildcat, since a male union steward not directly involved was also fired, though he won reinstatement. Forty-three of the women's grievances were dealt with together in a hearing headed by

Bora Laskin. Two issues were stressed in the union's presentation. The USWA tried to push discharge grievances in a new direction by insisting that dismissal should not result for an illegal work stoppage if the workers were 'provoked' into the walkout; this, in effect, 'mitigated [the] conduct' of those discharged. Second, the unsafe working conditions that women had repeatedly complained about, to no effect, were laid out as the context for the dispute. Even the arbitrators professed dismay with these conditions, including temperatures too cold to work in, water on the floor causing women to fall, an electric cord allowed to run along the wet floor, no screen around an aerosol gasser with cans flying off, and no rubber gloves for the hot-water bath. The written decision noted pointedly that safety was only taken seriously after the women walked out.

The precipitating spark of the wildcat, however, was a reorganization of production that discontinued the practice of job rotation on the line, which had allowed the balancing of heavy and lighter work. When the new schedule was first posted, many women walked out after their coffee break to protest; in their eyes, the current rotation was an integral part of their existing collective agreement and was not to be tampered with. The union pleaded for the status quo while it 'explained' the changes to the women, but the subsequent union meeting was taken up primarily with the case of the fired (male) shop steward. It is likely, however, that the union would have urged the women to accommodate the reorganization. When the new schedule was posted again for implementation, the women were told that it would be 'tried out,' then reviewed. It was not, however, which led to a second walkout, this time with pickets. One of the few English speakers in the crowd was chosen to explain the workers' concerns to a supervisor, who agreed to listen, then, according to witnesses, he 'turned his back and walked away.'

Although the events were more complicated, what is revealing here is the latitude that the arbitration decision gave the wildcatters in comparison to the electrical workers, and in a context in which illegal work stoppages, and wildcats in particular, were usually treated harshly. The judgment was classic Laskin in its call for a 'just balance between management authority and the worker's claim to security of employment.' Laskin was anxious to assert the arbitral distinction between those who instigated and those who participated in a wildcat, citing primarily US precedents. However, who was the instigator? There did not appear to be ringleaders, only wildcatters (though perhaps the leaders were astutely organizing in another language); international union leaders were hardly instigators unless one blamed their indifferent 'inaction,' duly noted by Laskin. Was there perhaps also an underlying sympathy for vulnerable workers, in this case immigrant women, many unable to speak English, doing unsafe work in difficult conditions, with lackluster union protection? Management, admitted the decision, was under no 'legal obligation' to keep the promises made to the women about reviewing the new system, but its rather cynical misleading of the women was viewed dimly: morally, they should not have disregarded the verbal 'accommodation that had been reached,' and at the very least, they owed the women an 'explanation.' Under such 'mitigating circumstances,'[175] the women were forgiven their wildcat. It is possible, then, that the women were the beneficiaries of a fleeting moment of chivalric justice, based on their appalling treatment and working conditions.[176]

If wildcats staged by women were rare, grievances of women fighting dismissal due to marriage and pregnancy were common. Employers' rules concerning the employment of married women varied across occupations. Regardless of marital status, women's (lower paid) labour in contingent, service, and part-time jobs was welcomed in this time period; the same was true for some feminized white-collar jobs. However, better remunerated, more secure jobs in industry, designated as 'male' jobs, were considered to be off limits to married women, not only by management but often by male workers too. Still, the memory of married women's work during wartime was fresh in some minds, and unions, as Pam Sugiman points out in the case of the UAW, felt bound to take up women's grievances when the contract was clearly violated. Many complaints about the marriage bar never made it to arbitration, as employers used more informal strategies to discourage married women's work (a fact evidenced by the packing-house worker discussed earlier who was simply refused time off for her marriage). When grievances did make it to arbitration, management's argument was often that past precedent and company rules should triumph, while unions countered that contract language – or the lack of it – should be the deciding issue.

This was already the pattern, four years after the war ended, when a UAW local faced off with a company over the dismissal of newly married Ina Barber. In its defence, the company cited a policy 'long in effect' before the war, while the union countered that the policy had now been abandoned and was nowhere to be seen in the contract. Even the employer-appointed member agreed with the union: marriage was not a stated, contractual cause for dismissal and there was 'no reason to believe that seniority should be lost by a female employee upon marriage,' since this too was *not* enshrined in the contract. Most of the arbitration, however, dealt with a second issue. Before the arbitration, the company conceded to reinstatement, on the condition that the union agree to negotiate language in the next contract allowing the employer to routinely lay off all married women. Two arbitrators claimed the company just wanted a guarantee the union would negotiate such a clause, but Drummond Wren insisted there was ample evidence that the company was offering a cynical quid pro quo: if Mrs Barber returned, in the future, other married women would not. The union understandably baulked at this future commitment, pushing the issue to arbitration. Though Mrs Barber was rehired, she received limited wage compensation, dating from the initial company offer to rehire: arguably, the union was standing up for a principle, but one that cost Mrs Barber her back wages.[177]

Even when married women were not automatically fired, they faced seniority discrimination. A well-documented case, that of auto worker Rosina Saxby, centred on General Motors' practice of recalling single women from layoff before their married peers, despite married women's higher seniority. The company was used to treating married women as a reserve army of labour, recalled as a last resort, and it did not want to abandon this source of flexible labour. The case was eventually heard by veteran liberal arbitrator Jacob Finkelman, who ruled that the company could not treat married women differently since the contract did not explicitly say married women had lesser or different seniority rights.[178] Saxby's grievance, however, also reveals how ambivalent mass-production unions were towards married working women. The local leaders and membership – even women unionists – were divided over the Saxby case; some leaders wanted to compromise with the company and set up a separate seniority list for married women. It took intervention from the International UAW, including the more progressive US Women's Department, to bring the Canadians in line with the union's official 'no discrimination' policy.

If married working women upset the dominant image of a male breadwinner, a pregnant woman was even more problematic, her swelling body a visible reminder of the prospect of working mothers. In the post–Second World War period, unionized women used a range of tactics, from ignoring workplace custom to launching grievances, in their efforts to break down prohibitions against women staying at work while pregnant, and also returning to claim back their jobs after the birth.[179] In grievances over pregnancy and maternity, voluntarist managerial control and labour's new grievance protections clashed repeatedly in arbitrations that also revealed a highly moralist discourse about sexuality, pregnancy, and working women. Some women clearly resorted to subterfuge to secure a maternity leave. Militant unions such as the UE backed them up. When a Westinghouse worker asked for a leave because she was pregnant, she was immediately turned down. She subsequently took a week's sick leave and produced a doctor's letter saying she needed a three-month leave due to a 'nervous condition brought about by other circumstances,' a rather ingenious way of aiding a woman who was going to be a sole-support mother. The UE won her arbitration, securing not only reinstatement, but also no loss of seniority since she had been discharged without cause to begin with. The doctor's letter and her request for a leave, two board members agreed, was an entirely different issue than her first request for pregnancy leave. They also added an editorial comment, suggesting that a company employing over a thousand women, 53 per cent of whom were married, had an 'inconsiderate [policy] seriously in need of revision by negotiation between the parties.'[180]

For many unions, though, maternity leave was not a priority in negotiations. An unusual contract might provide leave, but in one case it was limited to six months maximum, and when a female member went to arbitration to secure just one more month, the contract worked against her.[181] The main problem, however, was management's insistence that it was its prerogative to make the rules concerning pregnant women. When a woman at Essco Stamping Products, a predominately female workplace, requested a leave of absence in 1957, admitting she was pregnant, the UAW lost her grievance as arbitrator Hanrahan ruled that the 'leave' clause in question was 'permissive,' giving management the discretion to provide leaves – or not – as it saw fit. This employer was not unusual in articulating a fear of precedent and subscribing to the 'myth of perpetual pregnancy.'[182] Such a mindset assumed all employees would be reproducing so quickly that production would be disrupted and that 'an employee could only work a few months of the year between pregnancies and maintain full seniority rights.'[183] Less considered was the possibility that not all women in the plant were interested in giving birth every year.

Union victories in these pregnancy and maternity cases were not necessarily victories for the concept of maternity leave as much as they were clever defences of contract leave clauses.[184] A frontal challenge to pregnancy polices was less likely to succeed. In 1960, a pregnant woman working at Quaker Oats in Peterborough fought her dismissal when the company refused to allow her to work past six months. Its decision was based on three considerations: past practice, the managerial right to make policy in this area, and, third, the proven 'inefficiency and absenteeism' of pregnant women, a case it made at the hearing with statistics drawn from US employer studies. Quaker admitted that usually it refused to hire even married women, so the worker's re-employment would only be considered if she could prove she was separated from her husband and was the sole support of a dependent: for Quaker, the male-breadwinner ideology was sacred. Unfortunately, its rule barring pregnant women was only recorded in a management guide; employees were expected to absorb the rules by a process of osmosis. Most did, acquiescing to management requests for resignation without question, and so the company was miffed when Doris refused to follow suit obediently, or even to give the company nurse information about her due date.

With a sympathetic tribunal chair, the UPWA might have won her case, since requests for 'personal leave' were a contractual option, and there was certainly a body of arbitral opinion that saw company rules as second best to contract language.[185] But the majority ruled against her. The dissenting opinion, written by Mary Eady of the CLC, one of the emerging group of labour feminists in the labour bureaucracy, astutely pointed out that both the US statistics and management's detailed descriptions of Doris' personal life (including her common-law status and previous absences relating to an earlier pregnancy with a different partner) were irrelevant, used to 'cloud' the real issue.[186] This public display of one's personal life in a grievance arbitration, a forum usually dominated by men one did not know, must surely have dissuaded some women from going as far as Doris with their marriage and pregnancy grievances. Also, it is likely no accident that more than one arbitration involved women who did not conform to the dominant sexual script of pregnancy within marriage. Paternalist employers may have baulked at providing leaves to women whom they deemed less respectable; company rules then became a convenient form of 'industrial moral regulation.'

Some employers may have believed that pregnant women were a safety or efficiency issue, but the moralism that pervaded arbitrators' decisions revealed an ideological antipathy to women's continued work that reflected dominant gender norms, not safety standards. One management appointee stated unequivocally that pregnancy was a women's individual 'choice' (or fault?); she should thus accept the consequences, including policies that management had every right to make. Westinghouse's policy of not granting pregnancy leave was 'perfectly reasonable' given it employed over 1000 women, he wrote, and 'it is not reasonable that such a Company should be obliged to hold a job open for every pregnant woman, and give it back to her with accumulated seniority if and when she asks for it ... Pregnancy is not a misfortune brought upon a woman without her consent.'[187] In the case at Essco Stamping, the employer put forward multiple moralistic arguments against a leave, all relating to a woman's proper gender role. Since the griever's husband was 'gainfully employed,' she should not be working, but rather at home with her infant, and if she did work later, it should not 'interfere with her household duties.' If this arbitrator was moralistic, legal experts could be dismissive: as late as the 1970s, a book on discharge grievances treated pregnancy flippantly, citing a rare case involving a woman's four pregnancies, after which the ever 'absent' woman was 'gallantly' reinstated by a kind-hearted arbitrator.[188]

Management moralism was applied not only to proper household roles, but to sexual reputation as well. In another grievance challenging a company's right to refuse a leave to a single pregnant woman, the management appointee claimed it was an employer's right to 'maintain a reasonable moral standard' among his workers, especially if a woman was 'meeting the public' – in this case as a grocery cashier. State-sponsored studies indicated that the physical display of pregnant bodies was clearly a problem for some employers, though their decisions varied with the class designation of the job, with white-collar and professional women more of a concern than blue-collar workers.[189] Like Quaker, this grocery chain assumed its moral standards would be absorbed by osmosis, yet in this case, its failure to provide workers with a written policy resulted in the cashier winning her arbitration.[190] To be sure, counter-arguments put forth by unions were rarely either radical statements opposing such moralism or positive invocations that maternity was a social necessity; rather, unionists were defending contract language about 'leaves' for women, knowing full well that a victory might have indirect benefits for many other workers as well.

Management's concerns about pregnant women were also material in nature. Since women had to be rehired after a pregnancy, they started with no seniority at the bottom of the pay scale, providing a flexible, cheap labour force. For this reason, some pregnancy arbitrations centred on seniority, as in the Saxby case. Unions were well aware that seniority was 'gold,' a precious commodity, so defending it for both men and women in their separate spheres was a high priority. A grocery-store cashier who received a verbal leave of absence for pregnancy returned to work to find she had no seniority and a starting rate of pay. Although company policy stated that leaves had to be documented in writing, her bid to regain seniority was upheld, since it was deemed the company's responsibility to make sure written documents were in order.[191]

Conclusion

If unions had a bare 50 per cent chance of successfully fighting discharge, why did women continue to grieve? Grievance systems did provide workers with a conduit for their own notions of customary rights, fairness, and justice; indeed, they were ideologically effective precisely because they appeared to offer this accepted, legal channel for workers' values, rights, and interests. Moreover, like a predictable slot machine, there was always the promise, if not the reality, of a payoff, a small slice of justice, a temporary respite from someone berating you, or a last chance before dismissal. Yet over time, workers' daily experience with grievance machinery also bred an ideological perspective that subtly shaped their understanding of workplace relations, struggle, and, above all, what it was possible to struggle *for*.[192] The system encouraged individual, not collective, protest, and it fashioned a self-regulating worker whose investment in productivity and efficiency was supposed to be one and the same as that of management. Although a few radical unions and some radicals within unions saw grievances as a form of politicization, many began to see the 'the contract as an end in itself rather than a means of struggle.'[193] Moreover, grievance practices constituted workers not only as individual, consenting subjects, but as male subjects to boot. Grievance systems were shaped by gender as well as class relations: collective agreements, after all, codified gender inequality and outlined new 'rights'; grievance arbitrations were saturated with gendered assumptions; and discipline could be utilized as a means of industrial moral regulation that impacted quite differently on women than men. As Judy Fudge argues in the contemporary context, arbitration is not conducive to challenging forms of systemic discrimination, given the emphasis on 'private ordering, voluntarism and contractualism.'[194]

Critical legal and labour scholars, then, have in one sense made their case: the informal and formal practices associated with grievance law reshaped, but did not fundamentally unsettle, labour's role as commodity and capital's upper hand in the workplace. No amount of liberal hope or moral suasion could alter the reality of property relations that undergirded labour–capital relations: as economic instruments, contracts simply could not deliver political rights and industrial democracy to workers.[195] In the post-war Fordist accord, workplace discipline simply modernized its form; as David Brody wrote decades ago, 'A better definition of the rules did not mean their elimination.'[196] The state was an important player in this modernization process. It was undoubtedly pushed, reluctantly, into worker contractualism when faced with the frightening prospect of labour revolt and socialist electoralism in the aftermath of the Second World War, and confronted by legal experts who believed, quite hopefully, that grievance arbitration would facilitate industrial peace, stability, and prosperity for workers and corporations alike. Once implemented, however, grievance arbitration became a means of authenticating and justifying the labour-capital accord, with the state assuming the stance of the neutral, honest broker. While the state did not reinforce capitalist social relations in a direct, instrumental manner, it did help ideologically legitimize grievance arbitration and the accord as a supposed meeting of 'partners and equals.'

As contracts became exceedingly complex, the legalization of workplace struggles and union bureaucratization also transpired. The isolation of head offices from the rank-and-file was all too apparent in meat packing: company and union men sitting in offices in Toronto conferred over how to defuse grievances percolating up from the regions over what seemed to them to be minor matters such as women's unrestricted right to go to the bathroom. Grievance conflicts provide an excellent window into the interaction of the distinct, but overlapping 'inequality regimes' located within both unions and management. These institutionalized processes of ordering, envisaging, and justifying hierarchies within organizations, including the images and positioning of bodies, argues Joan Acker, are crucial means of reproducing 'control, compliance and domination.'[197] In the UPWA, opposing class interests intersected with shared management-union understandings of gender and ethnicity, though the dynamic of these intersections also varied over time and across unions.

There was often an ongoing tussle between local unions eager to take up some women's grievances (if only to make a point about fairness) and the labour bureaucracy at the centre, increasingly worrying about union time, money, and what was pragmatically possible. Moreover, as the women's wildcat indicated, not only were some locals little concerned with their female members, but in a more general sense, unions became managers of worker discontent, helping to 'normalize' workplace discipline.[198] This process is a cogent reminder of Gramsci's critique of law as a practice that subtly creates the illusion of common interest between the 'masses' and owners of production, a version of 'social conformism,' or homogenization of interests, at least in terms of ideology. In this schema, the state acts as 'educator, urging, inciting, soliciting, but also sometimes punishing' in order to fashion the law-abiding worker-citizen.[199]

The gap between workers' lives and legality, between their description of the problem and the legal solutions provided, is difficult to capture, but I believe it is expressed quite evocatively in the narratives found on the pages of many grievance files and arbitrations. Women's words attest to their physical discomfort, workplace frictions, unhappiness, pain, illnesses, dislike of co-workers, or anger over time or money felt to be their due, and such testimonials are offered in plain and direct language. Grievance panels and arbitrations sometimes offered sympathy and compassion, but the dominant language was a distanced, cut-and-dried one of precedent, industrial efficiency, and contract legalize. Workplace tensions were not translatable, let alone resolvable, with these two different dialects talking at cross purposes.

While endorsing this critical legal view of grievance systems, I also believe we need to take into account the meaning that grievances had for workers themselves, particularly at this historical moment. Because grievance systems had emerged from employees' struggles for dignity in the workplace, workers were determined to test them to their fullest, using grievances as a tool to voice their complaints, establish customary rights, articulate their own notion of justice, and defy the discipline of the time clock and the foreman's gaze. This is why Bell women pressed their demands for apologies when children were sick and meat-packing women walked off the job over relief time – even if the contract did not support their position. This is also why grievances are a rich historical source, revealing layers of contradictory forces: gendered workplace tensions; women's notions of fair play and customary rights; women's internalization of disciplinary rules; and yet also their subterranean tactics of individual and collective resistance.

For those working women covered by contracts – and they were a more privileged minority – grievance procedures could help temper overzealous discipline, alert employers that fired workers would not give up without a fight, and provide the option of refusing 'rehabilitation' by the company doctor. But arbitration decisions could also be capricious, and even their proponents began to concede that the legal machinery was slow, creaky, and cumbersome. For a woman whose paycheck was needed immediately to buy new winter snowsuits, it was probably easier to look for a new job than to weather a five-step grievance system. Nonetheless, women's determination to grieve over a wide range of issues, from misplaced wieners to spiders on the switchboard, reminds us that the system's appeal was its promise of a workplace 'just a little more bearable,' and that industrial legality never completely dampened all vestiges of worker resistance.

Whether or not women's grievances were taken up with vigour depended on the union's political outlook, as well as its local leadership and shop-steward system. What was considered fair and just, and thus worth fighting for, was also gendered and racialized. Grievances encoded not only economic relationships but also cultural assumptions about gender and ethnicity, from moral designations of good and bad girls to stereotypes of temperamental Europeans – though fewer grievances reveal assumptions about 'race,' in part because unionized jobs were so much the preserve of white, Anglo-European males.[200] Because the grievance system defended existing contractual rights, it tended to protect gender privileges, already codified in many contracts. Until women's discontent began to shake up the workplace in the late 1960s, this meant that male-dominated unions were often eager to defend their sisters' grievances as long as these were about women's seniority lists and not attempts to do men's jobs: union ideology thus mixed elements of male privilege with calls for women's rights.

Discipline and grievances naturally reflected the gendered nature of work culture and the work process: women's rebellions were less physical and profane, and in white-collar work especially, women could be disciplined on the basis of appearance, demeanour, and an appropriately feminine countenance. Lacking the designated skill of male knife wielders in meat packing or the physical mobility of telephone installers at the Bell, wage-earning women were subject to stiff surveillance, and some employers seemed to have a low threshold for female insubordination, perhaps because women were hired on the expectation they would be deferential and accommodating. By the early 1970s, however, there were indications that women workers were more assertively challenging both employers and their unions: they were filing grievances, pushing the issue of pregnancy rights, and, in some case, casting their eyes longingly at men's jobs.

The gendering of both discipline and grievance systems was displayed in the language and assumptions of official grievance arbitrations. Sexual harassment was not taken seriously, as it was classified as mere 'horseplay,' and it was assumed that women were less reliable, more likely to be absent with illnesses and 'natural' ailments. This is not to deny that women had difficulty balancing their paid and unpaid labour; this is apparent in women's rationales for absences and their flagrant disobedience regarding 'calling home.' Nowhere were the gendered premises of industrial legality more vividly illustrated than in arbitrations dealing with women's attempts to stay on the job after marriage or pregnancy. These tussles between women workers and employers reveal the saturation of the grievance system with the dominant – and moralistic – gendered norms, but they also capture the promise of the new industrial legality as women workers sought legal means to challenge those norms. Despite the limitations of liberal pluralist legal forms, despite the overwhelming dominance of masculine union hierarchies, women were looking for an opening to break free of long-standing limitations on their work lives. In the 1970s, their efforts would proliferate considerably.

Chapter 6

Aboriginal Women and Work in Prairie Communities[1]

In 1970 a young Anishinabe woman, Edna Manitowabi, published a short autobiographical narrative, *An Indian Girl in the City*, a painfully honest account of her early life on the reserve, her experiences in boarding school, and her search for work as a migrant to a large city. Arriving in the city with her sister when she was fifteen, she was only able to find domestic work and, as she says, 'drifted in and out of similar jobs, hanging out with young Indian kids who were working on shit jobs just like me.' At one point when she secured an interview at a hospital, the Catholic Sister told her, 'We don't like to hire Indian girls because they cannot be depended on.' Edna offered an angry reply, and then was promptly hired. 'I guess she felt guilty,' she wrote with some self-denigration. 'I really felt at the time that she was right and that she was doing me a favour. I *was* a person who could not be depended on.'[2] Manitowabi's memoir speaks to the social marginalization of Aboriginal women as workers, though it was also about much more, as the author provides a moving and complicated story of her social and cultural self-awakening as a Native person.

Despite the sadness articulated by Manitowabi, her story was far different from the many newspaper accounts of the time that portrayed Aboriginal women trapped on dying reserves characterized by 'futility and despair,'[3] or caught in an inevitable downward spiral into poverty and criminality in the city – not unlike recent sensational stories of urban areas such as Vancouver's downtown eastside.[4] Nor did it resemble the optimistic, promotional success stories that the Indian Affairs Branch (IA)[5] published in its *Indian News*. 'Indian Girls Achieve Successful Careers – Pave the Way for Others' was a typical headline, accompanied by pictures of beaming women who had come from remote reserves and surpassed all obstacles to become stenographers or hairdressers. The fact that similar stories appeared in the *Prairie Call*, the newsletter of the Winnipeg Indian and Métis Friendship Centre, suggests these women were seen as indicators of economic hope for Native peoples too.[6] Unlike these tales of rapid progress up or down the ladder of society, Manitowabi's story was a more complicated one of struggle, failure and success, enlightenment and confusion, and, ultimately, hope, for it ends with her going back to school and heading off to an Aboriginal camp to reconnect with her own culture.

Manitowabi's words remind us of how much more complex Aboriginal women's lives were than popular images and state publications suggested, and how important it is to heed their autobiographical writing and reminiscences. For researchers looking at state policies, though, the *Indian News* stories are also a useful index to government thinking at the time. IA believed that Aboriginal women would increasingly migrate to urban areas, that they needed to be integrated into permanent wage labour in service and clerical jobs (at least until marriage), and that white guidance was necessary as they shifted from traditional modes of living to modern employment. This chapter dissects these assumptions, exploring prairie women's labour within family economies of fish, fur, and beets, as well as in post-war, state-sponsored labour programs designed to counteract failing reserve economies with wage labour.

The notion of a Fordist accord, characterized by increased affluence and stable wage relations, had little resonance for the realities of Native life and labour, which reinforces the point that Fordism was a limited class accommodation that marginalized many working people, often on the basis of gender and race. In our contemporary era of so-called new flexible labour, contends anthropologist Gavin Smith, we should not forget that flexible labour, especially multi-occupational households and individuals, doing both paid and unpaid work, has long characterized the global workforce in its struggle for survival.[7] Similarly, for many Aboriginal peoples in the post–Second World War period, economic survival, profoundly altered by longer-term changes in the capitalist economy, entailed a variety of forms of work, including unpaid work, bartering and sharing, seasonal and casual wage labour, permanent wage labour, bush production for use, and bush production for market exchange.[8] Disentangling women's labour from that of kin and community, especially in bush production, is somewhat artificial; however, it is

Figure 12   The Indian Affairs Branch promoted white-collar work as a desirable and attainable occupation for Aboriginal women. Sally Jackson, a stenographer for the Yukon territorial government, ca 1959. (Photographer Richard Harrington. LAC, PA195137. Reproduced with the permission of the Minister of Public Works and Government Services)

important to integrate gender into a study of First Nations labour because the changing organization of work, and its regulation by the state, had different consequences for Aboriginal men and women.

Indeed, the social circumstances of contemporary Aboriginal women, including their criminalization, and the high levels of poverty and violence they experience, cannot be separated from a materialist history of their lives in post-war years, a period the Royal Commission on Aboriginal Peoples (RCAP) refers to as an era of deepening 'dependency.'[9] In this story, life and labour, colonialism and class, gender and race become interconnected categories of analysis. The denigration of Native culture and the racialization of Aboriginal women were indivisible from their economic exploitation and marginalization; we cannot separate material existence from social and cultural life, objective structures from subjective experience. Moreover, though hard times characterized Aboriginal women's lives in the post-war decades, they did not define them. Women's own accounts, like Manitowabi's, indicate how women negotiated increasingly difficult economic times with determined strategies for individual and family survival.

My analysis of state policy draws on insights from new Aboriginal and labour histories, and from feminist political economy, particularly its strong interest in the changing relationship of household to capitalist economies, social reproduction, and the state's role in gendering and racializing labour. Aboriginal and working-class history, both stimulated by political movements of the late 1960s and early 1970s, initially followed parallel but different paths. However, dialogue and mutual collaboration are increasingly evident, as labour historians' increased attention to 'race,' sympathy for First Nations organizing, and efforts to understand labour beyond the site of industrial production have stimulated more research on Aboriginal labour.[10] Scholars have explored Native labour in the context of regional economies, mercantile and industrial capitalism, changing modes of production, specific labour struggles, state policy, and Aboriginal organizing, to name only a few topics. Grappling with the varied and historically specific experiences of the many First Nations in Canada, however, is still a project in progress.[11] Anthropologists have a longer history of studying Aboriginal economies, though feminist anthropologists have been intensely critical of their discipline's analytic inattention to women, gender, and power relations within Aboriginal nations.[12] The invisibility of Aboriginal women in scholarship has thus increasingly been challenged, inspired also by

Aboriginal women's political organizing and their own testimonials to the destructive impact of colonialism on their lives.[13]

Like the First Nations themselves, research has been fruitfully comparative and transnational,[14] though borders did matter in terms of Aboriginal access to resources, legal regimes, and forms of repression. Nonetheless, there were some dominant North American trends in Aboriginal research during the immediate post-war period, when the labour placement programs described in this chapter took shape. Many social scientists were preoccupied with theories of cultural difference and acculturation, which was theoretically a two-way street of cultural exchange, though their focus was often on the one-way 'integration' of Aboriginal cultures (often homogenized and 'racialized') into more 'modern,' urban industrial ones. Influential Canadian anthropologists, for instance, stressed the value of preserving Aboriginal cultures, but nonetheless believed that the future for Indian 'citizenship' lay in economic equality and social integration.[15]

The theoretical shift that took place in the late 1960s and 1970s should not be underestimated: culture as a totalizing *explanation* for economic marginalization was replaced by questions of colonialism, inequality, and dependence. By placing Aboriginal history within the contexts of global capitalism and larger structural processes of economic and social formations, scholars took a dramatic left turn. Both theoretically and politically, analogies were drawn with the exploitation of the Third World colonies: reservations were described as satellites to metropolitan centres of political and economic power or as underdeveloped colonies created by capital and the state.[16] Marxist writing attempted to understand the economic dispossession and proletarianization of Native peoples, as well as those apparently cast outside the working class in marginalized communities.[17] Fur-trade studies increasingly stressed Aboriginal agency, while Aboriginal-authored exposés of their lived experience of colonialism had an immensely powerful impact on academic and popular thinking. Internal colonialism became both a Fanon-like description of the daily racist assaults on Native peoples' inner being, as well as an economic model that involved economic dispossession, political paternalism, and ideologies of racial superiority shaping Aboriginal lives.[18]

In the last two decades, explorations of colonialism from the perspective of identity, culture, and hybridity have assumed increased importance, and for non-Aboriginal scholars, issues of representation or delineations of state policy provide a means of contributing to, but not assuming, the voice of Aboriginal resistance. Marxism, once of interest to

Red Power advocates, is now portrayed, especially by American scholars, as economistic, inherently Eurocentric, and blind to Native culture, though Canadian political economy – where Marxism had the most impact – was never this rigidly reductionist. Cultural 'persistence' is an emerging keyword of research on Aboriginal labour. A recent American collection, for instance, lauds the ways in which Aboriginal communities preserved their cultures while '*adapting*' to capitalist economies.[19] Canadian political economists have accented these questions differently, asking if these adaptations benefited capital more so than Aboriginal peoples,[20] and also resisting a determining emphasis on culture rather than on Aboriginal peoples' rational economic strategies for survival.[21] The assumption that Aboriginal peoples' wage-labour strategies were fundamentally motivated by a desire to protect their culture, bearing little resemblance to the strategies of other working-class people, has thus garnered some compelling critiques.[22]

Understanding the 'work-culture dynamic' was also a central concern for the new (now old) labour historians. While critical of the rigid dichotomy drawn between (immigrant) folk and modern cultures, Herbert Gutman explored how immigrant workers negotiated structural economic changes in work with the cultural resources at hand – custom, rituals, belief – often drawing on the solidaristic ties of kin and community; culture was not the singular cause of change, but a crucial resource that 'confirms, reinforces, maintains, changes or denies particular arrangements of power, status and identity.'[23] While these insights on culture are very useful, the Aboriginal experience was also distinct, shaped by a history of colonialism, at its heart a form of domination that involved 'primitive' accumulation,[24] political subordination, and segregation, justified by ideologies of race and claims to cultural superiority.

The challenge, then, is to create a history that is both informed by political economy's understanding of capitalist social relations and critique of exploitation, and also cognizant of culture, identity, and human agency. We need to understand colonialism not only as a changing political and economic structure with its own contradictions, but also as a lived experience of domination, negotiation, and resistance – and a profoundly gendered one at that. Since the 1970s, social scientists have often described this relationship as one of 'internal colonialism'; however, the term has come under critical scrutiny for masking historical complexity, changing modes of production, Aboriginal agency, and differences within and between Aboriginal communities.[25] Other labels, such as 'colonized labour,' used in the Australian context, do not fit

Canadian conditions.[26] Indeed, the problem with these terms in general is that they suggest a model that may be too static, structured, and fixed to accord easily with the unfolding of human social relations. Thus, while not embracing wholesale the model of internal colonialism, I use the term as an apt political *metaphor*[27] for a historical relationship that, on the one hand, involved dispossession, segregation, and denigration, and yet also created forms of resistance, self-definitions, and longings for self-determination.

Fur, Fish, and Beets

Asking 'Where are the women workers?' is difficult when one examines Aboriginal communities whose economies involved multiple occupations and means of subsistence. While not limited to northern areas of the prairie provinces, such diverse economies were, nonetheless, particularly characteristic of northern Métis and Indian peoples. For that reason, I use northern trapping and fishing as examples of Aboriginal women's multiple work roles. As many studies of the period acknowledged, northern Aboriginals were especially hard hit in this period by economic change. For decades, they had adjusted their labour to new markets and resource extraction, but post-war industrial capitalism, changes in the fur trade, and geographical relocations resulted in considerable economic and social dislocation. The long-term impact of a paternalist, racially stratified fur trade, the commercialization and depletion of resources, and declining purchasing power in the interwar period, among other economic problems, set the scene for the increasing economic marginalization of Native peoples. In the post-war period, state intervention in the North, often framed by a paternalist mindset, also increased considerably, leaving a legacy of Aboriginal bitterness and limited economic benefits.[28]

Locating women workers in historical records bequeathed to us by the state is particularly difficult. The census, for instance, offers an inadequate measure of Aboriginal work; among other problems, some reserves may not have fully participated in reporting information, and statistic-gathering underestimated unemployment. Reflecting the dominant ethnographic and social perspectives of the time, these sources also enumerated male breadwinners earning money, yet ignored the work of homemakers, assuming such individuals neither produced goods nor generated any value. At a very general level, though, the census does indicate the continuing importance of trapping for Aboriginals (even if it was designated predominantly as men's work). It also shows women's increasing involvement, and over-representation, in service wage labour, such as domestic service or waitressing. In 1951, 57 per cent of Canadian women were in service work, yet 76 per cent of Aboriginal women on the prairies were clustered in these low-wage jobs.[29] Indian Affairs records, while only documenting status Indians, also offer an indication of the increasing importance of wage labour over time; by the 1940s, the proportion of Native income from wages had increased and was almost equal to the leading source of income, farming.[30]

The census, however, missed more than it documented. When Jean Lagasse used interviews with Native peoples for his 1959 study for the Manitoba government, the multiple and cyclical nature of Aboriginal occupations became visible.[31] Lagasse argued that many Aboriginal peoples were enmeshed in a 'cycle economy' consisting of serial occupations that changed with the seasons. Métis peoples interviewed in one rural area, for instance, participated in fishing, trapping, cutting pulpwood, guiding, digging seneca roots, picking frogs, harvesting wild rice, farm labour, and picking berries, as well as other kinds of seasonal and casual paid work. From women's oral histories, we know that they were partially, or centrally, involved in many of these occupations. Given this constant round of employment, many Aboriginal families, Lagasse said, had difficulty reporting an exact income, though statistical surveys *could* ascertain – not surprisingly – that Métis and Indian households always earned less than white ones in similar geographical areas.[32]

Nowhere was the discursive erasure of women's labour more striking than in the production of fur. In Saskatchewan, a massive fur conservation study kept copious records of trapping lines and outcomes. Perusing hundreds of pages of these records, I searched in vain for women, finding only a scattering of female names, probably widowed or single self-supporting women who carried on a family trap line.[33] In their studies of bush production in northern Saskatchewan, social scientists and state bureaucrats persisted in describing the fur economy as one in which 'male breadwinners' were responsible for all the trapping 'income,' while women were responsible for domestic 'affairs,' a rather vague term that carried less significance than 'income.'[34] Economists at the time also gathered income statistics for the government assuming a male breadwinner model.[35] Constrained by Western notions of the dichotomized private and public spheres, even anthropologists made gendered assumptions about the work of fur harvesting, perpetuating 'colonial and patriarchal' perspectives on women's trapping labour.[36]

Saskatchewan records are particularly voluminous thanks to an interventionist CCF government that wanted to cure capitalist ills in the North. While David Quirling is extremely critical of their solutions,[37] the government's concern at least left behind many community studies that can now be scoured for evidence of Aboriginal women's work. These post-war studies reflected the same gendered assumptions about work found in the census, yet they did attempt to analyse the 'colonial' relations underpinning northern poverty. Helen Buckley and her fellow economists doing these studies made it clear that the economic desperation they witnessed in northern Native communities was neither inevitable nor excusable. Drawing a forceful contrast between white and Aboriginal lives, they compared rising consumption in the south with Aboriginal 'debt' in the North: Aboriginal families could barely afford flour, the most basic staple needed for sheer survival.[38] The poverty Buckley and others described was related in part to the crisis in fur: an increasingly unfavourable and competitive international market and declining prices for pelts sent fur production into a tailspin from which it never fully recovered.[39] For Native trappers, problems originating in the interwar and especially Depression years worsened the situation. White trappers continued to expand their catchment areas, infringing on traditional Native trapping grounds; moreover, as seasonal/casual work in the North was de-casualized, with whites filling jobs previously done by Native men in construction, rail, and forestry, Native families became more dependent on trapping in a time of declining fur prices.[40] However one added up the multiple jobs and state payments to trapping households, the actual cash income was Third World in its final tally: some families eked out an existence on $300 to $400 a year.

State and social-science perspectives on the family trapping economy contrasted sharply with those of Aboriginal peoples. 'Women's labour,' summarized a government funded study of Cumberland House in 1960, 'is very limited as only four or five are HBC store clerks and a few others domestics in white households.'[41] Métis and Indian women, however, offered alternative perspectives in which their labour was hardly limited and peripheral. As well as contributing intermittent or casual wages to the family economy, women were instrumental in the collection of country food; they trapped small animals, prepared game, picked berries, smoked fish, and so on – and country food was, by some estimates, a large percentage of the family's diet. Second, women's role in social reproduction was crucial to bush production. Caring for children, cooking, repairing trapping and fishing equipment, making snowshoes, imparting knowledge to daughters and sons about the work processes of fur production – all this and more was critical, though this work changed significantly as settlements became more sedentary. As well, women played an important role in the chain of fur production: they were often the skinners, making a saleable pelt from the trapped animal. Much of this work was unpaid, but without it, families could not have survived. One could argue, as Marxists have, that women's social-reproduction work was an essential aid to the creation of profit, since low wages were 'subsidized' for capital by Aboriginal peoples when their basic subsistence needs were realized through unpaid, familial-based labour.[42] Indeed, even classical political economists lauded the importance of proletarianized workers' 'self provisioning,' since they recognized that this meant the costs of workers' daily reproduction were not entirely paid through wages.[43]

Women's work roles in the production of fur changed over this period, largely due to pressure from the federal and provincial governments to centralize Aboriginal populations in settlements in order to provide education and other services. Families who wished to avoid residential schools or benefit from promised health services complied, though this was also the era of coerced relocations.[44] Oral histories and ethnographic accounts of women's roles in the interwar period indicate Aboriginal people spent considerable time on the moving work site of the trap line; however, during the 1950s and especially the 1960s, men were more likely to trap alone (though sometimes accompanied in the summer by the family) in a smaller circle around the settlements. Even if women did not spend time on the trap line, they still did much of the skinning, preparing pelts for sale to the Hudson's Bay Company (HBC) or other companies. Some also worked directly for the local HBC post: at one northern Saskatchewan post, women received two to five cents for each muskrat skinned.[45]

In the post–Second World War period, Aboriginal women had no choice but to find more wage work to add to declining trapping and fishing income. They worked as clerks in HBC stores, cooks in construction camps, filleters in fish plants, waitresses in local restaurants or hotels, and as ward aides in hospitals. While cognizant of how meagre the total income was from this multiple-occupation family economy, women interviewed for oral history projects were anxious to stress the virtues of hard work and self-reliance, along with the benefits of learning labour as a cooperative family venture. As one woman remembered, this was 'dignified survival and communal living.'[46] In recalling the trapping economy, another Métis woman noted, 'We grew up learning various kinds of labour,' even though these did not necessarily involve remuneration. Women in her family, for example, emptied traps for her father while he worked on the railroad in the winter.[47] As trapping declined, some Aboriginal peoples lamented a past of economic independence and cultural dignity: a northern Métis woman recalled that she had been brought up knowing how to trap animals and use firearms by her father, who gave her 'ten traps to look after when she was ten ... He taught me to keep my dignity and accept nothing from the white man.'[48] Anthropologists at the time did fear that the shift from trapping and fishing to low-wage jobs had 'other than economic' consequences: trapping on the land was tied to a cosmology that was part and parcel of cultural life. Encouraging families to abandon trapping so that women could work as waitresses or men could combine welfare with intermittent road work thus resulted in not only economic poverty, but also a poverty of the spirit. Notions of social value and meaning attached to work could not be so easily and quickly transformed.[49]

Some observers at the time did recognize that the production of fur pelts was not an individual enterprise but a family one, and they were particularly concerned with the disintegrative effects of permanent settlement on the Native household as a unit of production.[50] Yet anthropologists also mused that settled life would benefit women, as they would have less arduous work, and more independence and leisure. Local economies varied far too much across the prairies to offer this general, optimistic view; for impoverished areas, the crisis of fur production was far more likely to result in social dislocation, not necessarily an easier life for women.[51] Even recent writing assumes a 'male provider' family model in trapping, which was then undermined by state nuclearization policies. While women's work raising children was undisturbed by nuclearization, argues David Quirling, Native men experienced declining prestige, status, and self-esteem as they lost their 'provider' role, resulting in 'dysfunctional' family breakdown and violence.[52]

The discourse of the male hunter-trapper-provider permeated business commentary as well. Hudson's Bay Company traders in the provincial prairie North usually dealt directly with Aboriginal men, designated in their minds as the heads of households in fur-producing families. Despite this masculinist point of view, HBC records disclose evidence of women's labour. Women, they recorded, remained in the bush working on the trap line while men came into the post for supplies; HBC men then complained to the government that the men should be able to cash the government family-allowance cheque, since the reigning system did not 'take into account the Indian way of life.'[53] As well as hiring women to prepare pelts, HBC traders also employed a 'family package' of labour to work at their posts; this involved women doing cleaning, cooking, or making clothes for the traders, though family wages were generally paid to the husband/father. While some traders were quick to assume that Aboriginal women looked for ways to escape work, they were less than supportive when women took the initiative as economic agents in their own respect, in one case rejecting a request by a woman for a post canoe so she could do her own fishing. The HBC men at the Nelson River post in Manitoba seemed especially perturbed when a woman tried to set up a rival trading post. They noted dismissively that she had to 'hire a man to drive her bombardier,' and, with some relief, that debt was doing her business in.[54]

Generally, however, women were not independent producers of fur: they worked with male kin to prepare pelts for sale. Their particular skill set should not be underestimated. The price attached to a pelt included how well it was prepared without flaws, wrinkles, or inordinate stretching. Cree women, indicated one source, used a 'frost drying' method of pelt preparation that led to 'larger cash returns' on the pelts. After skinning a beaver open, they had to carefully cut around all limbs and openings, sew these tiny openings shut with even stitches, wash the pelt, then stretch it on a home-made sapling hoop stretcher that let the air circulate freely, with no uneven stretching or wrinkling. After the pelt was hung out in freezing temperatures, it was ready for another scraping, thawing, a series of lathering and cleanings, and a re-stretching into its final form.[55] My short précis of the work process – omitting some steps – indicates a high level of skill that, if performed in an urban context by men, would have likely been described as impressively artisanal. However, because women's skill was integrated into the family economy, described as 'traditional' and a cultural carry-over from the past, it was not valued in the same way.

Many families combined fishing with trapping, especially in Manitoba, though Aboriginal fishing was also experiencing problems due to the increased commercialization of this resource. The contributions of women to fishing were not unlike those in fur: they looked after some of the tools of the trade, such as net repair, but also went out with husbands and families during the fish season, caring for the family, and aiding with the preparation of the catch, either for country food or subsequent sale (or both). As one federal agent near Oxford House reported, women caught all the fish 'for the table,' though men participated in the 'commercial side of the industry.'[56] In her oral history, Mary Whiteway recalled going out on the boat with her husband, watching his lines, and helping to pull the fish in; later, she worked with a large boiler in a shed, canning fish.[57] Even after nuclearization, families often worked together in fish camps for an intense period over the summer. Hilda, born in 1950, described her family's summer routine at a community fish camp: men brought the catch back to the women, who iced the fish in sheds where ice from the winter had been saved with moss coverings.[58] As one Manitoba Métis woman put it, fishing was a 'family project for two months of the summer' that families combined with taking in some country food, ducks and game, for the winter.[59]

Women involved in fur and fishing might also contribute to the family economy by making clothes for the local white traders, or by producing handicrafts such as rugs, hats, and moccasins; these were then traded or sold to various middlemen as part of a local 'doorstep economy.'[60] In the 1950s and 1960s, as more wage labour was added to this mixture, women's lives were characterized by more mobility and variety in work, with jobs, largely in the service sector, interspersed with work in the home. Outside of the family economy, women were likely to encounter more intensive racism. One Métis woman started working for a local farmer in the 1940s, then moved to a job in a local sanitarium, and later transferred to a hospital, where she received room and board. After working at home to raise children, she laboured in hotels in the kitchen, and then worked as a cook in the kitchen of a community club. It was here that she remembers a local health inspector demanding to see her hands, assuming that she was 'dirty' due to the 'colour of her skin.' 'I bet we are a hell of a lot cleaner than a restaurant in the city,' she told him.[61]

Northern Aboriginal men and women were well aware that trapping and fishing were in trouble. Native testimony and submissions to the 1947–8 Senate and House of Commons Joint Committee on the *Indian Act* made pleas for economic protection and development. They insisted that Aboriginal treaties and trapping rights be protected, and asked for aid to set up cooperatives (for instance, for fur farming), capital to outfit Aboriginal fishers with better boats and nets, and training so that northern Indians could be hired for public works, forestry, and Indian Affairs jobs.[62] While few women signed their names to any briefs, they occasionally sent letters, stressing the need for *community* economic support: in one case, a Manitoba woman invoked her role as mother to make her point: 'My main reason for writing is, it frightens me at time [*sic*] when I look at my three children when I don't see anything here that will save them from sickness and health ... We need [help] for our children. [We have n]o cows, no milk, no gardens, no vegetables, no health rules, no bathing, nothing to use to clean their teeth. No school to attend, no teacher ... We get plenty of fur but very unreasonable prices for the furs and the cost of living is rising at an alarming rate ... We don't make enough money to have a proper diet for the family.'[63]

Aboriginal speakers before the joint committee did not denounce the cyclical nature of their economy, as much as they decried the poverty that increasingly defined their multiple-occupation existence. Politicians listening, however, often assumed that Aboriginals were now faced with an either/or choice: traditional trapping or modern work roles. The fur trade was associated with bygone ways, and trapping supposedly prevented the development of modern work habits necessary for permanent employment. Many white politicians and social scientists appearing before the joint committee offered largely 'cultural' explanations for Native economic problems: 'sharing' in Indian cultures militated against upward mobility; Indians only lived for today, not tomorrow; and Indians needed to adopt the accumulative ethos of 'saving' for the future.[64] Indians, in other words, needed to internalize the ideological rules of the capitalist game – a prescription echoing previous generations of policymakers and commentators since the late nineteen century.

State efforts to aid economic development imagined male breadwinners as the answer; women's wage work was seen as ancillary. Indian Agents reported that some women secured the local contract to drive school buses, but this was obviously a seasonal, part-time job.[65] The production of Indian handicrafts was also offered up as a panacea especially suited to women, and their handicraft work was encouraged by missionaries and the state. Yet the amounts invested by the latter in handicraft development were paltry; ultimately, Indian Affairs admitted that only 'minor income' would result.[66] When one project for a garment factory was proposed for a Manitoba reserve, the Indian Agent dismissed this as rather useless, not only because it was 'low wage' labour, but because only women would be employed.[67]

In contrast, it was hoped that the corporate capital developing the North would offer waged employment to trappers and fishers, though it was soon clear that white workers were far more likely to be hired.[68] A number of federal relocation projects tried to move male Aboriginal breadwinners into permanent jobs in lumber cutting or mining.[69] Some IA officers did understand the crucial role women's domestic labour played in the success of these ventures. 'If Leo's wife can care more efficiently for the family,' wrote one such officer, 'he can work longer hours in the bush [lumber cutting].' In essence, this was an implicit acknowledgment that women's unpaid labour subsidized capital's cost of reproducing labour power.[70] Placement officers also recognized the importance of decent housing and household equipment for families, but some felt compelled to inspect Native women's work in the home. Surveillance slid easily into moral regulation similar to that visited upon welfare recipients. Marital or home problems were recorded as potential threats to men's fragile work habits. The ideal Aboriginal homemaker 'kept a clean house ... and [did] a family wash twice a week.' In contrast to the 'backward' Indians who refused to save, she also put money away for 'an electric iron and meat grinder.' Unsuitable for relocation, however, were a man and woman living 'common law,'[71] a sign that moral laxity had already set in. Morality was not simply about sexuality: it was seen as inseparable from economic 'initiative'[72] and the properly assumed work roles of male breadwinner and female homemaker.

Economic pressures on Native families also led to migrations in search of work. In the case of sugar-beet work, this migration was initially regulated by the federal state. Indian Affairs' promotion of sugar-beet work illustrates how an interventionist state perpetuated 'cycle employment,' even though politicians and policymakers talked about the virtues of permanent employment for Native peoples. Aboriginal peoples were pushed into seasonal sugar-beet work in the 1950s because the state saw them as particularly suited for migrant, seasonal, physical, low-paid work; moreover, bureaucrats knew the practices of kin-based labour – associated with fur and fish – could be incorporated into the regime of agricultural work, since this had already been the practice in agricultural migrations across the US border.[73] Once again, a male breadwinner figured prominently in the state's imagined workforce, rendering women's essential labour invisible.[74]

Aboriginal beet harvesting involved Manitoba Native peoples moving from the north to the south of the province, and to Alberta and southern Ontario; a second migration moved from northern Saskatchewan and central Alberta to the southern Alberta sugar-beet fields near Lethbridge. With as many as 1000 to 2500[75] workers migrating to the Alberta fields each year, this was the largest managed group migration of First Nations workers orchestrated by the state. Aboriginal workers in the Alberta fields had been preceded by European immigrants in the interwar period, and Japanese internees and POWs during the Second World

War. In Alberta, even Aboriginal peoples residing near the Lethbridge fields generally avoided this work, claiming it was 'a back breaking job with little reward.'[76] Similarly, when Ontario needed beet workers, Manitoba Aboriginals were seen as the answer, since 'this work is not considered acceptable to most of the labouring class in southern Ontario and no more attractive to the Indians of that region.'[77] Beet work was obviously a job that people with choices did not choose.

The sugar-beet migration, first suggested by Indian Affairs, was overseen by the Federal-Provincial Farm Labour Committee (FPFLC), aided by Canada Manpower Centres, Indian Agents, and Indian Affairs placement officers. Beet growers and their associations also had significant input, though they were initially wary of Indian labour: well into the 1950s, the growers asked the government why, with 'improved economic conditions'[78] in Europe, they could not secure the white European immigrant families they desired. Indian Affairs persistently promoted the value of Indian labour, even though its own agents in the field sent mixed reports to Ottawa on the outcome for the workers. Some individuals and families were willing to return next year, said a Manitoba agent, but others would not, since 'earnings were not as high as expected in view of the long hours and drudgery,' continuous employment was impossible, and the work was 'dull and uninteresting.'[79] The lack of unemployment insurance for agricultural work also dissuaded Native participation.

In Alberta, two groups of Native workers were used: those sponsored by the FPFLC and a growing number of 'freelancers' who came on their own. Men with families were actively recruited, but women without men were screened out, put in a category with other 'unemployables' and 'poor workers.'[80] In the first few years, women tried to participate, often in groups of women with small children, but they were deemed 'impossible to place' by the state and growers, presumably because of the smaller amount of acreage they could cover and shortages of housing. Not only were single women barred, but state officials and growers were adamant that pregnant women, especially those without 'male attendants,' stay at home, otherwise, they would be medical 'problems' to manage.[81] While pregnant women's inability to work was the main issue, the state and growers also complained about the presence of 'welfare' cases in their midst, whether this was hospitalized workers, unmarried abandoned women, fathers in jail, or pregnant women. A completely unencumbered labour force was the goal; this meant that the 'messier' work of social reproduction, as well as the welfare and medical needs of

Figure 13   'Workers sit down to lunch during sugar beet harvest.' (Photographer Nicholas Morant. LAC, NFB, PA116108)

families, would be assumed within Native peoples' home reserves – surely an economic aid to those buying Aboriginal labour.

As Ron Laliberte and Vic Satzewich argue, the state used both 'coercive' and 'paternalistic' measures to create the 'sponsored' workforce. One of the most effective (and later controversial) coercive measures was the cessation of welfare payments as a means of forcing families to accept sugar-beet work.[82] While ample archival sources indicate this tactic was employed, especially in Saskatchewan reserves, a fairly cautious investigation in 1970 by organized labour and some Native-rights groups claimed concrete, quotable evidence of this practice did not exist.[83] The state and growers also utilized paternalist recruiting tools, such as subsidized transportation to the site, hostel and housing accommodation (though critics later claimed it was substandard), and, in Alberta's case, a free rodeo trip.

Failure of the Ontario growers to provide similar entertainment was cited as one reason for their less successful experience with Aboriginal workers. While workers understandably wanted to build a social life around their temporary work site (and some remember migration as a 'community' time),[84] the tendency of white observers to equate Indians' migration solely with socializing (and with a tendency to 'blow' their earnings on sprees) seems overstated, a reflection of negative ideas of Indian work habits. One such study characterized the migration as downright pleasurable: 'Some [Indian] fellows from Pelican Narrows said they only came to see the country … [and join in] a fast way to make a few bucks … It would also appear to be a social event for some: a time for renewing and making acquaintances, for romancing and arranging marriages, and, it seems for a few, a time of orgies.'[85] If Aboriginal families wanted to have a party, I doubt they needed to travel 1000 miles to do so – while also working daily on their hands and knees.

Indeed, what kind of work was this? Almost everyone agreed it was tedious, arduous, physical labour: workers were responsible for rows of plants that they thinned and weeded by hand multiple times. Although the industry suggested machine thinners were the modern 'answer' to labour problems, it is likely that hand thinning actually provided a larger, more uniform crop.[86] Aboriginal workers had a set contract with the grower, specifying the price per row. Work was intermittent, rain could easily disrupt the work cycle, and some wages were held back until the job was done to the farmer's satisfaction (one way to keep a captive labour force). The process for addressing disagreements over wages paid was overseen by the growers, hardly a neutral group. Sugar-beet farmers, to be sure, were caught in their own economic squeeze, captive to one large sugar processor and an unfavourable international market. As a result, they were dependent on government handouts, direct and indirect, to subsidize their industry.

Yet the growers extolled the virtues of self-reliance when speaking about their labour force. In 1969–70, when labour and left-leaning writers tried to expose the exploitation involved in sugar-beet work, growers countered that they should be commended for offering Natives the opportunity to 'leave the confines of [the] reserve ... [to] get training experience' and 'better themselves.' One family was used as the model for a successful 'move into the mainstream': the father had worked in the industry for years, the mother now hung her 'white wash' out on the line, and the children were learning working-class occupations.[87] It is true that some families attempted to use sugar-beet earnings as a strategy to move out of poverty, but the notion that employers were doing Native labour a *favour*, when other employers were 'not willing to absorb Aboriginal labour' was paternalist to say the least. Nor was this claim limited to the growers: other employers in Alberta were celebrated for similar 'courage' in hiring Indians.[88]

Both the growers' profits and the incentive for workers to migrate relied heavily on kin-based labour, seldom analysed critically at the time. Indian agents noted that many men 'brought their families' to 'increase their earning power,'[89] but in fact, women and children were required on the team in order to make good wages. As one Native family told an interviewer, 'If the whole family cannot work, [we] will be unable to make much more than a bare livelihood.'[90] It was the spectre of child labour and truancy that finally sparked a controversy about family labour after critical media exposés were aired in the late 1960s. A commissioned study on the question of Native schooling, particularly the interviews with workers that formed part of this investigation, made it clear that male breadwinners were not the norm.[91] Some women interviewed, such as Ruby Ahenakew from the Sandy Lake Band, worked in the fields to begin with, but then later switched to caring for their children; in conditions of poor housing, with few pieces of furniture or appliances and lacking extended kin, women's reproductive labour was undoubtedly made more difficult. Other women primarily laboured in the fields, or combined field and domestic labour. In one interview, Thomas Lachance indicated that his welfare had been cut off, yet bush work was too hard for him at his age. He and his wife were thus compelled to work the sugar-beet fields. Since they 'could not earn enough by themselves,' their children worked alongside them. They did not want to leave the children at home as there was 'too much drinking,' though Lachance added he would 'stay home if he could support his family somehow.'[92] Far from cavalierly 'palming off' their children on relatives at home, as one reserve councillor commented in the 1960 joint Senate-House committee hearings,[93] women beet workers who left children on reserves were clearly worried about their welfare. They faced an impossible dilemma: how could they choose between economic need and their children's schooling, between doing their own motherwork or entrusting it to others? Some must have known only too well that children left behind might be removed by child-welfare authorities.

While women's work may have been subsumed under men's, Indian Affairs did implicitly admit it was important to the success of sugar-beet migrations. When women were absent, as they were in the Ontario migrations, the scheme was considered less successful. Many of the single male workers were in hostels, where less than ideal living conditions and tensions between 'Sioux and Salteaux groups' resulted in 'disturbances and damage to their living quarters.' Preference, recommended a Manitoba IA director, should be given to 'families, not single men in the future ... with at least 50% of the family able to work.'[94] The single male beet workers had actually earned less and less over time, and, according to IA, became demoralized and unmanageable, since they were 'isolated from the non-Indian community' and there was little supervision or entertainment offered. It is possible that Indian Affairs saw the presence of women and children as a stabilizing influence, keeping the men moral and labouring diligently, but there was also an economic bottom line: women and children's daily labour was necessary to make the total earnings enticing enough to attract Aboriginal families into this work.[95]

Aboriginal Concerns and State Responses: Labour Placement Programs

In the Senate–House of Commons Joint Committee hearings on Indian Affairs in 1959–60, economic betterment and wage labour were repeated themes in Aboriginal briefs and testimony. Aboriginal submissions sometimes employed the same analogies as the *Indian News* to make their case for economic aid, pointing to individual Native success stories such as the stenographer and nurse daughters of one chief.[96] Their proposals for economic development, however, ranged broadly, and included the protection of hunting and fishing rights, aid to small businesses, make-work projects on reserves, and 'a comprehensive plan to educate and train Indians so they can be employed off reserves.'[97] A gendered division of labour was taken for granted, with home aide, clerical, and nursing jobs cited as excellent employment options for women. Both Aboriginal women's and white lobby groups such as the Alberta Farm Women also wanted more, and better, home economics courses for Aboriginal women.[98] Still, taken together, Aboriginal submissions envisaged quite comprehensive and holistic answers to their economic problems that combined the protection of land-based production, the diversification of local economies, and the provision of more waged and salaried labour; respecting the treaties and training for new occupations were quite compatible in their view.

However, a lack of imagination, as well as persisting paternalism and parsimony, continued to hamper IA's attempts to deal with structural economic problems faced by Aboriginal peoples. Contradictions abounded. 'The primary economy of Northern Indians,' stated one Manitoba IA bureaucrat, 'will remain the development of fish and fur,'[99] and some programs were devised to bolster Aboriginal resource extraction. Yet other studies suggested that these economies could no longer support the Aboriginal population. It is not surprising, then, that a sense of fatality about failing 'traditional' economies was apparent in the Senate-House Committee hearings. Some politicians asked how the government could help 'dying' reserves, and the minister responsible, Ellen Fairclough, worried that reserves could become spaces for those who had 'failed' in the outside world. Why can't Natives be more like 'immigrants,' asked one politician, pulling themselves up by their own bootstraps.[100] In contrast, however paternalist Indian Affairs was, some Indian Agents at least recognized that lack of funding, not lack of initiative, was one reason for underdeveloped reserve economies.[101]

By the 1960s, the state increasingly touted 'full-time jobs, a steady income,' and 'integration into the industrial economy of Canada' as the solution to Aboriginal poverty.[102] Indeed, IA welfare policy had long been concerned with 'turning Indians into moral, thrifty workers.' IA was undoubtedly influenced by the prevailing social-science research on Aboriginal peoples, which was also communicated to the broader public through cultural venues ranging from magazines to NFB films documenting First Nations' necessary transition to the modern ways of a wage economy.[103] Anthropologist Harry Hawthorn's two studies are an interesting case in point, since IA must have read them selectively: he condemned casual agricultural labour such as beet work, arguing that its 'substandard pay and living conditions, along with the disorganization of family life' led to the creation of 'a lower caste' of labour.[104] Impervious to this critique, IA continued the sugar-beet program until 1981.

Hawthorn's second study condemned the 'assimilation and integration' of Indians as a state objective, but in fact many of his recommendations encouraged the integration of Aboriginal peoples into the industrial capitalist economy. This strategy, he believed, would aid, not destroy Aboriginal cultures, stemming the tide of 'personal and social disorganization plaguing Native communities.'[105] Hawthorn's anthropological accent on cultural preservation, however, was not necessarily embraced by IA, more inclined to favour integration as a means of replacing problematic Indian cultural practices with new ones better suited to the 'modern' workplace. Even Hawthorn tended to fall back on a model that posited a linear progression from failing subsistence economies to jobs within industrial capitalism; progress was equated with higher-paying wage labour, enhanced skills and training, and acceptance of new forms of work discipline.

Hawthorn's contention that traditional Aboriginal peoples who engaged in seasonal or cycle employment found modern, permanent wage labour a culturally alien concept was also influential at the time. In the joint-committee hearings, some Aboriginal groups framed their submissions with similar language, claiming they had been recently wrenched from traditional 'nomadic' lives and pushed into the modern 'atomic age' – and thus needed 'special help' to attain equality with other groups.[106] A Saskatchewan Aboriginal organization used the same cultural rationale offered by its own provincial government for Native peoples' inability to integrate into the wage economy: 'The employment *personality* of the Indian makes it difficult for him to adapt to the regular routine of daily employment ... a hangover from their nomadic life.'[107]

Unfortunately, a deterministic cultural reading of material life could become translated into prejudices impugning all Aboriginal work habits. In Winnipeg, for example, an advisory council on Indian employment, with provincial and federal authorities, labour, business, and community groups all represented, was set up to integrate Indians 'as individuals' into urban jobs as reserve economies 'were failing.' A garment manufacturer assured the first meeting that there were many jobs available in his industry if only Indian women would come to work on time and not quit at a moment's notice. Trade unionists agreed. Indian women, a union representative claimed, could be absorbed into the needle trades, dry cleaning, and other service jobs if only their work habits and 'social adjustment' improved.[108]

Hawthorn's thinking, like that of Indian Affairs, also took for granted a male breadwinner family, though he conceded that women's labour might be added to the family income, either in very poor or more aspiring circumstances.[109] He also surmised that women's training in clerical work might actually place them in more favourable positions in urban contexts, and indeed this was true for Indian Affairs' one in-house training program. However, other placement strategies and programs dominated the IA agenda. One of its long-standing employment solutions for Aboriginal women, before and after the Second World War, was domestic service. Since domestic work had long been associated with the necessary 'civilization' of Nature women, it is perhaps no surprise that some individuals wrote to the Indian Affairs Branch asking for an 'Indian girl' to work in their household. One wife of a civil servant from the Department of Finance, living in tony Rockliffe, wrote directly to the ministry in Ottawa, asking for an Indian maid. Although officials had to politely tell her that they could not find a maid for her, they did place other Aboriginal women in service.[110] Indian Agents and Regional Offices were also attempting to place young women in domestic positions. Girls coming out of residential schools were presumed to be especially well fitted for such work, since domestic training had been a central part of their education, and since they had done unpaid household work in the school or had worked in domestic placements during their summers.[111] What IA saw as the training benefits of residential schools are now seen in a different light: since the schools left some students with emotional scars as well as a limited education, they could also play a role in limiting, not expanding, women's employment options.[112]

The Calgary IA office, for example, had a domestic placement plan that paid women room and board for ten days in a city near their reserve so they could interview for domestic jobs. Domestic service was supposed to socialize young women to the world of wage labour, a first step towards other employment in service or factory jobs, though some IA bureaucrats also admitted it operated as a seasonal stopgap intended to supplement the 'meager' returns families received for trapping.[113] Despite the fact that, as some agents admitted, this was neither popular nor usually permanent work for women, domestic placements continued into the 1960s. Likely, some women used the program as a strategy to escape unemployment and surveillance by the Indian Agent on their reserves, or as the only means available to finance their urban migration in search of work. In its list of advertised achievements, IA pointed to its domestic courses in 'social living, clothes-making, buying and purchasing food and use of home equipment'[114] for Indian girls in agricultural schools in Saskatchewan and Alberta. Training for boys, by contrast, related to farming methods and equipment.[115] Minister Jack Pickersgill saw this as preparation for jobs as 'farm labourers and domestic workers,' and perhaps, he mused, if boys and girls went to agricultural school together 'we might stimulate some of them to get married and stay on farms where there are houses provided.'[116] His attempts to play Cupid likely had more to do with creating a casual labour supply than they did with romance.

The Superintendent of IA Welfare Services also promoted domestic jobs as a natural bulwark against female juvenile delinquency, keeping young women off the dangerous streets. The Calgary office was pleased when urban Indian girls were close enough to rural reserves to go home on weekends, away from the 'danger spots of the city.' Women presumed to be 'promiscuous' or poor workers – presumably designated so by their Indian Agents – were discouraged from entering the program, as the 'urban environment' would supposedly accentuate their bad habits.[117] Like earlier generations of working-class women, these domestic workers were viewed as morally fragile, always susceptible to the 'wrong kind of influence.'[118] However, race as well as class shaped the image of urban, working-class Aboriginal women. Their presence in the city was viewed as alien to the natural Indian character; they were literally out of place in urban spaces, or worse, 'trespassers' on white space, and thus 'fair game' for reform, removal, or retribution.[119] 'They are displaced persons in their own land,' wrote one well-intentioned reformer, 'trying to bridge the gap between generations when their proud race *was left behind.*'[120] The image of racial primitivism may have inspired the sympathy of some reformers, but it also encouraged contempt from others and, at worst, served as an invitation to discrimination and violence.

Aboriginal women new to the city did face economic and social problems, including difficulty finding jobs and housing, low wages, and isolation from their families; Métis women were also disadvantaged by their lack of access to IA funds for education. In many large cities, Aboriginal activists, in alliances with white supporters, created Friendship Centres, with programs intended to aid newcomers to the city. Aboriginal women's volunteer labour was instrumental in creating these organizations, which were also dedicated to revaluing Aboriginal identity and heritage.[121] The ability of such groups to address unemployment, education, and work issues, however, was limited. The same was true for white reformers. In Winnipeg, the United Church employed a social worker to help 'Indian

girls' locate jobs and other necessities such as clothing. Female church
volunteers were linked up with the girls as 'friends' and mentors, yet the
language of moral reclamation they used was reminiscent of earlier efforts of white, middle-class women to 'save' working-class girls: 'Beer par-
lours and dance halls are poor substitutes for homes when girls are
lonely and homesick,' intoned one reformer.[122]

Some state solutions to women's need for jobs were endorsed by
Aboriginal organizations. When the Indian Association of Alberta testi-
fied before the 1959 joint committee, it urged the government to en-
large its new labour placement program as the few placement officers
could barely begin to address the countless people needing training and
employment. Launched in 1957, this labour-placement program initially
hired officers in four large cities (three in the West) to provide employment counselling, arrange on-the-job training, find jobs, and facilitate
the relocation of Aboriginal men and women to either 'general' (casual)
or 'permanent' jobs.[123] While these efforts were referred to in shorthand
as 'placement programs,' relocation was generally involved, reflecting
IA's feeling that Aboriginals would and should increasingly move to
towns and cities in search of jobs, leaving behind reserves in decline.[124]
IA wanted to support this economic transition, seeing it as a more thorough cultural and political transformation. Young Indians, claimed one
report approvingly, are searching out urban employment, as they want
to move from 'the Indian mode of life to responsible citizenship,'[125] a
clear suggestion these were antithetical. Placement officers were to liaise
with other state agencies such as the National Employment Service, as
well as unions, industries, community organizations, and welfare groups,
to locate jobs and place Indians in 'urban-type' employment that would
expand the range of occupations available to them.[126] Loans and assistance with relocation, room and board, transportation, training, and in-
cidentals was often provided. Knowing that Indian women often faced
'prejudice' in the rental market, IA considered hostels for Indian girls,
but in the end thought it preferable for Native women to integrate with
other 'working-class girls' at the YWCA.[127]

There were some basic educational requirements and crucial character traits the placement officer was supposed to look for. Since urban
placements were assumed to involve stressful cultural adaptation, only
those with 'stable' personalities who were able to 'mix with non-Indians'
and withstand pressure without 'losing control or resorting to alcoholism' were to be selected.[128] Particular hope was placed on the young,
probably seen to be malleable in character, better able to integrate into

the white world. 'With considerable guidance and training,' wrote one Alberta report, 'this younger element could eventually integrate into the non-Indian communities and labour field but this will take patience and time.'[129] Integration, in other words, was another word for assimilation, a process to be aided through the careful surveillance of personality, character, and emotion – in Foucauldian terms, an exercise in governmentality and the management of conduct.

Placement officers put considerable stress on jobs for women in the white- and pink-collar sectors, and, to a lesser extent, domestic service. Hospital work, hairdressing, and clerical work were three hopeful areas for female employment. A small group of aspiring Aboriginal hairdressers were offered subsidized training; in Winnipeg, these women attended the Manitoba Technical Institute or the private Marvel Beauty School, then they were placed in salon jobs in various Manitoba cities. Two of the *Indian News*'s 'success stories' featured Manitoba hairdressers, and there were commonalities in the narratives IA presented: both women had migrated to the city from reserves, both relayed their dreams of property ownership, and both were provided with financial and job placement aid by IA. Readers were also told that Louise, a young woman from the North and a graduate of a residential school, had adjusted to the city with appropriately moral pastimes: she joined a 'local church group' and lived in a boarding house, where she was 'kindly' welcomed.[130] For some Aboriginal women, work in hairdressing was a step up the employment ladder from domestic work, but it was not a job that could easily sustain a breadwinner's household.[131] As Maria Campbell remembers in her autobiography, *Halfbreed*, she got a job in a beauty salon, but within two weeks it was clear that 'wages were so poor' she could never support herself and her children. She had no choice but to head to the welfare office.[132]

The number of women trained to be hairdressers, however, paled beside those who ended up in service jobs or the old standby, domestic work. Jean Lagasse's extensive survey of Métis and Indian employment in Winnipeg found that the largest groups of women who came to the city found their first job in restaurant kitchen work (38 per cent) or housework (38 per cent), with a much smaller group (4 per cent) in nurse's aide positions. In turn, most unemployed Aboriginal women in the city had come *from* these low-paid jobs. Indian women's wages put them at the bottom of the economic scale, followed closely by Métis women – statistics that remain similar today.[133] Giving a lie to notions of Indians' cultural inability to adapt to wage labour, Lagasse also found a higher than average labour-force participation rate for Aboriginal women:

55 per cent of Indian women and 44 per cent of the Métis women surveyed were working outside the home. Not surprisingly, a family economy of pooled wages existed: in over half of all the households there
were at least two adults employed outside the home.[134] Working Aboriginal families were squeezing by with few consumer luxuries (only 27 per
cent of Indians owed televisions) and little ability to save, not the least
because some were also aiding kin on reserves.

Lagasse called for special social support for Métis and Indian families,
such as dedicated housing and education programs, and an end to racial
discrimination, but he also relied on liberal individualist views of opportunity and social mobility. 'Adequate opportunities' for Aboriginals to
'share in the social and economic benefits' of society, not unlike the opportunities offered to immigrants, was the most rational policy in his
view. Like Hawthorn, he tended to see permanent, skilled work for men
as *the* solution. Aboriginal aspirations and discriminatory employment
barriers simply had to be altered so that Native peoples could integrate
into the working class. In such a schema, women's economic fate was
largely determined by their ties to men – despite Lagasse's own evidence
of their high labour-force participation rate. While recognizing that
Aboriginal women had their own employment dreams, such as nursing
jobs,[135] Lagasse mused that they – unlike Aboriginal men – could always
marry a white man and therefore 'move up' the social ladder. Some
urban Aboriginal women, he said, already 'pass' for white (using the
nomenclature of race associated with Blacks in the United States), having erased their Aboriginal heritage in order to meld into white society.
Such individuals either had the education and skills to make it in an
urban environment, or the will to seek out 'the more secure life of the
non-Indian middle class'; in any case, these women didn't need special
programs since they 'already fit into urban Canada as contributing members.'[136] Who, then, were the 'non-contributing' members? Women who
valued their heritage but were still working in a restaurant washing
dishes? Lagasse may have seen the 'passing' women as successful because
of their racial integration, but the response of one woman interviewed
who had 'passed' as Native was telling, if not horrific: 'My husband would
kill me' if he knew my true identity, she said.[137]

One of Lagasse's final recommendations concerning education was
that girls should be taught typing, stenography, and other commercial
skills in school. Business and commercial colleges were seen as important stepping stones to truly good employment for Aboriginal women,
and it was not simply Indian Affairs that lauded women's incursion into

clerical jobs. Gladys Bear, a columnist for the Winnipeg Friendship Centre's *Prairie Call*, also used her column to extol the successes of Aboriginal women who had secured steady jobs with employers such as Bell Telephone. One of IA's in-house placement programs did foster white-collar work training. In 1960 this program was developed at the cost of a mere $10,000, though IA lobbied strenuously to have the treasury board of Indian Affairs increase the figure to $25,000 so more than twenty-two people could be enrolled.[138] Status Indians with high-school or commercial-college education were given jobs in IA's local and regional agencies in order to gain employment experience, letters of reference, and extra job training. The purpose was to prepare as many people as possible, as quickly as possible, for permanent employment in industry, commerce, or government – and the program was justified using this language of economic efficiency, equal opportunity, and integration. Workers received a weekly allowance but not actual wages, so they were ineligible for unemployment insurance, certainly a downside of the program.

Since clerical jobs were heavily favoured, the program was theoretically biased towards young women workers; indeed, placement officers told one interviewer that 'the only consistently marketable group of job applicants are the Grade 12 women.'[139] And there was no question that these individuals were supposed to be single women. When one married woman wanted to participate, the local superintendent had to consult IA superiors, since the program was not intended for 'married women whose husbands were working.' He did plead her case: she faced 'family insecurity' as the husband was unemployed, so she wanted to be 'independent should the need arise,' able to support her family. While the local IA agency was solidly behind this sensible request, there is no evidence as to whether Ottawa bent the rules in response.[140]

The IA in-house training program assumed that young women could be integrated into permanent white-collar work, given the right education, incentives, and experience. Women in the program were usually required to try the federal civil-service exam as a means of encouraging them to move beyond the protective safety of the IA agency office. Although many women lacked the typing speed necessary for the civil-service exam, it was also their 'habits, shyness, [and] appearance' that were being assessed and managed. Assessments of the trainees repeatedly cited the problem of shyness and urged the inculcation of self-confidence if the women were to become integrated into the mainstream world of work: indeed, one IA promotional pamphlet explained to the public that the inherently 'non-aggressive' Indian 'character' meant these job seekers were 'unlikely to sparkle in a job interview.[141] There may certainly have been cultural differences that accounted for such shyness, though lack of education and proficiency in English, and the unfamiliarity of the office environment, may also have undermined these women's confidence.[142]

One problem with the labour placement programs was their limited reach. If the in-house program only aided 22 people a year, the larger labour placement program dealt with, at most, 500–600 people a year. This was not a comprehensive solution to unemployment. One critical assessment of 1968–9 placement statistics in Saskatchewan provided a dismal assessment of women's prospects: 79 per cent of the women could only obtain jobs as domestics or waitresses, and most women had to accept temporary not permanent positions. Placement officers supposedly tacitly helped employers fulfil provincial hiring targets, while in private interviews they admitted they did not think 'the vast majority of Indians employed would ... remain on the job.' As a result, this highly critical report claimed, some IA officers desperately 'adopted' certain 'promising' individuals or families, spending inordinate time trying to rid them of Indian 'traits' so they could integrate successfully into a respectable, white working-class life.[143] A less critical view might be extracted from census reports: although a substantial portion of Aboriginal women remained in service labour, there was a shift over the 1960s, as more moved into 'clerical' jobs, and fewer remained stuck in the service-work ghetto.[144]

While these labour placement programs were developing, an anxious discourse about the problem of the 'Indian in the City' was unfolding in state, social-science, social-work, and more popular venues.[145] The most pessimistic variant of this research was symbolized by studies of skid row that explored the subaltern cultures of Aboriginal poverty or offered critiques of 'old boy' networks of power and affluence within Aboriginal communities.[146] While this discussion about the Indian in the city is a topic unto itself, one aspect of it is especially relevant to Aboriginal women workers: the preoccupation with women as morally endangered or as purveyors of immorality. In the Lagasse report, for example, an 'interview' section that presented typical experiences of women coming to Winnipeg to work was excessively preoccupied with Native women's 'morality.' To be sure, men and alcohol were mentioned (in an effort to dispel negative images of Aboriginal drinking), and common-law marriage too was an issue. These unions, the report claimed, were frequent in *all* 'low class' populations; however, if Indians wanted to move up the social ladder, they would have to become respectable and get married.

Aboriginal women's sexuality was specifically discussed in many of the narratives the interviewers chose to feature – though filtered through the researchers' words, not those of the interviewees. One theme was the unfortunate discrimination that Aboriginal women faced in searching for work, which could be followed by a tragic downward spiral into crime. In one story, a young woman wishing to make good after getting into trouble as a teenager came to the city to find work in the needle trades. Despite her training in this area, she faced discrimination in her job search. The result: because she was easily led astray by companions, she was soon in conflict with the law again for prostitution. In another scenario, an 'unschooled girl' coming to the city to 'escape dreariness or hardship on the reserve discovers that her work as a maid puts her in a servant role and takes away her freedom.' 'She can try restaurant kitchen work,' and if she 'does not look Indian,' she may secure a factory sewing job, but trapped in low-paid, low-status work, she is faced with a difficult choice: to associate with other Indians whose social lives of questionable morals will prevent her upward mobility, or 'pass' and deny her background.[147]

Stories of naive Aboriginal women tricked, led, or forced into immoral lives paralleled 'white slave' stories circulating at the turn of the century in which working-class girls faced similar perils. Such accounts were also repeated to the later Royal Commission on the Status of Women.[148] While Aboriginal women's naivety was stressed, their 'promiscuity' was sometimes taken as a given. Such 'promiscuity' was equated with 'lower class' behaviour, but it 'differed' in that Aboriginal women seemed 'peculiarly' willing to sleep with men for the 'enjoyment of the relationship, or accommodation, rather than financial remuneration.' This 'willingness to have relationships with Caucasian men interested in sex rather than moral respect' made Indian women coming to the city to work especially vulnerable, claimed Lagasse's report. Even if couched in the language of concern, this image of an available, promiscuous Indian woman was a staple of racist ideology, and it became a licence for violence perpetrated against Aboriginal women. The Lagasse report might have claimed to be referring to class, but immorality was simultaneously constructed in racial terms. While decrying discrimination, on the one hand, the report thus perpetuated racist stereotypes, on the other. Any critique of Aboriginal women's imprisonment in low-wage job ghettos was compromised by recasting the key issue as one of 'morality.' Sexual regulation – and condemnation – was inextricably linked to material exploitation: the appropriation of Native women's labour cannot be separated from the expropriation of their sexual dignity.

Conclusion

This is one small part of the story of Aboriginal women's work in the post-war period. I could also have told the story of communities that continued to adapt to multiple forms of labour for survival, using the material and cultural resources at hand. I could have told the story of women coming to the city as migrant or commuting workers who developed effective strategies for survival, drawing on kin and community. I could have told the story of the establishment of organizations such as Friendship Centres, built with women's unpaid labour, and providing programs that would ultimately work against the state's assimilative programs. However, by concentrating on social-science writing and state policies, I have tried to emphasize that political choices were made that rested not only on cultural and racial assumptions, but also on assumptions about how the capitalist market should work, and, in fact, on the theory that it *did* work – for the better. Moreover, these political choices were a pale imitation of Aboriginal hopes and demands. Their vision of economic justice was more wide ranging, encompassing a program of economic development that ranged, broadly, from protection of their land to vocational and professional training for Aboriginal youth, while state-initiated programs were more narrowly designed, and thus ultimately unable to address the more pervasive economic and ideological legacies of colonialism.

While Aboriginal economic and social well-being varied considerably across the prairies, hardship and increasing dependency on the state were unmistakable in many northern areas. As Frank Tough argues in his study of northern Manitoba, the post-1945 period bore the legacy of underdevelopment that began in the interwar period, occasioned by changes to the fur trade, the dispossession of Aboriginal land title, and the expansion of resource industries. Contrary to the picture often painted at the time, there had not been a 'traditional' economy that was suddenly overcome by a 'modern' industrial wage economy, since Native peoples had for some time combined forms of wage and subsistence labour. However, the post-war period was characterized by the intensified 'integration of Native communities into the capitalist market on terms unfavourable to them.'[149] The social disruptions that resulted were accompanied by state interventions of a decidedly paternalist nature.

The increasingly interventionist role of the state in managing, reorienting, and reforming Aboriginal labour is thus an important theme in this period, and one that was fundamentally gendered, both in the conceptualization of the problem and in the creation of policy solutions. Informed in part by social-science studies of the time, but also by prevailing ideological images of the white, middle-class family, politicians and policymakers often assumed a male-breadwinner family as both the norm and the ideal. Women were seen as *ancillary* workers who worked when they were young and single, or brought in 'extra' money as handicraft producers. Moreover, the assumption that nuclearization simply made northern Métis and Indian women's lives easier ignored the ways in which the loss of their valued, skilled work on fur pelts or in fishing might have 'other than economic' repercussions for women's sense of value and well-being. Culture and work, as an earlier generation of labour historians argued, were dynamically interconnected; spatial and material changes in work were negotiated by workers with the cultural resources at hand, but economic upheaval might still be a destructive and damaging process.

State solutions to economic dependency took two general paths: on the one hand, there were relocation/labour programs to place male breadwinners in better-paid blue-collar jobs, and second, there was some (largely urban) job training in a small range of gender-specific jobs. The latter avenue involved both a continuation of earlier efforts to place Aboriginal women in domestic jobs as well as some new, though rather limited, programs to train them for pink- and white-collar work. It was probably in the latter category that some successes were attained. Still, state policy reinforced and reproduced lessons in gendered and racialized labour that left Indian and Métis women at the lower end of the employment ladder, where many remain today. The state's policy perspective on Aboriginal women workers and their appropriate place in the labour force bore some resemblance to its treatment of immigrants, such as the Dionne women; however, the positive celebration of these European women's culture was quite different from the state's image of Aboriginal women needing a cultural makeover. Non-Aboriginal women were similarly channelled into a very restricted range of sex-typed jobs by state employment policies, and working-class and poor white women experienced similar efforts to patrol and regulate their sexual morality. However, the moral and cultural explanations offered for Aboriginal women's supposed inability to adapt to wage labour, their poverty, or their criminalization were also racial arguments, even if they were dressed up as cultural difference. As a consequence, Aboriginal women were especially vulnerable to both material disadvantage and racist denigration as supposedly more primitive, backward, and promiscuous women, designations that also left them vulnerable to hostility and violence.

While scholarship has understandably focused on the *Indian Act*'s discriminatory classification of women's status, best exemplified by the 'marrying out' clause, the legislation, as Bonita Lawrence argues, was part of a much larger 'regulatory regime ... a way of seeing life ... that ultimately forms an entire conceptual territory on which knowledge is produced and shaped.' The state's image of women as ancillary workers in need of moral protection, and its active promotion of a patriarchal male-breadwinner model, were also ingredients of this regulatory regime; moreover, these ways of thinking, Lawrence adds, often come to 'permeate how Native peoples think of themselves ... [and] even [their] attempts to change the system itself.'[150]

Paradoxically, even though the state referred to male breadwinners, it promoted labour programs that actually relied on family labour, especially that of adult women. The sugar-beet program exemplifies this well. Women's work, both in caring for families and in the fields, was essential to a good economic return for Aboriginal families; however, state sources all but erased women's contribution, except when bureaucrats recorded their own attempts to keep single women out of these jobs. Both Aboriginal organizations and Indian Affairs were calling for better education, training, and permanent jobs, yet IA was pressing Aboriginal men and women into low-paid, seasonal agricultural work, historically reserved for those with few work choices, an indication of the resilience of a racialized ideology of appropriate work for Indians.

The case of beets, fur, and fish also underscore the importance of examining – in the vein of feminist political economy – both women's paid and unpaid work and the link between household and market economies. As the IA observer noted so astutely, if Leo's wife worked harder at home, the company would also get more 'value' from him. When work is redefined in broader terms that encompass social reproduction, Aboriginal women's labour becomes far more visible, though it is necessary for historians to read social-science, ethnographic, and state sources of the time against the grain, since a dominant discourse of the male trapper and male breadwinner permeates these documents so thoroughly.

Revaluing, even celebrating, women's crucial work roles in multi-occupational households, and their determined efforts to sustain themselves and their families in deteriorating economic conditions, is important, but again, this is only part of the story. Stressing Aboriginal agency and cultural persistence should not 'render capitalism invisible' or rule out a political-economy critique of exploitation. While women and men made difficult choices about survival, they did so, as Tough argues, within a larger framework of increasing economic dependency and the racial stratification of work.[151] Looking at adaptation is not enough; asking the classic political-economy question – 'Who benefits the most?' – is also important. The gendered and racialized division of labour experienced by Aboriginal women was inseparable from processes of capitalist accumulation and the contours of post-war economic development. Moreover, as radical Aboriginal critics pointed out in the 1960s and after, economic adaptations could also produce new inequalities within Aboriginal reserves and urban communities based on gender, family entitlement, or age.

By the late 1960s, Aboriginal activists were far more vocal in their critiques of Canadian state policies, the gender discrimination inherent in the *Indian Act*, and the church and state's long-standing pursuit of cultural assimilation, waged so tragically through the lives of children. While their use of the term 'internal colonialism' may not fit a fixed model, the *metaphor* is apt as a recognition of a historical relationship that involved dispossession, segregation, and violence, as well as the state's encouragement of a racialized and gendered labour force that, tragically, remains a fact of life today.

Chapter 7

Tackling the 'Problem' of the Woman Worker: The Labour Movement, Working Women, and the Royal Commission on the Status of Women

When the Royal Commission on the Status of Women (RCSW) began its cross-country hearings in 1968, much of the popular press was ready to gently – or not so gently – mock this public forum for women's views, complaints, and demands for equality. By the time the RCSW reported two years later, it had secured some grudging respect from journalists, not the least because the hearings brought to light countless personal examples of women's economic marginalization in Canadian society. Women's work for pay outside the home was one of the most important issues at stake for the commission: this topic assumed a central place in countless submissions as well as in the final report. This chapter uses the RCSW as a means of exploring changing and competing discourses about women and paid labour in the late 1960s, as well as the relationship between feminism and the labour movement. By looking not only at official union briefs and RCSW discussions, but also at the private letters submitted by women workers, we can see some seeds of discontent percolating below the supposedly serene surface of the post-war gender order.

In Canadian feminist historiography, the RCSW is often seen as a benchmark for feminist organizing, a 'watershed'[1] in the contemporary women's movement that supposedly ushered in 'second wave feminism.' While the RCSW did not, as some feminists have claimed, singularly 're-vive feminism,'[2] it represented both a transitional moment in which the cumulative impact of decades of economic and social change could be appraised, and a unique public space in which the meaning, experience, and political implications of women's labour could be debated. Moreover, throughout the next decade, the RCSW had a concrete impact on the shape of government legislation, and became a focal point of political organizing for liberal, labour, and socialist feminism.[3] In 1972, the

"Mum's out presenting a brief to. the Royal Commission on the Status of Women . . . "

Figure 14   Rusins cartoon, 1 October 1968. (Reproduced with permission of *The Ottawa Citizen*)

RCSW report was the catalyst for the creation of the National Action Committee on the Status of Women (NAC). NAC's 'liberal' feminist lobbying tactics and involvement in state programs did much to shape the public face of Canadian feminism, despite contending social-democratic visions within the organization that saw pressure at the top as less effective than grassroots protests.[4]

What the RCSW ignored, as much as what it covered, is significant. Race and ethnicity were not major feminist concerns in this period, though some commissioners became aware of the legal discrimination and abject social conditions endured by Aboriginal women. Nor, in essence, was class a key category of analysis. This may seem peculiar, given the commission's focus on paid work and female poverty; however, the RCSW, embedded in a liberal-feminist framework that sought equality within the prevailing economic system, simply did not see social class as an inherently unequal structural relationship. In fact, the final report intentionally conflated differences between women, assuming these could be divisive, and that it was more politically effective to advocate for women as an oppressed group with shared needs and rights.[5]

Our analyses need not replicate this classless view of women's lives and political organizing, implied by congealing 'second wave' feminism into one homogeneous movement. Indeed, the wave metaphor, so unfortunately ingrained in our vocabulary, is deeply problematic: it ignores women's equality-seeking efforts in the decades between first- and second-wave feminism, many of which were grounded in socialist or labour politics, and it downplays political continuities between generations of feminists.[6] It also centres our historical gaze on white women, ignoring minorities who organized outside the 'mainstream' women's movement in race-, ethnic-, or class-based groups. Throughout the twentieth century, different streams (rather than waves) of women's equality-seeking organizing waxed and waned, often promoting divergent visions of women's equality. Although the RCSW did capture a surging discontent with women's role in society in the late 1960s, even the feminists who appeared before it were not of one mind about why women were oppressed, or the political solutions needed to better their situation. Recognizing that radical ruptures and shifts may occur within feminism at certain times and in certain contexts does not lead us inevitably to a three-wave theory: we can acknowledge both continuity and change in feminist organizing, with movements ebbing and flowing in intensity, overlapping, but also embodying different – even oppositional – actors, political ideas, and objectives.

Historical reflections on the RCSW began within a decade of the final report. From within feminism, radical and socialist feminists penned critiques as soon as the report was issued, condemning its embrace of male-defined success, and dismissing its 'milktoast'[7] calls for 'women in Canada's board rooms' as mere tokenism that ignored an economic system built upon women's exploitation.[8] Feminist lobby organizations created a checklist of recommendations adopted and discarded,[9] while scholars began to critique the commission's 'idealist' assumptions and failure to address the tenacious structural basis of women's oppression.[10] Because the commission was recent history, some key players put in their two cents' worth, attempting to shape the historical record with first-hand reminiscences. Understandably, commission head Florence Bird's auto-biography portrays the RCSW's reform agenda as far-reaching but neces-sarily pragmatic,[11] while Monique Bégin, the civil servant who oversaw RCSW research, argues confidently that the commission 'changed the course of social history.' Indeed, Bégin, later a Liberal cabinet minister, not only echoes Bird's emphasis on the report's progressive and prag-matic character, she also creates a historical narrative in which the RCSW assumes a high point, after which feminism became divided and less rel-evant.[12] By the 1990s, when the report was seen increasingly as a histor-ical artefact, feminist academics offered a more distanced balance sheet of its weaknesses and strengths, attempting to situate its recommenda-tions in terms of the federal bureaucracy, political possibility, and the social landscape of the late 1960s and early 1970s.[13] Given its raison d'être and social origins, asked Cerise Morris, how could the RCSW be 'anything other than' a liberal feminist document?[14] Other critics, how-ever, are less forgiving, suggesting that the RCSW was a symbol of the deep-seated racism within Canadian feminism,[15] or that its progenitors contributed to the hegemony of a racially homogeneous, white women's movement in subsequent decades.[16]

When the RCSW was announced in 1967, royal commissions were the butt of Canadian political satire, portrayed as manoeuvres to bury con-tentious issues under years of hearings, mountains of paper, and droning experts. While these caricatures were exaggerations, governments some-times did use royal commissions to contain and redirect difficult issues. Faced with an increasingly vocal feminist lobby led by the newly or-ganized Committee for the Equality of Women (CEW), an umbrella organization dominated by white, professional, middle-class, and white-collar women's organizations, Lester Pearson established the RCSW in an effort, some believe, to both head off feminist critiques of his minor-ity government and also steer the emerging women's movement in a pragmatic, liberal direction. The timing of the CEW's campaign was op-portune: debates about civil rights, poverty, and equality, along with in-creasing numbers of women participating in the workforce, made the state particularly 'vulnerable'[17] to feminist lobbying in the late 1960s.

A similar feminist constituency had pushed after the Second World War for a federal Women's Bureau, eventually established in 1954 within the Department of Labour. The bureau began as a small research group and was justified by the Liberal government as an aid to the effi-cient use of woman power in the economy. However, under Marion Royce's leadership, the bureau gradually focused more attention on women's equality in the labour force: Royce emphasized women's rights and opportunity in a liberal-feminist vein, though she also increasingly called for special measures such as maternity leave, designed to help women balance paid work with their family responsibilities – and women's primary responsibility for the home was rarely questioned. The bureau, as Catherine Briggs argues, was one of the first instances of 'femcrats' working within the Canadian state, and it set a political tone and ideological agenda that the RCSW followed in the 1960s. Both saw issues of education, training, and the elimination of prejudicial attitudes as important; both drew on a post–Second World War concern with human rights; both referred to the effective use of 'womanpower' in building the nation.[18] By 1969 the bureau was aiding the commission's research endeavours, sharing information on legislative plans for reforms such as maternity leave.[19]

Whatever the political origins of the RCSW, it was an opportune opening for the public airing of feminist ideas at precisely the moment when the movement was gaining new adherents. Rather than asking why the RCSW was established, suggests Annis Timpson, we need to explore how women used it as a means of 'civic resistance' to challenge publicly the prevailing views on women's paid and unpaid work.[20] Moreover, royal commissions do not necessarily suppress all contentious issues: commissioners chosen for their 'safe' views might undergo a 'learning curve'[21] and change of heart, as was the case with RCSW commissioners Lola Lange and Jeanne Lapointe, who were 'converted' to feminism during the hearings. The unfolding of the commission as a media event may have also shifted public opinion. Even some reporters who had originally mocked the RCSW as the 'SOW' commission increasingly offered grudging acknowledgment that it was uncovering egregious inequalities and social problems. As Barbara Freeman's analysis of the press coverage indicates, there were many dismissals, denigrations, and instances of sexist humour directed at the RCSW, but it was also covered sympathetically by a few female journalists determined to put the commission on the front page rather than the woman's page, and by CBC's *Take Thirty,* which had a large female viewing audience.[22] The efforts of such proponents eventually bore fruit.

Assessing and Filtering the Evidence

As the RCSW unfolded, there was an ongoing tension between commissioners' attempts to speak for all women and their limited ability to do so, good intentions notwithstanding. The commissioners' political suppositions, methods of inquiry, and social backgrounds[23] all had a bearing on their individual understandings of women's work and, indeed, of working-class women – not a term they would have used. It is useful to trace the process by which 'official' RCSW knowledge about women and work was created, including the ways in which some stories were told or some analyses encouraged, and others not. This was, at heart, an ideological process in which the 'problem' came to be defined, class understood as structural inequality was obscured, and the state became legitimized as a positive instrument of liberal reform.

There was significant homogeneity in the commissioners' backgrounds. They were all white, well-educated, middle-class, and mostly professionals, though they did represent urban, rural, regional, and linguistic constituencies: to the extent that the government was worried about 'inclusiveness,' accommodating Quebec was its key concern. With the exception of the two male commissioners who remained unsympathetic to feminism, the appointees were comfortable with the RCSW's quintessentially liberal emphasis on equal opportunity, although Elsie Gregory MacGill, most definitely the radical in the commission crowd, pushed for more far-reaching economic changes and affirmative-action policies. Even though CUPE's Grace Hartman had been part of the CEW lobby, there was not one labour-identified commissioner appointed to the RCSW, to the dismay of the labour movement. The CLC president sent a telegram of protest to Lester Pearson, insisting that there were excellent trade-union women who would have 'provided a much-needed balance' to the RCSW.[24] To the CLC's chagrin, the Canadian commission was far less labour friendly than the 1961 Kennedy Commission on Women in the United States, which had emerged from that country's longer-standing Women's Bureau, and included trade unionists.[25] Perhaps the government feared being linked to left-wing politics or the 'partisan' interests of the NDP as much as to the labour movement. When commissioner Donald Gordon resigned early on, the cabinet 'agreed in principle' to approach Eugene Forsey, but it was human-rights specialist John Humphrey whom they finally agreed on. As Jane Arscott suggests, Forsey would have provided MacGill with a welcome ally, and his research expertise in labour matters, honed during his years at the CLC, might have resulted in a more progressive report. Tellingly, the royal commission swerved right, not left, when it replaced this 'male' appointment.[26]

The problem of the woman worker was also defined without significant attention to ethnicity and race. Whiteness was taken for granted, as was the notion that all European-born working women wanted to integrate into the dominant English (or French)-speaking majority. The RCSW's demographic research indicated that women of colour were still small minorities in a few large urban centres, and while this is true, these minority experiences were largely ignored.[27] When a commission study referred to Toronto's shift from a 'British' city to a cultural 'mosaic,' it was still referring to white European immigration; moreover, background studies on immigrant women sometimes differentiated primarily between native- and foreign-born women without even factoring in race and ethnicity.[28] Given that RCSW studies confirmed that foreign-born women had a higher labour-force participation rate than native-born women, it is surprising that the commissioners did not focus more attention on the needs of immigrant women, and on race and ethnicity, especially in the employment section of the report.

The commissioners were not unaware of their limited perspectives. Pressed by MacGill especially, they sought out the voices of working-class, racialized, and poor women: 'We need to tap into the experience of the less articulate woman who was not in an organized group ... those who have suffered discrimination ... those in lower social economic scale, new [C]anadians like West Indian domestics, low income mothers, those with social problems ... and [those] in prisons,'[29] they concluded during one discussion. Bird and Lange were insistent that the voices of Aboriginal women be heard. The recent Hawthorn report, Lange told her fellow commissioners, provided 'useful research,' but it 'lack[ed] something of the human element'; if commissioners wanted to discern the needs of Aboriginal women, they should 'attend Indian and Métis women's conferences' and listen to their voices.

For the time, the RCSW's attempts at outreach were innovative. It encouraged input by writing to four hundred women's organizations, advertising in the press, and publishing opinion surveys to be returned to the commission. Nor did the commission remain cloistered in Ottawa: it travelled to shopping centres and community halls, televised the hearings, and created a telephone hotline during the hearings. Aware of their woeful lack of knowledge about Aboriginal women, commissioners added northern hearings, using translators to record Inuit women's views. However, attempts at inclusiveness (not a term even used then) did not always translate into effective results. The RCSW was soundly denounced by an anti-poverty activist for being run by unrepresentatively 'well heeled' women who did not understand how poverty really felt. In Nova Scotia, African-Canadian crusader Carrie Best chastised the commission for its failure to reach out enough to poor women and women of colour,[30] criticisms that were undoubtedly both true.

The filtering process that took place as the RCSW amassed information was not only essential to the ideological construction of the problem of the working woman, it also determined what was bequeathed as evidence to future historians. When examining the studies commissioned by the RCSW, one is struck by how small a feminist academic research community there was at the time. (The commisioners did read Margaret Benston's famous 1969 piece on social reproduction and deemed it interesting, though it was probably too radical for their taste.)[31] The lack of feminist research had much to do with the prevailing discrimination against women university teachers, documented for the RCSW by four brave professors who presented a brief against the wishes of their own union, the Canadian Association of University Teachers (CAUT).[32] The commissioners' internal discussions indicated that they recognized the paucity of research options and were unhappy with some studies, yet they often isolated themselves from potential aid out of fear of 'partisanship.' Although the commissioners clearly put a high premium on research in labour studies, with Lange calling for special workshops with union women, they were so reluctant to be associated with organized labour that Florence Bird reneged on a telephone invitation to the CLC to join an advisory committee for the commission. Bird agreed with Bégin that such a committee would give the CLC a false sense of its importance, perhaps implying the commission would be bound to accept their advice. The RCSW saw labour as a constituency to be handled delicately, but not as a key resource.[33] Yet the commission was quite willing to hear the views of high-profile male academics, even if they were sometimes faced with disappointing results. Pressed to consult the communications guru Marshall McLuhan, Bird was seemingly relieved when he declined to write a speculative brief on women's future, telling her that 'women do not have goals, only men have goals,' and lamenting the 'orientalization' of the world as it became more and more 'feminine.' *Playboy*, he supposedly told her on the phone, was the last 'stronghold of the male in the north.'[34]

Several factors shaped the ideological filtering process that guided the commission's work. One was the internal dynamics of the RCSW. Two commissioners feared an overwhelming research focus on working women. John Humphrey, who made a point of publicly denying he was 'a feminist,'[35] claimed the RCSW was 'pressing' women into the workforce, and Jacques Henripin, who refused to sign the final report, likewise claimed inordinate attention was focused on married women's work outside the home when this was 'secondary' to women's role as mothers.[36] Even if the views of these men were in the minority, they acted as an ideological brake on more radical perspectives, particularly because Bird encouraged discussion and compromise in order to create a consensus on as many issues as possible. This cautious inclination not to rock the political boat was likely one reason she had appeared a safe choice in the first place to the Liberals.

Studies done for the RCSW by social-science experts were also heavily influenced by the dominant theories, assumptions, and methods of the time. One study of the impact of married women's work on the family, for instance, opened with a long discourse on Parsonian sociology: men generally handled the instrumental aspects of family life, but women had affective, intuitive roles that contradicted their identification with 'occupational roles.' This family 'equilibrium' was undermined by women's paid labour, and indeed married women workers might even become psychologically disturbed given the social view that they were 'deviants.' Although the researcher then suggested there was no evidence that children of working mothers suffered, any working mother reading the study would have been left with immense anxiety about her fundamentally contradictory dual role.[37] Moreover, the very questions posed were intrinsically biased: researchers continually asked if children of working mothers suffered, a question never posed of working fathers.

In studies done on immigrant working women, dominant assumptions about the benefits of cultural integration were similarly replayed: women immigrants sought, above all else, 'integration' or 'adjustment' to the dominant culture; racism was based in attitudes and 'prejudice' that human-rights laws could effectively address; and immigrant women from southern European came from patriarchal families with strongly enforced 'double standards' of morality. Not all the immigration studies ignored discrimination, and many recommended concrete programs of job counselling, training, and language classes; they also suggested that immigration policymakers desist from seeing all married women immigrants as dependents. Nonetheless, race and class were elided, as indicated by one study that suggested immigrant women were an undifferentiated group, 'sharing the same status problems'[38] as Canadian women, and a rather rosy picture of a welcoming Canadian nation sometimes prevailed, indicated by the conclusion that people of colour rarely encountered racism when looking for accommodation.[39] One rather doubts this.

The paucity of university researchers was a third factor affecting the commission's information-gathering efforts. This scarcity led the RCSW to private individuals and consulting firms whose unreflective assumptions influenced their methods and conclusions; as a result, reiterations of the dominant ideology were marketed as 'objective' research. One background study on department-store workers, written by a university commerce student and never published because it was so weak, relied on a mere six interviews with women workers to arrive at the rather mundane conclusion that they were 'generally satisfied' with their jobs.[40] A private firm did two of the major studies on working women. Hickling-Johnson's study of collective bargaining included copious comments on a vaguely defined female 'personality.' This firm's discussion of why women worked offered up the 'consumption conscious' woman, who wanted 'to keep up with the Jones' or had a precise economic 'objective of buying a fur coat, a new car or possibly helping with the mortgage.'[41] After stating that statistics on women's rate of unionization were difficult to come by, the authors jumped to the conclusion that women were simply 'harder than men to organize,' more apathetic about unions, and that their sense of 'insecurity and inferiority' or 'role incompatibility' (echoing Parsons again) precluded their involvement. To be sure, the authors also pointed to problems with gender-based seniority lists, lack of maternity leave, and sexist suspicions about female union leaders, but the tendency to psychologize women workers, or to proceed from an anecdote to a conclusion, was nonetheless troubling. The authors even misquoted Grace Hartman to make the point that women might not be adept at collective bargaining, something she would have been horrified to see.[42]

A fourth factor affecting the RCSW's work was that the choice of researchers, subjects for study, and the parameters of research, were moulded by the commission's cautious inclination not to antagonize powerful economic interests, or ask 'who benefits' from women's segregated and underpaid labour. This was epitomized well in a conflict over the research studies done on women in department stores and in chartered banks, both authored by Dutch-born economist Marianne Bossen. Bossen prided herself on her extensive empirical, archival, and statistical research examining gender differences in positions, promotions, attitudes, and compensation. Yet the commission pressed her to censor these studies before publication based on the advice of a Department of Justice lawyer who suggested that any comment the least bit critical of these businesses was considered potentially libellous.

Despite her initial resistance, libel chill forced Bossen to alter her reports. Even though she based her department-store data primarily on material given to her by Eaton's and the Hudson's Bay Company, the store names had to be removed (she could not even thank them), and her suggestion that women occupied 'inferior positions' in department stores had to be excised. Nor could she suggest that women would have to unionize to improve their status if they hoped to move outside their occupational 'ghettos,' because the latter term implied the 'firms were confining women to occupational ghettos because they were women,' a charge that the lawyer considered potentially 'distasteful and inflammatory.' Even the most minor comments were deleted. Bossen assented to the removal of the word 'outmoded' when referring to the tendency of banks only to 'think in terms of two occupational groups' (i.e., male managers and female clerks) because the lawyer thought this might 'slight their professional reputations.' He also worried about Bossen's implication that equal-pay laws were being circumvented – a reality simply taken for granted by working women and trade unionists. Most amusing, but depressingly revealing, was the lawyer's objection to Bossen's 'aside' comment that women in some service jobs were pressured to exhibit sex appeal and stress their subservient role to please men. The lawyer practically snorted his contempt for this 'manifestly untrue' idea, telling the author there was 'no male conspiracy involved ... The truth of the matter is that mini-skirted stewardesses, tellers and waitresses are pleasing to male customers, and that is good for business.'[43] Bossen removed her comment. No matter that the union of airline attendants said the same thing to the RCSW! Aside from indicating how libel laws favour power and money rather than the truth, these interventions indicated the government's and the RCSW's inordinate fear of affronting private enterprise.

A fifth element affecting the amassing of information was that commission evidence was also filtered through the RCSW's staff, who favoured briefs that were, in their view, politically measured and practical. To be sure, these employees had feminist sympathies; however, these were cultivated, shaped, and circumscribed by the liberal culture of the RCSW. This is well illustrated by the analysts' work summarizing briefs, providing sample questions for the hearings, and judging the veracity and usefulness of each submission. This screening process was intended to prep the commissioners and protect the commission from being discredited in the media because of weird and outlandish presentations. The analysts had little tolerance for radical claims-making: any political stance to the left of social democracy was considered wild and unrealistic. 'Less belligerently feminist than some,' one staff member wrote approvingly of the Saskatchewan Federation of Labour's submission, which was indeed pretty tame. Nor could this analyst disguise her contempt for the 'dogmatic' young socialist women from the League for Social Action who cited the capitalist economy as a key factor in women's exploitation.[44] Commission staff members were also critical of traditionalist submissions that extolled women's proper place in the home and decried all working mothers; their political impulse was to find an even-handed 'centre' that neither justified the status quo nor pushed too assertively to turn it on its head.[45]

Briefs that offered 'hard' social-science evidence, such as statistics (presumed never to lie), and that listed precise policy recommendations were looked upon favourably – and these were more likely to be submitted by well-educated, English- and French-speaking credentialed women from established occupational, club, and reform organizations. Conversely, briefs that were considered too personal were treated sceptically. One group of working mothers in white- and blue-collar jobs who were former servicewomen wrote a collective submission based on their day-to-day lives in order to highlight common problems faced by women workers. Although their examples pointed to systemic problems, they were not seen as good public-presentation material: questioning these women about their 'personal experiences' would be difficult, the analyst told the commission.[46] When a Montreal secretary and sole-support mother told her story, pointing to her low salary and lack of child care, her submission was designated as a very 'subjective' story,[47] but when a social worker drew conclusions from her interaction with a number of clients, her conclusions were treated as more substantive.

Perhaps the commission staff feared that some stories would confirm the press' portrayal of the commission as a group of whining women. Yet the personal narratives of poor and working-class women clearly moved some reporters and listeners in the hearings, and they provided object lessons in the systemic inequalities women faced. However, questions were prepared for the commissioners that steered presenters towards practical policy solutions, and commissioners did not hide their concern that even these might be difficult to secure. When an immigrant woman working as a secretary argued for tax breaks for working women, Bird replied: 'We agree with you [but] how do we get our legislators to agree?'[48] Trade-union presenters were asked to delineate where the funds would come from for programs such as child care, though when the more radical United Electrical Workers (UE) suggested that businesses should pay since they profited from women's labour, commissioners were rather sceptical.

While the commission saw unions as an important constituency to consult, it was also critical of them. When the Quebec Federation of Labour presented a rather long brief, Jeanne Lapointe interrupted the federation president, Fernand Daoust, challenging his contention that unions fought for women's equality, while employers resisted it: 'I have a feeling unions talk a lot about eliminating discrimination but don't fight for this in practice ... If you had 10% Negro or Indian workers in your union would you accept giving them lower pay?' she asked, putting the union in a decidedly negative light.[49] Similar critical questions were routinely asked of other unions, which were pressed to produce evidence that they put equity issues 'on the bargaining table.'[50] Granted, the press liked to report on these 'conflict moments' in the hearings, but RCSW documents also suggest that some commissioners were unconvinced of labour's claim to be at the forefront of the struggle for women's equality, or, at the very least, thought labour should attend to inequalities within its own house.

The Labour Movement Responds

If labour had secured a representative on the RCSW, would these questions have been different? Unions clearly thought so: many opened their public presentation by criticizing the commission's failure to appoint a labour-identified commissioner. Labour's eagerness to join the RCSW and showcase its commitment to gender-equality raises broader questions about the relationship between organized labour and feminism in the post-war period. Although the union movement, and especially craft unions, had devoted little attention to women's issues in the 1940s and 1950s, there were some labour feminists in staff and leadership positions scattered over the movement. Many of these individuals also made common cause with women in union auxiliaries, the CCF, or the Communist Party on rising prices, peace, or other social-justice issues – political work that contradicts the notion that 1945–68 was simply a trough in between 'waves' of feminism, a black hole of non-activism.

As we have seen, the UE nurtured a working-class feminism in its women's committees, packing-house workers were calling for equal pay, and in Quebec the CSN (Confédération des syndicats nationaux) investigated why few women were in its leadership. Yet Cold War politics, small numbers, the lack of a central coordinating body, and regional and language differences all militated against a strong national network of labour feminists. In contrast to the United States, there was not a long-standing federal Women's Bureau with the political will to bring union women from across the country together around a common agenda. Moreover, social-democratic women likely diverted their political energies into CCF women's committees, or even to keeping the CCF alive in some provinces where the party was in decline. In the 1940s and 1950s, women unionists were finding their voices at a local level, but they had not yet coalesced into a coherent, national pressure group. Nor was there a welcoming space within most labour federations for women to develop a critical view of their own unions: not only were women trade unionists themselves committed to a class-based politics, but, knowing their union brothers' antipathy to feminist-inspired gender rebellion, they continually reassured their comrades that 'women unionists don't want a special status ... only the same rights as other workers.'[51]

By the time of the royal commission, however, there were a few more, and more outspoken, feminists. The leadership of Grace Hartman, a feisty and militant unionist unafraid to advertise her parallel loyalty to feminism, made a difference. The growing numbers of unionized women in the public sector, the circulation of feminist ideas, and the disjuncture women felt between the rhetoric of union equality and the reality of their second-class citizenship provided fertile ground for the growth of labour feminism. During the 1960s, some unionists had been thrown together with feminists in new, if temporary, alliances. Women in the United Auto Workers, for example, supported a liberal-feminist lobby for legislation banning sex-based job advertising. From the mid-1960s on, women in some CLC unions were beginning to self-organize around gender-equality issues: in 1966 the Ontario Federation of Labour sponsored a women's conference that discussed day care, job training, and equal pay,[52] and in 1968 the CLC finally added prohibitions against sex discrimination to its constitution.

The royal commission gave this small group of labour feminists an opportunity to push an equality agenda within their unions, and also to lobby the state externally. Like their union brothers, labour women viewed the state with both suspicion and optimism, but ultimately in an instrumental manner.[53] Though labour rarely deliberated over abstract theories of the state, there was an implicit understanding that the state incorporated a number of structures, relations, and processes. Trade unions hoped to forge inroads of influence where they could, even though they presumed that, in general, the state was more sympathetic to capital.[54] Like other social democrats, they still placed considerable hope in the politics of parliamentary reform, but unlike liberal feminists, their view of government was often inflected with an implicit class critique. Women unionists, for instance, had been sceptical that the federal Women's Bureau – the product of middle-class women's lobbying – would have the power to make meaningful changes for women workers, yet they publicized its research and pressed for a more assertive approach to legislative reform. The RCSW was seen in a similar light: it represented a possibility not a panacea, an opportunity to advertise labour's platform and press a legislative reform agenda ahead.

By highlighting common keywords and silences in the union briefs, we can sketch out official union discourses on women's equality, and how these may have shifted over the post-war period. There was considerable uniformity in the trade-union briefs[55] – so much so that they make for boring reading. Few briefs ventured out on a socialist or radical limb; many offered similar statistics and legislative solutions. There was consensus that state action was needed on at least six issues: equal-pay laws were toothless and had to be altered to measure 'comparable worth'; legislated maternity leave with paid benefits was essential; 'sex' should be added to all human-rights and fair-employment statutes; women workers needed access to training and better education; tax laws had to be amended to allow deductions for working mothers, for instance, for housekeepers; child-care centres should be provided; and the narrow occupational segregation and lower pay of women needed to be rectified.

Certainly, political orientation, the nature of the workplace, and union constituencies did matter to some degree. Quebec's Confederation of National Trade Unions (in French, the CSN) placed considerable emphasis on a social critique of both the educational system as a negative tool of gender socialization and the media's objectification of women. Its study of sweated labour – an issue ignored by other unions – detailed substandard working conditions and called for the complete abolition of home-based labour. Although most unions avoided a critique of capitalism as a system, the (left-led) UE and the United Fishermen and Allied Workers Union both criticized corporate control of the economy and the way in which business drew 'extra' profit from women's lower-paid labour: surplus value was hinted at, though not named. Other unions were rather more timid, offering lacklustre calls for yet more studies of issues such as child care. Mass-production unions answering to a predominantly male membership were noticeably reticent about abolishing

separate seniority lists, though, ironically, a brave UAW women's auxiliary called for the abolition of all sex-based job classifications. CUPE's
submission was more honest than many others about the discrimination
women faced within their own unions, and it pulled no punches when
assessing the state's failures: in public, it referred to the Women's Bureau
as a useless. 'sop' to women, an allegation the media loved to repeat.
What came to be called sexual harassment was seldom mentioned; however, women whose jobs made them particularly subject to sexualization
were developing a political critique in this direction. The Canadian Air
Line Flight Attendants Association declared it wanted no more of the
'bunny club'[56] philosophy propagated by airline employers.

Rather than looking at these variations, it may be more useful to locate
shared assumptions, justifications, and discursive strategies used to promote unions as advocates of working women and also make the case for
legislative reform. Rhetorical references to family, nation, and citizenship were sometimes used to legitimate unions' support for gender
equality. According to the UAW, the country was wasting its woman
power, a great economic resource necessary for nation building: 'Swayed
by prejudice, employers did not make use of female talent which causes
resentment on the part of women and robs a competitive nation of much
expertise.'[57] References to human rights and equal citizenship appeared
often, buttressed with invocations of international human rights and
labour standards set out by the United Nations and the ILO. Unionists
knew that lofty international declarations often became hollow plati-
tudes at the national and provincial levels, but they could be used as
opportunities to shame the government. As a member of the United
Nations, Canada should embrace its resolutions on equality and discrimination passed by the General Assembly in 1967, the Canadian
Labour Congress argued. Similarly, many unions – as well as other organizations – chastised the government for not living up to ILO resolutions,
dating back to 1919, on equal pay and maternity leave.

Union arguments for change sometimes embraced the rhetoric of
liberalism, stressing individual rights, choice, equal opportunity, and human dignity: we should not discourage the development of 'human potential, place a limit on [women], or stifle individual opportunity,' said
the UAW.[58] Class was less visible, either as a method of explaining inequality or as a collective sense of identity and shared interests; undoubtedly, the language of class, associated as it was with communism, had
been suppressed by labour during the Cold War. Questions of race and
ethnicity were even more invisible: some unions saw immigrant workers

as more vulnerable, super-exploited workers (without differentiating by ethnicity), but racial and ethnic divisions of labour, unlike the sexual division of labour, were not the focus of sustained critique. And though the CLC was devoting some attention to Native workers in its own publications, this interest was not transferred to the organization's brief.[59]

The unions' emphasis on women's individual rights, opportunities, and choice is in part explained by their perceived audience – namely, the state, the liberal feminist RCSW, and the press. Such a focus also represented a growing sympathy on the part of those preparing briefs – union women's committees or research staff – with ideas of the emerging women's movement. Yet, this group represented a small current within the house of labour; indeed, there were some female unionists very uneasy with the idea of women's committees. One of the most progressive briefs, presented by CUPE, was largely the creation of its research director, Gil Levine, a leftist who also noted the important influence of his wife, a feminist scholar and activist, on his thinking.[60] There were still some important differences between unions and middle-class women's groups: one was labour's emphasis on collective bargaining as a key route to gender equality. Also, when unions tackled the perennial question 'Why do women work?' class-based arguments were implicit in their answers. Women went out to work because they had to support themselves, because husbands had low incomes, because the cost of living was rising, or because they simply had no other choice but to work, said the UE. CUPE dealt with the 'why women work' question by laying out all the prevailing myths – working mothers cause delinquency, working mothers are always late or absent, and so on – then carefully demolishing each one, ending with the claim that 'women should have the same rights and opportunities as men when they decide to seek employment.'[61] It was this head-on rejection of the male-breadwinner ethic that marked some submissions as radical departures from the past.

However forceful CUPE was, a few unions still offered rationales that reproduced stereotypical views of employed married women: the Saskatchewan Federation of Labour, for example, uncritically cited a sociological study that claimed women worked to provide 'extra luxuries for the family' or to relieve 'boredom and emotional problems.'[62] Exculpating the male breadwinner entirely from labour's imaginary vision of the family thus proved difficult. The OFL spoke of single women 'breadwinners' as distinct from married women, who needed to 'supplement their husband's income' as it was 'inadequate for the high cost of living,' or because they wanted to save for their children's education. A college education might be considered a necessity in the post-war years, unlike the standard trope of the luxurious fur coat, but women's 'supplementary' wages were still secondary wages.[63]

While economic need was emphasized in order to dispel negative views of married working women, the claim that 'generally women work out of economic necessity rather than choice' or that they should not be 'obliged to work because of low income' had contradictory ramifications.[64] A similar rationale was repeated in briefs from middle-class women's clubs: a picture emerged of working-class women (sometimes rather piteous single moms) pressed into wage labour by poverty, but who actually wanted to stay home like their middle-class sisters. This 'contingent' justification for women's labour downplayed women's unfettered right to paid work and opened the back door to a reconstituted male breadwinner.[65]

Another union blind spot was the double day. When discussing caring work in the home, almost no one imagined anyone other than women assuming the primary responsibility for children: women need social supports so they can go to work 'without hurting the well being of their children,' was the way the CNTU put it.[66] The royal commission did discuss internally how to recognize women's work in the home as a 'valid economic contribution,' and one idea floated was to make housekeeping a 'more respected vocation' by training women who would then aid mothers who were 'working, ill, or families in which the mother had died.' Potential candidates included 'mature' [read older] women, women with 'little education,' including Métis and Indian women, or any 'potential wife or mother,' suggesting women with few economic choices were being targeted – a depressingly old idea. However, when one public submission suggested Indian and Métis women be trained for domestic work, the RCSW analyst objected to this 'disturbing assertion.'[67] One might assume the call for paid homemakers was a class-based argument, yet some working-class women endorsed this as an ideal solution to their child-care needs.[68] A mother substitute was seen as a practical possibility; the idea of men doing domestic labour, including child care, was rarely mentioned, and judging by the newspaper cartoons that mocked men left at home while their wives attended the royal commission, this was still a rather outlandish idea.[69]

If there was one indication that the labour-movement discourse had shifted since the end of the war, it was unions' evolving critique of the male-breadwinner ideal and their attempts to dispel antipathy to married women workers. While few unions made any attempt to keep child-care centres open after the war, most now called for some form of state-subsidized child care – indeed, over half of the presentations to the commission favoured the social provision of non-maternal care.[70] These were official positions, however, and did not necessarily permeate rank-and-file views. The one study done for the RCSW on blue-collar male unionists' views revealed the reluctance of some male workers to abandon the male-breadwinner ideal, their ambivalence about women with small children working, and their fears that blue-collar work would endanger women's femininity. Of the men interviewed, there was a minority with a very 'egalitarian' outlook,[71] some with an 'awareness' of equality issues, and many who were struggling with their feelings of ambivalence about mothers' work for pay.

Labour feminists, in contrast, believed their full-fledged right to a breadwinner role was an absolutely key ideological issue. They astutely understood that this had the potential to challenge the gendered division of labour both at home and at work, since both spheres hinged on the notion that earning was a man's primary role. Vocal women unionists were making it clear they had simply had enough: they were tired of being criticized for working, having to justify their own hard-earned wages, and encountering criticism for abandoning children. 'We are tired of apologizing for being women [workers], for being married ... and seeing a veil drop over employers' eyes when we look for jobs,' Shirley Carr told the hearings.[72] Similar sentiments were voiced by ordinary women, unionized and not, who wrote the commission: 'I do not want to take over the world from men, but I DO want to be able to eat, feed, and clothe myself and my child,'[73] declared one woman. Why was it that women workers were invisible on TV? asked a female union representative; why was women's work in industry or the professions never validated, never offered any 'dignity'?[74]

If completely banishing the ideal of the male breadwinner was difficult for some unions, another problem was admitting that such organizations were dominated by males who sanctioned discrimination in some contracts and in their own leadership structures. In their critiques of the occupational segregation of women, many unions promoted a 'second wave' feminist argument that culture, socialization, and education (not biology or sex) produced gendered jobs. However, decrying the low wages of nurses' aides or waitresses was different than letting a woman bump into your own better-paid job on an assembly line. While many unions told the royal commission that women should be allowed to train for all jobs, some union contracts actually militated against this. Nor did unions dwell on the embarrassingly low numbers of women in union leadership positions. Granted, only 17 per cent of women were unionized, with lower numbers in the private sector than the public sector, but the numbers were still extremely embarrassing. CUPE's self-criticism on this issue was rare, and unfortunately, one suspects its admission garnered considerable press coverage only because it punctured unions' claims to be at the forefront of change.[75] Similarly, the press rather relished any gender tensions displayed during union presentations, as when CLC vice-president Hugette Plamondon (described only by her 'chic' appearance in one article)[76] interrupted and contradicted her own president, noting critically that unions had given leadership on gender-equality issues, but had hardly done enough in this regard.

Plamondon's outburst was unusual, especially given her earlier declarations in the 1950s that women were fully accepted in the labour movement. However, Plamondon had chaired the internal CLC committee that drafted this organization's brief to the RCSW, an experience that might have prompted both her remark and her increasingly vocal statements about gender equality. Five men, ten women, and two CLC staff were appointed to a CLC status-of-women committee that began meeting in January of 1968 to construct the CLC brief. In the first meeting, Plamondon struck a note the entire committee could agree on when she urged the CLC not to take a 'middle course,' but rather to write a powerful brief: 'Women are second class citizens,' she argued, and vague compromises would do little to 'end discriminatory practices.'[77] Disagreement surfaced, however, over how to face the criticism that unions did not practise what they preached – separate seniority lists being just one example. While some members wanted to admit union weaknesses, others wanted to paper them over, claiming these simply reflected wider social attitudes. Vice-president William Dodge excused the lack of female union reps with the very same rationale used by business for not hiring women: 'They don't want to move from one location to the other.'[78] There were other areas of debate, including the abolition of protective legislation, though this was hardly the divisive issue it had been in the United States. A compromise, stressing laws protecting men and women alike, with special health protection for pregnant women, was worked out in the final brief.

More significant differences arose over whether issues such as common-law relations, prostitution, and abortion should even be mentioned. Some committee members feared these issues would detract from the 'real' employment ones or be used to sully the CLC's reputation in the press. Abortion was not even put on the first meeting's agenda, since the male CLC researcher in charge opined that 'it was too sensitive an issue.'[79] A core of labour feminists immediately disagreed, arguing that a woman should have the right to control her body, and also that abortion should be seen as an economic issue, with Plamondon pointing out that 'wealthy women can obtain safe abortions abroad, while poor, single or married women must employ the services of unqualified personnel, often with tragic results.'[80] These feminists insisted that a pro-choice statement on abortion be included in the RCSW brief, and successfully pressed the CLC executive to do likewise in its upcoming presentation to the Senate Committee on Health. This position was endorsed at the CLC convention, and so the women were astounded when abortion was quietly excised from the RCSW brief. CUPE's Shirley Carr was extremely upset, convinced it was simply cowardice in the face of the Catholic Church, and she implored Plamondon to use her 'charm and powers of persuasion' to get the statement on abortion reinscrted by the leadership – to no avail.[81] No wonder the CUPE brief made a point of emphasizing that the right to choose was a CLC policy; privately, some CUPE leaders bemoaned the CLC's milktoast performance.[82] While the abortion issue was a small disagreement within the CLC, it symbolized a shift within the house of labour: emboldened by a sense of collective strength, labour women were becoming more vocal and more committed to a comprehensive feminist list of equality issues.

Other minor rebellions by union women surfaced during the hearings. A group of twelve autoworkers in St Catharines, laid off the year before by McKinnon Industries, publicly criticized their union's 'total disregard for women on the production line.' Their public submission claimed free trade had 'accelerated the Company's policy of eliminating women,' since the union would not tolerate women bumping into men's jobs. Once laid off, the women were left to fend for themselves by an indifferent union: they reported being told to either go on unemployment insurance or retrain as clericals, neither of which were strategies that addressed their immediate need to support themselves and their families. Probably knowing this complaint would be picked up by the press (as it was), the commission privately asked UAW president George Burt for his views. His response confirmed the union's lack of concern: the women, he said rather disingenuously, were 'protected by separate seniority lists,' and in any case, they could have been hired in 'girls' jobs in a new plant if they had not refused to move for 'family reasons.'[83]

Another submission from a blue-collar worker critical of her union was described by the RCSW analyst as a 'personal complaint,' yet it was actually an insightful analysis of contractual discrimination.[84] The men's benefit plan at Continental Can, where the woman worked, included dependents, yet hers did not; nor were life-insurance policies or required retirement ages the same for men and women. When this woman protested to the Ontario Human Rights Commission, it replied that nothing could be done, much to her indignation. Too often, she concluded, union 'brotherhood is interpreted as being for males only.' She was equally critical of her employer, pointing out that his objection to maternity leave rested on claims of high female turnover, a specious rationale contradicted by the many mothers she worked with who bore children *and* stayed on the job for up to twenty-seven years.[85]

White-collar unionized women also complained of union and employer discrimination that was simply taken for granted: two BC women sent in a survey showing the differential pay scales for men and women in their union, and one enraged Bell operator complained to the RCSW that the company's relocation program favoured men and discriminated against women. Even worse, she contended, the company managers 'lied to the [women workers] about their options,' exerted pressure on them to resign so the company could avoid paying a termination allowance, and threatened women with discipline, all the while reminding them that 'women don't need to work because they are supported by someone else.' Unafraid of controversy, this operator copied her letter to the president of Bell and the minister of transport, Jack Pickersgill.[86]

Dear Florence: Letters to the RCSW from Working Women

The Bell worker who complained to the commission was not alone. Many individual women gave public submissions or sent letters to commission chair Florence Bird. These letters, which had been solicited by the RCSW with newspaper ads, contain a wealth of information on working women's struggles, concerns, complaints, and strategies for daily survival. While the official briefs from organizations were formal, statistical, and distanced in tone, many of the private letters were more emotive, personal, and subjective. This is not to denigrate the letters as exemplars of emotional femininity, replicating a contemporary caricature of women: on the contrary, these letters suggest women's efforts to understand and negotiate the changing social and economic landscape around them, as well as the dominant discourses about women's work and their own complex reactions to them.

The letters were themselves examples of the commission's information-filtering practices. Though some clearly had 'private' on them, in other cases it was the commission staff who categorized them as private letters rather than submissions to be reprinted, based on their presentation and content.[87] As Jane Arscott suggests, this was yet another means of classifying women's 'experiential learning' as less important than social science style submissions.[88] The letters are also sometimes difficult to categorize, since they contain multiple themes, points of view, and even seemingly contradictory ideas: a letter might denounce married working women but then call for maternity leave. Ideology, however, is seldom a unified, seamless entity: it may incorporate ideals plucked from the dominant gender order, as well as notions drawn from lived experiences that undermine those ideals.[89] Women's personal narratives may thus simultaneously incorporate 'hegemonic tales' while also providing openings for 'subversive stories.'[90]

As historical sources, the letters have obvious limitations: they were geared to a precise audience – Florence Bird and the RCSW inner circle – and they came predominantly from English- and French-speaking literate (and semi-literate) women who had the confidence and skills to put their ideas on paper. There appeared to be a high number of white-collar women writing privately to the commission, in part, Bird suggested, because they wanted to avoid public exposure, fearing for their jobs. The anonymity of letter writing also meant they were skewed in political outlook: more women and men celebrating homemaking as women's God-given, natural role, and disapproving of married working women, wrote privately. As one Yukon writer explained in her letter criticizing married women for taking jobs away from Native youth, she did not want to voice these thoughts in public, 'since the tide of opinion is in favour of married women working.'[91] Yet, because letters such as this were not intended for public consumption, writers had the freedom to say the unspoken: not only did traditionalists write, but many women workers assumed the licence to complain and criticize; voice fear, anger, and cynicism; denounce other workers or bosses; and also speak out against 'the system.' Such statements and feelings would have been flattened out or 'contained' in a public context. Like the public briefs from organizations, the letters were strategic efforts on the part of women to persuade the RCSW that certain concerns were important. However, they addressed issues no other submissions did: there are more references in these letters to sexual harassment, abhorrent marriages, and violence, issues the commission simply sidestepped – and was later criticized for ignoring.

At the same time, we should be justifiably wary of seeing personal correspondence as an irrefutably privileged source of information from which we can easily discern women's voices. Indeed, to categorize the letters as documents revelatory of women's lives is to come up against postmodern feminist critiques of the 'the raw material of experience,'[92] or of a 'material' apart from the discursive, exemplified by Joan Scott's well-known characterization of experience as an epistemologically flawed foundational concept, a 'linguistic event' that 'doesn't happen outside established meanings.'[93] Critical of past feminist efforts to locate authentic, incontestable versions of women's voices, postmodern critics such as Craig Ireland see the concept of experience as a 'problematic building block' for social history, a form of 'foundationalism' that falsely assumes a pre-discursive reality and potentially leads us to the fetishization of the material body, and a dangerous 'neo-ethnic tribalism.'[94]

Although post-structuralist writing has productively complicated our writing on experience, I believe we can still read these letters to the RCSW with an eye to deducing women's experience as it was 'lived from the inside out,' shaped by material forces and social practices, yet also discursively mediated and interpreted.[95] Despite some confident historiographical assertions that the flawed concept of experience utilized by social historians such as E.P. Thompson has been effectively 'disposed of'[96] by Scott's critique, there is a rich lineage of materialist, Marxist, and feminist writing that suggests otherwise. Earlier socialist-feminist histories often struggled to enunciate a concept of experience that encompassed both lived events and women's understanding of them, recognizing that the former were always refracted through the partialities of historical recounting. While critical of the way in which masculinist ideologies had shaped the recording of history, they did not see this ideological 'contamination' as so thorough that they could not come to 'understand otherwise' about women's experiences in the past.[97]

Marxist and materialist-feminist scholars have described experience as a dialectical process that is both lived and construed, a 'point of origin' and an entity that is discursively constructed.[98] In E.P. Thompson's formulation, experience was a 'juncture point' and 'dialogue between social being and social consciousness moving in both directions.'[99] While Thompson's writing faced critique from both structuralist Marxists and later postmodernists, some feminists have developed rather than rejected this approach: drawing consciously on Thompson's writing, for instance, Rosemary Hennessy explores the 'dis-identification' that can transpire between lived experience and the identities promoted by the dominant culture, between feelings considered 'legitimate' under capitalism and those 'outlawed.'[100] To be sure, writing in this materialist vein often assumes a 'pre-discursive' domain, grounded in material relations, or presupposes certain 'kernels of truth' about the 'determining logic of capitalist relations.'[101] For postmodern critics, this is a key misconception at the heart of the concept of experience, but in my view, this is one legacy of historical materialism not to be jettisoned.

Any notion that we must choose between experience as either naive essentialism or as unknowable indeterminacy is also countered emphatically by a range of other feminist scholars, including standpoint theorists such as Nancy Hartstock, intersectionalist critical race theorists, and feminists recuperating existentialist feminism.[102] By denying experience, Sonia Kruks argues in the latter case, we risk reducing human subjects to a set of 'discursive effects,' prohibiting an understanding of both 'interiority' and 'the domain of affectivity.'[103] Similarly concerned about the 'affective' realms of history, Michael Pickering stresses not only the 'mutually constituting'[104] intersections of social structure, representation, and subjectivities that create lived experience, but the need for historians to eschew mechanical theories (whether Marxist or discursive) delineating society from above, in favour of efforts to listen to the collective voices of historical actors – however elusive that effort may be.

Scholars situated outside Marxist traditions are also voicing concerns that we are facing a historical 'crisis' as notions of social causality, human agency, and experience, long embattled by postmodern pessimism, are in need of re-theorization and recuperation.[105] The notion that experience is still 'epistemologically indispensable' to the recovery of history, that it does not inevitably lead down the slippery slope to repressive forms of identity politics, [106] is forwarded by post-positivist realists who fundamentally challenge attempts to de-legitimize a theoretical project that explores linkages 'between social location and identity.'[107] Experience may be mediated through culture and ideology, they argue, yet it is still shaped by cognitive processes, making humans capable of rendering relatively true and objective knowledge about the world – recognizing that objectivity does not mean neutrality.[108]

There are some overarching concerns expressed by many of these scholars concerning postmodern eviscerations of experience, including

their inattention to production relations/social context, the textualiza-
tion of social relations,[109] the slighting of human agency, and the notion
that discourse is inescapable, a 'closed circuit' of meaning.[110] All these
critiques informed my examination of women's letters to the RCSW.

First, at a most basic level, changes to the economy have to be taken
into account when reading the letters to Florence, not the least because
the RCSW came into being, in large part, as a response to the rapid increase in women working for pay. Changes in material life shape both
the formation of social groups and how such groups describe themselves.[111] The transformation in the labour force may have been interpreted differently, but it was not simply discursively constructed. Women's
expanding labour-force participation also meant they had different
timetables, hours of work, job definitions, and schedules with their children; in other words, the physical and mental mapping of their daily
lives was changing. As other feminist authors have argued, women's
physical and embodied experiences sometimes 'opened the way for a
transformation in consciousness.'[112] Second, the subtle alterations in
women's views of work that I sensed in the letters can be better understood by examining the fissures and frictions that may emerge in the
process of social change, and by the reflective responses of human subjects to those changes.[113] The ideological constructs of the male breadwinner and a fixed sexual division of labour rubbed up against women's
day-to-day needs and aspirations, resulting in their questions, resentments, and protests, even if these were often tentatively articulated. If we
are to understand historical 'transformations in collective consciousness,' suggests William Wilkerson in his critique of Scott, 'we have to accept the possibility that a group's reflections on the distorted ideological
constructions of their experiences might lead to a change in consciousness.'[114] Third, if we view women's narratives as only the product of the
available discourses, unconnected to the suffering and exploitation they
described, we may not only destabilize the truth claims of these concepts,
but also, in Catherine Hall's prescient words, diminish a sense of 'feeling
in historical writing.'[115] Granted, there is a social dimension to feeling: it
is not to be simply naturalized or made transhistorical. My political sensibilities and interpretive role need to be acknowledged in the process of
reading these letters. Nonetheless, particularly because the mode of letter writing in our culture permits emotion and affect, these letters do
offer a sense of human connection or 'emulative communication' with
women in the past.[116] In Raymond Williams's terms, they convey a provi-
sional, elusive 'structure of feeling,' that is, socially mediated patterns of

thought that were unfinished, partially articulated, and had yet to find 'the terms for their reflexive self-comprehension.'[117] A few examples drawn from the hundreds of letters might emphasize these points.

Working women often expressed their unhappiness, resentment, and desire for something better in individual terms, yet their life histories suggest far more than personal bitterness. The self-supporting woman had long had some social purchase as a 'deserving,' if pitied, wage earner, but single working women writing to Florence now consciously equated their needs and entitlements with those of self-supporting men. White-collar women bemoaned the fine line they faced between poverty and respectability, and with good reason. Women made up 61 per cent of all clerical workers, yet made just less than two-thirds of men's salaries, and some estimates of overall employment wage rates put women's pay at 50 per cent of men's.[118] This was not enough for many urban women to lease an apartment, leaving them in rented rooms or dependent on family. 'I want to speak for the unmarried female workers,' wrote one correspondent. 'How about some tax concessions so we can rent something better than housekeeping rooms, euphemistically called bachelor suites. After all, we are past the stage when dorm living is fun,' this writer continued.[119] This complaint about women's lack of access to the private 'home space' they deserved might occasionally be coupled with complaints about other women who were perceived to have more options. 'I have no pension,' wrote one woman, and it 'is well known that it is these marrieds with two incomes' and no responsibilities, who 'rent the high priced luxury apartments, [and] drive the prices up.'[120] Older women who had looked after aged parents also found themselves later in life without a house or pension, uncompensated for their years of caring work, and with few assets other than their high-school typing skills. They were resentful, but perhaps understandably so: they realized, in an inchoate way, that women's unpaid contributions to social reproduction had left them vulnerable to poverty and marginalization.

Resentment was directed not only at other women, but also at employers who made and policed the workplace rules that left women with a smaller paycheque than men. Women could see how unfair, if not irrational, the male-breadwinner ideal was when a young single man was paid more than an older, single mother – and they were not afraid to point out the contradiction. 'Women office workers in this small town,' wrote one woman, 'are so badly paid they cannot support their families, and their qualifications are not recognized. Take the young men out of university who are installed in higher positions and imperiously tell us where to put a comma when they can't write a sentence and are paid twice as much. So yes, women are discriminated against.'[121] It was not only white-collar workers who lamented this injustice: as one shoe sales-lady reported, 'They take a greenhorn man and pay him more [than me] right away.' These women understood that discrimination was systemic, not haphazard and occasional. As in the public submissions, the private letters criticized part-time employment agencies such as Drake Personnel that favoured young women and discriminated against older ones. 'Sorry,' they told one qualified woman, 'but we have had no requests for women over 50.'[122] This woman's angry letter of protest was copied to her Member of Parliament.

Letters that bridled with anger were also articulations of a sense of entitlement and rights. Many single women and self-supporting mothers suggested that every citizen had a right not to be forced into depend-ence on others. An immigrant woman working as a waitress protested that she could not secure a mortgage because she was single. Her anger was not only fuelled by this discriminatory insult, however, for she also resented the lack of dignity accorded her service work: there was 'no re-spect for waitresses, even less than [for] waiters'; despite providing an 'essential service,' she maintained, '[we are] too lowly to merit status.' [123] Similarly, a woman waiting on tables who learned of the RCSW from watching *Take Thirty*, lauded the commissioners for 'giving women more recognition.' She criticized only one aspect of her working life: her low wages. 'It bothers me that we only get one dollar an hour ... Other per-sonnel get raises, but not us,' she complained.[124]

Women also registered criticism of the feminization of some jobs, the lack of advancement for women in professions such as teaching, preg-nancy and marriage bars in employment, and the prevailing sexual div-ision of labour. White-collar women complained that employment agen-cies channelled women into a small number of clerical jobs, and that employers such as the banks slyly put a different title on a woman's job, then paid a man more to do it, while 'expecting us to live on a salary no single man would.'[125] Unconvinced that the sexual division of labour was based on inherent sex differences, some criticized the limitations placed on their earnings and decried their thwarted sense of fulfilment. A single office worker with dashed 'mechanical' ambitions told the RCSW she had been confined to female-typed jobs, barred from more technical, highly skilled, or highly paid ones in her company, even though she was 'fascinated with motor mechanics,' and had asked to work in the ware-house doing machinery orders. She believed that married women's place was primarily 'in the home' but that, as a single woman, she was in a different category: 'There are women like me who must make a living, not an existence, but a living, because we chose not to marry right out of high school.' She abandoned the company that prevented her from 'moving up or making equal' pay, and was still searching for a job where she felt she could secure the 'same benefits' as men without 'sacrificing [her] femininity.'[126]

Some letter writers had a more inherently politicized sense of who benefited from women's work in female job ghettos. 'I rise at dawn,' said one working mother, who then went on to outline her double day and her belief that 'employers take advantage of working mothers. They know [we have to work and] ... they discount [our] wages and job opportunities,' she wrote, further suggesting that employers used the excuse that women were 'short term' workers even though they actually worked for long periods of time. 'Why are girls only trained for nursing and teaching?' she asked. After all, 'women have brains too, yet they must outwork and outperform males.' As if to apologize for her radical views, she concluded more lightheartedly, 'I guess I was born thirty years too early.'[127] Even letters that urged individual 'bootstrapping' as a solution to women's inequality might simultaneously conclude that systemic sexism was the problem. One writer insisted that younger women just had to assume some 'backbone' in the quest for economic independence: 'Girls must see from the start that they must stand up for themselves ... Get all the knowledge you can and use it to be a full person and not lean on men as dependents ... Of course no husband is going to say you are worth your salt. I'd say find out what salt you are worth, and see you are worth it ... overlooking his snide remarks.' This self-help advocate, however, also blamed patriarchal ideology for women's problems: men would 'never do anything to help women as long as they can exploit them,' she wrote, ending with the essentialist but nonetheless amusing quip: 'Men are a race of cads.'[128]

While it is true that some working mothers voiced a sense of entitlement to wage work, others wrote defensively about their combined roles of wage and mother work. Using a strategy not unlike the CUPE brief's, such writers responded implicitly to all the myths about working moms. Working mothers felt they were the most stigmatized, misunderstood workers and they wanted the RCSW to hear their side of the story. One letter writer, for instance, countered the idea that women worked for unnecessary extras. A part-time worker living in the Maritimes, she reminded the RCSW that part-timers had 'few benefits and lower pay' and that her money was not 'spent on luxuries and riotous living … It goes to the dentist bill, buys shoes to replace a pair outgrown, new curtains, paint for the kitchen ceiling … and countless other items that deteriorate or disappear to the embarrassment of an already strained budget.'[129] The charge that working mothers neglected their children and created juvenile delinquents was the cruellest myth for most working mothers. One bookkeeper wrote to Bird denouncing a radio-show caller who had referred to mothers such as her as 'night time babysitters,'[130] insinuating they barely knew their children. Many working mothers invoked their experience as the countervailing evidence for these myths, and some suggested that working mothers were especially misunderstood by men who had never been in their shoes: 'Our legislators, predominantly male, fail to realize how hard the majority of women work to raise children, educate them, provide extras that are in no way luxuries, and ease the burden on the husband. Working mothers are helping to provide for the citizens of the future,' one individual wrote.[131] Historians may debate the notion of experience endlessly, but women at the time were convinced that their experiences produced a different understanding of the world: granted, this too was an interpretation, but certainly one that insisted on a connection between their social location and their emerging consciousness of oppression.

Fewer of these working women with families seemed to adopt the line of many service clubs, middle-class women's groups, and even some unions that suggested working moms would rather be homemakers but were forced to work due to their husband's low income or their own poverty. Understandably, these working women wanted to legitimate their labour and refuted the notion that bringing home a paycheque was a second-best option. Married women and mothers also lamented the barriers that kept them from paid work: first and foremost was usually the lack of child care, though other issues such as tax exemptions and low wages were routinely raised. The regional and racial complexion of Canadian poverty also revealed itself in submissions that simply asked for more paid work for women. 'There is little opportunity for women's labour in Newfoundland because of high unemployment,' wrote one woman.[132] While almost no Native women wrote letters, their public presentations voiced a similar unhappiness with lack of work available in their communities. An Alberta Métis woman expressed her concern for people in the next generation, should they not secure work: 'We need training and work … Men could work in sawmills, girls train as supervisors in local mission schools, or as waitresses, cooks and in beauty culture. It is sad to see so many young people walking around when so much could be done.'[133] The narrow list of work options she cited suggests that feminist critiques of the sexual division of labour did not have the same resonance for those who had long been denied any work. At least one Native woman also voiced her objection to being slotted into domestic labour. A self-described 'uneducated' Northwest Territories woman who had lost her treaty rights due to marriage, she told the commission that she could 'not stand long hours [of domestic work].' Since she had epilepsy, she 'could not operate machinery,' and the only work available was 'housekeeping for $100 a month, plus room and board.' 'Really,' she wrote, 'I just feel like committing suicide sometimes it's so tough, lucky I don't drink or I would have long ago.'[134]

While this short survey purposely favours the voices of working women who explained or defended their labour, there were also letters from those endorsing a natural sexual division of labour, denouncing married women workers, and idealizing the male breadwinner. The few letters truly steeped in misogyny, however, came predominantly from men. Even if no one had yet coined the term sexual harassment, the phenomenon was clearly visible: one man who insisted women over forty were 'not worth much,' bragged about his fun playing 'slap and tickle' with his 'cute typist.'[135] Another writer labelled feminists 'mentally sick, frustrated and unhappy.'[136] That even a minority wrote letters in this vein suggests how much the sexualization and ridicule of women was still taken for granted, though one could argue that these authors were on the defensive, fearful that an established gender order was in jeopardy.

Not all letters disparaging working women came from men; women criticized other women for their 'emotive' nature, their interest only in 'husband hunting,'[137] and their unsuitability for jobs; some opposed new maternity rights as misguided special status for women. Other critics did not denounce all working women, but rather laid out a hierarchy of the most virtuous, needy, and deserving women, assuming jobs should be given on the basis of need – though men were not assessed in the same way.[138] However, within the group of writers who defended male breadwinning as the cornerstone of the family and nation, there were important differences. Some individuals, usually men, endorsed a patriarchal family, relegating women to their role of 'pleasing men,' or striving to be 'experts in eroticism,' while many homemakers simply asked that their labour in the home be recognized for its importance and value. The most adamant opponents of women's equality were not taken seriously by the RCSW staff, though polite thank-you letters were required. Occasionally the staff had a little fun. When a rambling letter blamed Dagwood and Jiggs for patriarchy in crisis, the RCSW reply read: 'Thank you for your letter explaining 'the need for strong men and how Dagwood and Jiggs have demoted the father as the head of the household. Yours sincerely ...'"[139]

Although the RCSW was not inclined to value these private letters as solid, hard evidence (and indeed, staff members sometimes wrote 'no value' at the top of them), the topics they covered, the perspectives offered, the experiences invoked, and particularly the feelings they conveyed, did reveal something not found in the formal union briefs that divided up women's lives up into separate categories and charts. Some letters referred to violence, while others protested a whole series of problems that were interconnected. A sixty-eight-year-old widow with two sons wrote about tax relief, abortion, violence, job benefits, and equal pay. Her views, presented with both humour and indignation, are worth quoting at length. Calling for 'no laws at all' concerning abortion and birth control, she asked:

> Why should some 80 yr old cardinals decide [about abortion] for women. It's ridiculous ... might as well ask a eunuch to give his personal experience on sex ... Women have to work harder, usually have longer hours and perform monotonous jobs for less than their male counterparts in most industry and particularly in offices ... They are subject to dismissal after years of hard work by arbitrary bosses who would rather have a younger if less efficient worker, and [the one fired] has no protection. I hope you have many responses and something will be done for women who are pushed around, worked to death, beaten up (and too scared to say anything about it), and work at two jobs a day.[140]

Although many women offered their own opinions or framed their complaints within personal narratives, the letters can still be read collectively for evidence of women's attempts to understand the day-to-day experience of paid and unpaid work that so consumed their lives. Moreover, many women did not simply seek aid in becoming better individuals; rather, they voiced a sense of collective grievance, with their stories ending with calls for social change. 'We have to make things better for our daughters,' said one working mother, while another put it more forcefully: 'We need profound changes ... This is a generation of angry females who will be satisfied with nothing less.'[141]

Conclusion

During the commission hearings, a female journalist sympathetic to the RCSW published a piece in the *Star Weekly Magazine* exposing the hypocrisy underlying attitudes towards working mothers. While many men voiced 'outward encouragement' for women in the workforce, she detected a strong current of 'hidden disapproval' too; moreover, the women she interviewed indicated they had had enough of this subterranean disapprobation.[142] Another woman who sent an individual submission to the RCSW voiced her lament that working mothers were still misunderstood: despite the lack of evidence linking working mothers to juvenile delinquency, she wrote, 'this stigma is still out there.'[143] For both the reporter and the working mother, the RCSW provided a public space in which to question the prevailing gender order, and like many participants in the RCSW, they saw paid work as an absolutely crucial measure of women's equality. With the exception of the two male commissioners, the commission generally agreed. There was an implicit assumption that well-remunerated paid labour was one, if not *the*, path to emancipation; equality was not possible without the right to employment, equal access to occupations and training, and advancement up the ladder of success.

Despite the RCSW's emphasis on paid work, the word class was not in the vocabulary of the commission. The RCSW was conceived of, staffed, and implemented within a liberal feminist tradition that saw equality of opportunity as the means to liberation. Canada was not supposed to be a 'class ridden' society, and indeed, the notion of class as an essential category of analysis or as an inherently unequal relationship was largely foreign to the commissioners. Also, the ways in which information and knowledge was filtered through, and by, the RCSW created a perspective that was unlikely to see class, ethnicity, or race as critical determinants of inequality. As Dorothy Smith has shown, our methods, means, and assumptions of inquiry create powerful discourses that become their own 'relations of ruling.'[144] This social construction of knowledge was effected through the RCSW's own analysis of the submissions, its use of researchers raised on Parsonian sociology, its fear of being too critical of business, its absorption of prevailing cultural theories of immigrant 'integration,' and its placation of more conservative commissioners.

It is unlikely that the appointment of one labour commissioner would have changed this orientation, though the government's failure to do so symbolically marginalized labour as an important constituency. Unions were thus anxious to create their own knowledge legacy, offering well-researched, comprehensive briefs that laid out extensive plans for state reform, and simultaneously showed labour's role as a vanguard force for working women's struggles. Taken as a whole, the labour movement had a solid, social-democratic platform on working women's rights, and there were signs of political shifts since the war ended: to varying degrees, unions now challenged the notion of a singular male breadwinner, they began to insert 'woman' into their human-rights agenda, and they called for social recognition of the working mother with paid maternity leaves and child-care services. Some unions, however, were reluctant to challenge forms of male privilege embedded in their own contracts, and inclined to ignore their own male-dominated leadership structures as a problem. Given the numbers of non-English- and non-French-speaking immigrants who had come to Canada since the Second World War, not to mention abundant evidence that female immigrant workers were often trapped in low-wage service or 'sweated' labour, it is also surprising that trade unions spent so little time addressing the unorganized, the relationship between race, ethnicity, and work, and the particular needs of new immigrants.

CUPE's self-critical examination of gender inequality within its ranks was refreshingly honest, but also rare. Nonetheless, some rank-and-file women spoke out, using the RCSW as a forum for 'civic resistance,' criticizing inequalities structured into their contracts and workplaces. They were not anti-union as much as critical of unions' failure to live up to ideals of 'brotherhood' and equality. Within the union movement, a small group of labour feminists in leadership positions did use the RCSW as an opportunity to prod their own unions into action. The abortion squabble within the CLC was a small sign that labour feminists were ready to embrace a broader definition of feminism, a word that had always been seen suspiciously by unions. Although their view of the state was more cautious than that of some liberal feminists, accustomed as unionists were to this neutral 'umpire' siding with capital, they nonetheless maintained a fairly instrumentalist view that placed considerable hope in the possibility of lobbying and incremental reform. Arguably, labour feminism already had a presence within unions in the post-war period, but it was not well organized and coordinated across unions, in part due to Cold War hostilities. By the late 1960s, and after the RCSW, feminists in the mainstream union movement were far more intent on raising equality issues both inside and outside their unions. Ironically, however, they were soon challenged by a new cadre of feminists, educated in New Left, Marxist, and left-nationalist movements, who had a different analysis of class and union politics, who were more critical of the male-dominated labour bureaucracy, and whose socialist-feminist ideas posed a new challenge the CLC's embrace of 'social democracy as usual.'

The private letters addressed to the RCSW also suggested a shift had occurred in the meanings women assigned to wage labour. Traditionalist discourses stressing married women's place in the home and legitimizing a natural sexual division of labour were certainly voiced in private letters to the RCSW, but the fact that fewer women and men wanted to publicize these views suggests that such ideas did not have the social purchase they once did. Anonymity not only gave traditionalists a forum, it also provided an opening for dissatisfied women to say the unspoken, speak their unhappiness, vent their anger, complain about their second class status in the labour force, and press for change. One could argue that these letters of complaint were mediated by culture, crafted for the RCSW in a strategically emotional mode, and on one level that is true. But to interpret them only as complaints shaped by narrative convention, or only within a 'closed circuit' of pre-existing discursive possibilities, misses both the changing social and material conditions in which women were embedded and, perhaps most important, the fact that women had something to complain about. Rather, the letters reveal women's efforts to make sense of their day-to-day lives at a time when their labour was altering in significant ways, in a society that often denigrated their work, failed to recognize their unpaid contributions to social reproduction, and denied them the same entitlements as men.

If feminist historians once gave 'epistemic privilege to women's experience,'[145] we have increasingly expressed epistemic doubt about the concept. Yet experience need not, as postmodern critics suggest, become idealized and reified as an incontrovertible 'truth'; it can be interpreted in feminist and materialist veins, as a dialectical process that is both lived and construed, a 'point of origin' and discursively constructed.[146] The frictions, fissures, and contradictions that can emerge in the nexus of social being and social consciousness, and the power of reflective and rational human agency, are essential to this perspective. Women's resentments, unhappiness, and dissonant views were shaped in the liminal space and the contradictions they sensed between ideal and reality, legitimate and outlawed feelings, between the promise of work and its actual payoff. The ongoing friction between lived economic relations and 'imposed consciousness' offered some brief 'moments of openness and opportunity' in which alternative understandings might 'break through,' however temporarily or ephemerally.[147] These were not, in the words of the more misogynistic press, mere whining women, but rather daughters, aunts, mothers, and grandmothers who were developing a language of entitlement, who did not simply blame themselves, who equated their rights with men's rights, and who voiced a sense of collective grievance – and collective hope for the future.

Conclusion: Putting Contradictions into Context

To end the story of women's work and their involvement in the labour movement in 1970, the year the RCSW reported, is one appropriate chronological marker, but it prevents us from seeing the full impact of the long-term consequences of women's changing outlook and sense of discontent that were percolating below the surface of Canadian society. There were also significant changes that unfolded in the late 1960s and early 1970s. Due to the impact of a partially de-racialized immigration policy, there was a new demographic profile of working women emerging in the 1970s. Particularly in large urban centres, women of colour swelled the ranks of the labour force, slowly altering the face of the union movement as well. Organizations created by First Nations and women of colour also proliferated. Aboriginal women, for example, mounted independent challenges to the long-standing oppression they had endured under a patriarchal and colonial *Indian Act*, articulating a new women-centred politics that drew on both 'traditional' and emerging ideologies of equality.[1]

The challenges to the established order that had been brewing within the New Left, Red Power, women's liberation, student, and peace movements in the late 1960s persisted into the 1970s; indeed, some argue that radicalism across the globe was most intense during the 'glorious decade'[2] of the long sixties – from 1965 to 1975. After a self-critical assessment of their failure to analyse capitalist exploitation and recognize the importance of the working class to social transformation, some New Left and feminist activists shifted their focus to the labour movement, challenging what they saw as a comfortable, compliant, and conservative leadership. New Marxist Leninist parties, intent on radicalizing union members and winning workers to a socialist politics emerged, challenging the long-standing post-war standoff within the Left between the Communist Party and the CCF. A younger cadre of workers, who had already expressed their unhappiness with union complacency in the wildcat wave of the 1960s, as well as some working-class daughters in search of good, not 'female' wages, were also ready to challenge taken-for-granted labour movement ideas and practices.[3]

Feminism grew organizationally stronger after 1970, though it was not an ideologically homogeneous movement by any means; founded in 1972, the National Action Committee (NAC) was an uneasy coalition of liberal, socialist, and radical activists, with different visions and priorities. This apparent diversity in politics was not matched by diversity in NAC's constituency of predominantly white women, which led to subsequent challenges to its inadequate recognition of racial inequalities. Working-class and labour-movement women also created new, women-centred political organizations, starting in the mid-1960s, but picking up speed, and becoming more radical, in the 1970s. They formed women's committees that mobilized women to push for equality within their unions, and also founded new political organizations such as Ontario Working Women and Saskatchewan Working Women, dedicated to building a broader coalition of working women, often inspired by socialist-feminist politics that saw class analysis and union issues as a top priority.

There were clearly significant shifts in women's interpretations of their wage work, their consciousness, and their political sensibilities that became more visible, firmly articulated, and oppositional between the mid-1960s and 1970s. The sense of unfairness, the articulations of entitlement, the desire for change – the embryonic 'structure of feeling' – articulated in women's letters to the RCSW, were taking shape in forms that were better defined, publicly expressed, and consciously oppositional. Within this upsurge in new political organizing, younger women who came of age in the 1960s sometimes made common cause with older labour feminists, often Marxists and communists who had struggled through the dark years of the Cold War. The Canadian Textile and Chemical Union (CTCU) drew in younger socialist-feminists who imbibed the organizing know-how of Madeleine Parent, and in the Canadian Union of Public Employees, leader Grace Hartman found a new cadre of rank-and-file women, some Marxist Leninists, some not, eager to take up her long-standing interest in feminist issues. This rapidly expanding cadre of female public-sector unionists was to become a significant force in the labour movement's gradual embrace of feminist goals.

Yet, more established labour feminists also clashed with a younger generation of women who were mobilized around very different class politics and visions of feminism that eschewed reformism as an answer, and viewed change coming from the 'bureaucratic top' with considerable suspicion. In the West, for instance, innovative efforts to organize bank workers were undertaken by the Service, Office and Retail Workers Union of Canada (SORWUC), a grassroots, feminist, independent trade union, dedicated to rank-and-file democracy. Their underfunded, precarious, and courageous organizing campaign was opposed, and raided by CLC affiliates, with the full support of vice-president Shirley Carr.[4] The small group of labour feminists who had struggled into the union bureaucracy – and sometimes coped stoically with sexism – in earlier decades did not necessary comprehend radical political challenges from a new cadre of feminists. Recall the young telephone operator described in chapter 5 who wanted not only to file a grievance, but to circulate petitions and rally her co-workers to her cause; the established leadership in her all-female union was taken by surprise, and could not quite fathom her political style.

These changes in left-wing, feminist, and labour politics were illustrated well during a series of significant strikes beginning in the late 1960s. In 1967 a strike at Tilco, a small manufacturing plant in Ontario, became a national cause célèbre when the employer used an ex-parte injunction to usher strikebreakers into the plant, effectively crushing this small TWUA local, composed largely of women. An 'illegal' protest of employers' much-hated use of injunctions, led by an alliance of communist and CCF-affiliated male trade unionists, resulted in their public trial, convictions, and jail time. While they were cast as working class heroes, the women lost their jobs, and they did not testify at the hearings of the royal commission set up to investigate injunctions in the wake of this struggle. During the strike, unions condemned the super-exploitation of women workers, but gender was not a key organizing theme in the strike. Yet, in subsequent cause-célèbre strikes over the next decade, gender inequality became a vital issue; social democratic, left, and feminist sympathizers were mobilized as supporters precisely for this reason.[5] When immigrant women in the Puretex factory in Toronto struck in 1978, their protests over the invasive video monitoring of their every move in the plant incited protests from left-wing and feminist supporters, and there was no question that class, gender, and ethnicity were seen as interconnected points of oppression shaping these working women's lives. The CTCU took up their cause, protesting the 'double disadvantage' that women in these 'ghetto plants' lived with.[6]

To end in 1970, in other words, seems to miss all the fun: the excitement, change, tumult, and intoxicating feeling of hope that we felt, a tenuous sense that challenges to the gender order, class domination, and colonialism were not only necessary, but held out some hope of having a real impact. That, however, would be another book. Moreover, even though the long sixties represented a radical rupture with the feminist and labour politics of the post-war period, this need not suggest either a crude two-wave theory of feminist history, or that the years leading up to this rupture were merely a trough of inactivity. To see Canadian women workers in the post-war period simply as a conservative preview to the real drama of the 1970s misses the subtle changes that occurred in the twenty-five years after the war, the 'radical consequences of these incremental changes,'[7] and the contestations that did occur over women's paid work – in short, the specific dilemmas, struggles, and accomplishments of women workers in this era.

The word contradictory (along with fluid, fragmented, and contested) is currently overused in historical writing, yet it is does seem an apt descriptor of this era. While a revisionist current in North American scholarship has rightly challenged the notion that the post-war period was characterized overwhelmingly by an undifferentiated gender and political conservatism, we should not forget that there were repressive and constricting aspects to Canadian political and social life. Delineating the context for the contradictions of the post-war period is thus essential to understanding women's experiences of work. The Cold War, for one thing, put a damper on left-wing ideas and dissent, and its effect was felt beyond so-called communist unions and the Communist Party, for it offered rank-and-file women unionists object lessons in 'stepping out of line' by sounding like, or associating with, communists. The diffusion of fear and anxiety, and the encouragement of political conformity, associated with the Cold War were part of the ideological climate shaping the prevailing images of gender, work, unions, and resistance. The Cold War not only de-railed new union organizing in areas where many women worked, but it separated those few women activists promoting equality into rival political camps that disallowed collaborations, a problem compounded in Canada by the lack of institutional arrangements, such as a strong federal Women's Bureau and women's departments within unions, that existed in the United States.[8]

We must also acknowledge the existence of a powerful familialist ideology during this period that naturalized heterosexuality, emphasized women's feminine, domestic, and maternal roles, and justified the sexual division of labour both at work and at home. Granted, this was primarily a prescriptive, class- and race-based ideal. Many women were working for wages, supporting families, organizing, advocating, and protesting, but these social practices did not necessarily accord with the images that made up their world, and that were reproduced even within their own union newspapers. The effects of this ideology of sexual difference are difficult to identify with any certainty, but there was a clear dissonance between the rising numbers of married working women and a persisting idealization of home-centred motherhood. This image of femininity did not go completely unquestioned: a few feminist journalists lauded the working mother, union papers celebrated women workers on the picket line, and some discontented working women wrote to the RCSW, protesting society's unwarranted criticisms of working mothers. Yet the power of ideology is also its capacity to appeal, to seem legitimate and commonsensical. Given women's recent war experiences, the reality of the double day, and their responsibility for family care, these dominant ideals had a strong allure, and explain why a working mother might feel conflicted about her dual, overlapping work roles. In efforts to match their actual lives with the supposed norm, some working mothers legitimized their wage work by explaining that it was needed to supplement the family economy, or pay for a child's education.

That this dissonance between image and reality became a factor in the emergence of a renewed feminist movement is undeniable; however, one could argue that the same pressures had existed for much longer for single mothers, racialized minorities, and some working-class women, who had been combining home and wage work as a matter of sheer necessity. When the 'bad fit'[9] between ideal and reality became apparent for a much larger group of women, including professional, and other middle-class workers, the latter group did not necessarily see the difference between their lives and those of the women who babysat their children and cleaned their offices, or that their choices about work were premised on other women's lack of choice. This inattention to class and race inequalities was one theme running throughout the RCSW, despite some commissioners' desire to hear from more marginalized women.

This contradiction between representation and reality was captured well in beauty contests such as La Reine des Midinettes. The ILGWU saw this beauty contest as a way to unionize more women workers, appeal to them through a woman-centred culture, and recognize them as tireless wage workers contributing to social wealth. However, the cultural messages that were part and parcel of the contest simultaneously reinforced an equation of femininity with consumption, beauty, marrying up, and individual competition. These were polar opposites of the idealized attributes of masculinity that were equated with union activism and leadership: intelligence, political acumen, and militancy. By the 1970s, the contradiction of a labour movement publicly claiming to understand sexual inequality, but still representing women in bathing suits, was finally resolved when beauty contests were officially relegated to the past.

Invoking contradiction need not be an escape from causal explanations; rather, the concept can become a central element of them. Contradiction is crucial to many feminist efforts to reconstruct a new historical materialism with the transformative insights of feminism, to re-inscribe the 'social' in our explorations of women's lives in this post-, postmodernist academic era. Rather than lamenting the 'flawed' metanarrative of class associated with the white, male, paid worker, rather than seeing differentiation within categories such as class as a reason to abandon them, suggests Miriam Glucksmann, we should embrace contradiction and difference as stimuli to the 'conceptual refinement of class in the light of a complex social world.'[10] This intellectual project takes for granted the need to move beyond the 'closed circuit'[11] of discursive analysis, and stresses the importance of 'excavating'[12] lived experience as a way of understanding how class and gender are intertwined. By insisting on structure and agency as related, not dichotomous, and on a dialogue between theory and empirical work, these efforts draw not only on recent materialist-feminist theories, but they also harken back to early writing in working-class history that constructed class and gender as processes that also encompassed tradition, culture, and ideology. Clearly, not all past writing is passé.[13]

Contradiction is also central to our understanding of conflict and change. In any historical moment, there are contradictions that create 'possibilities for emancipatory struggle, as well as for reproduction of exploitation and domination.'[14] The contradictions in women workers' lives in post-war Canada were embedded in the existing social and material relations, but not determined by them; nor, on the other hand, were women the autonomous, 'Horatio Alger' agents of self-transformation, as suggested in the success stories presented in the *Indian News*. How and why different groups of women came to question the hegemonic definitions of womanhood and work in the post-war period had much to do with frictions, fissures, and seeming incongruencies that were part and parcel of their experience of work, as well as their active reflection on their labouring lives. Women workers' lives were bounded and 'pressured' by the material, to be sure, but lived experience was not then automatically 'translated' directly into political consciousness; rather, experience gave way to a range of possibilities that shaped how people handled those events. As in Gramscian writing, there existed the possibility of a disjuncture between dominant and submerged ideologies: the ongoing 'friction' between lived economic relations and 'imposed consciousness' from above occasionally offered people 'moments of openness and opportunity,' in which alternative understandings might break through, however temporarily and ephemerally.[15]

The ideological climate of the time did put boundaries and limitations on women's working lives, propping up the family-wage ideal. However, this male-breadwinner ideal (only ever partially realized) was evaporating for good, perhaps one of the more revolutionary aspects of this unrevolutionary period.[16] Until the 1960s, women rarely directly challenged the most resilient boundaries at work, such as the sexual division of labour, yet they still asserted their rights as workers and union members with new vigour. Although this book has argued that the Fordist bargain was a limited, gender- and race-biased accommodation, the accord did aid unionized workers, including women who had long been relegated to jobs that were considered less skilled, important, and secure, even by their own unions.

Women who had unionized jobs were anxious to enjoy the benefits of Fordism – as is indicated also by how receptive women were to public-sector unionism when it was legalized in the 1960s. New practices and cultures tied to worker contractualism constrained many forms of workplace protest and codified management discipline more effectively, but they also bolstered women's sense of entitlement and the possibilities for protest – a key contradiction of the accord. Women with unions to back them up used their new contractual rights to fight for more flexible, fair workplaces, to demand dignity on the job, and to secure some job security. In some cases, they also had to challenge masculinist practices and ideas within their own unions, but there is no doubt that these women welcomed the advantages of their new collective power, using them in strategic efforts to expand their rights as working women. Not only did the escalating number of arbitrations fought over pregnancy and marriage bars make this clear, but even within historically quiescent unions such as Bell Telephone's Traffic Employees Association, the leadership had to change its position on maternity leave within a matter of a few years, under pressure from their rank and file, who were part of a flood of women into new white-collar jobs, yet also full participants in the baby boom, no longer willing to accept the gender order the company had long dictated.

Of course, more women workers stood outside the virtuous circle of Fordism than within it: women in service work, the growing army of contingent clericals, and those in small manufacturing concerns, for instance, were often not so fortunate. During this period, many jobs in the service sector were feminized for both economic and ideological reasons, an indication of some continuities with the earlier twentieth century: women, for instance, were still described as 'until' (marriage) workers by the business press and employers who were interested in as flexible a workforce as possible. Even the vast category of white collar and service work was bifurcated: new Canadians were pressed to fill jobs such as waitressing or kitchen work that native-born women had fled from during the war, and expanding areas of work such as retail were constructed as higher-status jobs in part because they were equated with respectability and 'whiteness.'

Retail work, as the Dupuis Frères example indicated, had understandable appeal for women workers, both single and married, as employers made it time-flexible, and they also made every effort to link women's daily work to women's culture, stressing beauty, femininity, marriage, and consumption. Department stores were selling some of these very same products to their customers, utilizing the emotional and aesthetic labour of their women sellers to do so. This was also a process that involved ongoing management efforts to regulate and 'make over' the bodies of female saleswomen. Again, however, ideal and reality were not always a good fit. Women working at Dupuis Frères who complained of tired knees, refused to slim down, or talked back proved not to be so malleable, but perhaps the biggest shock for management was women's adamant rejection of traditional paternalism in favour of unionization, and their militant and spirited support for a strike in 1952. Department-store paternalism was not unusual across Canada, though retail unionization certainly was. The ideological contours of the Dupuis Frères strike were also politically distinct, reflecting the linguistic and ethnic inequalities at the heart of Quebec's political economy, the growing militancy in Quebec's Catholic union movement, as well as different understandings of nationalism within Quebec. This conflict, along with the Dionne one, underscores the importance of taking Quebec's distinct history, English-French tensions, and cultural differences into account in Canadian working-class history. Women retail workers in English Canada may have faced a similar work process and gendered hierarchy on the job, but

Quebec unions were already on their own distinct political trajectory that was to become even more divergent from English Canadian labour in the late 1960s and 1970s.

During the long sixties, the question of Quebec's self-determination was a crucial issue for many radicals, a touchstone for heated debates about difference and discrimination. Indeed, in the post–Second World War period, the Québécois were still sometimes referred to as a 'race' apart, even though the term seems anachronistic to our contemporary ears. By the 1980s and 1990s, however, a different feminist terminology and critique of race had emerged; feminists began to take a hard look at the way in which Canadian nation building had been equated with 'whiteness,' and how this racist ideal had been furthered by a discriminatory immigration policy. The NFB film described in chapter 2 that portrayed the archetypal 'good' immigrant woman worker as white, and northern European, destined for service or white-collar work, epitomized this policy. European immigrants from southern or eastern Europe, such as the Polish women brought to work in Dionne's mill, fit uneasily into this ethnic/racial hierarchy. Although these Polish newcomers were portrayed differently than they had been thirty years before, as more cultured, adaptable, and 'white,' notions about their appropriate and probable role in the labour force in service and manufacturing work indicated a lingering ethnocentrism. There is no doubt, however, that the Dionne women were preferred immigrants compared to women of colour; indeed, advocates of expanded eastern European immigration made precisely this argument to politicians, knowing its popular appeal.

Issues of race could not be so easily denied or obscured in the case of Canada's original inhabitants. For Aboriginal women, the dissonance between images of post-war affluence and actual experience was particularly sharp. Although First Nations women's experiences varied considerably from one region and nation to another, on the prairies, and especially in the provincial north, many women and their families faced worsening economic hardship and social dislocation. While the Fordist accord may have been a boon to some working-class men, it was quite the opposite for others. The decasualization of jobs, the commercialization of resources, declining fur prices, and white incursions on Native land – among other factors – created a climate of limited economic choices for families that had adapted to the market for some years as multi-occupational households. The state, often drawing on expert social-science opinion, perceived male breadwinners in these failing economies, ignoring women's crucial role in social reproduction and thus family survival, although paradoxically, policy makers were well aware that the low-paid sugar-beet work they promoted depended on family labour for profitability.

Other federal labour placement programs, which many Aboriginal people welcomed, were geared towards waged work, yet they were unfortunately limited in their scope, and they relegated women to a narrow range of jobs, usually in the service sector, as women were still imagined as ancillary workers, not breadwinners. These programs were also intended to remould a problematic Indian 'character' so these workers might 'integrate' or, in effect, assimilate; any failings could then be explained by Aboriginal peoples' cultural baggage from their traditional past. While the cultural worth of work, and ties to one's community and heritage were important for First Nations women, especially those migrating workers who found themselves in difficult, alien, urban surroundings, this 'culture blaming' could easily slide into a determinist, negative characterization. The portrayal of Aboriginal women, even by reformers *critiquing* discrimination, as morally endangered/endangering, shared some similarities with the prevailing construction of poor and working-class white women, but the lasting impact of colonialism also cast Aboriginal women in a 'primitivist' mould, with tragic consequences. Notions that Aboriginal women came from a 'race left behind,' and that part of their racial inheritance was a tendency to promiscuity, left them open not only to exploitation, but to racist denigration and violence; indeed, these economic and ideological processes were not distinct but interrelated. Perhaps it is this legacy of the post-war era that seems most at odds with the Happy Days image of the 1950s, and thus the most jarring and grievous contradiction described in this book.

Again, however, ending in 1970 leaves out a sequel story of Aboriginal women contributing to a renewed, militant, anti-colonial Indigenous movement, and also self-organizing to combat their particular history of patriarchal colonialism. This contradiction, eliciting as it does a sense of suffering and struggle, also reinforces my case for a feminist history that has neither abandoned a sense of 'feeling,' nor banished a sense of political commitment under the pressure of false claims to apolitical neutrality or postmodern pessimism. Rather than the latter, suggests Terry Eagleton, we should reflect critically on our interests and politics, striving for 'dispassionate judgement,' instead of succumbing to the 'liberal myth of even handedness.'[17] Contemplating affective links with women in the past also has certain perils: we may romanticize past actors, think in presentist terms, downplay differences based on class or race, or misinterpret women's interpretations of their experience. Yet, however fraught this form of emulative time travelling is, the effort is both politically and historically worthwhile.

Who, after all, cannot be moved by the letter from a daughter, addressed to Florence Bird, saying that her mother was 'too tired to even sit down and write at night,' so she would tell her story instead: and 'every word,' she assured Florence, 'is true.' Widowed unexpectedly at an early age, with no education, the mother worked at factory jobs, where she still laboured for $1.15 an hour in order to support three children. Yet these wages, said the daughter, 'barely pay the mortgage, food, oil, lights, clothing, medical.' Her mother raised them by working outside the home, but with significant, painful costs to her health, the daughter recounted. Indeed, the daughter indicated that she preferred her mother to remain at home. Above all, the daughter told Florence, her mother wanted to see her 'kids educated.'[18] This may seem like an ordinary, even commonplace story about women's low wages and lack of choice, but the daughter's letter also conveys a sense of injustice and regret, suffering and struggle, perseverance and pride, all of which were integral to the story of women's work in the post-war period.

Notes

Abbreviations and Shortened References

ALHI	Alberta Labour History Institute
AM	Archives of Manitoba
AO	Archives of Ontario
ASBGA	Alberta Sugar Beet Growers Association
BBP	Beatrice Brigden Papers
BOM	Bank of Montreal
CACSW	Canadian Advisory Council on the Status of Women
CL	*Canadian Labour*
CLC	Canadian Labour Congress Papers
CNTU	Confederation of National Trade Unions
CPHW	The Canadian Packinghouse Worker
CU	Cornell University
CU	*The Canadian Unionist*
CUC	Communications Union of Canada Papers
DFF	Dupuis Frères Fonds
DMI	Department of Manpower and Immigration
EGMF	Elsie Gregory MacGill Fonds
FLW	*The Fur and Leather Worker*
GA	Glenbow Archives
HBC	Hudson's Bay Company Records
HECA	Hautes Études Commerciales Archives
IFLWU	International Fur and Leather Workers Union Papers
IUE	International Union of Electrical Workers Fonds
JC	Joseph Cohen Papers

Kheel	Kheel Center for Labor-Management Documentation and Archives
LAC	*Labour Arbitration Cases*
LD	*Le Duprex*
MHSO	Multicultural History Society of Ontario
MOHC	Métis Oral History Collection
MPOH	Meatpacking Oral History Collection
MUSC	McMaster University Special Collections
NAC	National Archives of Canada
NFB	National Film Board
OFL	Ontario Federation of Labour
OTEU	Office and Technical Employees Association Papers
PE	Peterborough Examiner
Proceedings	Senate, Proceedings of the Standing Committee on Immigration and Labour, 10 March 1947
RCAP	Royal Commission on Aboriginal Peoples
RCEP	Royal Commission on Canada's Economic Prospects
RCSW	Royal Commission on the Status of Women
RH	Robert Haddow papers
SAB	Saskatchewan Archives Board
SpC	Special Collections
StC	Statistics Canada
TLCJ	*Trades and Labour Congress Journal*
UBC	University of British Columbia
UFCWU	United Food and Commercial Workers Union papers

Introduction

1 For a good description of this feeling see Kostash, *Long Way from Home.*
2 NAC, RG 33-89 (RCSW), vol. 8, Ontario file, WM.
3 Ibid, vol. 9, Ontario file, MW.
4 McInnis, *Harnessing Labour Confrontation*; Palmer, *Working Class Experience*, 336–9.
5 Albo, '"Competitive Austerity."'
6 Fudge and Tucker, *Labour Before the Law*, 310.
7 Vosko, *Temporary Work*, 26.
8 Cohen, *A Consumer's Republic.*
9 D. Miller, 'Shapes of Power.'

10 Research concentrating on workplaces shaped by the accord has also been influenced by the available sources. Union records in the post-1945 period, along with state records relating to those unions, are voluminous and rich. In fact, in order to find personnel records relating to retail workers, generally workers outside the 'accord,' I ended up using the records of one of the very few unionized department stores in the country.

11 Vosko, *Temporary Work*, 21–3; Forrest, 'Securing the Male Breadwinner.'

12 Sangster, '"We No Longer Respect the Law,"' 47.

13 Satzewich, *Racism and the Incorporation of Foreign Labour* and 'Unfree Labour and Capitalism.'

14 Vosko, *Temporary Work*, 91.

15 Here, I use the word feminization in its more general sense, i.e., a permanent increase in the numbers of women in the labour force. There is an extensive discussion about the nature of feminization (how it relates to sex segregation, for instance) in the political economy literature. See, for example, Vosko, *Temporary Work*; M. Cohen, 'The Implications of Economic Restructuring'; and Armstrong and Armstrong, 'The Feminization of the Labour Force.'

16 NAC, RCSW, vol. 9, Quebec, EP.

17 Williams, with Thorpe, *Beyond Industrial Sociology*, chap. 3.

18 For this definition, see Cossman and Fudge, *Privatization, Law, and the Challenge to Feminism*, 15. See also Luxton and Bezanson, eds., *Social Reproduction*; Luxton, *More than a Labour of Love*; and Corman and Luxton, *Getting By in Hard Times*. For a theoretical overview, see Picchio, *Social Reproduction*, chap. 5. In order to avoid a dualistic notion of social reproduction/production, Miriam Glucksmann suggests a more elastic term, the 'total social organization of labour,' i.e., all forms of labour divided up, and allocated to 'people, activities, structures, and institutions.' Miriam Glucksmann, *Cottons and Casuals*, 19. Historical examinations of household work in particular include Fahrni, *Household Politics*; and Strong-Boag, 'Home Dreams.'

19 Timpson, *Driven Apart*, 18.

20 A few examples include Bryden, *Planners and Politicians*; Litt, *The Muses*; Gauvreau, *The Catholic Origins*; Fahrni, *Household Politics*; Owram, *Born at the Right Time*; Whitaker and Marcuse, *Cold War Canada*; Adams, *The Trouble with Normal*; Gleason, *Normalizing the Ideal*; Behiels, *Prelude to Quebec's Quiet Revolution*; Struthers, *The Limits of Affluence*; and Strong-Boag, 'Home Dreams.'

21 Fahrni and Rutherdale, 'Introduction.'

22 For the former, see Christie, *Engendering the State*, chap. 7, and for the latter, see Finkel, *Sociological Policy*; see also Porter, *Gendered States*.

23 Finkel, *Our Lives*; Iacovetta, *Gatekeepers*; Adamoski, Chunn, and Menzies, eds., *Contesting Canadian Citizenship*.

24 Christie and Gauvreau, eds., *Cultures of Citizenship*.

25 An example of the former view is May, 'Pushing the Limits,' and of the latter, Meyorwitz, ed., *Not June Cleaver*. For a historiographical review, see Meyorwitz, 'Rewriting Postwar Women's History.'

26 Parr, ed., *A Diversity of Women*, 5.

27 Sugiman, *Labour's Dilemma*; Reiter, 'First Class Workers'; Guard, 'Fair Play or Fair Pay?'; Creese, *Contracting Masculinity*; Iacovetta, *Such Hardworking People*. American examples include Deslippe, 'Rights Not Roses'; Cobble, *The Other Women's Movement*; Kessler-Harris, *In Pursuit of Equity*; and Gabin, *Feminism in the Labor Movement*.

28 For example, Calliste, 'Canada's Immigration Policy'; Brand, *No Burden to Carry*; Kobayashi, 'For the Sake of the Children'; Flynn, 'Experience and Identity.'

29 MacLean, *Freedom Is Not Enough*.

30 Cobble, *The Other Women's Movement*. Although a Women's Bureau was set up by the Canadian government in 1954, the American one had a much longer history.

31 Nancy Gabin quoted in Deslippe, *'Rights Not Roses.'*

32 Satzewich and Wotherspoon, *First Nations*, 12. For an overview of Canadian feminist political economy, see Vosko, 'The Pasts (and Futures) of Feminist Political Economy'; Andrew, Armstrong, and Vosko, eds., *Studies in Political Economy*; and Clement and Vosko, eds., *Changing Canada*; and on historical materialism in Canada, Palmer, 'Historical Materialism.'

33 Acker, *Class Questions, Feminist Answers*, 38.

34 For more critical views of intersectionality, see Leslie McCall, 'The Complexity of Intersectionality'; Avtar Brah and Ann Phoenix, 'Ain't I a Woman? Revising Intersectionality'; and the special issue of *European Journal of Women's Studies* 31, no. 1 (2006).

35 Ibid. The term 'excavation' is used by Heidi Gottfried, 'Beyond Patriarchy?' 451.

36 Creese and Stasiulis, 'Introduction,' 7.

37 The eclipsing of agency and social causality have been central to long-standing Marxist critiques of postmodernism. For a discussion by non-Marxist historians of the problematic eclipsing of agency and social causality in historical writing see the special issue of *History and Theory* on 'Agency after Postmodernism,' including Shaw, 'Happy in Our Chains?' and Fitzhugh and Leckie, 'Agency, Postmodernism, and the Causes of Change.'

38 Camfield, 'Re-Orienting Class Analysis.' See also Camfield, 'Beyond Adding on Gender and Class.'

39 I have been influenced by discussions of feminist historical materialism by Pollert, 'Gender and Class Revisited'; Hennessy, *Profit and Pleasure*, and Soper, *Troubled Pleasures*; and also by Marxist-feminists, including Vogel, *Woman Questions*, and Brenner, *Women and the Politics of Class*. Materialist theories are not synonymous with Marxist ones, and there are distinctions between feminist materialism and feminist historical materialism. Indeed, there are different ways in which Marxist and feminist theory have been used and combined that are too extensive to go into here.

40 Gottfried, 'Beyond Patriarchy?' 464; see also Pollert, 'Gender and Class Revisited.'

41 Gimenez, 'Capitalism and the Oppression of Women,' 15. For a related discussion of the complexities (not economism) of Marx's method, see Fraccia, 'Marx's Aufhebung.'

42 Hennessy, drawing on Thompson; *Profit and Pleasure*, 17.

43 Thompson, *The Poverty of Theory*, 9.

44 Hartstock, 'Postmodernism and Political Change'; Wilkerson, 'Is There Something You Need to Tell Me?'; Hennessy, *Profit and Pleasure*, 230. Indeed, this insight was essential to earlier feminist history and historical materialism: Kelly, *Women, History and Theory*, chapter 4.

45 Barbara Foley, review of *Reclaiming Experience*.

46 Scott, 'The Evidence of Experience,' 387. See also Ireland, 'The Appeal to Experience.'

47 Fitzhugh and Leckie, 'Agency, Postmodernism, and the Causes of Change,' 65; and for the latter quote, Pickering, *History, Experience and Cultural Studies*, 224. See also Kruks, *Retrieving Experience*.

48 Moya, 'Postmodernism, "Realism" and the Politics of Identity,' 68. These post-positivists are not politically homogeneous, and as Foley points out, few deal with class exploitation or identity, an indication of how marginalized class analysis has become. Foley, review of *Reclaiming Experience*. On historians' long-standing critique of objectivity, see Zagorin, 'History, the Referent, and Narrative Reflections,' 2; and Haskell, *Objectivity Is Not Neutrality*, esp. chapter 6. For another useful discussion of objectivity see Eagleton, *After Theory*, 186.

49 Eley and Nield, *The Future of Class in History*, 106.

50 Kruks, *Retrieving Experience*.

51 Pickering, *History, Experience and Cultural Studies*, 177.

52 Gordon, 'Comments on That Noble Dream.'

53 Haskell, *Objectivity Is Not Neutrality*, 10.

54 Pickering, *History, Experience and Cultural Studies*, 16.

Chapter 1

1 I use the term 'married woman worker' in this chapter recognizing that it embodies heteronormative assumptions and technically leaves out, for example, common-law, lesbian, divorced, and widowed women. However, it was the term used at the time to denote non-single women workers, and it sometimes assumed that these 'wives' had children too.

2 Gleason, *Normalizing the Ideal.*

3 Fahrni and Rutherdale, 'Introduction'; Fingard, 'Women's Organizations'; Early, 'A Grandly Subversive Time.' On the United States, see Meyorwitz, ed., *Not June Cleaver*; and Coontz, *The Way We Never Were.*

4 Vickers, 'The Intellectual Origins'; Sangster, *Dreams of Equality.* For examples of women's labour activism, see Guard, 'Fair Play or Fair Pay'; and Sugiman, 'Unionism and Feminism.' US examples include Cobble, *The Other Women's Movement*; Kessler-Harris, *In Pursuit of Equity*; Deslippe, '*Rights Not Roses*'; Harrison, *On Account of Sex*; Horowitz, *Betty Freidan*; and Weingard, *Red Feminism.*

5 Shohat and Stam, *Unthinking Eurocentrism*, 178, quoting in the first instance Stuart Hall.

6 On the 'gender order' see Connell, *Gender and Power*, 87, who stresses that gender is not a thing, but a 'process' that is historically made and remade over time. The gender order takes into account relationships between institutions, power, and interests in historically specific contexts.

7 Pierson, *They're Still Women After All.*

8 Stephen, *Pick One Intelligent Girl*, 214.

9 Report of the Royal Commission on the Status of Women (RCSW), 55.

10 WB, *Women at Work, Canada*, 10.

11 Richard Edsall, 'More Married Women Work outside the Home Today,' *Canadian Business*, February 1958, 32.

12 J. White, *Sisters or Solidarity*, 45; Phillips and Phillips, *Women at Work*, 34.

13 Phillips and Phillips, *Women at Work*, 35.

14 WB, *Women at Work, Canada*, 7.

15 Armstrong and Armstrong, *The Double Ghetto*, 35.

16 McInnis, *Harnessing Labour Confrontation.*

17 For the former see Tomaskovic-Devey, *Gender and Racial Inequality at Work* and Reskin, *Job Queues, Gender Queues*; and for the latter, Armstrong and Armstrong, *The Double Ghetto.*

18 Calliste, 'Canada's Immigration Policy'; Iacovetta, '"Primitive Villagers."'

19 Armstrong and Armstrong, *The Double Ghetto*, 143.

20 Creese, *Contracting Masculinity.*

21 Arnopoulos, *Problems of Immigrant Women*, 5.

22 Indeed, the gender bias of evaluation schemes is an ongoing problem. See Fudge and McDermott, *Just Wages*.

23 On the former see Benston, 'The Political Economy of Women's Liberation' and on Communist orthodoxy, particularly its rejection of Mary Inman's work, see Sangster, *Dreams of Equality*, 182–7.

24 Creese, *Contracting Masculinity*, 19.

25 'Women Unionists,' *CL*, April 1966, 51. Among women union members, 47.8 per cent belonged to international unions, 33.8 per cent to national unions, and 18.4 per cent to government unions.

26 Briskin, 'Women and Unions in Canada,' 33.

27 For example, in 1961, 32 per cent of women were in the labour force in Ontario, compared to 18 per cent in Newfoundland, 24 per cent in Nova Scotia, and 28 per cent in British Columbia. WB, *Women at Work, Canada*, 15.

28 'Women Unionists,' *CL*, April 1966, 51.

29 *The CUPE Journal*, October 1969.

30 Porter, 'She Was the Skipper of the Shore Crew,' 122, and Vosko, *Temporary Work*, 14–15.

31 Vosko, 'Gender Differentiation.'

32 Boyd, 'At a Disadvantage.'

33 For statistics on Aboriginal women see chapter 6; for African-Canadian 'negro' women in Toronto (who were about 0.5 per cent of the population), see Canada, 1961 census, table 38-17, and also Brand, *No Burden to Carry*; on Asian women, see 1951 census, vol. 4, tables 12-1 to 12-8, and 1961 census, vol. 3, part 1, tables 21-1 to 21-16. In 1951 there were only 433 Asian women in the professional category across Canada.

34 This topic is covered in chapter 2. Although the point system was supposedly a racially neutral method of assessment, this does not mean that race ceased to be a category shaping immigration policy.

35 Green, *Immigration and the Postwar Canadian Economy*, 32.

36 Ibid., 32. There was a shift even within the category of white immigrants. Throughout the 1950s, the majority of new Canadians came from Britain and Northern Europe (65 per cent), though by the 1960s, this group represented only 41 per cent. Green, 97.

37 Canada, 1961 census, Population, vol. 1:2, table 38-5.

38 Porter, *The Vertical Mosaic*.

39 Estable, 'Immigrant Women in Canada,' 15; Pendakur, 'Immigrants in the Labour Force,' 63.

40 The highest labour-force participation rate for immigrant women was in Quebec. NAC, RG 33-89, Royal Commission on the Status of Women, vol. 28, Rioux, 'Female Immigrants in the Labour Force,' 6 Nov. 1969.

41 Boyd, 'At a Disadvantage,' 1101.

42 Pendakur, 'Immigrants in the Labour Force,' 59.
43 Estable, 'Immigrant Women in Canada'; Boyd, 'The Status of Immigrant Women in Canada'; Ng and Das Gupta, 'Nation Builders?'
44 Pendakur, 'Immigrants in the Labour Force,' 4.
45 NFB, *Women at Work*, dir. Gordon Sparling, 1958. See also Klein, 'How They Saw Us.'
46 See Prentice et al., *Canadian Women*, 98.
47 Luxton and Bezanson, eds., *Social Reproduction*.
48 Report of the RCSW, 32.
49 UBC, SpC, Elaine Bernard Collection [BC Telephone Workers], box 2-1, newspaper clippings.
50 UBC, SpC, Food and Service Workers Union of Canada Collection, Series A-1, 'Correspondence, 1971' file.
51 Christie and Gauvreau, 'Introduction,' in *Cultures of Citizenship*, 3–26.
52 Korinek, *Rouging It in the Suburbs*. Korinek makes the case for the importance of *Chatelaine* as a source, pointing, for instance, to its 'working class and middle class' (24) readership.
53 'Le deuxième sexe,' *Châtelaine*, April 1964, 19, 63–4. For an article on socialism see 'Que Promet le Socialisme au Québec?' *Châtelaine*, March 1964, 12, 78.
54 'Que font nos jeunes filles de leurs diplômes?' *Châtelaine*, July 1966, 4, 60–1.
55 My analysis uses magazines, though some authors' conclusions drawn from visual media are similar. On the very limited presentation of female types, including the 'sex object,' in television, see Rutherford, *When Television Was Young*, 200. The literature on Hollywood films is substantial. Two differing interpretations of women and Hollywood film in the 1950s are Molly Haskell, *From Reverence to Rape* and French, *On the Verge of Revolt*.
56 Weigand, 'The Red Menace'; Rosenberg, 'Foreign Affairs after World War II'; May, *Homeward Bound*.
57 May, 'Pushing the Limits,' 503. The word white is crucial here, as May argues that African American publications were more likely to present working women as 'heroic.' Some authors note that the famous women presented in women's magazines did not fit the domestic stereotype and were positive role models. While this is true, I am doubtful that 'celebrities' should be included in this category, or that such stories were the dominant message in *Chatelaine* reporting. See Meyorwitz, 'Rewriting Postwar Women's History' and, for a book that discusses famous women, Kaledin, *Mothers and More*.
58 Mary Jo Buhle, *Feminism and Its Discontents*. The individual, tragic repercussions of this social science and psychoanalytic proselytizing, suggests Wini

Breines, are apparent in the suicide of Anne Parsons, a 'failed' analyst and daughter of Talcott Parsons. Breines, *Young, White and Miserable*, chap. 5.

59 Weis, *To Have and To Hold*, 57.
60 On discontent percolating beneath the surface, see French, *On the Verge of Revolt* and Walker, 'Humour and Gender Roles.' Quote from Sara Evans, *Born for Liberty*, 248. Historians are also somewhat divided over whether the postwar period was one of 'sexual containment' or increasing rebellion and liberalism.
61 Buhle, *Feminism and Its Discontents*, 173.
62 Anne Fromer, 'What Will War Women Do When It's Over,' *Saturday Night*, June 1954, 6–7.
63 'Is a Woman Unfit as a Teacher When She Dons a Wedding Ring?' *Saturday Night*, 13 July 1946, 30–1.
64 Janet Tupper, 'Little Woman, What Now?' *Maclean's*, November 1944, 20, 32–3.
65 Charles Fulston, 'The Fallacy of Equal Pay for Equal Work,' *Saturday Night*, 7 Feb. 1945, 10.
66 'Careers and Marriage Don't Mix,' *Saturday Night*, 1 Nov. 1949, 32.
67 Strong-Boag, 'Home Dreams.'
68 Eva-Lis Wuorio, 'Two Years After,' *Maclean's*, 15 May 1950, 73
69 Mary Jukes, 'Seven Threats to Marriage,' *Chatelaine*, April 1949, 32.
70 Lee Peterson, 'Don't Educate Your Daughters,' *Chatelaine*, September 1954, 17–20.
71 Dorothy Manning, 'I Quit My Job to Save My Marriage,' *Chatelaine*, June 1955, 16–17, 78.
72 Rev. Lautenslager, 'A Minister's Frank Talk to Brides and Grooms,' *Chatelaine*, May 1954, 18–19, 96.
73 'Une mère moderne,' *Châtelaine*, May 1965, 39. See also 'Madame Châtelaine,' *Châtelaine*, May 1964, 33–4, and 'Madame Châtelaine,' *Châtelaine*, May 1966. One of the three runners up was portrayed at her workplace, something new.
74 Marion Hilliard, 'Stop Being Just a Housewife,' *Chatelaine*, September 1956, 90.
75 Doris Anderson, *Rebel Daughter*, 119, 139.
76 Sidonie Gruenberg and Hilda Krech, 'The Many Lives of Modern Woman,' *Chatelaine*, August 1952, 16–19.
77 Gruenberg and Krech, 'How to Lead a Happy Double Life,' *Chatelaine*, September 1952, 13–20.
78 McCall, 'Working Wives Are Here to Stay,' *Chatelaine*, September 1961, 31, 42, 72.

79 On career women see 'Voilà ce que j'en pense,' *Châtelaine*, March 1964, 4; and Michelle Tisseyre, 'La grande dame de la télévision,' *Châtelaine*, February 1964, 18. A rare article on a blue-collar mother is 'Cette femme forte,' *Châtelaine*, September 1964, 22–5.

80 Korinek, *Roughing It in the Suburbs*, 284.

81 'Cette femme forte,' *Châtelaine*, September 1964, 23.

82 Mollie Gillen, 'Back to Work,' *Chatelaine*, August 1969, 24–5, 36–8.

83 Mollie Gillen, 'Why You Still Can't Get Daycare,' *Chatelaine*, March 1970, 28, 70–8. For articles in *Saturday Night*, see Helen Moore, 'The Case for the Working Married Woman,' 11 Nov. 1961, 48–51, and Marguerite Ritchie and Mollie Gillen, 'How Canada Wastes Its Woman Power,' 2 April 1960, 17–19.

84 Korinek, *Roughing It in the Suburbs*.

85 John Walker, 'Are There Too Many Women in the Workforce?' *Canadian Business*, June 1961, 40–1. Walker cites a United Church minister who claimed working mothers were causing delinquency.

86 Audrey Gill, 'Lament for Wasted Resource,' *Financial Post*, 15 Oct. 1966, 1.

87 Wallace Gillespie, 'Women Earn More of Money They Spend,' *Financial Post*, 4 March 1950, 16, and 'Working Women Spur Spending,' *Financial Post*, 19 April 1958, 3.

88 Walker, 'Are There Too Many Women in the Workforce?' 41; Francis Baldwin, 'Wives with Paychecks,' *Canadian Business*, February 1954, 29.

89 Francis Baldwin, 'Wives with Paychecks,' *Canadian Business*, February 1954, 29.

90 Fred Philbrick, as told to Eileen Morris, 'How to Drive Your Boss Crazy,' *Chatelaine*, September 1955, 11–13.

91 'Women's Part in Industry,' *Financial Post*, 6 Sept. 1958, 49.

92 Nixon and Krushchev's public debate at the American National Exhibition in Moscow is covered in May, *Homeward Bound*, 16–17.

93 'Now Canadian Women Say They Work Too Hard?' *Financial Post*, 3 Sept. 1961, 39; see also Dean Walker, 'Women Have the Capacity for Executive Posts,' *Canadian Business*, August 1960, 90–2.

94 Walker, 'Are There Too Many Women in the Workforce?' 43.

95 This was a view that was repeated with some misogyny in *Playboy*. See Ehrenreich, *Hearts of Men*, 48.

96 On equal pay see Jack Scheeinee, 'Should Sex Get into the Act When Judging Pay Standards?' *Financial Post*, 3 Nov. 1962, 33, and Jack McArthur, 'Strong Opposition, Weak Voice: The Case against Legislating Equal Pay for Women,' *Financial Post*, 26 Feb. 1955, 7. On unemployment insurance, see

Francis Baldwin, 'Wives with Paychecks,' *Canadian Business*, February 1954, 53. On women and unemployment insurance, see Ann Porter, *Gendered States.*

97 For a photo of flight attendants on strike, see *CL*, July–August 1963, 37; 'Can Eatons Be Organized?' *CPHW*, November 1953, 12; 'OFL Demands Ban on Injunctions,' *Textile Labour*, May 1966, 1; 'Salute to Women,' *The Fur and Leather Worker*, April–May 1951, 14.

98 Ed Finn, 'The Story of a Hospital Strike,' *CL*, June 1963, 16.

99 'ILGWU Organizing Campaign,' *CL*, April 1966, 52–3.

100 *United Textile Worker*, August 1951.

101 UBC, Special Collections, Vertical Files, Vancouver Labour Committee for Human Rights, VFA, 442-b.

102 'Human Rights,' *CL*, December 1963, 9.

103 'Human Rights,' *CL*, May 1966, 29, and 'CLC Adopts,' *CL*, May 1968, 9.

104 For one example, see 'ICFTU Women's Charter,' *CL*, October, 1965, 39. It relied heavily on material submitted by the federal Women's Bureau as well, e.g., 'The Women's Bureau – An Anniversary and a Challenge,' *CL*, October 1964, 5–6. The question of why *Canadian Labour* feminists appear to be less numerous than American ones is discussed in chapter 7. One factor was the presence of the CCF in Canada, which became the alternative focus for women's social democratic work.

105 Elizabeth Faue argues that the labour press promoted images of men who were hyper-masculine, tough, and confrontational, to the point of 'romanticizing violence.' I found more diverse images, and less emphasis on the brute force of masculine power in confrontation with capital. However, Faue's discussion deals with the 1930s and with conflicts in which labour faced intense state and employer resistance, while my reading is of a range of publications in the post-war accord years. The latter, especially, likely led to different images. Faue, *In Suffering*, 71, 91.

106 *CU*, May 1955, 170.

107 Boyle, 'The Kiss,' 503. See also Meyer, 'Workplace Predators,' and for this argument about wartime papers, see Smith and Wakewich, '"Beauty and the Helldivers,"' 88.

108 *CU*, September 1954, 275.

109 Buzuk, *Pin-Up Girrrrls*, chapter 6; Howard, '"At the Curve Exchange"'; Ehrenreich, *Hearts of Men*, chapter 4; Meyerowitz, 'Women, Cheesecake and Borderline Material.'

110 'They're Your Brothers ... They Sure Are' was the headline above the bunnies. *CUPE Journal*, April 1968, 2. Masculinist or misogynist work

cultures also became a difficult barrier for women attempting to do 'men's' jobs in the 1970s. Gray, 'Sharing the Shop Floor'; Easson, Field, and Santucci, 'Working in Steel.'

111 See, for example, 'The Rod and Gun Club' and 'Invading Port Perry,' *The Oshaworker*, 7 April and 2 August 1944. For the role of the Rod and Gun Club in aiding unionization see Christine McLaughlin, 'The McLaughlin Legacy,' 99. My thanks to her for providing copies of *The Oshaworker* to me.

112 'Office Automation,' *CL*, April 1964, 37.

113 'Health Problems of Women in Industry,' *CU*, August 1948, 142; emphasis mine.

114 Geoffry and Sainte-Marie, *Attitudes of Union Workers*, 25, 98, 56.

115 Cobble, *The Other Women's Movement*, 60–8.

116 Forrest, 'Securing the Male Breadwinner'; Porter, *Gendered States*.

117 John Lee, 'Do Working Women Cause Unemployment?' *CL*, March 1961, 26–7.

118 'Le Mari Canadien-Français,' *Châtelaine*, April 1967, 31; 'Autoportrait de la Canadienne Française 68,' *Châtelaine*, June 1968, 25.

119 Geoffry and Sainte-Marie, *Attitudes of Union Workers*, 55.

120 Eileen Robins, 'An Election Issue,' *CPHW*, March 1957, 5.

121 McLaughlin, 'The McLaughlin Legacy,' 116.

122 Thorn, 'Visions of the New World Order'; Sangster, *Dreams of Equality*, 91.

123 Peg Stewart, 'Flying the Coop,' *CPHW*, May 1953, 5.

124 Peg Stewart, 'Another Language,' *CPHW*, January 1954, 5.

125 Peg Stewart, 'My Dear, You Should Have Seen Her Kitchen Floor,' *CPHW*, January 1956, 5.

126 John Lee, 'Do Working Women Cause Unemployment?' *CL*, March 1961, 20–1; Kessler-Harris, 'Where Are the Organized Women Workers?'

127 'The UPHW in Canada,' *CL*, February 1959, 6–8.

128 'PWA Students Discuss Problems of Women Workers,' *CPHW*, March 1957, 11.

129 'OFL Conference on Women Workers,' *CL*, July/August 1966, 48.

130 'Who's Who in the CCL,' *CL*, June 1956, 30.

131 Yet many women involved in the union movement at a leadership level were single career women – Grace Hartman being an exception – a fact that perhaps indicates the difficulty of combining three kinds of labour: paid, home, and political.

132 'Hugette Plamondon,' *CPHW*, March 1955, 7.

133 Dorothy Sangster, 'The Lady Is a Labour Leader,' *Maclean's*, 8 Dec. 1956, 16–17, 100–3.

134 Geoffry and Sainte-Marie, *Attitudes of Union Workers*, 101.

135 Hickling-Johnston, 'A Report on the Status of Women in the Field of
     Collective Bargaining,' study for the RCSW, 1968, 14.
136 Joan Sangster, *Earning Respect.*
137 Heron and Penfold, *The Workers Festival*, 207–8. For employer-sponsored
     contests, see Sobel and Meurer, *Working at Inglis*, 73–5, and, for depart-
     ment stores, Belisle, 'A Labour Force.'
138 On a non-unionized workplace, see Gentile, '"Government Girls."'
139 Holliday and Taylor, 'Aesthetic Surgery,' 188. Even postmodern feminists
     find this trend alarming: Banet-Weiser and Portwood-Staver, 'I Just Want to
     Be Me Again,' 263. A post-structuralist approach influences Davis, *Reshap-
     ing the Female Body* and Banet-Weiser, *The Most Beautiful Girl in the World.* For
     a longer discussion of feminist theory, beauty contests, and labour, see
     Sangster 'Queen of the Picket Line.'
140 Young, 'Feminism and the Power of Politics,' 176. This is also the basic
     contention in Felski, 'Because It Is Beautiful,' 280, and in Banet-Weiser,
     The Most Beautiful Girl.
141 Examples of this approach might include Freeman, *Beauty Bound*;
     MacCannell and MacCannell, 'The Beauty System'; and Wolf, *The Beauty
     Myth.* Historians of the working class also explored the appeal of fashion
     and beauty culture in working-class contexts: Roberts, *Honest Womanhood*;
     Peiss, *Cheap Amusements*; Ruiz, *Cannery Women, Cannery Lives.*
142 Tice, 'Queens of Academe,' 250.
143 Kozol, 'Miss Indian America'; Barnes, 'Face of a Nation'; Yano, *Crowning
     the Nice Girl*; Craig, *Ain't I a Beauty Queen*; Cohen and Wilk, with Stoeltje,
     eds., *Beauty Queens on the Global Stage.*
144 Foley, *Undressed for Success*, 99.
145 'Fashion Show and Tea Staged by UPWA Women,' *CPHW*, 12 Dec. 1957,
     12.
146 Belisle, 'A Labour Force.'
147 *CL*, February 1962, 20.
148 *Canadian Congress Journal*, July 1949, 16–17.
149 'Queen of the Midinettes,' *Justice*, 15 Nov. 1963, 1; 'Serez-Vous la Prochaine
     Reine?' *Justice*, October 1950, 4.
150 *CL*, January 1961, 31.
151 Cornell University, Kheel Centre for Labor-Management Documentation
     and Archives, ILGWU Papers, box 295, file 1b, Bernard Shane to David
     Dubinsky, 3 Dec. 1959; 'Le Bal des Midinettes,' *Justice*, November 1947, 1.
152 Cornell University, ILGWU Papers, box 64, file 2, Shane to Dubinsky, 18
     Oct. 1950.
153 NFB, *Pins and Needles*, dir. Anne Pearson and Roger Blais, 1954.

154 Foley, *Undressed for Success*, 156.
155 'Le Bal des Midinettes,' *Justice*, October 1950, 4. On 'self-improvement,'
     see *Pins and Needles*. The 'Cinderella myth' suggests beauty is all a woman
     needs for success, and that contest winners could 'marry up,' out of their
     class. Banner, *American Beauty*.
156 *UE News*, 27 Feb. 1948.
157 *Textile Labor*, October 1955, 1.
158 *CUPE Journal*, September 1971, cover.
159 Douglas, *Where the Girls Are*.
160 Skeggs, 'The Toilet Paper.'
161 'Sex? It's Disgusting,' *CPHW*, May 1963, 12.
162 Ibid.
163 On the Women's Bureau , see Briggs, 'Fighting for Women's Equality';
     Burt, 'Organized Women's Groups and the State.'
164 The first director of the bureau was initially hesitant to endorse legislated
     maternity leave, as it appeared to be special protection, but she later
     embraced it as a health-protection measure not incompatible with an
     equal-rights approach. Briggs, 'Fighting for Women's Equality.' See also
     Burt, 'Organized Women's Groups.'
165 Some articles talked only of women isolated within their own language and
     culture within the home, though occasionally bad working conditions were
     addressed: Staebler, 'The Other Canadians,' and Drea, 'Lucia's Trying
     Love Affair with Canada,' *Chatelaine*, April 1961, 41, 61–4.

Chapter 2

  1 An estimated 160,000 displaced persons came between 1946 and 1952.
     After 1952, continental European recruitment centred on Holland,
     Germany, Greece, Italy, and Portugal, and due in part to a narrowing US
     policy, the numbers of immigrants climbed significantly after 1952. The
     largest group of newcomers in this period (1945–70) came from Britain,
     followed by the United States, Italy, and Germany. Avery, *Reluctant Host*,
     167, 171.
  2 While the majority were Polish, there were a few Ukrainian, Hungarian,
     and Lithuanian women as well. Although young working women were
     often referred to as 'girls' at this time, the term may also have been used
     since there were some teenagers as young as 17 in the group. For a brief
     mention of the Dionne affair, see Helen MacDonald, 'The Power of
     Polonia,' 205–8, and for a discussion based on newspaper sources, see
     Courville et al., *Histoire de Beauce-Etchemin-Amiante*.

3 On pre–Second World War immigration see, for example, Avery, *Reluctant Host*; Hoerder, *Creating Societies*; essays in Burnet, ed., *Looking into My Sister's Eyes*; and Epp, Iacovetta, and Swyripa, eds., *Sisters or Strangers*.

4 On human rights see Frager and Patrias, "'This Is Our Country, These Are Our Rights.'"

5 On integration, see Zay, 'Adaptation of the Immigrant,' and on integration and 'diversity,' see Allen, 'Helping Immigrants Belong,' 109. The concern about 'integration' could also take a more paternalist turn: e.g., Edna Staebler, 'The Other Canadians,' *Chatelaine*, March 1965, 64, 109–10. This is not to argue that Canada became a haven of tolerant multiculturalism. Interestingly, the word 'integration' also replaced 'assimilation' in discussions of Aboriginal peoples.

6 It was not until the 1960s, argues José Igartua, that the high value put on 'Britishness' was truly displaced by a more 'de-ethnicized,' English-Canadian 'civic identity.' Igartua, *The Other Quiet Revolution*, esp. 4–15. I am not suggesting this process was inevitable or emanated from one date, but rather that it was an uneven one occurring over the post-war period.

7 Roediger, *Working towards Whiteness*, 9. Roediger suggests this was a process in the United States stretching from the New Deal era to the end of the Second World War, and reminds us that 'any periodization of when new immigrants ... ceased to be victimized on "racial" grounds ... is bound to be vexed.' See also Jacobson, *Whiteness of a Different Colour*.

8 Abella and Troper, *None Is Too Many*.

9 The early importation of Polish refugees became a template for future policies on displaced persons. See Satzewich, 'Unfree Labour and Capitalism,' 103. On Displaced Persons domestic schemes, see Harzig, 'MacNamara's DP Domestics.'

10 Iacovetta, *Gatekeepers*; Hawkins, *Canada and Immigration*; Whitaker, *Double Standard*; Knowles, *Strangers at Our Gates*.

11 NAC, Dept. of Labour, RG 27, vol. 3022, Immigration Policy file, 17 March 1947, A.L. Jolliffe to Raymond Ranger about cabinet discussions.

12 Ibid., Immigration Policy file, general correspondence.

13 King made the statement in May of 1947. Hawkins, *Canada and Immigration*, 92–3.

14 NAC, Dept. of Labour, RG 27, vol. 3022, 'General Correspondence on Immigration Policy, pt. 3, Committee for the Repeal of the Chinese Immigration Act submission,' c. 1947. See also Proceedings, 10 March 1947. Only some family members could join Chinese citizens in Canada, who were small in numbers precisely because of the Exclusion Act. See Pendakur, *Immigrants in the Labour Force*, 23.

15 Abu-Laban and Gabriel, eds., *Selling Diversity*, 43. For these schemes see
   Calliste, 'Canada's Immigration Policy' and 'Women of Exceptional Merit.'
   This is not to say that race was not important after 1967. See, for example,
   Bakan and Stasiulis, *Not One of the Family*, *Atlantis* special issue vol. 24, no. 2
   (Spring 2000); and Bannerji, *The Dark Side of the Nation*.
16 Danys, *Lithuanian Immigration*, 83.
17 'Unfree labour involves workers whose ability to circulate in the labour
   market is restrained through political or legal compulsion.' Basok, quoting
   the classic definition in *Tortillas and Tomatoes*, 4. Basok suggests a more
   extensive definition: premised on workers' basic needs and the structure of
   policies, the definition should include those 'unfree to refuse employers'
   requests for their labour whenever need arises.'
18 Abella and Troper, *None Is Too Many*, 217, 232. The poll asked what national-
   ities people wanted to exclude, and Poles only secured 15% of this unpopularity vote. The authors suggest that earlier antipathy to Poles emerged in
   part because this geographical region was associated with Jews.
19 Mitchell, House of Commons, *Debates*, 3 June 1947, 3768–9.
20 The word 'racial' was still used by many politicians. For example, John
   Diefenbaker used the term when he referred to his Polish and Ukrainian
   constituents as 'fine citizens.' Ibid., 3701.
21 Proceedings, 14 May 1947. See also 'Congress Submission on Immigration,'
   Trades and Labour Congress Journal, 13 May 1947.
22 Lambertson, 'The Dresden Story.'
23 The CCL continued to offer its 'guarded support,' calling for tripartite
   planning to match immigration and employment needs, and also criticizing
   racial discrimination. See MacDonald, 'Canadian Labour and Immigration'
   and 'Congress Policy on Immigration.'
24 In presentations to the standing committee, for instance, statistics were
   presented on 'race' that included Negroes, Hebrews, Albanians, English,
   Dutch, Slovaks, and so on. Ukrainian spokesmen talked of all the 'Slavic
   races' in Canada, including the Ukrainians. Proceedings, 7 May 1947 and
   12 June 1947. These examples demonstrate how 'race' operates as a socially
   and historically constructed category.
25 Dickinson and Young, *A Short History of Quebec*, 275. The protests of
   Quebec politicians seemed at times to use coded language. One MP, for
   instance, decried the 'millions' spent bringing 'fur merchants' and those
   involved in ladies garment manufacturing to Canada, when money could
   be spent on 'our' workers. Those working in fur and garments were
   predominantly Eastern European Jews. Quoted in Pendakur, *Immigrants in
   the Labour Force*, 25.

26 'Politique d'immigration: Illogique, ridicule et révoltante,' *Le Travail,* June 1947.

27 For example, 'Le manque de main-d'œuvre et l'immigration,' *Le Travail,* 6 March 1951 and 'Un scandale de l'immigration?' *Le Travail,* 18 Jan. 1952. A few articles did recommend ways to integrate immigrants into society: e.g., 'Pour aider nos immigrants,' *Le Travail,* 26 Jan. 1951. Between 1921 and 1949, the CTCC sent 21 resolutions to Ottawa calling for an end to immigration, except in the case of agricultural workers. See Pâquet, *Tracer les marges,* 176.

28 Anti-communist views sometimes overlapped with anti-Semitism and ethnocentrism. Certainly Fred Rose and Sam Carr were known as Jews, though Tim Buck was not. In Quebec, Premier Maurice Duplessis combined anti-communism with denunciations of 'foreigners.' On anti-communism in Quebec, see Whitaker and Marcuse, *Cold War Canada* and, on anti-communism and immigration, Finkel, 'Canadian Immigration Policy.' On anti-Semitism see Davis, ed., *Antisemitism in Canada* and Abella and Troper, *None Is Too Many,* esp. 162. Tulchinsky (*Branching Out,* 269–70) argues that anti-Semitism declined in Quebec in the post-war period.

29 'Politique d'immigration: Illogique, ridicule et révoltante,' *Le Travail,* June 1947.

30 Proceedings, 7 May 1947.

31 Ibid. See Ukrainian Canadian Committee testimony about immigrants also curing those 'infected' with communist ideology, 12 June 1947.

32 Proceedings, 24 April 1947.

33 Mitchell, House of Commons, *Debates,* 3 June 1947, 3768; Proceedings, 12 June 1947.

34 NAC, RG 27, vol. 1300, press clippings file, *Ottawa Evening Citizen,* 30 April 1947.

35 NAC, RG 27, vol. 3531, file 3-24-38, pt 1. This file included one unusual letter of protest from the secretary of the United Church of Canada concerning the Dionne scheme that cited religious concerns. The secretary agreed with the prime minister's goal of keeping the basic 'character' of the country the same, including its 'racial ... religious and social outlook.'

36 'Immigration of workers from displaced persons camps,' *Labour Gazette* 47, October 1947, 1407; NAC, RG 27, vol. 3022, General Correspondence file, vol. 3, Interdepartmental Labour-Immigration Committee, 17 March 1948.

37 NAC, Dept. of External Affairs, RG 25, vol. 3952, Dionne file, Dionne to Lester Pearson, 9 Sept. 1947, and Undersecretary of External Affairs to Dionne, 16 Sept. 1947. Dionne wanted to pass on advice to the Americans.

38 Dionne, House of Commons, *Debates*, 13 June 1947, 4121. Mackenzie King had experienced his own run-in with a Polish maid two years later. He lamented the lack of 'Anglo' domestics, and when his Polish maid appeared to be stealing his cigarettes, he pressured his head housekeeper to have the maid confess, saying he would overlook the wrong if she was honest. When she did confess through an interpreter, he promptly fired her, saying he could 'see how foreigners of this kind have the habit of lying to their employers out of fear. It would have been a mistake to have let her go without admitting her fault.' NAC, MG 26-J, M. King Diaries, 7–8 Mar. 1949.

39 NAC, RG 27, vol. 1300, press clippings file, *Ottawa Evening Citizen*, 30 April 1947. These tests may also have indicated a fear that the women would become 'public charges.' Harzig, 'MacNamara's DP Domestics,' 33.

40 Ruth Hamilton, interviewed by 'Miss Goold,' in 'In a Strange Land,' *Canadian Welfare* 23 (January 1948): 11–14. Another author reassured his readers in another manner; many Canadians expected the displaced to look emaciated and were surprised to find 'attractive blond Estonian girls or bright-eyed Polish tailors,' who 'look very much like native-born Canadians.' Stuchen, 'Canadian Newcomers.'

41 Finkel, 'Canadian Immigration Policy.'

42 Coldwell, House of Commons, *Debates*, 3 June 1947, 3671.

43 Iacovetta, 'Freedom Lovers' and 'Many Model Citizens.'

44 Quoted in Behiels, *Quebec and the Question of Immigration*, 11.

45 Pâquet, *Tracer les marges*, 178. Beyond general fears that immigrants were a 'destabilizing' force undermining Quebec's distinct society and culture, there were differences of opinion between employers and labour, between those who believed the province could (constitutionally) do little and those who urged some action, between some xenophobic nationalists and those who promoted the integration of new Canadians into Quebec society.

46 Bureau du Service des Néo-Canadiens, *Canadiens-Français et Néo-Canadiens*, 11. For example, Duplessis enthusiastically endorsed aid for the Hungarian refugees of 1956 because they were fleeing communism. See Pâquet, *Tracer les marges*, 182.

47 It was obviously taken for granted that these European newcomers would be Catholic, not Jewish, immigrants.

48 Dionne letter quoted in Canada, House of Commons, *Debates*, 3 June 1947, 3779.

49 NAC, RG 27, vol. 3022, Immigration Policy file, A.R. MacNamara to Minister of Labour, 27 March 1947.

50 Ibid., General Correspondence on Immigration Policy file, vol. 1, A.L. Jolliffe to A.R. MacNamara, 27 March 1947.

51 The IGCR was founded in 1938 in response to the pre-war refugee problem. By 1947 its work had been largely absorbed into the new United Nations organization, the International Refugee Organization (IRO). Marrus, *The Unwanted*, 163, 340, 343.

52 Satzewich, *Racism and the Incorporation of Foreign Labour*, 86.

53 Dionne, House of Commons, *Debates*, 13 June 1947, 4119.

54 Myers, *Caught*.

55 *La Presse*, 2 June 1947.

56 Coldwell, House of Commons, *Debates*, 3 June 1947, 3668.

57 The statute, for instance, forbade the solicitation and importation of 'aliens' under contract, including the practice of prepaying transportation for these workers. Canada, *Revised Statutes of Canada*, 1952, vol. 1, chap.7, s. 2, 45. On the history of the law see Fudge and Tucker, *Labour before the Law*.

58 McInnis, House of Commons, *Debates*, 3 June 1947, 3779, and Strum, ibid., 3704.

59 Proceedings and vol. 1300, press clippings, Dionne case, *Canadian Tribune*, 27 May 1947.

60 On earlier debates about 'wage slavery' see Roediger, *Colored White*, 108, and, on white slavery, Donovan, *White Slave Crusades*.

61 Coldwell, cited in *La Patrie*, 2 June 1947. The marriage issue was perhaps a misunderstanding that resulted when the mill manager told the press that married women workers would not be accepted in the factory. On trade-union views on this issue at the time, see Tremblay, *Le syndicalisme québécois*, 100. 'Help Wanted: Female,' *Time Magazine*, 19 May 1947, 40.

62 Mavis Gallant, 'DP Test Case – A Failure.' *Montreal Standard*, 28 August 1948.

63 *La Presse*, 3 June 1947.

64 Mitchell, House of Commons, *Debates*, 3 June 1947, 3769; and St Laurent, ibid., 3788.

65 Dionne, House of Commons, *Debates*, 13 June 1947, 4117, 4118.

66 Dionne interview, *L'Éclaireur*, 5 June 1947. Paternalist workplaces were not limited to Quebec: see Parr, *The Gender of Breadwinners* and Sangster, 'The Softball Solution.'

67 *Globe and Mail*, 31 May 1947.

68 The English press was often quick to condemn Quebec's view of immigration. See Igartua, *The Other Quiet Revolution*, 60.

69 *Le Soleil*, 3 June 1947; *Le Devoir*, 3 June 1947; *La Presse*, 2 June 1947.

70 Pierre Vigeant served as an assistant to a Conservative minister in R.B. Bennett's government, then as a parliamentary correspondent. In 1946 he lobbied for immigrant representation on the Montreal Catholic school

board, challenging the assumption that immigrants should automatically assimilate into English Catholic schools. See *Le Devoir*, 31 Oct. 1946.

71 *Le Devoir*, 3 June 1947. The statement by the UAW's George Burt that the Catholic girls had to be 'selected by the Vatican,' though somewhat idiosyncratic, did suggest some anti-Catholic feeling in English Canada. *Le Soleil*, 29 May 1947.

72 Courville et al., *Histoire*, 659.

73 *L'Éclaireur*, 5 June 1947 and 29 May 1947.

74 *L'Éclaireur*, 12 June and 19 June 1947.

75 Angus McInnis, quoted in *Le Devoir*, 3 June 1947. Special animosity was directed towards John Diefenbaker's 'francophobe' views.

76 *Le Travail*, May 1947.

77 *Le Travail*, May 1947 and June 1947.

78 'The Importation of Contract Labour,' *CU*, June 1947: 125. Individual unions also intervened with resolutions. 'Local 222 Asks Immigrants to Come as Free Persons,' *CU*, 18 June 1947.

79 Rouillard, *Histoire de la CSN*, 176.

80 According to Tremblay (*Le syndicalisme Québécois*, 30–2), they were also sympathetic to a more 'pancanadian' nationalism, stressing the idea of two nations within Canada.

81 NAC, Dept. of External Affairs, RG 25, vol. 3952, Dionne file, Escott Reid to L.B. Pearson, 15 Dec. 1947, and Dionne file, Pearson to Ken Kirkwood, 19 June 1947. The reference to chestnuts seems to have been used originally by Assistant Deputy Minister of Labour A.R. MacNamara to Reid in conversation, then later repeated to others as an apt description of the whole affair. Escott Reid memo, 17 Nov. 1947 in the Dionne file.

82 Escott Reid believed in the need for collective Western defence in the face of Soviet aggression, but this did not mean shutting down relations with other communist countries. Reid, *Radical Mandarin*, 224–6.

83 Marrus, *The Unwanted*, 340–2.

84 NAC, RG 25, vol. 3952, Dionne file, pt. 2, A. Fiderkiewica to Secretary of State for External Affairs, 3 June 1947.

85 Ibid., Kirkwood translations of Polish press stories.

86 Ibid., 'Report of Conditions,' 9.

87 NAC, RG 25, vol. 3952, Dionne file, Memo of E. Reid, 17 Nov. 1947, and Chance to Reid, 10 Dec. 1947.

88 Ibid., Louis St Laurent to M. Bielski, 16 Jan. 1948.

89 Ibid., St Laurent to Dionne, 9 Nov. 1948: 'I cannot give you an official passport.'

90 Dionne, quoted in House of Commons, *Debates*, 3 June 1947, 3886.

91 Rouillard, 'La révolution tranquille' and *Le syndicalisme Québécois.*
92 Numbers differ according to the source – employer or union. The former says there were 200 women and 130 men, the latter 177 women and 125 men. The leadership of the CTCC union was dominated by men, although one woman served as secretary. On other strikes see Baillargeon, 'Les grèves du textile.'
93 *La Patrie,* 29 July 1948; *La Presse,* 2 August 1948; *Toronto Star,* 21 July 1947.
94 *Le Soleil,* 4 Aug. 1948.
95 Proposition du Conciliateur, NAC, RG 27, Strikes and Lockouts files, vol. 465, # 91. This is the only remaining document from the provincial government concerning the adjudication of the strike. When a meeting of textile unions within the CTCC was held in 1949, there was no representative from the Beauce area. It appears that the region finally secured a union in the late 1960s. *Le Travail,* September 1949.
96 'Non satisfait d'avoir exploités ses employés, Dionne s'en prend à leur syndicat,' *Le Travail,* September 1948. See also *L'Éclaireur,* 30 Sept. 1948.
97 Eva-Lis Wuorio, 'Two Years After,' *Maclean's,* 15 May 1950, 71.
98 *Ottawa Morning Journal,* 23 Sept. 1947.
99 *Montreal Gazette,* 13 May 1949.
100 Gallant, 'DP Test Case.'
101 This is exemplified well by another DP case. A well-educated Polish couple met Dionne when he was recruiting in Europe. He was sympathetic to their plight and arranged for a job for the former lawyer at the mill. The wife worked for Dionne as a housekeeper and cook 'for nothing.' In September 1948 they left with other Polish women for Toronto. See Eva Lis Wuorio, 'We Can't Go Back,' *Maclean's,* 1 June 1948, 26, and 'Two Years After.'
102 'Ce bon paternalisme,' *Le Travail,* August 1947.

Chapter 3

1 Palmer, *Canada's 1960s,* 52.
2 Scher, *The Un-Canadians;* Weisbord, *The Strangest Dream.*
3 This may serve as an example of Gramsci's claim that both coercion and consent were important to ideological hegemony.
4 John Harbron, 'The Red Threat of Our Pacific Gateway,' *Financial Post,* 12 Dec. 1953, 1.
5 'Outlaw the Communist Party,' *Canadian Business,* October 1950, 8; B.K. Sandwell, 'Section 98 Was a Bad Law but We Might Draw a Better One,' *Saturday Night,* 16 Aug. 1947, 16. See also Hal Tracey, 'Canadian Shop Newspapers Are Communist Poison,' *Saturday Night,* May 1951, 7–8.

6 Scott Young, 'Should I Keep My Commie Friend?' *Saturday Night*, 10 Nov. 1951, 11.

7 'Outlaw the Communist Party.' This was an issue when George Drew introduced federal legislation to create a legal version of McCarthyism in Canada. Those arguing against this tactic spoke of freedom, but they seldom stressed communists' civil rights and almost never expressed any political sympathies for communist politics. A communist conspiracy was often assumed: P.M Richards, 'Communists in Our Midst,' *Saturday Night*, 20 March 1951; Wilfrid Eggleston, 'How to Deal with Communists,' *Saturday Night*, 16 May 1950, 3; 'What Way with Communists?' *Saturday Night*, 16 May 1950, 5; 'How the Reds Are Using Our Youth,' *Financial Post*, 11 Aug. 1951, 13.

8 Valerie Korinek argues that *Chatelaine* articles on the Cold War revealed 'grey' areas and 'ambivalence,' but this was not the case in magazines such as *Saturday Night*. See 'It's a Tough Time to Be in Love,' 177. This may be, in part, because some of the articles she cites are dated 1960 – after the time the Cold War was at its height in the 1950s.

9 Whitaker and Marcuse, *Cold War Canada*. A similarly influential American study is Schrecker, *Many Are the Crimes*.

10 Finkel, 'Canadian Immigration Policy.'

11 The term insecurity state was first used by Wesley Wark, and taken up by Reginald Whitaker and Gary Marcuse in their title. They note that the term security state inevitably implies insecurity as well; *Cold War Canada*, xi.

12 Ibid., 241.

13 McInnis, 'Teamwork for Harmony.'

14 In Canada, a few studies partisan to the CCF/NDP suggest the purges were needed: Morton, *Working People*; Copp and Knipfel, *The IUE in Canada*. A more balanced approach is Abella, *Nationalism, Communism, and Canadian Labour*. American books include Meyer, *Stalin over Wisconsin*; Keeran, *The Communist Party*; Halpern, *UAW Politics*; Cochran, *Labor and Communism*; Levenstein, *Communism, Anticommunism*; Rosswurm, ed., *The CIO's Left-led Unions*; and Cherny, Issel, and Taylor, eds., *American Labor*. While the American literature is too vast to cite, one difference is its concern with the Cold War's effect on the collapse of organizing in the South in the post-war period: e.g., Kornstad, *Civil Rights Unionism*; Honey, 'Operation Dixie.'

15 Whitaker and Hewitt, *Cold War Canada*, 43. I have referred to the trade-union opposition to communists as 'social democratic' since it was often led by CCFers, though it did take in those with Liberal and Conservative politics. On the anti-socialist campaign, see Boyko, *Into the Hurricane*.

16 Canadian examples include Manley, 'Starve, Be Damned'; Sangster, *Dreams of Equality*; and Steedman, 'The Promise.' US examples are Naison, *Communists in Harlem* and Kelley, *Hammer and Hoe*. This tradition is not confined to an earlier New Left. One example of a recent book that emphatically stresses the local is Storch, *Red Chicago*.

17 Nor is Stalinism simply defined as 'Moscow control.' Palmer, 'Rethinking the Historiography.'

18 This chapter deals primarily with the TLC and CCL. The CTCC's attitude towards communism is dealt with in the next chapter.

19 *TLCJ*, November 1952, 11.

20 *CU*, June 1950, 111; April 1948, 75.

21 *CU*, Nov. 1948, 261.

22 Prentice, 'Workers, Mothers, Reds.'

23 Advertisers such as the Pacific Brewers Agents of British Columbia and Canadair (Aircraft Manufacturers) ran ads referring to the fight against communism. As a military supplier, the latter's interests are clear. In an ad that equated athletic prowess with military might, entitled 'Communists: World's Finest Athletes,' Canadair warned that the Soviet 'Spartans' were physically training, while 'we' were 'sipping sodas and watching sports on television,' enjoying the 'soft' life of the West. This particular ad, however, was rare in these union papers. *TLCJ*, May 1955, back cover. For the ad about education, see *TLCJ*, April 1955.

24 American writing has effectively probed the local factors that shaped Cold War battles between various liberals and leftists within the labour movement. For example, Cherny et al., *American Labor and the Cold War*.

25 *TLCJ*, October 1950, 11; January 1951, 4; March 1951, 5.

26 Rouillard, *Histoire du syndicalisme Québécois*, 260–1. Solski and Smaller, *Mine Mill*; Kaplan, *Everything That Floats*.

27 May, *Homeward Bound*; D'Emilio, *Sexual Politics, Sexual Communities*. Since these books appeared, the Cold War has been examined in relation to a much wider range of topics, from moral regulation and delinquency to culture, literature, and film. A few examples include Adams, *The Trouble with Normal*; Kinsman, *The Regulation of Desire*; and Cavell, ed., *Love, Hate, and Fear*.

28 Cobble, *The Other Women's Movement*. On this era see also Deslippe, *Rights Not Roses*.

29 Kannenberg, 'The Impact of the Cold War.'

30 The Taft-Hartley (1947) law, or the *Labor Management Relations Act*, limited the power of unions in a number of ways, and included one provision that required union leaders to sign anti-communist affidavits. Union leaders

could be prosecuted, and their unions would be made, in effect, 'illegal,' in
that they were left without any access to state labor-relations protections.
Quebec had a similar act, discussed in the next chapter.

31 The International Fur Workers Union was founded in 1912 in the United
States as an American Federation of Labour (AFL) affiliate. In 1938 it
merged with the Leather Workers to become the International Fur and
Leather Workers Union, and it moved to the CIO. The official pro–Ben
Gold history of the US left–led union is Foner, *The Fur and Leather Workers
Union.*

32 McShane, *International Labour and the Cold War.*

33 On the 1930s see Frager, *Sweatshop Strife*, 210–10.

34 Strauss, 'The Canadian Fur Manufacturing Industry.'

35 CU, Kheel, IFLWU, box 25, folder 29, Winnipeg Fur Workers Local 91
Membership List.

36 For a more detailed analysis of these divisions, see Frager, *Sweatshop Strife.*

37 This recruitment effort, supported by unions and businesses, sought
primarily single men. Of the approximately 500 immigrants, only 60 per
cent were supposed to be from the same religious group, a behind-the-
scenes quota requested by the federal government. NAC, RG 27, vol. 279,
file 1-26-5-2. See also AO, MHSO, Series 85-023, MU 9011, interview with
Al Hershkovitz, n.d.

38 NAC, JC, vol. 16, file 9.

39 *Toronto Star,* 7 May 1937. In Winnipeg there were not dual unions, but the
existing one was faced were immense employer hostility. See CU, Kheel,
IFLWU, vol. 7, file 4 and vol. 25, file 24. The adamantly anti-union Hurtig
Furs won a suit for $2869.

40 See one court case in which the CIO group sued the AFL one for office
property. NAC, JC, vol. 11, file 2688.

41 AO, MHSO, interview with Al Hershkovitz.

42 On Pearl Wedro and Freda Coodin, see Sangster, *Dreams of Equality*, 79, 131,
78; on Wedro, see Frager, *Sweatshop Strife*, 156–7. After her stay in jail,
Coodin died of tuberculosis, becoming something of a communist martyr.

43 Documents showed, among many things, attempts to hide the books in the
Royal York Hotel, and self-incriminating statements that clearly suggested a
measure of guilt. On Federman's illegal actions, including a copy of the
Toronto District Labour Council trial (and condemnation) of him and his
associates, see AO, MHSO, MU 9021, Muni Taub papers, file 8428; MU
9001, Federman papers; and NAC, JC, vol. 13, file 2701.

44 AO, MHSO, Fur Workers Union, F 1405, Series 85-023, MU 9021, file 8428,
letter to President of the Independent Fur Manufacturers Association from

AFL union and pamphlet of 24 April 1940. As a former communist unionist who later joined Federman in the union as a business agent noted, 'Federman just stuck it out' after he was caught playing 'hanky panky' with the books. AO, MHSO, interview with Al Hershovitz.

45 UBC, SpC, Trade Union Research Bureau, box 39, IFLWU, file 39-5.
46 CU, Kheel, IFLWU, vol. 28, file 1, Haddow to Gold, 25 Jan. and 11 June 1954, and Haddow to Abe Feinglass, 28 Dec. 1954.
47 Haddow was actually a machinist, not someone who knew the fur business. Al Hershkovitz referred to Haddow as a 'party hack.' AO, MHSO, interview with Al Hershovitz.
48 NAC, RH, MG 39, A118, vol. 1, Fur Workers file, District 10 statement on merger, 1954.
49 CU, Kheel, IFLWU, vol. 28, file 1, Haddow to Fineglass, 5 Oct. 1954 and 11 June 1954. For a far more detailed analysis of this battle in fur, see Sangster, 'Canada's Cold War in Fur.'
50 AO, MHSO, interview with Al Hershkovitz. Hershkovitz lobbied Communist Party leader Dave Kashtan, urging him to oppose this option of Canadian autonomy.
51 Brody, *The Butcher Workmen*, 259–67; Levenstein, *Communism, Anticommunism*, 67.
52 AO, MHSO, Abella Oral History Collection, interview with Muni Taub, n.d.
53 NAC, UFCWU, MG 28 I 186, acc. 1992/0101, vol. 2, *The Anti-Communist Fur Workers Voice* file, April 1957.
54 Ibid.
55 Such 'patriotism' was used to defend a raiding attempt in Montreal. NAC, UFCW Papers, acc. 1992, vol. 2, AFL pamphlet for Montreal fur workers, 1950.
56 NAC, UFCW Papers, acc.1992/0101, vol. 4, Federman file, address on 50th anniversary, 1956, and AO, F 1405, Series 85-031, Fur Workers Union Papers, Fur Workers Union of Toronto, 50th Anniversary Pamphlet. Note that a Montreal historical publication at least recognized that Robert Haddow had been a pioneer leader in the union; in Toronto, former communist union leaders were left out of all histories. NAC, UFCW, acc. 1992, vol. 4, file 16, Programme souvenir, 65th anniversary of Montreal union.
57 AO, MHSO, MU 9001, Federman papers. Gold was also described as 'El Duce' in pamphlets characterized by virulent anti-communism.
58 Wedro was also on the Toronto Labour Council, where she was outspoken on such issues housing and prices. It is interesting that in one battle she was simply 'drowned out' with shouts from the largely male crowd. *Toronto Star*, 28 Sept. 1948.

59 'New Officers Installed by Sister Wedro,' *FLW*, June 1949.
60 AO, Abella Oral History Collection, Pearl Wedro interview, n.d.
61 'Ten Month Struggle Wins Pact at Humberstone Shoe,' *FLW*, March/April 1952; 'Militant 10 Day Strike Wins Gains at Winnipeg,' *FLW*, June 1949; 'Richmond Shoe Strike in 14th Week and Montreal Local 500 Shop Wins 5 c Raise,' *FLW*, May 1950.
62 CU, Kheel, IFLWU 1946 Convention Minutes, 217.
63 Ibid., 1950 Convention Minutes, 268.
64 Ibid., 1944 Convention Minutes, 209.
65 NAC, RCMP Papers, RG 18, vol. 3526, pamphlets, *Toronto Furriers Newsletter*, June 1954.
66 *The Beaver*, a newsletter of the Toronto union. CU, Kheel, IFLWU Papers, vol. 25, file 20.
67 'Women's Parley Maps New Activities,' *FLW*, April–May 1951.
68 CU, Kheel, IFLWU Convention Report, 1946, 219.
69 Ibid., IFLWU, vol. 28, file 2. See letters from Gold pressuring Gauthier not to resign and counselling her on her state of health: Gold to Gauthier, 16 Jan., 19 April, and 19 Dec. 1945.
70 *The Butcher Workman*, August 1955, 8–10.
71 My reading of gender politics is taken from not only Canadian sources, but also American ones, including IFLWU papers, annual convention reports, and the IFLWU paper, *The Fur and Leather Worker*, though this contained a limited number of Canadian stories.
72 UBC, SpC, Trade Union Research Bureau, box 39, IFLWU, file 39-5.
73 'IFLWU Delegation Asks Parliament to Act on Jobless,' *FLW*, March–April 1952. On the industry's troubles in the 1950s, see Strauss, 'The Canadian Fur Manufacturing Industry.'
74 The same may have been true for the United States; see Cochran, *Labor and Communism*, 331.
75 Writing on women in the Communist Party in the United States tends to focus on the pre-1945 period. An important exception is Weigand, *Red Feminism*. Her historiorgraphical claim that previous writers simply concluded that women 'abandoned' (4) their feminism once in the party does not do credit to the nuances of previous writing. On the efforts of the Canadian Communist Party to address gender inequality in this post-war period, see Sangster, *Dreams of Equality*; Thorn, 'Visions of the New World Order'; and Guard, 'Women Worth Watching.'
76 To the public at large, but also in private letters to fur owners (in efforts to get them not to recognize the CIO union), the AFL union denounced IFLWU members as Nazis, traitors, betrayers of the war effort, a fifth

column, and so on. Equating them with Nazis was bound to have maximum impact in an industry with so many Jewish workers and employers. AO, MHSO, F 1405, Series 85-031, MU 9021. Maurice Wax to Fur Manufacturers Association, 27 May 1940; 24 April 1940.

77 On electrical workers in Canada, see Guard, 'Fair Play.' On the United States, see Schatz, *The Electrical Workers*; Kannenberg, 'The Impact of the Cold War'; and Milkman, *Gender at Work.*

78 Copp and Knipfel, *The IUE in Canada.*

79 Doug Smith, *Cold Warrior.* On the United States, see Matles and Higgins, *Them and Us* and Abella, *Nationalism, Communism, and Canadian Labour.*

80 Copp and Knipfel, *The IUE in Canada,* 54.

81 Cherny et al., *American Labor and the Cold War.*

82 Mercier, 'Instead of Fighting the Common Enemy.' See also Alken, 'When I Realized.' The equation of masculinity and breadwinning with both sides of the Cold War battle in western US mining towns might therefore have been less a universal truism than the product of a historically masculine workforce, union, and local context.

83 Maurutto, 'Policing and Surveillance of Catholics.'

84 Letter to the editor, *PE,* Nov. 1949.

85 MUSC, IUE, box 1, file 2a, undated transcript of Thelma Cromie, probably 1952.

86 *PE,* 19 June 1951.

87 *PE,* 22 June 1951.

88 Nor did (American) Tom Fitzpatrick's anti-communist speech to the IUE convention in Peterborough address gender issues. His 1963 call to start yet another new raiding campaign on the UE, termed a 'farce' of a union, did not seem to garner much interest from the Canadian delegates. MUSC, IUE, box 1, file 6, Convention, 24–6 Oct. 1963.

89 There were more women in the electrical industry than manufacturing as a whole. The 1955 Conference on the Problems of Working Women noted they were about 28% of the workforce in the 1950s to that date, while in manufacturing they constituted about 20%.

90 Cobble, *The Other Women's Movement.*

91 Stepan-Norris and Zeitlin, *Left Out,* 195. See also Zeiger, *The CIO, 1935–55,* 349.

92 'Four women presidents elected by UE locals,' *UE News,* 17 Jan. 1966.

93 Guard, 'Fair Play,' 156.

94 The first IUE annual convention in Canada was held in 1952. Numbers were not obtained for every year, but they were consistently low. In 1952 there was only one woman elected to the executive; ten years later,

two women were elected to the 15-member board. MUSC, IUE, box 1, files 2, 4, 6. Note that the International said its female membership was about one-third of its total, while the Canadian district put the percentage as high as 40%.

95 Ibid., file 6, Convention, 24–6 October 1963.

96 NAC, IUE Papers, box 1, file 1-2, District Five Annual Convention Minutes, 9–11 Oct. 1959.

97 *PE*, 22 June 1951. See also the major coverage of the UE's victory in a grievance fought for women working on induction motors. *PE*, 13 Jan. 1949.

98 In this case, the leadership was not simply appealing to the majority at the local level, but was standing on principle. This position won them the wrath of the local *single* women, who claimed that their democratic rights to establish priorities were violated.

99 NAC, CLC, MG 28 I103, vol. 29, UE file, pamphlet 'Win the Peace: The UE plan for Canadian Prosperity in the Post War Period,' 1944. This pamphlet had 18 points, including 'full freedom in job opportunity for women in every trade, government subsidized child care and equality of wages.' See NAC, UE, reel 2339, letter to George Drew from UE District Council, 28 April 1946. Note that some of the UE papers were used before microfilming, so I have tried to provide the right reel number.

100 Kannenberg, 'The Impact of the Cold War,' 316–17.

101 Sangster, *Dreams of Equality*.

102 NAC, UE papers, 1954 UE Conference on the Problems of Working Women, Minutes, 14–17 October, 2.

103 NAC, UE Papers, reel 2362. While written in the United States, it seemed to have been used in Canada as well. Radio Script #6, 'Women in Industry,' 1955.

104 NAC, UE Papers, reel 2362, C.S. Jackson, 1955 Conference on the Problems of Working Women, Minutes, 17–18 September, 2.

105 Foreign-policy priorities of the UE leadership, for instance, were always on the agenda. Ibid., 15.

106 In 1961, such washroom complaints and issues were still being discussed. See *UE News*, 'Clearwater Women's Weekend,' 25 Sept. 1951. On federal unemployment insurance, see Ann Porter, *Gendered States*, and on the Ontario equal-pay bill that the UE criticized, Tillotson, 'Human Rights Law as a Prism.'

107 NAC, UE, reel 2362, submission to Hon. Charles Daley on the *Fair Remuneration Act 1951* by the UE, 23 March 1955.

108 Ibid., reel 2356, Minutes of annual convention, 8–11 Oct. 1953.

109 Ibid., reel 2358, Minutes of annual convention, 14–17 Oct. 1954, 4.
110 NAC, Cohen papers, vol. 47, file 3183, GE/UE bargaining 1949. US workers had a similar experience. Milkman, *Gender at Work.*
111 NAC, UE, reel 2337, District Council Minutes, report by Evelyn Armstrong on the Problems of Working Women. For a number of examples see Guard, 'Fair Play,' 149–50.
112 Guard, 'Fair Play.'
113 *UE News*, 20 March 1953.
114 NAC, RCMP Records, RG 146, UE files, UE local 507 (Toronto), report of 21 Jan. 1966.
115 *UE News*, 23 April 1948.
116 Evelyn Armstrong, quoted in *UE News*, 2 Jan. 1953.
117 *IUE News*, 21 Sept. 1967.
118 MUSC, IUE, box 1, F2, Guelph Convention, 25–26 Oct. 1952.
119 When IUE organizer Jeanine Theoret was sent to Washington to discuss the white-collar campaign, she reported back that the major difference with white-collar workers in the United States was the fact they were 'closer' to the boss and might be wary of joining a union. MUSC, IUE, box 1, file 3, District Council Minutes, 17–19 May 1962.
120 Cobble, *The Other Women's Movement*, 5; Hartmann, *The Other Feminists*, chap. 2. It is important to stress the differences between the unions. The IUE was larger and stronger in the United States due to the earlier defeat of the UE under Taft-Hartley and CIO pressures. Race and gender issues, and alliances with civil-rights groups, emerged in the American union earlier, giving it a more progressive cast despite the continued irrational anti-communism of some of its leaders. See also Hartmann, *The Other Feminists.*
121 *IUE News*, 10 April 1969.
122 MUSC, IUE, box 2, file 13, District Council Meeting, October 1967
123 Note the following recollection of a male UE activist: 'I wasn't really involved until the meeting when I took a swing at Jack Morton.' And this from a unionist who was *sympathetic* to women's equality issues. Interview with RP, Peterborough, 19 March 1989.
124 Guard, 'Fair Play,' 161.
125 *PE*, 5 Sept. 1950.
126 NAC, CLC, vol. 319, files 9-13 and 9-14. American TWUA leader Rieve to Pat Conroy, 13 June 1947.
127 Even during the war years, the two unions clashed over certification battles; after the Cold War heated up, these skirmishes intensified, often with ugly sideshows attached, including lawsuits and picket-line violence.

When Val Bjarnason denounced Baron as a 'stool pigeon' for having outed former comrades in the Socialist Party before the anti-communist Dies Committee in the United States, Baron successfully sued for slander. NAC, Amalgamated Clothing and Textile Workers Union [TWUA papers], Acc 84 0013, box 2, file 14, History.

128 Kent Rowley was 'in the communist youth movement,' but was not a party member by the end of the Second World War. Salutin, *Kent Rowley*, 19–20.

129 Canada, Royal Commission on the Textile Industry Report (Ottawa 1937). In 1955 some similar patterns existed: on the declining employment in the fifties see Canada, Royal Commission on Economic Prospects, 'Canadian Primary Textile Industry,' prepared by the National Industrial Conference Board, 1956. On women and textile work, see Brandt, 'The Transformation'; Parr, *The Gender of Breadwinners*; Scheinberg, 'The Tale of Tessie'; and Sangster, *Earning Respect*.

130 'Cut to the Red Cloth,' *Saturday Night*, 31 July 1951.

131 Fred Rose was first elected to parliament for a Montreal constituency in a 1943 by-election under the LPP banner. Post-Gouzenko, a royal commission on espionage was set up and targeted Rose as a suspect. He claimed innocence but refused to testify, and was imprisoned and stripped of his parliamentary seat. After his release from prison and a move to Poland, he was stripped of his citizenship as well.

132 Baillargeon, 'Les grèves du textile au Québec,' 66.

133 'Cut to the Red Cloth.'

134 See, for example, NAC, Madeleine Parent and Kent Rowley Collection, MG 21 B19 (Parent-Rowley), vol. 3, file 13, copy of TWUA Conference proceedings. Disparaging references to the UTWA's LPP (Labour Progressive Party) lawyer, Bernard Morgler, also suggest that anti-semitism may have been used in the anti-UTWA campaign. See also vol. 15, file 7, copy of UTWA information sheet on TWUA raiding. During the war, Ellen Scheinberg argues, the Cornwall UTWA had a less than stellar record on women's equality. It then switched to the TWUA. Scheinberg, 'The Tale of Tessie.'

135 On the Catholic Church in Peterborough, see Doug Smith, *Cold Warrior*, 217; on the US Catholic Church and communism, see Rosswurm, 'The Catholic Church.'

136 For one example, see Joy Parr's description of the 1949 Penman's strike: Parr, *The Gender of Breadwinners*, chap. 5.

137 NAC, Parent-Rowley, vol. 9, 'April 1946, Bates and Innes strike.'

138 Ibid., vol. 1, TWUA Silknit file.

139 NAC, TWUA papers, Acc 84 0013, box 2, file 14, 'History' Report of Sam Baron, 7 June 1950.

140 Briskin and McDermott, *Women Challenging Unions*; Stepan-Norris and Zeitlin, *Left Out.*

141 Interview with Ed Seymour, Hamilton, 26 Jan. 2005.

142 NAC, TWUA Papers, box 14, file 18.

143 Ibid., box 12, 'Texpack' file, and box 14, file 27.

144 Ibid., box 12, 'Texpack' file, letter from George Watson to staff, 1 Oct. 1971. For more details see Sangster, 'Remembering Texpack.'

145 Interview with L and C, 23 Nov. 2004.

146 Parr, *The Gender of Breadwinners*, chap. 5.

147 Sangster, '"We No Longer Respect the Law."'

148 Lizabeth Cohen, *A Consumer's Republic*, 8. She nonetheless shows the negative consequences for women workers of labour's pursuit of purchasing power over workplace militancy.

149 Homer Martin, *A Life in Fishing*, 93.

150 NAC, CLC Papers, vol. 46, OPWU file, Barbara Cass-Beggs to Pat Conroy, 14 and 16 1950.

151 Kaplan, *Everything That Floats.*

152 McInnis, 'Teamwork for Harmony.'

153 When many workers began to revolt in the 1960s through wildcats or other protests, they were coming to the realization that industrial legality had its limits. This was exactly the position taken by 'communist' unions such as the UE in the 1950s. On wildcats, see Palmer, 'Wildcat Workers.'

Chapter 4

1 *Montreal Gazette*, 19 May 1952 and *Le Devoir*, 20 May 1952. On the history of the CTCC, see Rouillard, *Histoire de la CSN*. See also his *Histoire du syndicalisme Québécois* and 'Major Changes.' On the changing political ideas of the CTCC, see Tremblay, *Le syndicalisme Québécois.*

2 HECA, DFF, box 21707, 'Syndicat Catholique et National des employées' file, letter from Aumonier General Jean Bertrand of the union to Albert Dupuis, 23 February 1937, and reply of Dupuis, n.d., with donation for the union enclosed. (Hereafter, all HECA references are to DFF.)

3 *LD*, October 1946. During the election that took place during the Dupuis Frères strike, the union newspaper also published advertisements paid for by Premier Duplessis that lauded his record in combating communism.

4 Parr, *Domestic Goods*; Christie and Gavreau, 'Recasting Canada's Post-war Decade.'

5 Struthers, *The Limits of Affluence.*

6 Cowan, *More Work for Mother*. Domestic labour also differed according to class: see Luxton, *More than a Labour of Love*.
7 Lizabeth Cohen, *A Consumer's Republic*. On Canada, see McInnis, *Harnessing Labour Confrontation* and Belisle, 'Exploring Postwar Consumption.'
8 Canada, StC, *Department Stores*, 18.
9 On this modernization plan see HECA, box 21707, 'Historical' file, clipping from *Canadian Variety Merchandising*, December 1950.
10 Glazer, *Women's Paid and Unpaid Labor*, xiv.
11 BOM, *The Service Industries*, RCEP study, March 1956, 20. In another study, women went from less than a third of the selling workforce to over half of those employed; Canada, DMI, *Manpower in Canada*, 60, 128. Measuring 'occupation' before 1951 is, however, difficult, as sales clerks were combined with service-station attendants in the census.
12 Macdonald and Sirianni, 'Introduction.'
13 BOM, *The Service Industries*, 71.
14 Ibid., 69.
15 Bossen, *Patterns of Manpower Utilization*, 19.
16 NAC, RCSW, box 24, Labour file, Deputy Attorney General to Florence Bird, 27 Jan. 1970.
17 HECA, box 21662, employee 2785.
18 *LD*, 14:4, August 1950. See also *LD*, 14:7, June 1951, and 14:8, October 1951.
19 *LD*, 14:4, August 1950. Note that quotes taken from *LD* appear in English and French; the English ones are my own translations that convey the meaning and intent of the quote. Where that was difficult, I kept the French.
20 A similar phenomenon is described by Natalie Zemon Davis, though in the case she describes the inversion of roles was both a reinforcement of, and challenge to, the gender order. See her 'Women on Top' in *Society and Culture*, 124–51.
21 Bossen, *Patterns of Manpower Utilization*, 73.
22 On the CCL, see Belisle, 'Exploring Postwar Consumption.'
23 BOM, *The Service Industries*, 70.
24 For an excellent analysis of the unsuccessful Eaton drive see Belisle, 'Exploring Postwar Consumption.' An insider's account is found in Sufrin, *The Eaton Drive*.
25 Shilling, *The Body and Social Theory*. The current academic preoccupation with the body has focused far less on the 'labouring' body than the 'libidinal' one. See Eagleton, *The Illusions of Postmodernism*, 71. See also Sangster, 'Making a Fur Coat.'

26 Benson, *Counter Cultures*. For recent writing on service labour see Cobble, 'A Spontaneous Loss of Enthusiasm'; Reekie, *Temptations*; Boris, 'Desirable Dress'; and Barry, *Femininity in Flight*.

27 Macdonald and Sirianni, 'Introduction,' 3; Lan, 'Working in a Neon Cage.'

28 Leidner, *Fast Food*, 2–3.

29 Hochschild, *The Managed Heart*.

30 Macdonald and Sirianni, 'Introduction,' 3–4.

31 Glazer, *Women's Paid and Unpaid Labor*, 66.

32 Macdonald and Sirianni, 'Introduction,' 11.

33 Leidner, *Fast Food*, 18.

34 Bourdieu, *Distinction*. Bourdieu's work on the social reproduction of class also illuminates the repeated, taken-for-granted gestures and inflections of embodied behaviour that characterize the hierarchical encounter between the consumer and the retail worker, reflecting one axis of power in the workplace.

35 Witz, Wsarhurst, and Nickson, 'The Labour of Aesthetics.' This concept was developed to describe the late-twentieth-century service economy, and may thus be somewhat historically limited. It nicely encapsulates the difference between modern and postmodern views of the worker. Hochschild's worker is 'mindful and feeling' (36) despite her exploitation, while the aesthetic worker's commercial embodiment comes to define the inner self.

36 *LD*, 9:2, March 1937.

37 *LD*, 4:4, January 1930.

38 Bryan Palmer, *Capitalism Comes to the Backcountry*, 17. On paternalism see also Sangster, 'The Softball Solution'; Parr, *The Gender of Breadwinners*; and, for the US context, Zahavi, *Workers, Managers and Welfare Capitalism* and Tone, *The Business of Benevolence*. The paternalism of Dupuis Frères is discussed more extensively in a thesis based on *Le Dupront*: Matthews, 'Working for the Family.'

39 Welfare benefits were available to all; discretionary paternalism offered certain special favours to the whole workplace at various times (e.g., early closing) or to individual employees. See Sangster, 'The Softball Solution,' 181. On retail, see Benson, *Counter Cultures*

40 HECA, box 21707, 'Syndicat' file, letter from Le Syndicat to M.J. Émilien Frechette, 14 April 1951.

41 *LD*, 4:8, May 1930.

42 *LD*, 9:1, January 1937, was entirely taken up with the former; for 'Saint Dugal,' 'our idol,' see *LD*, 13:6, December 1947.

43 *LD*, 12:1, March 1943.

44 For example, the family donated books on history to the schools, and Albert Dupuis sat on the Montreal committee for the Troisième Centenaire de Montréal. This is not to say that they were not on good terms with governments in Ottawa. They read out letters from Mackenzie King and other federal politicians at celebrations, and the family supported the war effort, commending employees serving during the Second World War. The family endorsed many of the values associated with 'traditional Quebec elites,' described by Michael Behiels, though it championed liberal values of individualism and, of course, private property. See Behiels, *Prelude to Quebec's Quiet Revolution.*

45 *LD*, 14:6, February 1951; 11:8, April 1942.

46 The Mohawk came to 'pay tribute' to Dugal in a public celebration, giving him a feather headdress. The curate of the parish thanked Dupuis Frères for what it had done for the reserve, acting as 'an interpreter for his children [the Natives]'; *LD*, July 1941. Northern Quebec Inuit were brought to the store (as were dwarfs at Christmas time) more for display than anything else. When promoting sports activities, Dupuis Frères also linked workers to the physical prowess of the 'colonizers of the west,' thereby situating its employees within the vexed history of settlers occupying First Nations land. *LD*, 11:8, April 1942.

47 Matthews, 'Working for the Family,' 67. Matthews points out that Dupuis Frères supported the 'Achat Chez Nous' campaign, with its xenophobic overtones, in the 1930s.

48 Dugal claimed that anyone spreading such rumours was a traitor to the race. *LD*, 4:6, March 1930.

49 HECA, box 21707, 'Historique' file. Albert Dupuis was given the Croix de L'Ordre Latin de France in recognition of this work.

50 *LD*, 3:5, February 1929.

51 *LD*, 3:6, March 1929.

52 *LD*, 4:9, June 1930. There was also similarity to working-class novels in which the heroine discovers her love interest is wealthy, or that she herself has been lost or abandoned, and raised by a poor family, only to discover her wealthy family. See Denning, *Mechanic Accents* and McMaster, *Working Girls in the West.*

53 *LD*, 5:7, April 1931.

54 *LD*, 15:6, March 1956.

55 *LD*, 11:1, February 1941.

56 *LD*, 16:2, December 1956.

57 *LD*, 14:6, February 1951.

58 *LD*, 11:1, February 1941. See also 'Twelve Ways to Irritate a Client,' *LD*, 14:7, June 1951.

59 *LD*, 14:6, February 1951.

60 *LD*, 11:2, May 1941.

61 *LD*, 6:12, December 1932.

62 *LD*, 5:7, April 1931.

63 *LD*, 13:3, February 1957.

64 *LD*, 13:3, February 1947.

65 McLaughlin, 'The McLaughlin Legacy.'

66 *LD*, 11:3, June 1941. As one issue said, 'women are the life of the nation, raising children in French, teaching them their culture, languages, songs.'

67 *LD*, 11:1, February 1941.

68 *LD*, 13.2, October 1946.

69 'God's purpose in uniting a man and a woman is for them to procreate children.' *LD*, 5:3, December 1930. This was not only an interwar preoccupation.

70 *LD*, 9:4, July 1937.

71 Lan, 'Working in a Neon Cage,' 29.

72 *LD*, 13:5, September 1947.

73 Belisle, 'A Labour Force.'

74 *LD*, 13:4, June 1947.

75 HECA, box 21656, employee file 2040.

76 Morton, *Working People*, 219. As Willis points out, there is no real evidence to support this.

77 Eighty-seven personnel files were examined. All the women at some time worked on the selling floor, and all worked during the 1950s. They were randomly sampled, with an effort to secure a range of ages as well. Files of men were examined to gage contrasting working conditions for men. While there were differences in the long-timers' files between the interwar and postwar period, I have tried to concentrate on themes found in the 1940s and 1950s.

78 On the earlier period, see Roberts, *Honest Womanhood*, Peiss, *Cheap Amusements*; Enstad, *Ladies of Labor*; and Benson, *Counter Cultures*. On the postwar period, see Howard, 'At the Curve Exchange' and Belisle, 'A Labour Force,' and on cultural capital, see Skeggs, 'The Toilet Paper.'

79 I have concentrated on the work of selling, though women also worked in clerical jobs, including at the catalogue office.

80 HECA, employee file 2101.

81 HECA, employee file 2059.

82 HECA, employee file 2221.

83 HECA, employee file 442.

84 HECA, employees files 4993, 11, 322, 2537.

85 NAC, CUC Fonds, MG 28 I 329, vol. 33, grievance files.
86 HECA, employee file 2537.
87 HECA, employee files 2463 and 2221.
88 HECA, employee file 2221.
89 HECA, employee files 485, 2188.
90 HECA, employee file 4975.
91 HECA, employee file 21260.
92 HECA, employee file 2090.
93 HECA, employee file 2303.
94 HECA, employee file 2040.
95 HECA, employee files 2089, 2100.
96 HECA, employee file 2059.
97 Five cases were available for examination. An employer could be liable for injuries sustained by a co-worker or customer due to a worker's negligence. Technically, the employee was also liable, but employers knew there was not much point in suing for money the employee did not have. If the store was found negligent because of an employee, no doubt the employer would be very unhappy with the worker in question; moreover, things as small as not cleaning up spills or toys in the aisles could cause falls and lawsuits.
98 HECA, employee file 2090.
99 HECA, employee file 436.
100 HECA, employee file 2747.
101 HECA, employee file 21657.
102 Benson, *Counter Cultures*, chap. 6.
103 HECA, box 2168, 'Syndicat Catholique et National des Employés' file.
104 HECA, Le Syndicat Catholique et National des Employés de Magasin, Avant-propos, ca 1921, and 4 April 1927.
105 In the interwar period, Matthews notes only one woman elected to the position of assistant secretary, in 1928. Given the number of Dupuis Frères female employees, this was very low compared with other international unions with sizable female memberships. Matthews, 'Working for the Family,' 30.
106 Moreover, the tone of the letters to Dupuis Frères in 1943–4 from Alfred Charpentier was one of deference, in contrast to letters only years later from the CTCC's Gérard Picard. HECA, 21707, Syndicat file, Alfred Charpentier to Albert Dupuis, 23 Jan. 1943; Dupuis to Charpentier, 29 Jan. 1943; Le Syndicat to CTCC, 23 March 1944.
107 Brosseau, 'L'histoire.'
108 Boucher was also the son-in-law of the former VP, Dugal. On Chagnon, see

Dupuis-Leman, *Dupuis Frères*, 246–7. Raymond's sister offers an unhappy account of a will that shut the sisters out of the business, and of Raymond's subsequent 'folie de grandeur.'

109 Confédération des Syndicats Nationaux (CSN) Archives, CTCC Executive minutes, 6 March 1952, letter from Marcel Lanouette to attorney general asking that legal procedures be taken against Dupuis Frères regarding unjustified transfers and dismissals. Chagnon had informed them that he wanted to make salary and other adjustments the year before; see Executive minutes, 19 Feb. 1951.

110 Chagnon's order 'met le feu aux poudres.' Foisey, *Michel Chartrand*, 163.

111 Bryan Palmer, *Canada's 1960s*. See also Ralph Guntzel, 'Rapprocher les lieux du pouvoir.'

112 Gray, 'The Greatest Canadian Shit Disturber,' 18.

113 Since the detailed events of the strike have been described elsewhere, I have not given a full account here. See Willis, 'Cette manche au syndicat' and Vadboncoeur, 'Dupuis Frères.'

114 HECA, box 21712, 'Sentence Arbitrale' file, 7 April 1952.

115 CTCC, 'Pourquoi ils sont en grève,' 4–6.

116 The employer and union numbers given to the government differed. Dupuis Frères said there were 1036 and the union 1300. The numbers were probably closer to the latter. In both statistics women were the majority. NAC, RG 27, Department of Labour, Strikes and Lockouts file, reel T4117, #61.

117 Willis, 'Cette manche au syndicat'; Vadboncoeur, 'Dupuis Frères.'

118 'Pourquoi ils sont en grève,' *Le Travail*, 9 Mai 1952; Vadboncoeur, 'Dupuis Frères,' 114.

119 'Vous faites votre devoir chez Dupuis,' *Le Travail*, 16 Mai 1952.

120 In 1949 the store introduced Friday evening work, but paid time-and-a-half; later it integrated these hours into the regular pay schedule. Vadboncouer, 'Dupuis Freres,' 11.

121 Foisey, *Michel Chartrand*, 165.

122 Ibid., 113.

123 Dupuis-Leman, *Dupuis Frères*, 241.

124 The mayor inhibited the strikers by refusing to allow them to book public space for meetings; Houde and his wife had long been supporters of the Dupuis family.

125 Vadboncoeur, 'Dupuis Frères,' 124.

126 For similar comments in the 1984 Eaton's strike, see McDermott, 'The Eaton's Strike.'

127 'Intervues avec les femmes grévistes,' *Le Travail*, 9 May 1952.
128 Vadboncoeur, 'Dupuis Frères,' 115–16.
129 *The Gazette*, 19 May 1952; *Le Devoir*, 20 May 1952.
130 *Le Devoir*, 31 May 1952. Filion implied that Dupuis Frères did not have resources to pay. The paper did allow the union to have a rebuttal on 7 June 1952.
131 *Le Devoir*, 31 May 1952. Simmons was organized by the CCL. The number of strikes taking place at the same time in Quebec must have concerned the government. On Simmons, see *Le Devoir*, 5 and 11 June 1952.
132 'Joe Louis refuse de traverser les lignes de piquetage,' *Le Travail*, 30 May 1952.
133 Glazer, *The Work Transfer*.
134 *Financial Times*, 23 May 1952; *Montreal Gazette*, 5 May 1952; HECA, box 21712, 'Syndicat Grève 1952' file.
135 HECA, box 21712, 'Syndicat' file, Robitaille, Hurteau and Desmarais Ltd. to Roland Chagnon, 8 July 1952.
136 'Vous faites votre devoir,' *Le Travail*, 16 May 1952.
137 Behiels, *Prelude to Quebec's Quiet Revolution*.
138 Vadboncoeur, 'Dupuis Frères,' 121 and 127.
139 Jeremy Milloy, 'A Battle Royal.'
140 Vadboncoeur, 'Dupuis Frères,' 119.
141 'Deux actions en dommages,' *Le Devoir*, 16 May 1952.
142 HECA, box 21712, 'Strike 1952' file, Dupuis Frères vs. Philippe Girard et al., 14 May 1952.
143 Ibid. Dupuis Frères vs. Syndicat National des Charpentiers Meunisiers de Montreal et al., 13 June 1952, 10; 'Injonction de Dupuis rejetée quant à la forme,' *Le Devoir*, 13 June 1952.
144 *Le Devoir*, 28 July 1952.
145 Sangster, 'The Softball Solution'; Parr, *The Gender of Breadwinners*.
146 Willis, 'Cette manche au syndicat,' 90.
147 Rouillard, *Histoire de la CSN*. The CTCC granted there were some 'exceptional' cases, such as widows.
148 Ibid., 171.
149 Brosseau, 'L'histoire,' 483.
150 Rouillard, *Histoire de la CSN*.
151 Gagnon, 'Women in the Trade-Union Movement,' 161–2.
152 'La femme au travail,' *Le Travail*, May 1951.
153 For example, 'Les différentes attitudes et reactions de la femme dans l'atelier s'y mieux adapter,' *Le Travail*, November 1949.

154 Two examples are 'Les problèmes du travail feminine,' *Le Travail,* 8 Feb. 1952, and 'La femme et le syndicalisme au Canada,' *Le Travail,* 2 Nov. 1951.

155 'Session intensive feminine à Chicoutimi,' *Le Travail,* 2 Dec. 1951.

156 The title of the article was significant: 'Émancipation de la femme et syndicalisme,' *Le Travail,* 18 Jan. 1952. The author, Laure Gaudreault, who appears to have been one of the teachers of the previously cited special course for women, was associated with the Fédération des Institutrices Rurales in Quebec.

157 Gauvreau, *The Catholic Origins,* 225.

158 It ran until 1966 and was revived in 1974. Confédération des Syndicats Nationaux, *Portrait.*

159 NAC, RG 33-89, RCSW, reel 4881, brief #347.

160 HECA, box 21712, 'Syndicat griefs 1952' file.

161 Even the 1984 strike at Eaton's, which had immense labour and feminist support, was not a victory. McDermott, 'The Eaton's Strike.'

162 Belisle, 'The Rise of Mass Retail.'

163 See, for example, Dupuis Frères' submission to the Royal Commission on Canada's Economic Prospects, which made a strong case for the cultural development of the eastern and French part of the city, as western (Anglo) areas were favoured. Though this would aid Dupuis Frères' enterprise, the store did believe that it should use its economic interests to sustain French culture. LAC, RG 33-30, Royal Commission on Canada's Economic Prospects, reel 1541, exhibit 191.

164 Schilling, *The Body in Culture,* 72.

165 Butler, *Gender Trouble* and *Bodies That Matter;* Lovell, 'Thinking Feminism.' For a materialist-feminist critique of performance see Hennessy, *Profit and Pleasure,* 115–20.

Chapter 5

1 *LAC,* Toronto: Central Ontario Industrial Relations Institute, United Electrical, Radio and Machine Worker of America (UE) Local 505 and The International Silver Company of Canada, 30 June 1949, 252.

2 Edwards, *Contested Terrain,* 105–7.

3 Thompson, 'Time, Work-Discipline and Industrial Capitalism.'

4 Examples of the first might be George Adams, *Grievance Arbitration,* and of the second, Edwards, *Contested Terrain.*

5 Examples of the first group are Sugiman, *Labour's Dilemma* and Taylor, 'The Struggle for Rights at Work.' The second group ranges from Logan,

State Intervention and Carrothers, *Labour Arbitration* to Brown and Beatty, *Canadian Labour Arbitration*, 3rd ed. and Palmer and Palmer, *Collective Agreement Arbitration in Canada*, 3rd ed. The third is represented by Drache and Glasbeek, *The Changing Workplace*.

6 This is a simplified version of the Ontario process. Processes across the country did not differ in fundamental ways. See Ontario, RSO, *Labour Relations Act*, c. 232, s. 37(2).

7 Carrothers, *Labour Arbitration*; Arthurs, Carter, and Glasbeek, *Labour Law*, 278.

8 Girard, *Bora Laskin*, 226.

9 As David Miller points out, 'stability' rather than 'reform' often lay behind the creation of Labour Relations Boards, and they also left countless workers outside the Fordist accord. See Miller, 'Shapes of Power.'

10 This quote from Aaron Mosher refers to a proposal for labour courts. See Fudge and Tucker, *Labour before the Law*, 272.

11 Ibid., 299.

12 Girard, *Bora Laskin*, 230.

13 Brody, 'Workplace Contractualism.'

14 Ironically, the interwar precedents for compulsory arbitration and grievance systems came from industries, such as garment making, with many women workers, but these union agreements had also solidified gendered wage differentials, just as other mass-production industries, such as auto, meat-packing, and steel did. On clothing see Steedman, *Angels of the Workplace*.

15 Fudge, 'Gender Issues in Arbitration.'

16 Etherington, 'Arbitration, Labour Boards and the Courts.' Some of the more critical views include Stanton, *Labour Arbitrations*; Haiven, 'Hegemony and the Workplace'; and Glasbeek, 'The Utility of Model Building.' American discussions include Lichtenstein, 'Great Expectations' and Brody, 'Workplace Contractualism.'

17 Stone, 'The Post-War Paradigm,' 1580.

18 Stanton, *Labour Arbitrations*, 51. While Stanton's statistics are more compli-cated, showing better results for public-sector unions, private-sector unions were sometimes losing 50% or slightly more of their cases.

19 Haiven, 'Past Practices' and 'Workplace Discipline.' I have used his work as an example, but the critical literature is more extensive.

20 Glasbeek, 'The Utility of Model Building,' 136.

21 Lichtenstein, 'Great Expectations,' 114.

22 Etherington, 'Arbitration, Labour Boards and the Courts,' 445.

23 See Girard, *Bora Laskin*, chapter 10 for a longer analysis and Beatty and Langille, 'Bora Laskin.'

24 Palmer and Palmer, *Collective Agreement Arbitration*, 172; Arthurs, 'The New Economy,' 53. See also Weiler, *Reconcilable Differences*, 92 and his *Labour Arbitration*.

25 Weiler suggested Labour Relations Boards be given the ability to create conditions of 'fairness' where contracts are silent, while Beatty implied that labour arbitration might be even more useful than collective bargaining in securing some workplaces gains. See Beatty, 'The Role of an Arbitrator.'

26 Bilson, 'Calling Them as You See Them.'

27 Stanton, Drache, and Glasbeek all note that the success rate hovers around 50%. Adams's study is far more optimistic about the role of grievance arbitration

28 Arthurs, 'The New Economy,' 50–1.

29 I looked at approximately 100 grievance files for the UPWA from 1948–68, most of which were unprocesssed and uncatalogued. Files included everything from letters from locals asking for advice on grievances to grievances at the fifth stage, where head office was involved. Both men's and women's grievances were examined in equal numbers for comparative purposes, but I took detailed notes on women's grievances. Oral histories and other union records were also used.

30 MacLachlan, *Kill and Chill*, 233. For other descriptions of the sexual division of labour see Fink, *Cutting into the Meatpacking Line*, 82–90 and Fehn, 'Striking Women.'

31 On the sexual division of labour in the United States see Horowitz, *Putting Meat on the American Table* and *Negro and White*; Rick Halpern, *Down on the Killing Floor*; and Deslippe, 'Rights Not Roses,' chap. 6.

32 Given the nature of the 'occupation' category in the census, exact numbers are difficult to ascertain. The 19% was taken from 1961 and the 16% from 1971, although in Alberta, women's share seemed to plummet to 11%. Canada, Dominion Bureau of Statistics, General Review of Manufacturing Industries of Canada, 1961 and 1971. Cynthia Loch-Drake's research on Alberta indicates that women's share of packing-house jobs climbed again in the 1970s due to the oil boom.

33 Census results are imprecise, given the changing categories for meat-plant workers by 'occupation' and 'industry.' In some cases, statistics broke down into butchers and meat cutters separate from meat packers, with far more men in the former – but this took in butchers not working in plants. In some census years, the statistics on ethnic identification ('origin') were collected by broader industry categories (e.g., food), but not by precise reference to 'meat packing.' Industry numbers would have taken in some non-production workers, and one presumes that immigrants were more

likely in production work. Nonetheless, there is evidence that immigrants were not in the majority across Canada in the years I cover, nor were those identifying their origin as eastern or southern 'European' as opposed to British and French. However, numbers of immigrants were clearly increasing over the entire period. Ethnic origin did vary across the country in the plants studied here, which accounts for the greater emphasis on class and gender in this chapter. Census of Canada, 1951, vol. 4, table 12 shows 79% of women in meat packing were Canadian-born; 35% identified as British and 16% as French, the two largest categories. With respect to men, 62% were Canadian-born, but among butchers and meat cutters (more skilled jobs), 74% were Canadian-born. In the 1961 census, those in food manufacturing were still largely Canadian-born. The 1971 census indicated a shift, more so for men: see vol. 111:4, table 2 and vol. 111:3, table 4, which indicates that for 'slaughtering and meat cutting' across Canada, now only 49% of men were Canadian-born.

34 'Centre left' refers to how American historian Roger Horowitz describes the leadership. See Horowitz, *Negro and White*, chap. 8. The CCF was strongly represented, one might say in control, in the Canadian union.

35 The TLC's Packinghouse Butcher and Allied Food Workers Union, which retained some strength in Quebec, but was eventually eclipsed by the UPWA. See Montague, 'Trade Unionism.'

36 See Horowitz, *Negro and White*.

37 Deslippe, 'Rights Not Roses' and Fehn, 'Striking Women'; Warren, *Struggling with Iowa's Pride*.

38 *Canadian Packing House Worker* (*CPHW*), 'Pledge to Aid Women' (about women organizing in United States), 5 June 1952, 5, and 'Members Forum' (on equal pay), 8 Aug. 1956, 4.

39 Montague, 'Trade Unionism,' 215–16.

40 Fehn, 'Striking Women,' 223–6; *CPHW*, 'Members Forum.'

41 NAC, UFCW, MG 28 I 186, Acc. 1985. On severance pay, see vol. 13, Peterborough Canada Packers local; on strike pay, see example of 1965 Presswood strike, vol. 44; on women in the union leadership, vol. 20; the ca 1968 district staff of 28 included six women, but only two (Iona Samis and Hugette Plamondon) worked above the secretarial level.

42 ALHI, interview with May Fingler. She termed 'free thinkers' those in the union, like Borsk, who were progressive on women's activism. Borsk was a paid official for many years. See Montague, 'Trade Unionism,' 105.

43 NAC, UFCW, Acc. 1974-0536, vol. 14, Grievances file.

44 NAC, UFCW, vol. 20, Local 551 file.

45 AM, MPOH, interview with Ronald Matthewson, 18–24 June 1985.

46 Meyer, 'Work, Play, and Power' and 'Rough Manhood.'

47 AM, MPOH, interview with Sophie Malinowksi, 11 July 1985.

48 ALHI, interview with May Finkler.

49 AM, MPOH, interview with Vera Slobodian, 2 July 1985.

50 AM, MPOH, interview with Patricia McFadzen, 30 July 1985.

51 ALHI, interview with May Finkler.

52 NAC, UFCW, vol. 44, Local 219 file, letter from Sam Hughes to Charles Daly, 18 Nov. 1949.

53 *LAC*, International Union of Brewery, Flour, Cereal and Soft Drink Distillery Workers vs. O'Keefe, 8 Sept. 1948, 193–5.

54 NAC, UFCW, Acc. 84-536, vol. 21, 1959 file (unless otherwise noted grievances files are from Acc. 84-536.)

55 *LAC*, 8, Canadian General Electric and UE, 238. The same company successfully discharged a man for falsifying a piecework ticket by 80 cents. Yet, when a canteen attendant was found to be overcharging *his fellow employees* for chocolate milk by 1 cent he was reinstated. He was stealing from other employees, not the company. *LAC*, Canada General Electric vs. UE, 25 April 1949, 32–4.

56 Since no letter announced victory, the local probably lost. NAC, UFCW, vol. 21, 1959 file. It was common in such cases for unions to want proof equivalent to that required under criminal law, with employers opposed. Decisions began to settle 'somewhere in between.' Arthurs, Carter, and Glasbeek, *Labour Law*, 266.

57 NAC, UFCW, vol. 11, 1964 file.

58 NAC, UFCW, vol. 43, Swifts grievances file.

59 NAC, UFCW, vol. 11, 1963 grievances file.

60 NAC, UFCW, vol. 44, Local 208 file.

61 Ibid.

62 NAC, UFCW, vol. 21, 1953 file.

63 NAC, UFCW, vol. 13, 1965 grievances file, Sam Hughes to Vancouver local.

64 On the importance of washroom grievances, see Sugiman, *Labour's Dilemma* and Ignagni, 'Processing Discontent.'

65 NAC, UFCW, vol. 44, 1968 grievances file.

66 Such was UPWA's Fred Dowling's description of a 'nervous' man whose outburst in the plant was akin to expressing 'the wish to a colleague to burn down the school house.' By creating an image of the man as 'human' with the occasional outburst of 'temper,' the union was able to fight his dismissal. This too appears a gendered defence, not so easily used for women, though the union was trying to use any argument it could to get the man's job back. *LAC*, UPWA vs. Canada Packers, 25 May 1949, 340–1.

67 NAC, UFCW, vol. 13, grievances file.

68 NAC, UFCW, vol. 20, Burns file.

69 *LAC*, 9, United Packing House Workers, Local 114 and Canada Packers, 1958, 200–4. Laskin reiterated his right to order redress if the issue had been arbitrable.

70 Ibid.

71 NAC, UFCW, vol. 29, Swifts file.

72 NAC, UFCW, vol. 21, 1956, Grievances file.

73 AM, MPOH, Vera Slobodian, 2 July 1985.

74 NAC, UFCW, vol. 21, Grievance file, letter of 17 April 1956, Roland St Arnaud to UPWA head office.

75 *LAC*, 1/2, Amalgamated Meat Cutters and Butcher Workmen, Local 470 and Choice Chicken Ltd., 14 Dec. 1950, 661–5.

76 NAC, UFCW, vol. 44, Local 219 file.

77 NAC, UFCW, vol. 12, 1965 grievances file.

78 NAC, UFCW, vol. 11, Grievances file.

79 Haiven, 'Workplace Discipline,' 78.

80 This was not out of keeping with the trend of labour arbitrations after the war. Girard notes that Laskin was not sympathetic about protecting women's right to work (*Bora Laskin*, 238).

81 Job loss varied across the country, depending on the plant. Canada-wide, women's percentage of the workforce seemed to drop from about 19% in 1961 to 16% in 1971, but the numbers remained higher in Ontario, and plummeted more in Alberta. Dominion Bureau of Statistics, General Review of the Manufacturing Industries of Canada, 1961, 24 and 1971, 30.

82 NAC, UFCW, vol. 11, Grievances file.

83 NAC, UFCW, vol. 44, Grievances file.

84 Arthurs, Carter, and Glasbeek, *Labour Law*, 272.

85 Fink, *Cutting into the Meatpacking Line*, 88.

86 NAC, UFCW, vol. 14, Grievances file, Burns.

87 NAC, UFCW, vol. 14, Grievances file, 1960.

88 NAC, UFCW, vol. 44, Local 244 file.

89 NAC, UFCW, vol. 44, Grievances file, Hughes to Moncton local 288, 15 March 1967.

90 NAC, UFCW, vol. 44, Grievances file, Local 280.

91 NAC, UFCW, vol. 63, Everleigh Cleaners file. The business agent worked for the Amalgamated Meat Cutters and Butcher Workmen. This grievance lends weight to the argument in chapter 3 that women in the Fur Workers union gained little by amalgamation.

92 Ibid., handwritten letter, 20 Feb. 1957, 'Dear Sirs' from 'girls in local 750,' as well as letters to and from the business agent and the company.

93 Creese, *Contracting Masculinity*.

94 *LAC*, United Steelworkers vs. The John Inglis Company, 31 March 1953, 1249–54.

95 The sources used for this section include files of the Traffic Employees Association, renamed the Communications Union of Canada in 1974. These workers later became part of the Communications Workers of Canada (CWC). Second, some mixed-gender workplace grievance files from British Columbia, collected by the Office and Technical Employees Association (OTEU), Local 378, and Canadian Union of Public Employees (CUPE), Local 881, all held in the University of British Columbia Special Collections, were also examined. Two sets of hospital grievances were consulted as well, but omitted only for space reasons: they did not necessarily show fundamentally different patterns. On the origins of the OTEU, see Creese, *Contracting Masculinity*, 58–9.

96 There was also a second group, the Canadian Telephone Employees Association (CTEA) that represented office workers.

97 NAC, CUC, MG 28 I 329, vol. 33, file 1: TEA Informative Meeting, 12–13 April 1960.

98 On the earlier feminization see Sangster, 'The Bell Telephone Strike' and Michèle Martin, 'Hello Central?'

99 NAC, CUC, vol. 33, file 1: TEA Informative Meeting, 4–5 Dec. 1956.

100 Kuyek, *The Phone Book*, 22.

101 Ibid., 24.

102 NAC, CUC, vol. 33, file 1: Informative Meeting, 9 March 1960.

103 Of about 68 disciplinary cases, the most frequent charge noted first was absenteeism, then performance, then various kinds of 'fraud.' However, often letters contained more than one problem, so it is not easy to quantify. Although names are given on the letters I have chosen to identify women not by name, but simply by the file their letter was in.

104 NAC, CUC, vol. 33, file 5.

105 A Snarky Operator and Lippy Representative, 'Working at the Bell,' *Canadian Dimension* 8, no. 7 (June 1972), 13.

106 NAC, CUC, vol. 33, file 6.

107 Ibid., file 5.

108 'She has a bad attendance record ... and the other girls will be upset if she is reinstated' stated her own union rep, who also expressed her desire not to fight this one out. NAC, CUC, vol. 35, file 35.

109 NAC, CUC, vol. 33, file 5.

110 Ibid.
111 NAC, CUC, vol. 38, file 17.
112 NAC, CUC, vol. 33, file 5.
113 NAC, CUC, vol. 33, Final Warnings file.
114 NAC, CUC, vol. 34, file 17.
115 'Working at the Bell,' 13.
116 NAC, CUC, vol. 33, file 5.
117 Ibid.
118 NAC, CUC, vol. 33, file 6.
119 Ibid. This use of medical experts was not unlike state efforts to create 'healthy' and efficient girl workers in the 1920s. See Strange, *Toronto's Girl Problem.*
120 The Bell files would suggest that women were analysed more as having unstable 'personality' problems, but these files obviously did not offer a group of comparable male workers. Another group of grievance files I examined suggests to me that 'male' alcoholism was treated in a similar medical-rehabilitative manner.
121 NAC, CUC, vol. 34, file 42.
122 NAC, CUC, vol. 43, file 5.
123 NAC, CUC, vol. 35, file 39.
124 NAC, CUC, vol. 38, file 12.
125 NAC, CUC, vol. 16, file 9.
126 NAC, CUC, vol. 35, file 46.
127 NAC, CUC, vol. 33, file 1, Informative Meeting, 4–5 Dec. 1956.
128 NAC, CUC, vol. 33, file 2, Staff Adjustment Policy, c. 1962. See also views on pregnancy benefits in 1962, ibid., Informative Meeting, 21 June 1962.
129 NAC, CUC, vol. 36, file 6; vol. 38, file 17.
130 The two unions were in British Columbia.
131 UBC Special Collections, OTEU, vol. 2, 1 Dec. 1964, union president to C.G. Devonshire.
132 Ibid., vol. 2, female ticket sellers grievance, 1 March 1949.
133 Ibid., vol. 2, Mrs M. to union president, 18 Feb. 1949.
134 UBC Special Collections, OTEU, vol. 2, letter of Mrs K. to union president, 15 March 1949.
135 UBC Special Collections, Trade Union Research Bureau, CUPE Local 881, vol. 9, Grievance file.
136 Miller, 'Shapes of Power,' viii.
137 Glasbeek, 'The Utility of Model Building,' 141.
138 The 2 per cent is from Haiven, 'Hegemony in the Workplace.' See also Arthurs, Carter, and Glasbeek, *Labour Law*, 255.

139 Adams, *Grievance Arbitration*, 2, 19.

140 Ibid., 26, 35. The term 'rehabilitation' was coined by long-time arbitrator O.B. Shime, quoted in Young, *At the Point*, 35.

141 These significant cases were collected by the Central Ontario Industrial Relations Institute, an employer group. Some later cases had employer 'footnotes' that betrayed this bias, but most of these cases did not. I looked at all discharge cases in volumes 1–20 (about 1948–69) to ascertain the gender of the griever and the cause for dismissal. I looked at both men's and women's cases, but I have concentrated here on 35 women's cases.

142 Glasbeek, 'The Utility of Model Building,' 139.

143 Of the 35 women's cases, 43% were lost and another 22% were reinstated but with some kind of penalty, e.g., suspension, lost wages. Only three received full compensation. For similar though sometimes varying numbers, see Stanton; Drache and Glasbeek; and Taylor. Adams's study found that discharge was upheld in 46.5% of the cases, but in 37.5% a lesser penalty was imposed with reinstatement, and only 17% represented complete 'successes' (42–3).

144 *LAC*, 13, Sudbury General Workers, Local 902 and Loblaw Groceterias Co., 17 Sept. 1962, 2.

145 There were no thefts among the women's cases, but two issues involving dishonesty: one woman punched in for her supervisor, and one was discharged for what we might call 'corruption,' though it was not named as such (the woman was trying to 'solicit building materials' from contractors coming into the office). *LAC*, 17, UE and Canada Wire and Cable Co., 3 July 1950, 492–7, and 17, Office and Professional Employees International Union, Local 343 and United Brotherhood of Carpenters, Local 18, 21 Nov. 1966, 417–18. The other two most common charges cited in grievance arbitrations were insubordination and lack of attendance. Adams, *Grievance Arbitration*, 45.

146 *LAC*, 16, United Automobile Workers Local 27 and Minnesota Mining and Manufacturing of Canada, 16 Nov. 1965, and 20, Retail and Food Employees Local 175 and Steinbergs, 20 Oct. 1969.

147 As Gramsci noted many years before this, employers' increasing surveillance of workers' personal lives was not simply 'puritanical' in nature, but was linked to Taylorism and Fordism. Gramsci, *Selections*, 303–4.

148 Emphasis mine. *LAC*, 5, Building Service Employees, Local 210 and Hotel Dieu Hospital, 4 March 1958, 2091–6.

149 *LAC*, 2, UE and American Optical Co. of Canada Ltd., 1 March 1950, 427–31.

150 *LAC*, 1, Massey Harris vs. UAW Local 439, 30 June 1948, 11–12.

151 *LAC*, 1, UE and American Optical Co. of Canada Ltd., March 1950, 427–31.

152 *LAC*, 20, Amalgamated Meat Cutters and Butcher Workmen vs. Power Supermarket, 11 Jan. 1969, 73.

153 Employers could argue that an incident, however small, was a 'culminating' one after a history of minor problems and warnings not heeded.

154 Adams attests that 35% of discharge cases received a lesser penalty, though 81% of all discharge cases were found 'guilty' of some offence overall (*Grievance Arbitration*, 43).

155 Bruce Young, *At the Point*, 19.

156 Goldblatt, *Justice Delayed*, 44.

157 *LAC*, 15, International Woodworkers of America and Brunswick of Canada, 14 Sept. 1964, 232. Studies done in the 1970s differed over whether single or multiple arbitrators aided workers, but there was evidence in Adams and especially Goldblatt that a single arbitrator was more likely to lead to reinstatement.

158 Adams lists this as the primary cause, and in my sample, insubordination came second after the marriage/pregnancy grievances. Adams, *Grievance Arbitration*, 45

159 *LAC*, 2, Aeronautical Lodge 717, International Association of Machinists and A.V. Roe, 1950, 669–73. Adams used the phrase primarily in reference to men (*Grievance Arbitration*, 54).

160 *LAC*, 20, Building Service Employees International Union, Local 268 and Central Park Lodge, 18 March 1969, 186.

161 *LAC*, 18, Retail, Wholesale and Department Store Union Local 1002 and Smiths of Windsor, 16 June 1967, 253.

162 Arbitrators and employers were most likely to disagree over insubordination. Young, *At the Point*, 44–5. Substitution was practised until it was challenged successfully in the Supreme Court in 1969, at which point it was added to the legislation in most provinces.

163 *LAC*, 19, Retail Wholesale and Department Store Union, Local 1002 and Sentry Department Store Ltd., 378.

164 *LAC*, 16, UAW Local 673 and De Havilland Aircraft of Canada, 24 Jan. 1966, 383–4.

165 Distinctions made explicitly by Shime, quoted in Young, *At the Point*, 38.

166 The sample is too small to tell. In the immediate post-war years, local JPs and magistrates were used, as well as some 'professional' arbitrators with legal or other training. By the 1960s, the former were being replaced, and the latter dominated.

167 *LAC*, 17, UAW and Leepo Machine Products, 24 Feb. 1966, 33.

168 *LAC*, 12, Canadian Food Workers, Local 1105 and Canada Packers, 1970, 21.

169 This may also have been seen differently as woman vs. woman animosity. *LAC*, 3, Johnstel Metal Products and UAW, 4 Dec. 1951, 923–4.

170 *LAC*, 20, Retail, Wholesale and Department Store Union Local 5791 and Northern Foodmart, 214.

171 *LAC*, 17, Hotel, Restaurant Employees International Union and Westminister Hotel, 28 June 1966, 212. Yet, a man might be excused for his actions because of a 'domestic quarrel' that day. Young, *At the Point*, 72.

172 LAC, 13, National Public Service Employees Local 13 and Chatham Memorial Centre Commission, 13, 2 Nov. 1962, 167–8. The question is, was it wife assault or the string of alcohol offences (or both) that concerned the employer? The treatment of discharge grievances involving a man's criminal conviction outside the workplace changed over time, with earlier rulings supportive of discharge, while later ones applied more stringent questions of 'impact' for the employer.

173 *LAC*, 1, UAW local 195 and Motor Products Ltd., 12 Nov. 1949, 393–6.

174 Taylor, 'The Struggle for Rights'; on women at GE see Sangster, *Earning Respect*, chap. 7.

175 The arbitration noted that some management people did not show up to testify, perhaps in order to escape from admitting guilt. LAC, 16, USWA and Aerocide Dispensers Ltd., 15 April 1965, 57–72.

176 Wildcats were largely male events, wrapped up in masculinized images of 'toughness' and physical confrontation. Although the nature of this walkout was different, it suggests that women shared some of the rank-and-file discontent with the union bureaucracy that shaped the broader wildcat movement in the mid-1960s, itself directly related to the limitations of the Fordist accord. See Palmer, 'Wildcat Workers.'

177 *LAC*, 1, UAW Local 28 and Canada Cycle and Motor Co. Ltd., 1, 2 June 1949, 16.

178 NAC, Jacob Finkelman papers, MG 31 E 27, vol. 9, UAW grievances file.

179 For oral-history evidence see Sangster, 'Doing Two Jobs.' On women trying to use the UI system, see Ann Porter, *Gendered States*, 63–91.

180 *LAC*, 5, UE Local 504 and Canadian Westinghouse, 7 May 1954, 1825 (1824–7).

181 *LAC*, 15, United Brewery Workers, Local 173 and Dare Foods, 13 April 1964, 44.

182 Finley, 'Transcending Equality Theory,' 1131.

183 *LAC*, 8, UAW and Essco Stamping Products Ltd., 19 Dec. 1957, 26.

184 See, for example, *LAC*, 5, UE Local 504 and Canadian Westinghouse, 7 May 1954, 1825 (1824–7).

185 *LAC*, 2, CGE and UE, Local 524, 688.

186 *LAC*, 1, UPWA and Quaker Oats, 9 Sept. 1960, 87–94.

187 *LAC*, 5, UE and Canadian Westinghouse, 7 May 1954, 1824.

188 Young noted that 'few absenteeism cases ... involve pregnancies,' but these arbitrations did not necessarily fall under that category (*At the Point*, 128). In a rare footnote to a case, the Central Ontario Industrial Relations Institute added its moralist language to a pregnancy case, referring to a woman's 'bastard' child. *LAC*, 8, UAW and Essco Stamping Products Ltd., 19 Dec. 1957, 26.

189 AO, Dept. of Labour, RG 7, Women's Bureau, Series VIII, box 1, 'What Is Maternity Leave,' 7.

190 *LAC*, 13, Sudbury General Workers, Local 902 and Loblaw Groceterias Co. Ltd., 17 Sept. 1962, 96.

191 *LAC*, 7, Sudbury General Workers Local 902 and Loblaw Groceterias Co. Ltd., 20 June 1956, 3.

192 See Hugh Collins, *Marxism and Law.*

193 Matheson, 'The Canadian Working Class,' 204.

194 Fudge, 'Gender Issues,' 130.

195 Glasbeek, 'The Utility of Model Building.'

196 Brody, *Workers in Industrial America*, 210.

197 Acker, *Class Questions, Feminist Answers*, 109, 122.

198 Drache and Glasbeek, *The Changing Workplace*, 127, chap. 7.

199 Gramsci, *Selections*, 242, 247.

200 In white-collar work, low levels of non-white immigration before the 1970s and racial exclusion meant that office, stores, and switchboards were also racialized and gendered spaces of work. Whiteness was ensconced as an assumed privilege in many unionized jobs; however, local studies of specific unionized plants or regions would provide one means of exploring the intersection of ethnicity and language with class and gender in more depth: for example, looking at French and English workers in New Brunswick plants.

Chapter 6

1 Like the Royal Commission on Aboriginal Peoples (RCAP), I use the term 'Aboriginal' to encompass both Métis and Indian peoples. For the sake of variety, I also use the terms First Nations or Native in the same vein. When I am referring directly to sources of the period I sometimes adopt the language used at that time, i.e., 'Indian' or 'Métis.'

2 Manitowabi, *An Indian Girl.* A slightly different version was 'An Ojibway Girl
   in the City.'
3 AM, HBC, RG 7/1/760, Reports from Posts, Newspaper clippings, 12 and
   20 July 1966.
4 Culhane, 'Aboriginal Women.'
5 I have consistently referred to Indian Affairs (short for the Indian Affairs
   Branch) as the federal body responsible for Indians, although the branch
   came under different ministries during this period: in the 1940s it was
   under Mines and Resources, then in 1950 moved to Citizenship and
   Immigration, and in 1966 to Northern Affairs and Natural Resources.
6 'Indian Girls Achieve Successful Careers – Pave the Way for Others,' *Indian
   News,* June 1958, 6–7. See also *Winnipeg Free Press,* 18 Jan. 1958; AM, BBP,
   P 6829, file 5, *Prairie Call,* issue 5.
7 Gavin Smith, 'Writing for Real.'
8 This roughly follows Michael Asch's terminology: there is bush production
   related to both capitalism and subsistence. See Asch, 'Capital and Economic
   Development.'
9 Canada, RCAP, vol. 2 (Ottawa, 1996), 777.
10 Some earlier works did exist: for example, Knight, *Indians at Work.* For one
   review of the literature see High, 'Native Wage Labour.' An excellent
   discussion of economic history that takes issue with High is Tough, 'From
   the "Original Affluent Society."' The emphasis on the fur trade and
   resource extraction in Canadian writing inevitably necessitated discussion of
   Aboriginal labour, though there was more emphasis on the eighteenth and
   nineteenth centuries. Some examples are Ray, *Indians in the Fur Trade;*
   Newell, *The Tangled Webs;* Muszynski, *Cheap Wage Labour;* Van Kirk, *Many
   Tender Ties;* Burley, *Servants of the Honourable Company;* and Produchny,
   'Unfair Masters.'
11 Some examples include Lutz, 'After the Fur Trade'; Bourgeault, 'Aboriginal Labour'; Fiske, 'Fishing Is Women's Business'; and Parnaby, 'The Best
   Men.'
12 For example, Fiske and Sleeper, eds., *New Faces of the Fur Trade.*
13 Anderson, *Recognition of Being;* Acoose, *Iskwewak;* Campbell, *Halfbreed;*
   Lawrence, 'Real' Indians; *American Indian Quarterly,* special issue, 27: 3 and 4
   (2004).
14 For example, Raibmon, 'The Practices of Everyday Colonialism,' and
   Hosmer, *American Indians.* Other examples of American scholarship include
   O'Neill, *Working the Navajo Way;* Hosmer and O'Neil, eds., *Native Pathways;*
   Knack and Littlefield, eds., *Native Americans;* M'Closkey, *Swept under the Rug;*
   Berman, *Circle of Goods;* and Albers, 'Labor and Exchange.'

15 AM, BBP, P 6829, file 7, clippings, sections of Douglas Leechman, *The Indian in Transition*. It is likely this was the 1964 work in a series published by IA.
16 The metropolis/satellite theory was used more in the United States: Jorgenson, 'A Century.' Other American examples range from Richard White, *The Roots of Dependency*, which was not explicitly Marxist, to Cardell Jacobson, 'Internal Colonialism'; see also Wilkins, 'Modernization, Colonialism, Dependency.' An excellent early piece in the political-economy tradition was Albers, 'Autonomy and Dependency'; Canadian examples are Watkins, *Dene Nation*; Dobbin, 'Prairie Colonialism'; Loxley, 'The Great Northern Plan'; and Lithman, *The Practice of Underdevelopment*.
17 Elias, *Metropolis and Hinterland*.
18 Harold Adams, *Prison of Grass*.
19 Champagne, 'Tribal Capitalism.'
20 For a critical view of Marxist and dependency theories, see O'Neill, 'Rethinking Modernity' and, in contrast, Muszynski, *Cheap Wage Labour*; see also Abele and Stasiulis, 'Canada as a "White" Settler Colony.'
21 In some ways this debate harkens back to an earlier discussion by Bruce Trigger of romantic versus rationalistic images of Aboriginal Native–newcomer relations. Trigger, 'Early North American.'
22 See, for example, Tough, 'From the "Original Affluent Society"' and Brownlie, 'Living the Same.'
23 Gutman, *Work, Culture and Society*. For more recent discussion of parallels and differences between immigrants and Native American migrants to the city, see Lagrand, *Indian Metropolis*.
24 What Marx called original accumulation was translated as primitive accumulation. See Perelman, *The Invention of Capitalism*.
25 Satzewich and Wotherspoon, *First Nations*, 6–8.
26 The Australian term was devised for a historical context in which violence, compulsion, and forced labour were more prevalent – indicating the importance of looking at transnational differences as well as similarities. Williams and Thorpe, *Beyond Industrial Sociology*, 97–8, and Curthoys and Moore, 'Working for White People.'
27 Gordon, 'Internal Colonialism and Gender.'
28 On the fur trade and the way state paternalism replaced that of the HBC, see Ray, *The Canadian Fur Trade*. As well, see Tough, *As Their Natural Resources Fail*. My discussion of state policy is not an argument that policy alone 'caused' economic problems, which, as Tough argues, had deep and long roots.
29 In 1951, 36% of Aboriginal men across Canada were involved in fishing/trapping and 11% in agriculture. On the prairies, these patterns were

accentuated: fishing and trapping occupied 44% of men in Manitoba, and 66% in Saskatchewan, though only 27% in Alberta. Canada, Census of Canada, 1941, vol. 7, table 26, 12; 1951, vol. 4, table 20; 1961, vol. 3:1, table 22.

30 Satzewich and Wotherspoon, *First Nations*, 48.

31 Lagasse, *The People of Indian Ancestry in Manitoba*, vol. 3.

32 Ibid., 54.

33 SAB, Institute for Northern Studies, G S 213.

34 Kew, *Cumberland House, 1960*, 31, 90.

35 Buckley, *Trapping and Fishing.*

36 Fiske and Sleeper-Smith, 'Introduction,' and Fiske and Mufford, 'Hard Times and Everything Like That.' Earlier works on women's role in the fur trade focused on the eighteenth and nineteenth centuries; see, for instance, Van Kirk, *Many Tender Ties.*

37 Quirling, *CCF Colonialism.* A different approach that recognizes the government's mistakes and paternalism, but acknowledges its (misguided) good intentions and disputes the idea that wholesale assimilation was the CCF goal, is Barron, *Walking in Indian Moccasins.*

38 Worsely, Buckley, and Davis, *Economic and Social Survey*, 13. Economist Buckley was a co-author of many of these studies and later wrote *From Wooden Ploughs to Welfare.*

39 Strauss, 'The Canadian Fur Manufacturing Industry.'

40 Ray, *I Have Lived Here*, 291.

41 Kew, *Cumberland House, 1960*, 61.

42 See Muszynski, 'Race and Gender,' 103.

43 Perleman, *The Invention of Capitalism*, 95.

44 RCAP, *Restructuring the Relationship*, vol. 2.

45 Marsh, *The Swampy Cree.*

46 Poelzer and Poelzer, *In Our Own Words*, 19.

47 SAB, Saskatoon Native Women's Association Métis Oral History Project, interviews with Evelyn Whitfield, Rose Fleury, and Josephine Tarr, n.d.

48 SAB, Saskatoon Women's Centre Society, GS 105, file b 112, clipping, *Time Magazine*, 21 Jan. 1964. The idea of independence was probably relative; Aboriginal people had been integrated into a market economy of fur production for a long time.

49 Hongiman, 'Incentives to Work,' 26.

50 Marsh, *The Swampy Cree*, 57.

51 Moreover, nuclearization brought other problems: in the case of one Manitoba community, it created tensions between Métis and Indians, since the latter had different housing, and all families became more dependent on store-bought goods, leading to nutrition problems. Sealey, 'Fish Lake.'

52 Quirling, *CCF Colonialism*, 48.
53 AM, HBC Records, RG 7/1 1764, R.H. Cheshire to Mr Mackay, 5 Oct. 1950.
54 AM, HBC Records, RG 7, file 18, Nelson River Reports, 7 Jan. 1958.
55 'Careful Fur Preparation Brings Bigger Cash Returns,' *Indian News*, January 1956, 4.
56 NAC, Indian Affairs Records (RG 10), vol. 8464, file 901/23-21, pt 1, Report of Manitoba Social Worker, January 1951.
57 AM, MOHC, interview with Mary Whiteway.
58 Ibid., interview with Hilda Hysart.
59 Ibid., interview with Sandra Anderson.
60 Carol Williams, 'Between Doorstep.'
61 AM, MOHC, interview with Mary Pottinger.
62 Canada, Senate and House of Commons Joint Committee on the Indian Act, 1947. For a discussion of the images of Indians projected in committee discussions, see Sheffield, *The Red Man's*, chap. 6.
63 Canada, Senate and House of Commons Joint Committee on the Indian Act, 1947, Mrs Charles Franklin for Popular River Reserve, Man., Appendices, 221.
64 Canada, Senate–House of Commons Joint Committee on Indian Affairs, 1958–9, 1035–6. Social-science studies pinpointed similar cultural problems, though without the condemnatory language. For example, a study of northern Manitoba resource jobs listed some problems with Indian integration into the workforce, including Native peoples' inability to adapt to new work processes, time discipline, and work rhythms after engaging in bush production. One of the authors also worked on Hawthorn's study. See Jamieson and Hawthorn, 'The Role of Native People,' quoted in Hawthorn, *A Survey*, 155.
65 Canada, Report of the Department of Citizenship and Immigration, Indian Affairs Branch, 1956–7.
66 One hundred dollars was given to one reserve. NAC, RG 10, vol. 8443, 674/23-4, Saskatoon District Semi-Annual Reports, Superintendent, Shellbrook Agency to Regional Supervisor, 2 April 1965.
67 Ibid., vol. 8442, 501/23-4, Superintendent, Fisher River to Regional Director, 31 Oct. 1966.
68 Some hope was placed in tourist operations as employers of Aboriginal men as guides, though the profits, as Helen Buckley astutely observed, went into white pockets, leaving Native men dependent on uncertain work. Buckley, *Trapping and Fishing*, 51.
69 As the records of one of these programs makes clear, placement officers could become deeply invested in having families they worked with succeed.

Worrying that one relocated family would be drawn back to the reserve, one officer told the reserve Indian Agent to make sure 'cheerier' letters were sent to 'his' relocated family so they would not return home. NAC, RG 10, Alberta Regional Office Correspondence, vol. 7988, 701/19-4, Field Officer R.L. Ekland to Regional Supervisor Alberta, 7 Feb. 1963. For a critical assessment of placement officers singling out and 'adopting' promising families in an almost 'symbiotic' relationship, see SAB, GS 105, Saskatoon Women's Centre Society, 'Native Women, Perpetuation of the Poverty Cycle' file. This is an earlier draft of Dosman, *Indians*, 133.

70 NAC, RG 10, Alberta Regional Office Correspondence, vol. 7988, 701/19-4, Edland to Regional Supervisor, 7 Feb. 1963, though he is writing about a different family than the one above. In another clear instance of Aboriginal workers being expected to use subsistence practices for self-provision (and to isolate them from whites), the placement officer suggested that if there was no housing, the Native family could live in tents on the outside of town.

71 Ibid., Regional Supervisor, Alberta, to Indian Affairs Branch, 20 Nov. 1962.

72 Ibid., Field Officer R.L. Ekland to Regional Supervisor Alberta, 7 Feb. 1963.

73 NAC, RG 10, vol. 842, 671/23-4, North Battleford District, Semi-Annual Reports, C.C. Bell to Indian Affairs Branch, 15 Sept. 1951.

74 The Alberta sugar-beet migration is discussed in other secondary literature, so I have concentrated on family and gender issues. See Laliberte, 'The Canadian State' and his 'The "grab-a-hoe" Indians'; Laliberte and Satzewich, 'Native Migrant Labour.'

75 In the 1950s there were only hundreds, but by 1965, there were 2500 migrant workers.

76 NAC, RG 10, Acc. 1985, 'Economic Development Research and Surveys of Alberta Regional Office,' file 701/19-2, part 1, Labour Force Survey, 11 Jan. 1967.

77 NAC, RG 10, vol. 8414, file 1/21-1, pt. 6, Memo to the Director from Chief, Welfare Division, 26 March 1959.

78 GA, ASBGA, M7474, box 2, file 19, Annual report, 1956. Similar laments were heard in the 1958–9 Senate hearings as politicians lamented that Indians could not 'do well like immigrants.' Canada, Joint Committee, 1958–9, 1098. In later years, the Indian labour force was praised, at least publicly: 'Indian Workers Praised,' *Lethbridge Herald*, 18 May 1960.

79 NAC, RG 10, vol. 8421, 501/21-1, Manitoba Region, General Correspondence Regarding Placement of Indian Labour, H.M. Jones to Deputy Minister, 2 Dec. 1954.

80 NAC, RG 10, vol. 8429, file 701/21-5, Alberta Region Employment of Indians Seasonal and Casual, Memorandum to the Deputy Minister, 2 Dec.

1954 and 29 Aug. 1958; Minutes of the Meeting of the Federal-Provincial Farm Labour Committee, 22 Sept. 1958.

81 NAC, RG 10, vol. 8429, file 701/21-5, Minutes, 22 Sept. 1958.

82 Although some researchers have argued that Aboriginals, pushed out of other blue-collar jobs after the Second World War, served as a 'reserve army of labour' for employers, others designated Aboriginal workers on social assistance with little hope of permanent employment as the more marginalized, 'permanently unemployed,' and it was often those on social assistance who made their way to the beet fields. On the former see Patrias, 'Race, Employment Discrimination,' and on the latter, see Elias, *Metropolis.*

83 This investigation was far more conservative than exposés on sugar-beet work. Groups such as the Alberta Federation of Labour, the Indian Association of Alberta, the Métis Association of Alberta, and the Alberta Human Rights Association were involved. Some criticisms were made, for instance, about child labour and bad housing, but the authors also defended the growers 'who gave their migrant labour force a fair deal.' The Métis Association later said the report was too soft. Organized labour was rather dismissive about the prospects of such workers ever becoming organized as part of their own movement. For the report, see GA, ASBGA, M 7474, box 8, file 88, 'Report of the Independent Committee of Inquiry Established to Examine the Conditions of Migrant Workers in the Sugar Beet Industry in Alberta,' 1970, and on organized labour's views and Métis objections, box 12, file 134, 'Migrant Labour Report Too Mild – Métis Head,' clipping, n.d.

84 When delivering part of this chapter at a conference, I was preceded by a Native elder who spoke of migrant hop-picking labour in the past as a good community time. It was a lesson in how a state-focused view (like this chapter) is partial: it cannot capture the complexities of Aboriginal life or the way historical memory is constructed.

85 GA, ASBGA, Herman French, 'A Study Conducted during May and June Regarding the Education of the Children of Saskatchewan Treaty Indians Who Become Transient Labourers in the Sugar Beet Fields of Alberta.'

86 *Silver Sunshine* [published by the Canadian Sugar Factories Ltd.] 12, no. 1 (Spring 1953), 8 and picture on 25. Thanks to Will Knight for analysing the pictures.

87 GA, ASBGA, M 7474, box 8, file 88: Indian Beet Labour.

88 NAC, RG 10, vol. 8443, 774/23-4, Edmonton Hobbema District Semi-Annual Reports, Report by K.R. Brown, 30 Sept. 1965.

89 NAC, RG 10, vol. 8421, 501/21-1, Manitoba Region General Correspondence, 5 March 1957.

90 GA, ASBGA, M 7474, box 8, file 88, French, 'A Study,' 19.

91 In fact, a far more comprehensive study had been suggested in 1962 to the FPFLC, but it was not undertaken. For the long list of research questions, see RG 10, vol. 8429, 701-2-5, Memo from Regional Supervisor, Alberta, to Indian Affairs, Ottawa, 12 April 1962.

92 GA, ASBGA, M 7474, box 8, file 88, French, 'A Study,' 39, 34.

93 Saddle Lake Band Councillor Ralph Steinhouser, quoted in Canada, Senate-House Joint Committee on Indian Affairs, 1959–60, 917. He did acknowledge the problems of taking children out of school. One white politician thought there was no problem with transferring these children to a new school in May, as it might be an 'integrative' experience, though another declared it was a 'breeding ground for juvenile delinquency' (917).

94 NAC, RG 10, vol. 8421, 501/21-1, J.F. Kristiansen, Unemployment Insurance Commission to Regional Supervisor of Indian Affairs, 14 April 1958.

95 Ibid., Manitoba Region General Correspondence, J.H. Gordon to Chief, Welfare Division, 29 Aug. 1958.

96 Canada, Senate–House of Commons Joint Committee, 1959–60, 460.

97 Ibid., 144–54 (Brief from Indian Association of Alberta).

98 Some white women's lobby groups also called for protection of treaties as well. See Canada, Joint Committee, 1959–60, Farm Women's Union of Alberta brief, 1021–2; and on requests of Saskatchewan Native women for homemaking instruction, see Stahl, 'Marvelous Times.'

99 NAC, RG 10, Manitoba, vol. 8421, 501/21-1, General Correspondence Regarding Placement of Indian Labour, 1959–61.

100 For both comments, see Canada, Senate-House Joint Committee, 1959–60, 1098, 178, 1141.

101 NAC, RG 10, vol. 8442, 574-23-4, Memo to Regional Director, Manitoba, from Superintendent, Fisher River, 31 Oct. 1966: 'It is time we realized that the modern farmer cannot make a living with a hoe, a shovel, a rake, and a broken down tractor.'

102 Shewelll, *Enough to Keep Them Alive*, 328. See also Canada, *The Indian in Transition*, 10, 17.

103 Sangster, 'The Beaver as Ideology.'

104 Hawthorn, *A Survey*, vol. 1, 179.

105 Ibid., 127.

106 Canada, Joint Committee, 1959–60, Saddle Lake Band, Alberta, brief, 913, 917.

107 Ibid., Federation of Saskatchewan Indians, 460. For the provincial government's views, see 1035–6 (my emphasis).

108 NAC, RG 10, vol. 8574, 1/1-2-2-17, 14 Feb. 1963.

109 Hawthorn, *A Survey*, vol. 1, 94.

110 NAC, RG 10, vol. 8424, file 1-2-2, pt 1, G. Armstrong, Welfare Division to unknown, 29 Oct. 1945. On the earlier 'production of domesticity,' see Pamela White, 'Restructuring the Domestic Sphere,' and on the United States, Simonsen, *Making Home Work.*

111 Ibid., vol. 8415, 1/21-1, Summer Placement from Mohawk Residential School, 1961.

112 While Joanne Fiske's study of one BC school argues there were some unintended employment benefits of residential schooling for girls, J.R. Miller's larger study concludes that the 'protective and exploitative attitudes' towards Aboriginal girls' 'socioeconomic horizons' were intensified in residential schools. Fiske, 'Gender and the Paradox'; J.R. Miller, *Shingwauk's Vision,* 249. See also John Milloy, *A National Crime.*

113 NAC, RG 1, 8414, 1-21-1, R.F. Davey, Superintendent of Education, to J.E. Morris, 17 June 1955.

114 Canada, Annual Report (Indian Affairs Branch), Department of Citizenship and Immigration, 1956.

115 See also Canada Annual Report, Department of Citizenship and Immigration, 1958, on training girls in 'home economics' and boys in 'agriculture' (1957), providing 'trade and vocational training to help fit men to earn a better living and women make better housewives' (1958).

116 To be fair, he credited his colleague Jean Lesage with the idea. NAC, RG 10, vol. 8414, 1-21-1, Jack Pickersgill to Deputy Minister, 13 June 1955. For similar ideas in the residential schools, see Miller, *Shingwauk's Vision,* 229–30.

117 NAC, RG 10, vol. 8413, 1-21-1, correspondence regarding the placement of Indian labour, G. Gooderham, Regional Supervisor, to H.M. Jones, 14 Aug. 1952.

118 Ibid., Hilda Holland, Havergal College, to Mr Matters, Indian Affairs, 18 March 1948.

119 Peters, '"Urban" and "Aboriginal"'; on the racialization of space see Razack, *Race, Space and the Law.*

120 AM, Brigden, P 820, f . 2, clipping, *Winnipeg Free Press,* 18 Jan. 1958; my emphasis.

121 For an excellent discussion of Native women in Toronto see Howard-Bobiwash, 'Women's Class Strategies.'

122 Ibid. Beatrice Brigden, a former social gospeller and CCFer, was very involved with the Winnipeg Indian and Métis Friendship Centre as well as this church work. On Brigden's early years see Sangster, 'The Making of a Socialist Feminist.'

123 NAC, RG 10, vol. 915, f. P 2168-8-6/2, pt. 1, Employment and Recruiting Equal Opportunities. For their definition of general and permanent, see Canada, IA, *The Indian in Transition,* 11.

124 Lagrand, *Indian Metropolis*; MacKay, 'Warriors into Welders.' The Canadian program initially designated three areas of activity: general, rural, and urban placements. However, there was an emphasis on the latter, especially for youth.

125 NAC, RG 10, reel C 13809, f. 1/23-21, General – Social Worker Report, 18 March 1953.

126 Ibid., vol. 8515, file 1-21-1, pt. 7, Placement Manual, Saskatchewan Region.

127 Ibid., reel C 13809, f. 1/23-21, General – Social Worker Report, 18 March 1953.

128 Ibid.

129 NAC, RG 10, Acc. 1985, f. 701/19–2, pt 1, 14 April 1966, Memo to Regional Director, IA, from Development Officer, Calgary.

130 'Indian Girls Achieve Successful Careers – Pave the Way for Others,' *Indian News*, June 1958, 6–7, and 'How Louise Found Her Job,' *Indian News*, May 1960, 4.

131 In the United States, jobs in beauty culture provided much-needed employment for African American women, sometimes leading to small-business ownership. The latter did not happen in Canada, probably because there were far fewer women involved, nor was there the same geographical segregation as in the United States. See McCallum, 'The "Permanent Solution,"' and on the United States, Peiss, *Hope in a Jar*; Blackwelder, *Styling Jim Crow*; and Willett, *Permanent Waves*.

132 Campbell, *Halfbreed*, 154.

133 Lagasse, *The People of Indian Ancestry*, 3: 65. See Gerber, 'Multiple Jeopardy.'

134 Lagasse, *The People of Indian Ancestry*, 3: 71.

135 Ibid., 77.

136 Ibid., 129.

137 Ibid., 129.

138 A case was being made for success, since fifteen moved on to other jobs within six months. NAC, RG 10, vol. 8428, f. 1-2-4-2, p. 2, Deputy Minister to Treasury Board, 5 Feb. 1962.

139 Dosman, *Indians*, 133.

140 NAC, RG 10, vol. 8428, file 1-21-4-2, Superintendent, Cowichan Agency, to Indian Commissioner, BC, 25 Sept. 1962.

141 Mortimore, *The Indian in Industry*, 7.

142 Trent University Archives, Clare Brant, A Collection of Chapters, Lectures, Workshops and Thoughts.

143 Dosman, *Indians*, 138.

144 The percentage of Aboriginal women in white-collar work was still less than for Canadian women in general, but the shift towards more clerical

jobs for Aboriginal women was nonetheless noticeable. Between 1961 and 1971 the percentage in clerical work went from 7 to 17%, while the numbers of those in service work declined significantly. The percentage of nurses who were Aboriginal also increased substantially from 1961–71. The overall numbers of Aboriginal women working for wages increased over time, but the percentage of Aboriginal women as a part of the female labour force remained small – fewer than 1% of all working women in 1971. Canada, Census of Canada, 1951, vol. 4, table 20; 1961, vol. 3:1, table 21; 1971, vol. 3, pt. 3. The figures on clerical work might support Joanne Fiske's contention that Aboriginal women's education could provide better access to jobs than Aboriginal men's education did. Fiske, 'Gender and the Paradox.'

145 *A National Conference on Indians in the City* (Ottawa: Dept. of Indian Affairs and Northern Development, 1966).

146 Brody, *Indians on Skid Row*; Dosman, *Indians.*

147 Lagasse, *The People of Indian Ancestry*, 3: 111–12.

148 NAC, RG 33/89, Royal Commission on the Status of Women, box 29, Nan Shipley, Report on the Status of the Indian and Métis Women of Manitoba.

149 Tough, *As Their Natural Resources Fail*, 299.

150 Lawrence, 'Gender, Race,' 3, 4. The marrying-out clause was section 12 (1) (b) of the *Indian Act*, which took women's Indian status away if they married a man without Indian status. This part of the act was amended in 1985.

151 Ibid., 301.

Chapter 7

1 Paltiel, 'State Initiatives,' 27.

2 Bégin, 'The Canadian Government,' 14. See also Timpson, 'Royal Commissions,' 124.

3 I use the word 'feminist' to denote women who analyse, or are committed to, gender equality. The term was seldom embraced by female trade-union activists in the 1940s and 1950s, as it was associated with middle-class women's organizations whose interests did not accord with those of working-class women. Labour feminists, in Dorothy Sue Cobble's useful definition, were women of various class backgrounds active in, or working for, the labour movement. Cobble, *The Other Women's Movement.*

4 Findlay, 'Facing the State.'

5 NAC, EGMF, MG 31 K7, box 3, Commission Minutes, 30–31 Oct. 1968.

6 Sangster, *Dreams of Equality*; Vickers, Rankin, and Appelle, *Politics as if Women Mattered.*

7   NAC, RG 33-89, RCSW, vol. 44, clippings, *Toronto Star Weekly.*

8   Marchak, 'A Critical Review'; Canadian Women's Educational Press, 'Pie in the Sky'; Kowaluk, 'The Status of Women.'

9   CACSW, *The Royal Commission.*

10 Armstrong and Armstrong, *The Double Ghetto,* 135–40.

11 Bird, *Anne Francis.*

12 Bégin, 'The Canadian Government,' 27, 21.

13 See many of the essays in Andrew and Rogers, eds., *Women and the Canadian State.*

14 Morris, 'More than Simple Justice,' 319. Other discussions of the commission include Speers, 'The Royal Commission' and McLeod, 'Laying the Foundation.'

15 See, for example, Turpel-Lafond, 'Patriarchy and Paternalism.'

16 Nadeau, 'Enterprizing Nationals.'

17 Findlay, 'Facing the State,' 48.

18 Briggs, 'Fighting for Women's Equality'; Burt, 'Organized Women's Groups.'

19 The bureau was criticized by some unions for being underfunded and lacking in real power. The RCSW effectively sidelined the bureau by recommending other state machinery to oversee the RCSW report's implementation.

20 Timpson, 'Royal Commissions,' 123.

21 Jenson, 'Commissioning Ideas,' 54.

22 Freeman, *The Satellite Sex.*

23 The commissioners were Mrs John (Florence) Bird, journalist; Miss Elsie Gregory MacGill, aeronautical engineer; Mrs Lola Lange, volunteer for women's farming organizations; Miss Jeanne Lapointe; Mrs Robert (Doris) Ogilvie, judge; Mr Jacques Henripin, academic/demographer; and Mr John Humphrey, professor of law.

24 'No Working Women on the Royal Commission,' *Canadian Labour,* February 1967, 26.

25 Harrison, *On Account of Sex,* 135, and Cobble, *The Other Women's Movement,* 159–61.

26 Jane Arscott suggests that they were looking for gender balance as well. My thanks to Jane, who generously provided this information from her research notes. Her reference is LAC, RG 2, Privy Council Office, series A-5-a, vol. 6323, meeting 1967/12/1.

27 However, seeing the RCSW *only* through our current political eyes and with respect to issues that are important today can, as Jane Arscott argues, cloud a historical understanding of the commission's meaning and impact.

Arscott, 'Twenty-Five Years.' Commissioner Humphrey repeatedly noted his
interest in human-rights issues relating to race and met with Indian women
concerning their unequal treatment in the 1969 white paper. However, this
concern with race remained somewhat separate from the RCSW's concerns.

28 NAC, RCSW, box 28. There were three immigration studies: Rioux, 'Female
    Immigrants'; Hawkins, 'Women Immigrants'; and Ferguson, 'Immigrant
    Women in Canada.'

29 NAC, EGMF, box 3, Minutes, 15–16 Feb. 1968.

30 NAC, RCSW, vol. 41, clippings, *Victoria Province*, 17 April 1968; vol. 43, *Pictou
    Advocate*, 18 Sept. 1968.

31 Benston, 'The Political Economy.'

32 NAC, RCSW, vol. 18, brief 443, Marion Smith, Pauline Jewett, Helen
    McCrae, Madeline Gobeil.

33 NAC, RG 33-89, vol. 36, 'Relations with Associations,' inter-office memo of
    6 Sept. 1967 and Bird to Bégin, 7 Sept. 1967. Bird and Bégin were quite
    sure they had inside knowledge of the labour movement and informed
    other commissioners not to even mention the CNTU (Confederation of
    National Trade Unions) in front of the CLC due to 'jealousy and rivalry.'
    One wonders about such so-called inside knowledge on reading Bégin's
    memo: 'Mr. MacDonald may very soon become the President [of the CLC].
    (He could be moody. He was in the Miners Union).'

34 NAC, EGMF, box 4, Minutes 13–15 March 1968. They were also dis-
    appointed with a massive study done by University of Toronto professor
    Arthur Porter on technology, claiming it made a number of unexamined
    assumptions about women's mental abilities.

35 NAC, RCSW, vol. 43, *St John's Evening Telegraph*, 19 Nov. 1968.

36 NAC, EGMF, vol. 3, Henripin to Commissioners, Minutes, 14 Aug. 1968;
    Humphrey to Commissioners, Minutes 25–27 Feb. 1968.

37 NAC, RCSW, vol. 30, Robert Stirling, 'A preliminary review of research
    concerning the effects of a wife's employment on family relations.'

38 Ibid., microfilm reel C-6800, Hawkins, 'Women Immigrants,' 19.

39 Ferguson, 'Immigrant Women,' 16.

40 NAC, RCSW, vol. 28, Robert Hyndman, 'An occupational study of Depart-
    ment store saleswomen.'

41 Hickling-Johnson, 'The Status of Women,' 7.

42 Ibid., 9–10, 18.

43 For a full list of all the objections, see NAC, RCSW, vol. 24, Labour file,
    Deputy Attorney General to Florence Bird, 27 Jan. 1970.

44 When the League for Social Action women tried to draw connections
    between sexism and imperialism, Bird forbade them from speaking about

the Viet Nam War as she deemed this too political an issue. If the RCSW was anything, surely it was 'political.'

45 They probably also became bored. Many contributors liked to draw references to potted histories of suffragettes and other female heroines such as Eleanor Roosevelt. After one such brief, the analyst wrote: 'an unoriginal synopsis of the history of women in the workforce with the usual complaints about the unequal treatment of women in the workforce.' NAC, RCSW, vol. 14, brief 223, Eleanor Lynch.

46 NAC, RCSW, vol. 12, brief 115, Tri-vettes brief.

47 Ibid., vol. 11, brief 28, Sherrill Jackson.

48 Ibid., vol. 12, brief 95, Kay Cornish.

49 Ibid., vol. 41, *Ottawa Journal,* 12 June 1968.

50 Ibid., vol. 11, brief 69, analyst questions for Ontario Federation of Labour.

51 'OFL Conference on Women Workers,' *Canadian Labour,* July/August 1966, 48.

52 Ibid. and 'Human Rights,' *Canadian Labour,* May 1966, 29.

53 For a discussion of instrumentalist views of the state, see Jessop, *The Capitalist State,* 13–14.

54 On women workers and the state, see Armstrong and Armstrong, *Theorizing Women's Work,* 113–30, and on the post-war welfare state, see Ann Porter, *Gendered States.* For a discussion of the welfare state's contradictory approach to male breadwinning in New Zealand, see Nolan, *Breadwinning.*

55 Eleven unions provided substantial written briefs. About another seven submissions came from nurses' and teachers' associations.

56 NAC, RCSW, reel C 4882, brief 441, Canadian Air Line Flight Attendants Association.

57 Ibid., vol. 17, brief 374, United Automobile Workers, Canadian Council.

58 Ibid.

59 'Human Rights of Indians and Eskimos,' *CL,* December 1967, 12–15; 'Prejudice Hurts Indians, Saskatchewan Federal Seminar Told,' *CL,* February 1968, 41; 'Canadian Sugar Beet Cutters,' *CL,* February 1970, 20–3.

60 Author's interview with Gil Levine, Ottawa, 18 March 2006.

61 NAC, RCSW, vol. 18, brief 437, CUPE.

62 Ibid., vol. 15, brief 296, Saskatchewan Federation of Labour.

63 Ibid., vol. 11, brief 69, OFL.

64 Ibid., and vol. 17, brief 347, CNTU.

65 These same concepts were used by neo-conservative political arguments for child care for working mothers in the 1990s. Teghtsoonian, 'Work and/or Motherhood,' 429.

66 NAC, RCSW, CNTU brief.

67 Ibid., vol. 17, brief 353, Alison McAteer. The report did offer a recommendation that Household Workers Bureaus be provincially established, along with safeguards for good pay and working conditions, but provided no mention of who would be recruited for such work. Canada, *Royal Commission on the Status of Women Report*, 404.

68 So too did groups such as the NDP. NAC, RCSW, vol. 12, brief 133, NDP Provincial Women's Committee (Saskatchewan).

69 One example was a cartoon showing a henpecked husband (with a picture on the wall of an overbearing woman with a rolling pin) looking after many children while the wife was at the RCSW. *Ottawa Citizen*, 4 Oct. 1968.

70 Timpson, *Driven Apart*, 37.

71 Geoffrey and Sainte-Marie, 'Attitudes of Union Workers,' 103. This was one of the better studies that used both quantitative and qualitative methods and tried to offer conclusions that had some nuance.

72 NAC, RCSW, vol. 42, *Winnipeg Free Press*, 1 Oct. 1968.

73 Ibid., vol. 11, brief 62, anon.

74 Ibid., vol. 41, *Victoria Province*, 17 Apr. 1968.

75 'CUPE Chief Admits Discrimination,' *Globe and Mail*, 1 Oct. 1968.

76 'Officer Looked Chic,' *Ottawa Citizen*, 2 Oct. 1968.

77 NAC, CLCF, MG, 28 I 103, reel H 575, file 7, Minutes of the CLC Advisory Committee on the Status of Women, 29 Jan., 1968.

78 Ibid.

79 Ibid.

80 Ibid.

81 NAC, CLC, reel H 575, file 7, Shirley Carr to Hugette Plamondon, 11 Sept. 1968.

82 Other labour briefs avoided or sidestepped abortion. For example, the OFL spoke vaguely of 'liberalizing' abortion laws, and at the same time affirmed its dedication to 'preserving the family and marriage as an institution,' while the Saskatchewan Federation of Labour women's committee did not mention abortion at all.

83 NAC, RCSW, vol. 11, brief 8, Anne Thomson.

84 Ibid., vol. 13, brief 150, Christine Bennett.

85 Ibid.

86 NAC, RCSW, vol. 9, Ontario letters. I have chosen to give the file name, but not the personal name. Despite the fact that these boxes are entirely open, the women felt they were writing personal letters, and I don't feel enough time has elapsed yet to use the names.

87 The RCSW stated that it had received '468 briefs and 1000 letters of opinion.' *Report of the Royal Commission*, ix. Having seen the two-and-a-half

boxes of letters, 1000 seems high to me. I looked at the majority of letters in order to locate ones that dealt with work. I read 200 of these from all provinces, although there are more in my sample from Ontario, due to the sheer number coming from that province. The majority of these letters were penned by women, with a small minority written by men.

88 Her suggestion is based on the information she provided me on how mail submissions were sorted. Arscott to Sangster, personal correspondence.

89 Eagleton, *Ideology*, 36.

90 Ewick and Silbey, 'Subversive Stories.'

91 NAC, RCSW, vol. 8, NWT letters.

92 E.P. Thompson, *The Making of the English Working Class* (London· Gollancz, 1964), 9.

93 Joan Scott, 'The Evidence of Experience' *Critical Inquiry* 17, no. 4 (Summer 1991), 793. Scott claims that 'experience was reintroduced into historical writing in the wake of critiques of empiricism.' This was not the situation with Marxist exponents of the word, and feminists were often committed to validating a non–male-centred view of history, less concerned with questions of empiricism. Scott does note the problem of experience being a term almost impossible to do without, and she too uses it: Scott, *Only Paradoxes to Offer: French Feminists and the Rights of Man* (Cambridge: Harvard University Press, 1996), 14.

94 Ireland, 'The Appeal to Experience,' 95. The difference between postmodern critiques of identity politics and materialist-feminist ones should be noted: see Hennessy, *Profit and Pleasure*, 229.

95 Sonia Kruks, quoting Elizabeth Grosz in *Retrieving Experience*, 138. Another comment on Scott and experience is Laura Lee Downs, 'If "Woman" Is Just an Empty Category.'

96 Eley and Nield, *The Future of Class*, 106. For a review of earlier debates about experience within history, and also Scott's relation to them, see Jay, *Songs of Experience*, 424.

97 Pickering, *History, Experience and Cultural Studies*, 183.

98 Kruks, *Retrieving Experience*, 141.

99 Thompson, *The Poverty of Theory*, 362.

100 Hennessy, *Profit and Pleasure*, 317.

101 Ibid., 17.

102 For example, Hartsock, 'Postmodernism and Political Change,' 24, 27; Collins, *Black Feminist Thought*; Kruks, *Retrieving Experience*.

103 Kruks, *Retrieving Experience*, 140.

104 Pickering, *History, Experience*, 176.

105 Note that these are not the traditional Marxist critics of postmodernism. For example, see the whole issue of *History and Theory* 40 (2001) and Shaw's introduction, 'Happy in Our Chains?' in which he writes that 'it is time for historians to show how these attempts to understand the self as constituted in social history were not misguided but were essential to historical work' (3).

106 Moya, 'Postmodernism,' 68.

107 Ibid., 69.

108 Haskell, *Objectivity Is Not Neutrality*, esp. chapter 6. On pre-postmodern historical critiques of objectivity, see Zagorin, 'History, the Referent,' 2.

109 Or as Pickering terms Scott's approach, 'linguistic determinism.' *History, Experience*, 230, 225.

110 Fitzhugh and Leckie, 'Agency,' 65. See also Moya, 'Postmodernism,' 68.

111 Holt, 'Experience.'

112 Canning, *Gender History in Practice*, 79.

113 Wilkerson, 'Is There Something,' 277.

114 Ibid.

115 Hall, 'Politics,' 204–10.

116 Gordon interview, in *Visions of History*, 77.

117 On structure of feeling see Williams, *Marxism and Literature*, 130–1.

118 Canada, Department of Labour, *Women at Work*, 51, 58.

119 NAC, RCSW, vol. 9, Ontario.

120 NAC, RCSW, vol. 8, Ontario; vol. 9, Ontario letters.

121 NAC, RCSW, vol. 9, Ontario.

122 NAC, RCSW, vol. 8, Ontario.

123 NAC, RCSW, vol. 11, brief 14, anon.

124 NAC, RCSW, vol. 8, Ontario.

125 NAC, RCSW, vol. 8, Ontario and Nova Scotia.

126 NAC, RCSW, vol. 8, Alberta.

127 NAC, RCSW, vol. 8, Ontario.

128 NAC, RCSW, vol. 8, Ontario.

129 NAC, RCSW, vol. 8, New Brunswick.

130 NAC, RCSW, vol. 9, Nova Scotia.

131 NAC, RCSW, vol. 9, Nova Scotia.

132 NAC, RCSW, vol. 18, brief 424, Ella Manuel.

133 NAC, RCSW, vol. 14, brief 253, Clara Yellowknee.

134 NAC, RCSW, vol. 17, brief 394, Marie Anne Lahache.

135 NAC, RCSW, vol. 9, Quebec.

136 NAC, RCSW, vol. 8, Saskatchewan.

137 NAC, RCSW, vol. 8, Ontario.

138 For discussion of earlier views on the hierarchy of need, see Kessler-Harris, 'Gender Ideology.'

139 NAC, RCSW, vol. 8, Ontario.

140 NAC, RCSW, vol. 8, Ontario.

141 NAC, RCSW, vol. 8, Saskatchewan.

142 Janice Tyrwhitt, 'Why the Hell Can't We Provide Daycare for Working Mothers' Kids?' *Star Weekly*, 27 July 1968.

143 NAC, RCSW, vol. 11, brief 85, Joan McKenna.

144 Smith, *Texts, Facts and Femininity*.

145 Pierson, 'Experience, Difference, Dominance,' 85.

146 Kruks, *Retrieving Experience*.

147 Thompson, 'The Politics of Theory,' 406.

Conclusion

1 Fiske, 'The Womb Is to the Nation as the Heart Is to the Body.'

2 Tariq Ali, 'Where's the Rage?' *The Guardian*, 22 March 2008.

3 Palmer, *Canada's 1960s*; Easson et al., 'Working in Steel.'

4 Bank Book Collective, *An Account to Settle*, 115–24.

5 Joan Sangser, '"We No Longer Respect the Law"'; Maroney, 'Feminism at Work'; Luxton, 'Feminism as a Class Act.'

6 NAC, Frank and Libbie Park papers, MG 31 K9, vol. 33, file 428, Puretex file article by Laurel Ritchie.

7 Kessler-Harris, *Out to Work*, chap. 11.

8 Judging from Nancy MacLean's *Freedom Is Not Enough*, the presence of a stronger civil-rights movement also made a difference in the United States.

9 De Hart, 'The New Feminism,' 544.

10 Glucksmann, *Cottons and Casuals*, 17.

11 Fitzhugh and Leckie, 'Agency, Postmodernism,' 65; Gottfried, 'Beyond Patriarchy?' 453.

12 Gottfried, 'Beyond Patriarchy?' 451.

13 Discussions of feminist historical materialism are also differentiated; in some cases, they lean far more towards a neo-Marxism, others are sympathetic to feminist standpoint theory, and some draw heavily on Gramsci, others on E.P. Thompson. The notion of class as a 'making' or process is obviously indebted to Thompsonian social history, while a parallel discussion of gender can be found in Kessler-Harris, 'A New Agenda for American Labor History.'

14 Gottfried (drawing on Marx and Gramsci), 'Beyond Patriarchy?' 458.

15 Thompson, 'The Politics of Theory,' 406.
16 MacLean, 'Postwar Women's History.'
17 Eagleton, *After Theory*, 136.
18 NAC, RG 33-89, RCSW, vol. 9, Ontario letters.

Bibliography

Archival and Library Collections

Archives of Manitoba
Beatrice Brigden Papers
Hudson's Bay Company Records, RG 7/1/760
Meatpacking Oral History Collection
Métis Oral History Collection

Archives of Ontario
Federman papers, MU 9011
Fur Workers Union papers
Multicultural History Society of Ontario, Series 85-023, MU 9011
Muni Taub papers, MU 9021

National Archives of Canada
Amalgamated Clothing and Textile Workers Union papers
Canadian Labour Congress papers
Communications Union of Canada papers
Department of External Affairs, RG 25
Department of Labour, RG 27
Elsie Gregory MacGill Fonds
Frank and Libbie Park Collection
Indian Affairs Records, RG 10
International Union of Electrical Workers papers
Jacob Finkelman papers
Joseph Cohen papers
Parent and Rowley Collection

RCMP papers
Robert Haddow papers
Royal Commission on the Status of Women, RG 33-89
United Electrical, Radio and Machine Workers of America papers
United Food and Commercial Workers Union papers

Saskatchewan Archives Board
Institute for Northern Studies, GS 213
Saskatoon Native Women's Association Métis Oral History Project
Saskatoon Women's Centre Society, GS 105

Other
Cornell University, Kheel Centre for Labor-Management Documentation and
    Archives, International Fur and Leather Workers Union papers
– Unite-Here [ILGWU] papers
Glenbow Archives, Alberta Sugar Beet Growers Association files
Hautes Écoles Commerciales Archives, Dupuis Frères Fonds
McMaster University Special Collections, International Union of Electrical
    Workers Fonds
Trent University Archives, Clare Brant Collection
University of British Columbia, Special Collections, Elaine Bernard Collection
    [BC Telephone Workers]
– Food and Service Workers Union of Canada Collection, Series A-1
– Office and Technical
    Employees Association papers
– Trade Union Research Bureau
– Vertical Files, Vancouver Labour Committee for Human Rights, VFA, 442-b

Publications of Government Departments and Agencies

Brody, Hugh. *Indians on Skid Row.* Ottawa: Department of Indian and Northern
    Affairs, 1971.
Buckley, Helen. *Trapping and Fishing in the Economy of Northern Saskatchewan,
    Report #3, Economic and Social Survey of Northern Saskatchewan.* Saskatoon:
    Centre for Community Studies, University of Saskatchewan, 1962.
Canada. Census of Canada, various years.
– Department of Citizenship and Immigration, Indian Affairs Branch. Annual
    reports, 1956–7.
– Department of Citizenship and Immigration. *The Indian in Transition.* Ottawa:
    Dept. of Citizenship and Immigration, 1962.

– Department of Indian Affairs and Northern Development. *A National Conference on Indians in the City.* Ottawa: Dept. of Indian Affairs and Northern Development, 1966.
– Department of Labour, Women's Bureau. *Women at Work, Canada.* Ottawa, 1964.
– Department of Manpower and Immigration. *Manpower in Canada, 1931–61.*
– Parliament. House of Commons. *Debates.* Various years.
– *Report of the Royal Commission on the Status of Women.* Ottawa, 1970.
– Royal Commission on Aboriginal Peoples. Ottawa, 1996.
– Royal Commission on Aboriginal Relations. Vol. 2, *Restructuring the Relationship.* Ottawa, 1996.
– Royal Commission on Canada's Economic Prospects *The Canadian Primary Textile Industry* and *The Canadian Electrical Manufacturing Industry.* Ottawa, 1956.
– Senate, Proceedings of the Standing Committee on Immigration and Labour, 10 March 1947.
– Senate and House of Commons, Joint Committee on the Indian Act, 1947.
– Senate and House of Commons, Joint Committee on Indian Affairs, 1958–9.
– Statistics Canada. *Department Stores in Canada, 1923–76.*
Canadian Advisory Council on the Status of Women. *The Royal Commission Report: Ten Years Later.* Ottawa: CADSW, 1979.
Estable, Alma. 'Immigrant Women in Canada – Current Issues.' Ottawa: CACSW, 1986.
Ferguson, Edith. 'Immigrant Women in Canada.' Study prepared for the RCSW. Ottawa, 1970.
Hawkins, Freda. 'Women Immigrants in Canada.' Study prepared for the RCSW. Ottawa, 1970.
Hawthorn, Harry B. *A Survey of the Contemporary Indians of Canada: Economic, Political, Educational Needs,* vol. 1. Ottawa: Indian Affairs Branch, 1966.
Hickling-Johnson Ltd. 'The Present Role of Women in the Canadian Labour Force.' Study prepared for the RCSW. Ottawa, 1970.
– 'The Status of Women in the Field of Collective Bargaining.' Study prepared for the RCSW. Ottawa, 1970.
Kew, J.M. *Cumberland House, 1960, Report #2, Economic and Social Survey of Northern Saskatchewan.* Saskatoon: Centre for Community Studies, University of Saskatchewan, 1962.
Lagasse, Jean. *The People of Indian Ancestry in Manitoba,* vol. 3. Winnipeg: Department of Agriculture and Immigration, 1959.
Mortimer, George. *The Indian in Industry: Roads to Independence.* Ottawa: Dept. of Citizenship and Immigration, 1965.

Rioux, Marcela. 'Female Immigrants in the Labour Force.' Study prepared for
    the RCSW. Ottawa, 1970.
Worsely, P.M., Helen L. Buckley, and A.K. Davis. *Economic and Social Survey of
    Northern Saskatchewan*. Saskatoon: Centre for Community Studies, University
    of Saskatchewan, 1961.

Newspapers and Magazines

The Anti-Communist Fur Workers Voice
The Beaver
Canadian Dimension
Canadian Labour
The Canadian Packinghouse Worker
The Canadian Unionist
Chatelaine and Châtelaine
Le Duprex
The Fur and Leather Worker
Globe and Mail
Indian News
Lethbridge Herald
Peterborough Examiner
Prairie Call
Saturday Night
Silver Sunshine
Time Magazine
The Toronto Furriers Newsletter
Toronto Star
Trades and Labour Congress Journal
UE News
Vancouver Sun

Secondary sources

Abele, Frances, and Daiva Stasiulis. 'Canada as a "White" Settler Colony: What
    about Natives and Immigrants?' In *The New Canadian Political Economy*, ed.
    Wallace Clement and Glen Williams, 240–77. Montreal: McGill-Queen's
    University Press, 1989.
Abella, Irving. *Nationalism, Communism, and Canadian Labour*. Toronto: Univer-
    sity of Toronto Press, 1973.

Abella, Irving, and Harold Troper. *None Is Too Many: Canada and the Jews of Europe, 1933–48.* Toronto: Lester & Orpen Dennys, 1982.

Abelove, Henry, ed., *Visions of History.* New York: Pantheon Books, 1983.

Abu-Laban, Yasmeen, and Christina Gabriel, eds. *Selling Diversity: Immigration, Multiculturalism, Employment Equity and Globalization.* Peterborough: Broadview Press, 2002.

Acker, Joan. *Class Questions, Feminist Answers.* Oxford: Roman and Littlefield, 2006.

Acoose, Janice. *Iskwewak: Neither Indian Princesses nor Easy Squaws.* Toronto: Women's Press, 1995.

Adamoski, Robert, Dorothy Chunn, and Robert Menzies, eds. *Contesting Canadian Citizenship: Historical Readings.* Peterborough: Broadview Press, 2002.

Adams, George. *Grievance Arbitration of Discharge Cases.* Kingston: Industrial Relations Centre, Queen's University, 1978.

Adams, Harold. *Prison of Grass: Canada from the Native Point of View.* Toronto: New Press, 1973.

Adams, Mary Louise. *The Trouble with Normal: Postwar Youth and the Making of Heterosexuality.* (Toronto: University of Toronto Press, 1997.

Albers, Patricia. 'Autonomy and Dependency in the Lives of Dakota Women: A Study in Historical Change.' *Review of Radical Political Economics* 17, no. 3 (1985): 109–34.

– 'Labor and Exchange in American Indian History.' In *A Companion to American Indian History,* ed. Philip J. Deloria and Neal Salisbury, 269–86. Oxford: Blackwell, 2004.

Albo, Greg. '"Competitive Austerity" and the Impasse of Capitalist Employment Policy.' In *Socialist Register 1994: Between Globalism and Nationalism,* ed. R. Milliband and L. Panitch, 144–70. London: Merlin Press, 1994.

Alken, Katherine. '"When I Realized How Close Communism Was to Kellogg, I Was Willing to Work Day and Night": Anti-Communism, Women, Community Values, and the Bunker Hill Strike of 1960.' *Labor History* 36, no. 2 (1995): 165–86.

Allen, G.P. 'Helping Immigrants Belong.' *Canadian Welfare,* May 1961, 108–12.

American Indian Quarterly, special issue, 27, nos. 3&4 (2004).

Anderson, Doris. *Rebel Daughter: An Autobiography.* Toronto: Key Porter Books, 1996.

Anderson, Kim. *Recognition of Being: Reconstructing Native Womanhood.* Toronto: Sumach Press, 2000.

Andrew, Caroline, Pat Armstrong, and Leah Vosko, eds. *Studies in Political Economy: Developments in Feminism.* Toronto: Women's Press, 2003.

Andrew, Caroline, and Sandra Rogers, eds. *Women and the Canadian State.* Montreal: McGill-Queen's University Press, 1997.

Armstrong, Pat, and Hugh Armstrong. *The Double Ghetto: Canadian Women and Their Segregated Work.* Toronto: McClelland and Stewart, 1984.

– 'The Feminization of the Labour Force: Harmonizing Down in a Global Economy.' In *Invisible,* ed. M. Hessing et al. Charlottetown: Gynergy Books, 1995.

– *Theorizing Women's Work.* Toronto: Garamond Press, 1990.

Arnopoulos, Sheila. *Problems of Immigrant Women in the Canadian Workforce.* Ottawa: Canadian Advisory Council on the Status of Women, 1979.

Arscott, Jane. 'Twenty-Five Years and Sixty-Five Minutes after the Royal Commission on the Status of Women.' *International Review of Canadian Studies* 11 (Spring 1995): 33–58.

Arthurs, Harry. 'The New Economy and the New Legality: Industrial Citizenship and the Future of Labour Arbitration.' *Canadian Labour and Employment Law Journal* 7, no. 1 (1999): 45–64.

Arthurs, Harry, D.D. Carter, and Harry Glasbeek. *Labour Law and Industrial Relations in Canada.* Toronto: Butterworths, 1981.

Asch, Michael. 'Capital and Economic Development: A Critical Reappraisal of the Recommendations of the Mackenzie Valley Pipeline Commission.' In *Interpreting Canada's North,* ed. Kenneth Coates and W. Morrison, 299–308. Toronto: Copp Clark, 1989.

Atlantis, special issue, 24, no. 2 (Spring 2000).

Avery, Donald. *Reluctant Host: Canada's Response to Immigrant Workers, 1898–1994.* Toronto: McClelland and Stewart, 1995.

Baillargeon, Denyse. 'Les grèves du textile au Québec: 1946, 1947, 1952.' In *Madeleine Parent, Militante,* ed. A. Lévesque, 59–70. Montreal: Éditions du Remue Ménage, 2003.

Bakan, Abigail, and Daiva Stasiulis. *Not One of the Family: Foreign Domestic Workers in Canada.* Toronto: University of Toronto Press, 1997.

Bank Book Collective. *An Account to Settle: The Story of the United Bank Workers (SORWUC).* Vancouver: Press Gang, 1979.

Banner, Lois. *American Beauty.* New York: Knopf, 1983.

Banet-Weiser, Sarah. *The Most Beautiful Girl in the World: Beauty Pageants and National Identity.* Berkeley: University of California Press, 1999.

Banet-Weiser, Sarah, and Laura Portwood-Staver. 'I Just Want to Be Me Again: Beauty Pageants, Reality Television and Post-feminism.' *Feminist Theory* 7, no. 2 (2006): 255–72.

Bannerji, Himani. *The Dark Side of the Nation: Essays on Multiculturalism, Nationalism and Gender.* Toronto: Canadian Scholars Press, 2000.

Barnes, Natasha. 'Face of a Nation: Race, Nationalisms, and Identities in Jamaican Beauty Pageants.' In *Gender and Consumer Culture Reader*, ed. Jennifer Scanlon, 355–71. New York: Routledge, 2000.

Barron, F. Laurie. *Walking in Indian Moccasins: The Native Policies of Tommy Douglas*. Vancouver: UBC Press, 1997.

Barry, Kathleen. *Femininity in Flight: A History of Flight Attendants*. Durham: Duke University Press, 2007.

Basok, Tanya. *Tortillas and Tomotoes: Transmigrant Mexican Harvesters in Canada*. Montreal: McGill-Queen's University Press, 2002.

Baxandall, Rosalyn. 'The Question Seldom Asked: Women and the CPUSA.' In *New Studies and the Politics and Culture of U.S. Communism*, ed. Michael Brown. New York: Monthly Review Press, 1993.

Beatty, David. 'The Role of an Arbitrator: The Liberal Version.' *University of Toronto Law Journal* 34 (1984): 136–69.

Beatty, David, and Brian Langille. 'Bora Laskin and Labour Law: From Vision to Legacy.' *University of Toronto Law Journal* 35 (1985): 627–727.

Bégin, Monique. 'The Canadian Government and the Commission's Report.' In *Women and the Canadian State*, ed. Caroline Andrew and Sandra Rogers, 12–26. Montreal: McGill-Queen's University Press, 1997.

Behiels, Michael. *Prelude to Quebec's Quiet Revolution: Liberalism versus Neo-nationalism, 1945–60*. Montreal: McGill-Queen's University Press, 1985.

– *Quebec and the Question of Immigration: From Ethnocentrism to Ethnic Pluralism, 1900–1985*. Ottawa: Canadian Historical Association, 1991.

Belisle, Donica. 'Exploring Postwar Consumption: The Campaign to Organize Eaton's in Toronto, 1948–52.' *Canadian Historical Review* 86, no. 4 (2005): 641–72.

– 'A Labour Force for the Consumer Century: Commodification of Canada's Largest Department Stores, 1890–1940.' *Labour/Le Travail* 58 (2006): 107–44.

– 'The Rise of Mass Retail: Canadian Department Stores, 1890–1940.' PhD thesis, Trent University, 2007.

Benson, Susan Porter. *Counter Cultures: Saleswomen, Managers and Customers in American Department Stores, 1890–1940*. Urbana: University of Illinois Press, 1988.

Benston, Margaret. 'The Political Economy of Women's Liberation.' *Monthly Review* 21 (1969): 13–27.

Berman, Tressa. *Circle of Goods: Women, Work and Welfare in a Reservation Community*. Albany: SUNY Press, 2003.

Bilson, Beth. 'Calling Them as You See Them: Sources of Legitimacy in Labour Arbitration.' *Canadian Labour Law Journal* 2 (1994): 184–230.

Bird, Florence. *Anne Francis, An Autobiography*. Toronto: Clarke, Irwin and Co., 1974.

Blackwelder, Julia. *Styling Jim Crow: African-American Beauty Training during Segregation.* College Station: Texas A&M University Press, 2003.

Boris, Eileen. 'Desirable Dress: Rosies, Sky Girls and the Politics of Appearance.' *International Labor and Working Class History* 69 (Spring 2006): 123–62.

Bossen, Marianne. *Patterns of Manpower Utilization in Canadian Department Stores.* Study prepared for the Royal Commission on the Status of Women, Ottawa 1971.

Bourdieu, Pierre. *Distinction: A Social Critique of the Judgement of Taste.* Trans. Richard Nice. Cambridge: Harvard University Press, 1984.

Bourgeault, Ron. 'Aboriginal Labour in the North-West.' *Prairie Forum* 31, no. 2 (Fall 2006): 273–304.

Boyd, Monica. 'At a Disadvantage: The Occupational Attainments of Foreign Born Women in Canada.' *International Migration Review* 18, no. 4 (Winter, 1984): 1091–119.

– 'The Status of Immigrant Women in Canada.' In *Women in Canada,* ed. Marylee Stephenson, 228–44. Don Mills: General Publishing, 1977.

Boyko, John. *Into the Hurricane: Attacking Socialism and the CCF.* Winnipeg: J. Gordon Schillingford, 2006.

Boyle, Kevin. 'The Kiss: Racial and Gender Conflict in a 1950s Automobile Factory.' *Journal of American History* 84 (Sept. 1997): 496–523.

Brah, Avtar, and Ann Phoenix. 'Ain't I a Woman? Revising Intersectionality.' *Journal of International Women's Studies* 5, no. 3 (May 2004): 75–86.

Brand, Dionne. *No Burden to Carry: Narratives of Black Working Women in Ontario, 1920s–1950s.* Toronto: Women's Press, 1991.

Brandt, Gayle. 'The Transformation of Women's Work in the Quebec Cotton Industry, 1920–50.' In *The Character of Class Struggle,* ed. Bryan D. Palmer, 115–37. Toronto: McClelland and Stewart, 1986.

Breines, Wini. *Young, White and Miserable: Growing Up Female in the Fifties.* Chicago: University of Chicago Press, 1992.

Brenner, Joanna. *Women and the Politics of Class.* New York: Monthly Review Press, 2000.

Briggs, Catherine. 'Fighting for Women's Equality. The Federal Women's Bureau, 1945–67: An Example of Early "State Feminism" in Canada.' PhD thesis, University of Waterloo, 2001.

Briskin, Linda. 'Women and Unions in Canada' In *Union Sisters,* ed. Briskin and Yanz, 28–43.

Briskin, Linda, and Pat McDermott. *Women Challenging Unions: Feminism, Democracy, and Militancy.* Montreal: McGill-Queen's University Press, 1993.

Briskin, Linda, and Lynda Yanz, eds. *Union Sisters: Women in the Labour Movement.* Toronto: Women's Press, 1983.

Brody, David. *The Butcher Workmen: A Study in Unionization.* Boston: Harvard University Press, 1964.
– *Workers in Industrial America: Essays in the Twentieth Century Struggle.* New York: Oxford University Press, 1980.
– 'Workplace Contractualism in Comparative Perspective.' In *Industrial Democracy in America: The Ambiguous Promise*, ed. Nelson Lichtenstein and Howell John Harris, 176–205. Cambridge: Cambridge University Press, 1993.
Brosseau, Madeleine. 'L'histoire de ma vie syndicale.' *Vie Ouvrière* 29 (Oct. 1979): 481–6.
Brown, Donald J.M., and David M. Beatty. *Canadian Labour Arbitration*, 3rd ed. Aurora: Canada Law Book, 2006.
Brownlie, Robin. 'Living the Same as White People: Mohawk and Anishinabe Women's Labour in Southern Ontario, 1920–40.' *Labour/Le Travail* 61 (Spring 2008): 41–68.
Bryden, Penny. *Planners and Politicians: Liberal Politics and Social Policy, 1957–1968.* Montreal: McGill-Queen's University Press, 1997.
Buckley, Helen. *From Wooden Ploughs to Welfare: Why Indian Policy Failed in the Prairie Provinces.* Montreal: McGill-Queen's University Press, 1992.
Buhl, Mary Jo. *Feminism and Its Discontents: A Century of Struggle with Psychoanalysis.* Cambridge: Harvard University Press, 1998.
Bureau du Service des Néo-Canadiens. *Canadiens-Français et Néo-Canadiens.* Montreal: Bureau du Service des Néo-Canadiens, 1950.
Burley, Edith. *Servants of the Honourable Company: Work, Discipline, and Conflict in the Hudson's Bay Company, 1790–1879.* Toronto: Oxford University Press, 1997.
Burnet, Jean, ed. *Looking into My Sister's Eyes: An Exploration in Women's History.* Toronto: Multicultural History Society of Ontario, 1986.
Burt, Sandra. 'Organized Women's Groups and the State.' In *Policy, Communities and Public Policy in Canada: A Structural Approach*, ed. William Coleman and Grace Skogstad, 191–211. Toronto: Copp Clark Pitman, 1990.
Butler, Judith. *Bodies That Matter: On the Discursive Limits of Sex.* New York: Routledge, 1993.
– *Gender Trouble: Feminism and the Subversion of Identity.* New York: Routledge, 1990.
Buzuk, Maria. *Pin-Up Girrrls: Feminism, Sexuality and Popular Culture.* Durham: Duke University Press, 2006.
Calliste, Agnes. 'Canada's Immigration Policy and Domestics from the Caribbean: The Second Domestic Scheme.' In *Race, Class and Gender: Bonds and Barriers*, ed. Jesse Vorst, 136–68. Toronto: Garamond Press, 1991.
– 'Women of Exceptional Merit: Immigration of Caribbean Nurses to Canada.' *Canadian Journal of Women and the Law* 6, no. 1 (1993): 85–102.

Camfield, David. 'Beyond Adding on Gender and Class: Revisiting Feminism and Marxism.' *Studies in Political Economy* 68 (Summer 2002): 37–53.
– 'Re-Orienting Class Analysis: Working Classes as Historical Formations.' *Science and Society* 68, no. 4 (Winter 2004–5): 421–6.
Campbell, Maria. *Halfbreed*. Toronto: Seal Books, 1973.
Canning, Kathleen. *Gender History in Practice: Historical Perspectives on Bodies, Class, and Citizenship*. Ithaca: Cornell University Press, 2006.
Carrothers, A.W.R. *Labour Arbitration in Canada*. Vancouver: Institute of Industrial Relations, University of British Columbia, 1961.
Carter, Sarah. *Capturing Women: The Manipulations of Cultural Imagery in Canada's Prairie West*. Montreal: McGill-Queen's University Press, 1997.
Cavell, Richard, ed. *Love, Hate, and Fear in Canada's Cold War*. Toronto: University of Toronto Press, 2004.
Champagne, Duane. 'Tribal Capitalism and Native Capitalists: Multiple Pathways of Native Economy.' In *Native Pathways: American Indian Culture and Economic Development in the Twentieth Century*, ed. Brian Hosmer and Colleen O'Neill, 308–29. Boulder: University of Colorado Press, 2004.
Cherny, Robert, William Issel, and Kieran Taylor, eds. *American Labor and the Cold War: Grassroots Politics and Postwar Political Culture*. New Brunswick, NJ: Rutgers University Press, 2004.
Christie, Nancy. *Engendering the State: Family, Work, and Welfare in Canada*. Toronto: University of Toronto Press, 2000.
Christie, Nancy, and Michael Gavreau. *Cultures of Citizenship in Post-War Canada, 1940–55*. Toronto: University of Toronto Press, 2003.
– 'Recasting Canada's Post-war Decade.' In *Cultures of Citizenship in Post-War Canada*, 3–26.
Clement, Wallace, and Leah Vosko, eds. *Changing Canada: Political Economy as Transformation*. Montreal: McGill-Queen's University Press, 2003.
Cobble, Dorothy Sue. *The Other Women's Movement: Workplace Justice and Social Rights in Modern America*. Princeton: Princeton University Press, 2004.
– 'A Spontaneous Loss of Enthusiasm: The Workplace, Feminism and the Transformation of Service Jobs in the 1970s.' *International Labor and Working Class History* 56 (Oct. 1999): 23–44.
Cochran, Bert. *Labor and Communism: The Conflict That Shaped American Unions*. Princeton: Princeton University Press, 1977.
Cohen, Colleen Ballerino, and Richard Wilk, with Beverly Stoeltje, eds. *Beauty Queens on the Global Stage*. New York: Routledge, 1996.
Cohen, Lizabeth. *A Consumer's Republic: The Politics of Mass Consumption in Postwar America*. New York: Knopf, 2003.

Cohen, Marjorie. 'The Implications of Economic Restructuring for Women: The Canadian Situation.' In *The Strategic Silence: Gender and Economic Policy*, ed. I. Bakker, 117–29. London: Zed Books, 1994.

Collins, Hugh. *Marxism and Law*. New York: Oxford University Press, 1984.

Collins, Patricia Hill. *Black Feminist Thought: Knowledge, Consciousness, and the Politics of Empowerment*. Boston: Allen and Unwin, 1993.

Confédération des Syndicates Nationaux. *Portrait d'un movement*. Montreal: CSN, 2000.

Connell, Robert. *Gender and Power*. Stanford: Stanford University Press, 1987.

Coontz, Stephanie. *The Way We Never Were: American Families and the Nostalgia Trap*. New York: Basic Books, 1992.

Copp, Terry, and Al Knipfel. *The IUE in Canada. A History*. Flora, ON: Cumnock Press, 1980.

Corman, June, and Meg Luxton. *Getting By in Hard Times: Gendered Labour at Home and on the Job*. Toronto: University of Toronto Press, 2001.

Cossman, Brenda, and Judy Fudge, eds. *Privatization, Law, and the Challenge to Feminism*. Toronto: University of Toronto Press, 2002.

Courville, Serge, et al. *Histoire de Beauce-Etchemin-Amiante*. Sainte Foy: Les Éditions de l'IQRC, 2003.

Cowan, Ruth Schwartz. *More Work for Mother: The Ironies of Technology from the Open Hearth to the Microwave*. New York: Basic Books, 1983.

Craig, Maxine Leeds. *Ain't I a Beauty Queen: Black Women, Beauty and the Politics of Race*. New York: Oxford, 2004.

Creese, Gillian. *Contracting Masculinity: Gender, Class, and Race in a White-Collar Union, 1944–94*. Toronto: Oxford University Press, 1999.

Creese, Gillian, and Daiva Stasiulis. 'Introduction: Intersections of Gender, Race, Class and Sexuality.' *Studies in Political Economy* 51 (Fall 1996): 5–15.

Culhane, Dara. 'Aboriginal Women in Eastside Vancouver: Emerging into Invisibility.' *American Indian Quarterly* 27, nos. 3&4 (2003): 593–606.

Curthoys, Ann, and Clive Moore. 'Working for White People: An Historiographic Essay on Aboriginal and Torres Strait Islander Labour.' *Labour History* 69 (1995): 1–29.

Danys, Milda. *Lithuanian Immigration to Canada after the Second World War*. Toronto: Multicultural History Society of Ontario, 1986.

Davis, Alan, ed. *Antisemitism in Canada: History and Interpretation*. Waterloo: Wilfrid Laurier University Press, 1992.

Davis, Kathy. *Reshaping the Female Body: The Dilemma of Cosmetic Surgery*. Berkeley: University of California Press, 1999.

Davis, Natalie Zemon. *Society and Culture in Early Modern France*. Stanford: Stanford University Press, 1975.

De Hart, Sherron Jane. 'Second Wave Feminists and the Dynamic of Social Change.' In *Women's America: Refocusing the Past*, ed. Linda Kerber and Jane Sherron De Hart, 598–623. New York: Oxford University Press, 2003.

D'Emilio, John. *Sexual Politics, Sexual Communities: The Making of a Homosexual Minority in the United States, 1940–70*. Chicago: University of Chicago Press, 1983.

Denning, Michael. *Mechanic Accents: Dime Novels and Working Class Culture in America*. New York: Verso, 1987.

Deslippe, Dennis. '*Rights Not Roses': Unions and the Rise of Working Class Feminism, 1945–80*. Urbana: University of Illinois Press, 2000.

Dickinson, John, and Brian Young. *A Short History of Quebec*. Montreal: McGill-Queen's University Press, 2008.

Dobbin, Murray. 'Prairie Colonialism: The CCF in Northern Saskatchewan, 1944–64.' *Studies in Political Economy* 16 (Spring 1985): 7–40.

Donovan, Brian. *White Slave Crusades: Race, Gender, and Anti-vice Activism, 1887–1917*. Urbana: University of Illinois Press, 2006.

Dosman, Edgar. *Indians: The Urban Dilemma*. Toronto: McClelland and Stewart, 1972.

Douglas, Susan. *Where the Girls Are: Growing Up Female with the Mass Media*. New York: Times Books, 1994.

Downs, Laura Lee. 'If "Woman" Is Just an Empty Category Why Am I Afraid to Walk Alone at Night? Identity Politics Meets the Postmodern Subject.' *Comparative Studies in Society and History* 35, no. 2 (1993): 414–47.

Drache, Daniel, and Harry Glasbeek. *The Changing Workplace: Reshaping Canada's Industrial Relations System*. Toronto: James Lorimer, 1992.

Drees, Laurie Meijer. 'Citizenship and Treaty Rights: The Indian Association of Alberta and the Indian Act, 1946–48.' *Great Plains Quarterly* 20 (Spring 2000): 141–58.

Dupuis-Leman, Josette. *Dupuis Frères: Le Magasin du Peuple*. Montreal: Stanké, 2001.

Eagleton, Terry. *After Theory*. New York: Basic Books, 2003.

– *Ideology: An Introduction*. London: Verso, 1991.

– *The Illusions of Postmodernism*. Cambridge: Blackwell Publishers, 1996.

Early, Frances. 'A Grandly Subversive Time: The Halifax Voice of Women in the Early 1960s.' In *Mothers of the Municipality: Women, Work and Social Policy in Post–1945 Halifax*, ed. Judith Fingard and Janet Guildford, 253–80. Toronto: University of Toronto Press, 2005.

Easson, Jeannette, Debbie Field, and Joanne Santucci. 'Working in Steel.' In *Hard Earned Wages*, ed. Jennifer Penney, 210–11. Toronto: Women's Press, 1983.

Edwards, Richard. *Contested Terrain: The Transformation of the Workplace in the Twentieth Century*. New York: Basic Books, 1979.

Ehrenreich, Barbara. *The Hearts of Men: American Dreams and the Flight from Commitment.* New York: Anchor Books, 1984.

Eley, Geoff, and Keith Nield. *The Future of Class in History: What's Left of the Social?* Ann Arbour: University of Michigan Press, 2007.

Elias, Peter. *Metropolis and Hinterland in Northern Manitoba.* Winnipeg: Manitoba Museum of Man and Nature, 1975.

Enstad, Nan. *Ladies of Labor, Girls of Adventure: Working Women, Popular Culture, and Labor Politics at the Turn of the Century.* New York: Columbia University Press, 1999.

Epp, Marlene, Franca Iacovetta, and Frances Swyripa, eds. *Sisters or Strangers: Immigrant, Ethnic, and Racialized Women in Canadian History.* Toronto: University of Toronto Press, 2004.

Etherington, Brian. 'Arbitration, Labour Boards and the Courts in the 1980s: Romance Meets Realism.' *Canadian Bar Review* 68 (Sept. 1989): 405–47.

Evans, Sara. *Born for Liberty: A History of Women in America.* New York: Times Books, 1989.

Ewick, Patricia, and Susan Silbey. 'Subversive Stories and Hegemonic Tales: Toward a Sociology of Narrative.' *Law and Society Review* 29, no. 2 (1995): 197–226.

Fahrni, Magda. *Household Politics: Montreal Families and Postwar Reconstruction.* Toronto: University of Toronto Press, 2005.

Fahrni, Magda, and Robert Rutherdale. 'Introduction.' In *Creating Postwar Canada, 1945–75,* ed. Magda Fahrni and Robert Rutherdale, 1–20. Vancouver: UBC Press, 2008.

Faue, Elizabeth. *In Suffering and in Struggle: Women, Men and the Labor Movement in Minneapolis, 1915–45.* Chapel Hill: University of North Carolina Press, 1991.

Fehn, Bruce. 'Striking Women: Gender, Race and Class in the United Packinghouse Workers of America (UPWA), 1938–68.' PhD thesis, University of Wisconsin, 1991.

Felski, Rita. 'Because It Is Beautiful: New Feminist Perspectives on Beauty.' *Feminist Theory* 7, no. 2 (2006): 273–82.

Findlay, Susan. 'Facing the State: The Politics of the Women's Movement Reconsidered.' In *Feminism and Political Economy: Women's Work, Women's Struggles,* ed. Heather Jon Maroney and Meg Luxton, 31–50. Toronto: Methuen, 1987.

Fingard, Judith. 'Women's Organizations: The Heart and Soul of Women's Activism.' In *Mothers of the Municipality: Women, Work and Social Policy in Post-1945 Halifax,* ed. Judith Fingard and Janet Guildford, 25–48. Toronto: University of Toronto Press, 2005.

Fink, Deborah. *Cutting into the Meatpacking Line: Workers and Change in the Rural Midwest.* Chapel Hill: University of North Carolina Press, 1998.

Finkel, Alvin. 'Canadian Immigration Policy and the Cold War, 1945–80.' *Journal of Canadian Studies* 21, no.3 (Fall 1986): 53–86.

– *Our Lives: Canada after 1945.* Toronto: Lorimer, 1997.

– *Sociological Policy and Practice in Canada: A History.* Waterloo: Wilfrid Laurier University Press, 2005.

Finley, Lucinda. 'Transcending Equality Theory: A Way Out of the Maternity and the Workplace Debate.' *Columbia Law Review* 86, no. 6 (1986): 1118–83.

Fiske, Jo-Anne. 'Colonization and the Decline of Women's Status: The Tsimshian Case.' *Feminist Studies* 17, no. 3 (Fall 1991): 509–35.

– 'Fishing Is Women's Business: Changing Economic Roles of Carrier Women and Men.' In *Native People/Native Lands: Canadian Indian, Inuit and Métis,* ed. Bruce Cox, 186–98. Ottawa: Carleton University Press, 1988.

– 'Gender and the Paradox of Residential Education in Carrier Society.' In *Women of the First Nations: Power, Wisdom, Strength,* ed. Christine Miller and Patricia Churchryk, 167–82. Winnipeg: University of Manitoba Press, 1996.

– 'Mothers of the Nation: Aboriginal Women and Maternalism.' *Studies in Political Economy* 51 (Fall 1996): 65–95.

– 'The Womb Is to the Nation as the Heart Is to the Body: Ethnopolitical Discourses of the Canadian Indigenous Women's Movement.' In *Feminism, Political Economy and the State: Contested Terrain,* ed. Pat Armstrong and M. Patricia Connelly, 293–326. Toronto: Canadian Scholars Press, 1999.

Fiske, Jo-Anne, and Caroline Mufford. 'Hard Times and Everything Like That: Carrier Women's Tales of Life on the Trapline.' In *New Faces of the Fur Trade,* ed. Jo-Anne Fiske, Susan Sleeper-Smith, and Bill Wicken, 28–37. East Lansing: Michigan State University Press, 1998.

Fiske, Jo-Anne, and Susan Sleeper-Smith, eds. *New Faces of the Fur Trade: Selected Papers of the North American Fur Trade Conference.* Lansing: Michigan State University, 1998.

Fitzhugh, Michael L., and William H. Leckie, Jr. 'Agency, Postmodernism, and the Causes of Change.' *History and Theory* 40, no. 4 (Dec. 2001): 59–81.

Flynn, Karen. 'Experience and Identity: Black Immigrant Nurses to Canada, 1950–1980.' In *Sisters or Strangers? Immigrant, Ethnic, and Racialized Women in Canadian History,* ed. Marlene Epp, Franca Iacovetta, and Frances Swyripa, 381–98. Toronto: University of Toronto Press, 2004.

Foisey, Fernand. *Michel Chartrand: Les voies d'un homme de parole.* Montreal: Lanctôt Éditeur, 1999.

Foley, Barbara. Review of *Reclaiming Experience, Cultural Logic: An Electronic Journal of Marxist Theory and Practice* (ISSN 1097-3087) 4, no. 2 (Spring 2001).

Foley, Brenda. *Undressed for Success: Beauty Contestants and Exotic Dancers as Merchants of Morality*. London: Palgrave/Macmillan, 2005.

Foner, Philip. *The Fur and Leather Workers Union: A Story of Dramatic Struggles and Achievements*. Newark: Nordan Press, 1950.

Forrest, Anne. 'Securing the Male Breadwinner: A Feminist Interpretation of PC 1003.' In *Labour Gains, Labour Pains: 50 Years of PC 1003*, ed. Cy Gonick, Paul Phillips, and Jesse Vorst, 139–62. Winnipeg: Fernwood, 1995.

Fox, Bonnie, and John Fox. 'Canadian Occupational Segregation, 1931–81.' *Canadian Review of Sociology and Anthropology* 24, no. 3 (August 1981): 374–97.

Fraccia, Joseph. 'Marx's Aufhebung of Philosophy and the Foundation of Materialist Science of History.' *History and Theory* 30, no. 2 (May 1991):153–79.

Frager, Ruth. *Sweatshop Strife: Class, Ethnicity and Gender in the Jewish Labour Movement of Toronto, 1900–1939*. Toronto: University of Toronto Press, 1992.

Frager, Ruth, and Carmela Patrias. '"This Is Our Country, These Are Our Rights": Minorities and the Origins of Ontario's Human Rights Campaigns.' *Canadian Historical Review* 82, no. 1 (2001): 1–35.

Freeman, Barbara. *The Satellite Sex: The Media and Women's Issues in English Canada, 1966–71*. Waterloo: Wilfrid Laurier University Press, 2001.

French, Brandon. *On the Verge of Revolt: Women in American Film of the Fifties*. New York: Frederick Ungar, 1978.

Freeman, Rita. *Beauty Bound*. Lexington, MA: Lexington Books, 1986.

Fudge, Judy. 'Gender Issues in Arbitration: An Academic Perspective.' *Labour Arbitration Journal* 1 (1991): 119–31.

Fudge, Judy, and Patricia McDermott. *Just Wages: A Feminist Assessment of Pay Equity*. Toronto: University of Toronto Press, 1991.

Fudge, Judy, and Eric Tucker. *Labour Before the Law: The Regulation of Workers' Collective Action in Canada, 1900–1948*. Toronto: Oxford University Press, 2001.

Gabin, Nancy. *Feminism in the Labor Movement: Women and the United Auto Workers, 1935–75*. Ithaca: Cornell University Press, 1990.

Gagnier, Regenia. *Subjectivities*. New York: Oxford University Press, 1992.

Gagnon, Mona-Josée. 'Women in the Trade-Union Movement in Quebec.' In *Quebec since 1945: Selected Readings*, ed. Michael Behiels, 157–77. Toronto: Copp Clark Pitman, 1987.

Gauvreau, Michael. *The Catholic Origins of Quebec's Quiet Revolution, 1931–70*. Montreal: McGill-Queen's University Press, 2005.

Gentile, Patrizia. '"Government Girls" and "Ottawa Men": Cold War Management of Gender Relations in the Civil Service.' In *Whose National Security? Canadian State Surveillance and the Creation of Enemies*, ed. Gary Kinsman, Dieter K. Buse, and Mercedes Steedman, 131–42. Toronto: Between the Lines, 2000.

Geoffry, Renée, and Paule Sainte-Marie. *Attitudes of Union Workers to Women in Industry*. Ottawa: RCSW, 1971.

Gerber, Linda. 'Multiple Jeopardy: A Socio-Economic Comparison of Men and Women among the Indian, Métis and Inuit Peoples of Canada.' *Canadian Ethnic Studies* 22, no. 3 (1990): 69–84.

Gimenez, Martha. 'Capitalism and the Oppression of Women: Marx Revisited.' *Science and Society* 69, no. 1 (Jan. 2005): 11–32.

Girard, Philip. *Bora Laskin: Bringing Law to Life*. Toronto: University of Toronto Press, 2005.

Glasbeek, Harry. 'The Utility of Model Building: Collins Capitalist Discipline and Corporatist Law.' *Industrial Law Journal* 13 (1984): 133–52.

Glazer, Nona. *Women's Paid and Unpaid Labor: The Work Transfer in Health Care and Retailing*. Philadelphia: Temple University Press, 1993.

Gleason, Mona. *Normalizing the Ideal: Psychology, Schooling, and the Family in Postwar Canada*. Toronto: University of Toronto Press, 1999.

Glucksmann, Miram. *Cottons and Casuals: The Gendered Organization of Labour in Time and Space*. Durham, Eng.: Sociologypress, 2000.

Goldblatt, Howard. *Justice Delayed: The Arbitration Process*. Toronto: Labour Council of Metropolitan Toronto, 1974.

Gordon, Linda. 'Comments on That Noble Dream.' *American Historical Review* 96, no. 3 (June 1991): 683–4.

– 'Internal Colonialism and Gender.' In *Haunted by Empire: Geographies of Intimacy in North American History*, ed. Ann Laura Stoler, 427–51. Durham: Duke University Press, 2006.

– 'Interview.' In *Visions of History*, ed. Harry Abelove. New York: MARHO, 1976.

Gottfried, Heidi, 'Beyond Patriarchy? Theorizing Gender and Class.' *Sociology* 32, no. 2 (August 1998): 451–68.

Gramsci, Antonio. *Selections from the Prison Notebooks of Antonio Gramsci*. Ed. and trans. Quintin Hoare and Geoffrey Smith. New York: International Publishers, 1971.

Gray, Stan. 'The Greatest Canadian Shit Disturber.' *Canadian Dimension*, Nov.–Dec. 2004, 18.

– 'Sharing the Shop Floor.' *Canadian Dimension*, June 1984: 17–36.

Green, Alan. *Immigration and the Postwar Canadian Economy*. Toronto: Macmillan, 1976.

Guard, Julie. 'Fair Play or Fair Pay: Gender Relations, Class Consciousness, and Union Solidarity in the Canadian UE.' *Labour/Le Travail* 37 (Spring 1997): 149–77.

– 'Women Worth Watching: Radical Housewives in Cold War Canada.' In *Whose National Security? Canadian State Surveillance and the Creation of*

Enemies, ed. D. Buse, G. Kinsman, and M. Steedman, 73–88. Toronto: Between the Lines: 2000.

Guntzel, Ralph. 'Rappocher les lieux du pouvoir: The Québec Labour Movement and Québec Sovereigntism, 1960–2000.' *Labour/Le Travail* 46 (Fall 2000): 369–95.

Gutman, Herbert. *Work, Culture and Society in Industrializing America*. New York: Alfred Knopf, 1976.

Haiven, Larry. 'Hegemony and the Workplace: The Role of Arbitration.' In *Regulating Labour: The State, Neo-Conservatism and Industrial Relations*, ed. Larry Haiven, Stephen McBride, and John Shields, 79–117. Winnipeg: The Society for Socialist Studies, 1990.

– 'Past Practices and Customs and Practice: "Adjustment" and Industrial Conflict in America and the U.K.' *Comparative Labour Law Journal* 12, no.3 (Sept. 1991): 300–34.

– 'Workplace Discipline in International Comparative Perspective.' In *Workplace Industrial Relations and the Global Challenge*, ed. Jacques Belanger, P.K. Edwards, and Larry Haiven, 70–102. Ithaca: Cornell University Press, 1994.

Hall, Catherine. 'Politics, Post-structuralism and Feminist History.' *Gender and History* 3, no. 2 (1991): 204–10.

Halpern, Martin. *UAW Politics in the Cold War Era*. Albany: SUNY Press, 1988.

Halpern, Rick. *Down on the Killing Floor: Black and White Workers in Chicago's Packinghouses, 1904–54*. Urbana: University of Illinois Press, 1997.

Harrison, Cynthia. *On Account of Sex: The Politics of Women's Issues, 1945–68*. Berkeley: University of California Press, 1988.

Hartmann, Susan. *The Other Feminists: Activists in the Liberal Establishment*. New Haven: Yale University Press, 1998.

Hartsock, Nancy. 'Postmodernism and Political Change: Issues for Feminist Theory.' *Cultural Critique* 14 (1989/90): 15–33.

Harzig, Christiane. 'MacNamara's DP Domestics: Immigration Policy Makers Negotiate Class, Race, and Gender in the Aftermath of World War II, 1945–68.' *Social Politics* 10, no. 1 (Spring 2003): 23–48.

Haskell, Molly. *From Reverence to Rape: The Treatment of Women in the Movies* (Chicago: University of Chicago Press, 1987).

Haskell, Thomas. *Objectivity Is Not Neutrality: Explanatory Schemes in History*. Baltimore: Johns Hopkins University Press, 1998.

Hawkins, Freda. *Canada and Immigration: Public Policy and Public Concern*. Montreal: McGill-Queen's University Press, 1988.

Hennessy, Rosemary. *Profit and Pleasure: Sexual Identities in Late Capitalism*. New York: Routledge, 2000.

Heron, Craig, and Steven Penfold. *The Workers Festival.* Toronto: University of Toronto Press, 2005.

High, Steven. 'Native Wage Labour and Independent Production during the "Era of Irrelevance."' *Labour/Le Travail* 37 (Spring 1996): 243–64.

Hochschild, Arlie. *The Managed Heart: Commercialization of Human Feeling.* Berkeley: University of California Press, 1983.

Hoerder, Dirk. *Creating Societies: Immigrant Lives in Canada.* Montreal: McGill-Queen's University Press, 2000.

Holliday, Ruth, and Jacqueline Sanchez Taylor. 'Aesthetic Surgery as False Beauty.' *Feminist Theory* 7, no. 2 (2006): 179–95.

Holt, Thomas, 'Experience and the Politics of Intellectual Inquiry.' In *Questions of Evidence: Proof, Practice and Persuasion across the Disciplines,* ed. James Chandler, A. Davidson, and H. Harootunian, 393–5. Chicago: University of Chicago Press, 1994.

Honey, Michael. 'Operation Dixie, the Red Scare and the Defeat of Southern Labor Organizing.' In *American Labor and the Cold War: Grassroots Politics and Postwar Political Culture,* ed. Robert Cherny, William Issel, and Kieran Taylor, 216–44. New Brunswick, NJ: Rutgers University Press, 2004.

Hongiman, John. 'Incentives to Work in a Canadian Indian Community.' *Human Organization* 8, no. 4 (1949): 23–30.

Horowitz, Daniel. *Betty Freidan and the Making of the Feminine Mystique: The American Left, the Cold War, and Modern Feminism.* Amherst: University of Massachusetts Press, 1998.

Horowitz, Roger. *Negro and White, Unite and Fight: A Social History of Industrial Unionism in Meatpacking, 1930–90.* Urbana: University of Illinois Press, 1997.

– *Putting Meat on the American Table.* Baltimore: Johns Hopkins University Press, 2006.

Hosmer, Brian. *American Indians in the Marketplace: Persistence and Innovation among the Menominees and Metlakatlans, 1897–1920.* Lawrence: University of Kansas Press, 1999.

Hosmer, Brian, and Colleen O'Neill, eds. *Native Pathways: American Indian Culture and Economic Development in the Twentieth Century.* Boulder: University of Colorado Press, 2004.

Howard, Vicki. 'At the Curve Exchange: Postwar Beauty Culture and Working Women at Maidenform.' In *Beauty and Business: Commerce, Gender and Culture in Modern America,* ed. Philip Scranton, 195–216. New York: Routledge, 2001.

Howard-Bobiwash, Heather. 'Women's Class Strategies as Activism in Native Community Building in Toronto, 1950–75.' *American Indian Quarterly* 27, nos. 3&4 (Summer-Fall 2001): 566–82.

Iacovetta, Franca. 'Freedom Lovers, Sex Deviates, and Damaged Women: Iron Curtain Refugee Discourses in Cold War Canada.' In *Love, Hate and Fear in Canada's Cold War*, ed. Richard Cavell, 77–107. Toronto: University of Toronto Press, 2004.

– *Gatekeepers: Reshaping Immigrant Lives in Cold War Canada.* Toronto: Between the Lines, 2006.

– 'Many Model Citizens: Gender, Corrupted Democracy, Immigration and Refugee Reception Work in Cold War Canada.' In *Whose National Security?: Canadian State Surveillance and the Creation of Enemies*, ed. Gary Kinsman, Dieter K. Buse, and Mercedes Steedman, 154–67. Toronto: Between the Lines, 2000.

– '"Primitive Villagers and Uneducated Girls": Canada Recruits Domestics from Italy, 1951–52.' *Canadian Women's Studies* 7, no 4 (Winter 1986): 14–18.

– *Such Hardworking People: Italian Immigrants in Postwar Ontario.* Montreal: McGill-Queen's University Press, 1992.

Igartua, José. *The Other Quiet Revolution: National Identities in English Canada, 1945–71.* Vancouver: UBC Press, 2006.

Ignagni, Sandy. 'Processing Discontent: Women's Organizing and the Newfoundland Fisherman, Food and Allied Workers Union, 1971–87.' MA thesis, Trent University, 2003.

Ireland, Craig. 'The Appeal to Experience and Its Consequences: Variations on a Persistent Thompsonian Theme.' *Cultural Critique* 52 (Autumn 2002): 86–107.

Jacobson, Cardell. 'Internal Colonialism and Native Americans: Indian Labor in the United States from 1871 to World War II.' *Social Science Quarterly* 65, no. 1 (1984): 158–71.

Jacobson, Matthew Frye. *Whiteness of a Different Colour: European Immigrants and the Alchemy of Race.* Cambridge: Cambridge University Press, 1998.

Jay, Martin. *Songs of Experience: Modern American and European Variations on a Universal Theme.* Berkeley: University of California Press, 2006.

Jenson, Jane. 'Commissioning Ideas: Representation and Royal Commissions.' In *How Ottawa Spends: Making Change*, ed. Susan Phillips, 39–70. Ottawa: Carleton University Press, 1994.

Jessop, Bob. *The Capitalist State.* New York: New York University Press, 1982.

Jorgenson, Joseph. 'A Century of Political Economic Effects on American Indian Society, 1880–1960.' *Journal of Ethnic Studies* 6, no. 3 (1973): 1–82.

Kaledin, Eugenia. *Mothers and More: American Women in the 1950s.* Boston: Twayne, 1984.

Kannenberg, Lisa. 'The Impact of the Cold War on Women's Trade Union Activism: The UE Experience.' *Labor History* 34 (1993): 309–23.

Kaplan, William. *Everything That Floats: Pat Sullivan, Hal Banks, and the Seamen's Unions of Canada.* Toronto: University of Toronto Press, 1987.

Keeran, Roger. *The Communist Party and the Autoworkers Unions.* Bloomington: Indiana University Press, 1980.

Kelley, Robin. *Hammer and Hoe: Alabama Communists during the Great Depression.* Chapel Hill: University of North Carolina Press, 1990.

Kelly, Joan. *Women, History and Theory.* Chicago: University of Chicago Press, 1984.

Kessler-Harris, Alice. 'Gender Ideology in Historical Reconstruction: A Case Study from the 1930s.' *Gender and History* 1, no. 1 (Spring 1989): 31–49.

– *Gendering Labor History.* Urbana: University of Illinois Press, 2006.

– 'A New Agenda for American Labor History: A Gendered Analysis and Questions of Class.' In *Perspectives on American Labor History: The Problems of Synthesis,* ed. J. Carroll Moody and Alice Kessler-Harris. DeKalb: Northern Illinois University Press, 1990.

– *Out to Work: A History of Wage-earning Women in the United States.* New York: Oxford University Press, 1982.

– *In Pursuit of Equity: Women, Men, and the Quest for Economic Citizenship in 20th-Century America.* New York: Oxford University Press, 2001.

– 'Where Are the Organized Women Workers?' In *Gendering Labor History,* ed. A. Kessler-Harris, 21–37. Urbana: University of Illinois Press, 2007.

Kinsman, Gary. *The Regulation of Desire: Homo and Hetero Sexualities.* Montreal: Black Rose, 1996.

Kinsman, Gary, Dieter K. Buse, and Mercedes Steedman, eds. *Whose National Security? Canadian State Surveillance and the Creation of Enemies.* Toronto: Between the Lines, 2000.

Klein, Yvonne Matthews. 'How They Saw Us: Images of Women in National Film Board Films of the 1940s and 1950s.' *Atlantis* 4, no.2 (Spring 1979): 20–33.

Knack, Martha, and Alice Littlefield. *Native Americans and Wage Labour: Ethno-historical Perspectives.* Norman: University of Oklahoma Press, 1996.

Knight, Rolf. *Indians at Work: An Informal History of Native Labour in British Columbia 1858–1930.* Vancouver: New Star Books, 1996.

Knowles, Valerie. *Strangers at Our Gates: Canadian Immigration and Immigration Policy, 1540–1997.* Hamilton: Dundurn Press, 1997.

Kobayashi, Audrey. 'For the Sake of the Children: Japanese/Canadian/Mothers/Workers.' In *Women, Work and Place,* ed. Audrey Kobayashi, 45–72. Montreal: McGill-Queen's University Press, 1994.

Korinek, Valerie. 'It's a Tough Time to Be in Love: The Darker Side of Chatelaine during the Cold War.' In *Love, Hate, and Fear in Canada's Cold War,* ed. Richard Cavell, 159–82. Toronto: University of Toronto Press, 2004.

– *Roughing it in the Suburbs: Reading Chatelaine Magazine in the Fifties and Sixties.* Toronto: University of Toronto Press, 2000.

Kornstad, Robert. *Civil Rights Unionism: Tobacco Workers and the Struggle for Democracy in the Mid-Twentieth-Century South.* Chapel Hill: University of North Carolina Press, 2002.

Kostash, Myrna. *Long Way from Home: The Story of the Sixties Generation in Canada.* Toronto: Lorimer, 1980.

Kowaluk, Lucia. 'The Status of Women in Canada.' In *Mother Was Not a Person,* ed. Margaret Anderson, 210–20. Montreal: Our Generation Press, 1972.

Kozol, Wendy. 'Miss Indian America: Regulating Gazes and the Politics of Affirmation.' *Feminist Studies* 31, no.1 (Spring 2005): 64–94.

Kruks, Sonia. *Retrieving Experience: Subjectivity and Recognition in Feminist Politics.* Ithaca: Cornell University Press, 2001.

Kuyek, Joan Newman. *The Phone Book: Working at the Bell.* Toronto: Between the Lines, 1979.

Lagrand, James. *Indian Metropolis: Native Americans in Chicago.* Urbana: University of Illinois Press, 2002.

Laliberte, Ron. 'The Canadian State and Native Migrant Labour in Southern Alberta's Sugar Beet Industry.' MA thesis, University of Saskatchewan, 1994.

– 'The "grab-a-hoe" Indians: The Canadian State and the Procurement of Aboriginal Labour for the Southern Alberta Sugar Beet Industry.' *Prairie Forum* 31, no.1 (Fall 2006): 305–24.

Laliberte, Ron, and Vic Satzewich. 'Native Migrant Labour in the Southern Alberta Sugar-Beet Industry: Coercion and Paternalism in the Recruitment of Labour.' *Canadian Review of Sociology and Anthropology* 36, no. 1 (Feb 1999): 65–86.

Lambertson, Ross. 'The Dresden Story: Racism, Human Rights, and the Jewish Labour Committee of Canada.' *Labour/Le Travail* 47 (Spring 2001): 43–82.

Lan, Pei-Chia. 'Working in a Neon Cage: The Bodily Labour of Cosmetics Saleswomen in Taiwan.' *Feminist Studies* 29 (2003): 21–45.

Lawrence, Bonita. 'Gender, Race, and the Regulation of Native Identity in Canada and the U.S.: An Overview.' *Hypatia* 18, no.2 (Spring 2003): 3–31.

– *'Real' Indians and Others: Mixed-Blood Urban Native Peoples and Indigenous Nationhood.* Vancouver: UBC Press, 2004.

Leechman, Douglas. *The Indian in Transition.* Ottawa: Queen's Printer, 1961.

Leidner, Robin. *Fast Food, Fast Talk: Service Work and the Routinization of Everyday Life.* Berkeley: University of California Press, 1993.

Levenstein, Harvey. *Communism, Anticommunism and the CIO.* Westport, CT: Greenwood Press, 1981.

Lichtenstein, Nelson. 'Great Expectations: The Promise of Industrial Jurispru-
dence and Its Demise.' In *Industrial Democracy in America: The Ambiguous
Promise*, ed. Nelson Lichtenstein and Howell John Harris, 113–41.
Cambridge: Cambridge University Press, 1993.

Lithman, Yngve Georg. *The Practice of Underdevelopment*. Stockholm: Stockholm
Studies in Social Anthropology, 1982.

Litt, Paul. *The Muses, the Masses, and the Massey Commission*. Toronto: University
of Toronto Press, 1992.

Logan, Harold. *State Intervention and Assistance in Collective Bargaining: The
Canadian Experience*. Toronto: University of Toronto Press, 1956.

Lovell, Terry. 'Thinking Feminism with and against Bourdieu.' *Feminist Theory*
1 (2000): 11–32.

Loxley, John. 'The Great Northern Plan.' *Studies in Political Economy* 6 (Autumn
1981): 151–82.

Lutz, John. 'After the Fur Trade: The Labouring Classes of British Columbia,
1849–90.' *Canadian Historical Association Papers* (1992): 69–93.

Luxton, Meg. 'Feminism as a Class Act: Working-Class Feminism and the
Women's Movement in Canada. *Labour/Le Travail* 48 (2001): 63–88.

– *More Than a Labour of Love: Three Generations of Women's Work in the Home*.
Toronto: Women's Educational Press, 1980.

Luxton, Meg, and Kate Bezanson, eds. *Social Reproduction: Feminist Political
Economy Challenges Neo-liberalism*. Montreal: McGill-Queen's University Press,
2006.

McCall, Leslie. 'The Complexity of Intersectionality.' *Signs* 30, no. 3 (2005):
1771–800.

McCallum, Mary Jane. 'The "Permanent Solution": Aboriginal Hairdressers in
Post-War Manitoba,' unpublished paper.

MacCannell, Dean, and Juliet Flower MacCannell. 'The Beauty System.' In *The
Ideology of Conduct: Essays in the Literature and the History of Sexuality*, ed. Nancy
Armstrong and Leonard Tennenhouse, 206–36. New York: Methuen and Co.,
1987.

M'Closkey, Kathy. *Swept under the Rug: A Hidden History of Navaho Weaving*.
Albuquerque: University of New Mexico Press, 2002.

McDermott, Patricia. 'The Eaton's Strike: We Wouldn't Have Missed It for the
World!' In *Women Challenging Unions: Feminism, Democracy and Militancy*, ed.
Linda Briskin and Patricia McDermott, 23–43. Toronto: University of
Toronto Press, 1993.

Macdonald, Cameron Lynne, and Carmen Sirianni. 'Introduction.' In *Working
in the Service Society*, ed. Cameron Lynne Macdonald and Carmen Sirianni, 14.
Philadelphia: Temple University Press, 1996.

MacDonald, Donald. 'Canadian Labour and Immigration.' *Canadian Unionist*, December 1953: 481–4.

– 'Congress Policy on Immigration.' *Canadian Unionist*, July–August 1955: 238–9, 250.

MacDonald, Helen. 'The Power of Polonia: Post WWII Polish Immigrants to Canada: Survivors of Deportation and Exile in Soviet Labour Camps.' MA thesis, Trent University, 2001.

McInnis, Peter. *Harnessing Labour Confrontation: Shaping the Postwar Settlement in Canada*. Toronto: University of Toronto Press, 2002.

– 'Teamwork for Harmony: Labour-Management Production Committees and the Post-War Settlement in Canada.' *Canadian Historical Review* 77 (Sept. 1996): 317–52.

MacKay, Kathryn. 'Warriors into Welders: A History of Federal Employment Programs for American Indians, 1898–1972.' PhD thesis, University of Utah, 1987.

MacLachlan, Ian. *Kill and Chill: Restructuring Canada's Beef Commodity Chain*. Toronto: University of Toronto Press, 2001.

McLaughlin, Christine. 'The McLaughlin Legacy and the Struggle for Labour Organization: Community, Class, and Oshawa's UAW Local 222, 1944–49.' MA thesis, Trent University, 2007.

MacLean, Nancy. *Freedom Is Not Enough: The Opening of the American Workplace*. New York: Russell Sage Foundation, 2006.

– 'Postwar Women's History: The "Second Wave" or the End of the Family Wage?' In *A Companion to Post-1945 America*, ed. Jean-Christophe Agnew and Roy Rosenzweig. (Oxford: Blackwell Publishing, 2002), 235–59.

McLeod, Kathryn. 'Laying the Foundation: The Women's Bureau, the Royal Commission on the Status of Women and Canadian Feminism.' MA thesis, Laurentian University, 2006.

McMaster, Lindsey. *Working Girls in the West: Representations of Working-class Women*. Vancouver: UBC Press, 2007.

McShane, Denis. *International Labour and the Cold War*. Oxford: Clarendon Press, 1992.

Manitowabi, Edna. *An Indian Girl in the City*. Buffalo: Friends of Malatesta, 1971.

– 'An Ojibway Girl in the City.' *This Magazine Is About Schools*, 4, no. 4 (1970): 9–22.

Manley, John. 'Starve, Be Damned: Communists and Canada's Urban Unemployed.' *Canadian Historical Review* 79 (Sept. 1998): 466–92.

Marchak, Pat. 'A Critical Review of the Royal Commission on the Status of Women Report.' *Canadian Review of Sociology and Anthropology* 9, no. 1 (1972): 73–96.

Maroney, Heather Jon. 'Feminism at Work,' *New Left Review* 141 (Sept.–Oct. 1983): 51–71.

Marrus, Michael. *The Unwanted: European Refugees in the Twentieth Century*. New York: Oxford University Press, 1985.

Marsh, Leonard. *The Swampy Cree: A Study in Acculturation*. Ottawa: National Museum of Man, 1967.

Martin, Homer. *A Life in Fishing*. Madeira Park, BC: Harbour Publishing, 1992.

Martin, Michèle. *'Hello Central?' Gender, Technology, and Culture in the Formation of the Telephone System*. Montreal: McGill-Queen's University Press, 1991.

Matheson, David. 'The Canadian Working Class and Industrial Legality, 1939–1949.' MA thesis, Queens University, 1990.

Matles, James, and James Higgins. *Them and Us: Struggles of a Rank and File Union*. Englewood Cliffs, NJ: Prentice Hall, 1974.

Matthews, Mary Catherine. 'Working for the Family, Nation and God: Paternalism and the Dupuis Frères Department Store, Montreal, 1926–52.' MA thesis, McGill University, 1998.

Maurutto, Paula. 'Policing and Surveillance of Catholics: Anti-communism in the Roman Catholic Archiocese of Toronto, 1920–60.' *Labour/Le Travail* 40 (1997): 113–36.

May, Elaine Tyler. *Homeward Bound: American Families in the Cold War Era*. New York: Basic Books, 1988.

– 'Pushing the Limits, 1940–1961.' In *No Small Courage: A History of Women in the United States*, ed. Nancy Cott, 473–528. New York: Oxford University Press, 2000.

Mercier, Laurie. 'Instead of Fighting the Common Enemy: Mine Mill versus the Steelworkers in Montana, 1950–67.' *Labor History* 40, no. 4 (1999): 459–80.

Meyer, Steven. 'Rough Manhood: The Aggressive and Confrontational Shop Culture of U.S. Auto Workers during World War II.' *Journal of Social History* 36, no. 1 (2002): 125–47.

– *Stalin over Wisconsin: The Making and Unmaking of Militant Unionism, 1900–50*. New Brunswick, NJ: Rutgers University Press, 1992.

– 'Workplace Predators: Sexuality and Harassment on the U.S. Automotive Shop Floor, 1930–1960.' *Labor: Working Class History of the Americas* 91 (2004): 77–93.

– 'Work, Play, and Power: Masculine Culture on the Automotive Shop Floor, 1930–60.' In *Boys and Their Toys? Masculinity, Class and Technology in America*, ed. Roger Horowitz, 13–32. New York: Routledge, 2001.

Meyorwitz, Joanne. *Not June Cleaver: Women and Gender in Postwar America, 1945–60*. Philadelphia: Temple University Press, 1994.

– *'Rewriting Postwar Women's History.'* In *A Companion to American Women's History*, ed. Nancy A. Hewitt. Wiley-Blackwell Publishing, 2005. Blackwell Reference Online. At http://www.blackwellreference.com/subscriber/tocnode?id =g9781405126854_chunk_g978140512685423.

– 'Women, Cheesecake and Borderline Material: Responses to Girlie Pictures in the Mid-Twentieth-Century U.S.' *Journal of Women's History* 8, no. 3 (Fall 1996): 9–35.

Milkman, Ruth. *Gender at Work: The Dynamics of Job Segregation by Sex during World War II.* Urbana: University of Illinois Press, 1987.

Miller, David. 'Shapes of Power: The Ontario Labour Relations Board, 1944–1950.' PhD thesis, York University, 1980.

Miller, J.R. *Shingwauk's Vision: A History of Residential Schools.* Toronto: University of Toronto Press, 1996.

Milloy, Jeremy. 'A Battle Royal: Service Work Activism and the 1961–62 Royal York Strike.' *Labour/Le Travail* 58 (2006): 13–40.

Milloy, John. *A National Crime: The Canadian Government and the Residential School System, 1879–1986.* Winnipeg: University of Manitoba Press, 1999.

Montague, John Tait. 'Trade Unionism in the Canadian Meat Packing Industry.' PhD thesis, University of Toronto, 1950.

Morris, Cerise. 'More than Simple Justice: The Royal Commission on the Status of Women in Canada.' PhD thesis, McGill University, 1982.

Morton, Desmond. *Working People: An Illustrated History of the Canadian Labour Movement.* Montreal: McGill-Queen's University Press, 1998.

Moya, Paula. 'Postmodernism, "Realism" and the Politics of Identity.' In *Reclaiming Identity: Realist Theory and the Predicament of Postmodernism*, ed. Paula Moya and Michael Hames-Garcia, 67–101. Berkeley: University of California Press, 2000.

Muszynski, Alicia. *Cheap Wage Labour: Race and Gender in the Fisheries of British Columbia.* Montreal: McGill-Queen's University Press, 1996.

– 'Race and Gender: Structural Determinants in the Formation of B.C.'s Salmon Cannery Labour Force.' In *Class, Gender and Region: Essays in Canadian Historical Sociology*, ed. Gregory Kealey, 3–20. St John's: Canadian Committee on Labour History, 1988.

Myers, Tamara, *Caught: Montreal's Modern Girls and the Law, 1869–1945.* Toronto: University of Toronto Press, 2006.

Nadeau, Mary Jo. 'Enterprizing Nationals: The Coalition for the Equality of Women of Canada and the Racial Politics of Managed Dissent in the Women's Movement.' Forthcoming.

Naison, Mark. *Communists in Harlem during the Depression.* Urbana: University of Illinois Press, 1983.

National Film Board. *Pins and Needles*. Dir. Anne Pearson, Roger Blais, 1954.

Newell, Dianne. *The Tangled Webs of History: Indians and the Law in Canada's Pacific Coast Fisheries*. Vancouver: UBC Press, 1997.

Ng, Roxanna, and Tania Das Gupta. 'Nation Builders?: The Captive Labour Force of Non-English Speaking Immigrant Women.' *Canadian Women's Studies* 3, no. 1 (1981): 83–5.

Nolan, Melanie. *Breadwinning: New Zealand Women and the State*. Canterbury: Canterbury University Press, 2006.

O'Neill, Colleen. 'Rethinking Modernity and the Discourse of Development in American Indian History, an Introduction.' In *Native Pathways: American Indian Culture and Economic Development in the Twentieth Century*, ed. Brian Hosmer and Colleen O'Neil, 1–26. Boulder: University of Colorado Press, 2004.

– *Working the Navajo Way: Labor and Culture in the Twentieth Century*. Lawrence: University of Kansas Press, 2005.

Owram, Doug. *Born at the Right Time: A History of the Baby-Boom Generation*. Toronto: University of Toronto Press, 1996.

Palmer, Bryan D. *Canada's 1960s: The Ironies of Identity in a Rebellious Era*. Toronto: University of Toronto Press, 2009.

– *Capitalism Comes to the Backcountry*. Toronto: Between the Lines, 1992.

– 'Historical Materialism and the Writing of Canadian History: A Dialectical View.' *Journal of the Canadian Historical Association* 17, no. 2: 33–60.

– 'Rethinking the Historiography of United States Communism.' *American Communist History* 2, no. 2 (2003): 139–73.

– 'Wildcat Workers in the 1960s: The Unruly Face of Class Struggle.' In *Labouring Canada: Class, Gender and Race in Canadian Working-Class History*, ed. Bryan Palmer and Joan Sangster, 373–93. Toronto: Oxford University Press, 2008.

– *Working Class Experience*. 2nd ed. Toronto: Oxford University Press, 1998.

Palmer, Earl, and Bruce Palmer. *Collective Agreement Arbitration in Canada*. 3rd ed. Toronto: Butterworths, 1991.

Paltiel, Frieda. 'State Initiatives: Impetus and Effects.' In *Women and the Canadian State*, ed. Caroline Andrew and Sandra Rogers, 27–51. Montreal: McGill-Queen's University Press, 1997.

Pâquet, Martin. *Tracer les marges de la Cité: Étranger, immigrant et état au Québec, 1627–1981*. Montreal: Boréal, 2005.

Parnaby, Andrew. 'The Best Men That Ever Worked the Lumber: Aboriginal Longshoremen on Burrard Inlet, 1863–1939.' *Canadian Historical Review* 87, no. 1 (March 2006): 53–78.

Parr, Joy. *A Diversity of Women, Ontario, 1945–1980*. Toronto: University of Toronto Press, 1995.

– *Domestic Goods: The Material, the Moral and the Economic in the Postwar Years.* Toronto: University of Toronto Press, 1999.

– *The Gender of Breadwinners: Women, Men, and Change in Two Industrial Towns, 1880–1950.* Toronto: University of Toronto Press, 1990.

Patrias, Carmela. 'Race, Employment Discrimination and State Complicity in Wartime Canada, 1939–45.' *Labour/Le Travail* 59 (Spring 2007): 9–42.

Peiss, Kathy. *Cheap Amusements: Working Women and Leisure in Turn-of-the-Century New York.* Philadelphia: Temple University Press, 1986.

– *Hope in a Jar: The Making of America's Beauty Culture.* New York: Metropolitan Books, 1998.

Pendakur, Ravi. *Immigrants in the Labour Force: Policy, Regulation, Impact.* Montreal: McGill-Queen's University Press, 2000.

Perleman, Michael. *The Invention of Capitalism: Classical Political Economy and the Secret History of Primitive Accumulation.* Durham: Duke University Press, 2000.

Peters, Evelyn. '"Urban" and "Aboriginal": An Impossible Contradiction?' In *City Lives and City Forms: Critical Research and Canadian Urbanism,* ed. J. Caulfield and L. Peake, 47–62. Toronto: University of Toronto Press, 1996.

Phillips, Paul, and Erin Phillips. *Women at Work: Inequality in the Canadian Labour Market.* Toronto: Lorimer, 1993.

Picchio, Antonella. *Social Reproduction: The Political Economy of the Labour Market.* Cambridge: Cambridge University Press, 1992.

Pickering, Michael. *History, Experience and Cultural Studies.* New York: St Martin's Press, 1997.

Pickles, Katie, and Myra Rutherdale. *Contact Zones: Aboriginal and Settler Women in Canada's Colonial Past.* Vancouver: UBC Press, 2006.

Pierson, Ruth Roach. 'Experience, Difference, Dominance, Voice in the Writing of Canadian Women's History.' In *Writing Women's History: International Perspectives,* ed. Karen Offen, Ruth Roach Pierson, and Jane Rendall. Bloomington: Indiana University Press, 1991.

– *They're Still Women After All: The Second World War and Canadian Womanhood.* Toronto: McClelland and Stewart, 1986.

Poelzer, Dolores and Irene Poelzer. *In Her Own Words: Northern Saskatchewan Métis Women Speak Out.* Saskatoon: One Sky Books, 1986.

Pollert, Anna. 'Gender and Class Revisited or the Poverty of Patriarchy.' *Sociology* 30, no.4 (1996): 639–59.

Porter, Ann. *Gendered States: Women, Unemployment Insurance, and the Political Economy of the Welfare State in Canada, 1945–97.* Toronto: University of Toronto Press, 2003.

Porter, Marilyn, 'She Was the Skipper of the Shore Crew: Notes on the History of the Sexual Division of Labour in Newfoundland.' *Labour/Le Travail* 15 (1985): 105–23.

Prentice, Alison, et al. *Canadian Women: A History.* Toronto: Harcourt, Brace Jovanovich, 1988.

Prentice, Susan. 'Workers, Mothers, Reds: Toronto's Postwar Daycare Fight.' *Studies in Political Economy* 30 (Autumn 1989): 115–41.

Produchny, Carolyn. 'Unfair Masters and Rascally Servants: Relations among Bourgeois, Clerks, and Voyageurs in the Montreal Fur Trade.' *Labour/Le Travail* 43 (Spring 1999): 43–70.

Quirling, David. *CCF Colonialism in Northern Saskatchewan.* Vancouver: UBC Press, 2004.

Raibmon, Paige. 'The Practices of Everyday Colonialism: Indigenous Women at Work in the Hop Fields of Puget Sound.' *Labor: Studies in Working Class History of the Americas* 3, no. 3 (Fall 2006): 23–56.

Ray, Arthur. *The Canadian Fur Trade in the Industrial Age.* Toronto: University of Toronto Press, 1990.

– *I Have Lived Here since the World Began.* Toronto: Key Porter Books, 1996.

– *Indians in the Fur Trade: Their Role as Hunters, Trappers, and Middlemen in the Lands Southwest of Hudson Bay, 1660–1870.* Toronto: University of Toronto Press, 1974.

Razack, Sherene. *Race, Space and the Law: Unmapping a White Settler Society.* Toronto: Between the Lines, 2002.

Reekie, Gail. *Temptations: Sex, Selling and the Department Store.* Sydney: Allen and Unwin, 1993.

Reid, Escott. *Radical Mandarin: The Memoirs of Escott Reid.* Toronto: University of Toronto Press, 1989.

Reiter, Ester. 'First Class Workers Don't Want Second Class Wages.' In *A Diversity of Women,* ed. Joy Parr, 168–99. Toronto: University of Toronto Press, 1995.

Reskin, Barbara. *Job Queues, Gender Queues: Explaining Women's Inroads into Male Occupations.* Philadelphia: Temple University Press, 1990.

Roberts, Wayne. *Honest Womanhood: Feminism, Femininity and Class Consciousness among Toronto Working Women, 1893–1914.* Toronto: New Hogtown Press, 1976.

Roediger, David. *Colored White.* Berkeley: University of California Press, 2002.

– *Working towards Whiteness: How America's Immigrants Became White.* New York: Basic Books, 2005.

Rosenberg, Emily. 'Foreign Affairs after World War II: Connecting Sexual and International Politics.' *Diplomatic History* 18, no.1 (1994): 59–70.

Rosswurm, Steve. 'The Catholic Church and Left-Led Unions: Labor, Priests, Labor Schools and the ACTU.' In *The CIO's Left-Led Unions*, ed. Steve Rosswurm, 119–37. New Brunswick, NJ: Rutgers University Press, 1992.

Rosswurm, Steve, ed. *The CIO's Left-led Unions*. New Brunswick, NJ: Rutgers University Press, 1992.

Rouillard, Jacques. *Histoire de la CSN, 1921–81*. Montreal: Boréal Express–CSN, 1981.

– *Histoire du syndicalisme Québécois*. Montreal: Éditions du Boréal, 1989.

– 'Major Changes in the Confédération des Travailleurs Catholiques du Canada, 1940–60.' In *Quebec since 1945: Selected Readings*, ed. Michael Behiels, 111–32. Toronto: Copp Clark, 1987.

– 'La Révolution tranquille: Rupture ou tournant?' *Journal of Canadian Studies* 32, no. 4 (1998): 23–51.

– *Le Syndicalisme Québécois: Deux siècles d'histoire*. Montreal: Boréal, 2004.

Ruiz, Vicki. *Cannery Women, Cannery Lives: Mexican Women, Unionization and the California Food Processing Industry, 1930–50*. Albuquerque: University of New Mexico Press, 1987.

Rutherford, Paul, *When Television Was Young: Primetime Canada, 1952–1967*. Toronto: University of Toronto Press, 1990.

Salutin, Rick. *Kent Rowley: The Organizer, A Canadian Union Life*. Toronto: James Lorimer, 1980.

Sangster, Joan. 'The Beaver as Ideology: Constructing Images of Inuit and Native Life in Post-World War II Canada.' *Anthropologica* 49 (2007): 191–209.

– 'The Bell Telephone Strike of 1907: Organizing Women Workers.' *Labour/ Le Travailleur* 3 (1978): 109–30.

– 'Canada's Cold War in Fur.' *Left History* 13, no. 2 (Spring 2009): 10–36.

– 'Doing Two Jobs: The Wage-Earning Mother, 1945–70.' In *A Diversity of Women: Ontario, 1945–80*, ed. Joy Parr, 98–134. Toronto: University of Toronto Press, 1995.

– *Dreams of Equality: Women on the Canadian Left, 1920s to 1950s*. Toronto: McClelland and Stewart, 1989.

– *Earning Respect: The Lives of Women in Small-town Ontario, 1920–60*. Toronto: University of Toronto Press, 1995.

– 'Making a Fur Coat: Women's Labour, the Body and Working Class History.' *International Review of Social History* 52 (2007): 241–70.

– 'The Making of a Socialist Feminist: The Early Career of Beatrice Brigden.' *Atlantis* 13, no. 1 (Fall 1987): 13–28.

– 'Remembering Texpack: Nationalism, Internationalism and Militancy in Canadian Unions in the 1970s.' *Studies in Political Economy* 78 (2006): 41–66.

– 'The Softball Solution: Female Workers, Male Managers and the Operation of Paternalism at Westclox, 1923–60.' *Labour/Le Travail* 32 (1993): 167–200.
– '"We No Longer Respect the Law": The Tilco Strike, Injunctions and the State.' *Labour/Le Travail* 53 (2004): 47–88.
Satzewich, Vic. *Racism and the Incorporation of Foreign Labour: Farm Labour Migration to Canada since 1945.* London: Routledge, 1991.
– 'Unfree Labour and Capitalism: The Incorporation of Polish War Veterans.' *Studies in Political Economy* 28 (Sept. 1989): 89–110.
Satzewich, Vic, and Terry Wotherspoon. *First Nations: Race, Class, and Gender Relations.* Regina: Canadian Plains Research Centre, 2000.
Schatz, Ronald. *The Electrical Workers: A History of Labor at GE and Westinghouse, 1923–60.* Urbana: University of Illinois Press, 1983.
Scheinberg, Ellen. 'The Tale of Tessie the Textile Worker: Female Textile Workers in Cornwall during World War II.' *Labour/Le Travail* 33 (Spring 1994): 153–86.
Scher, Len. *The Un-Canadians: True Stories of the Blacklist Era.* Toronto: Lester Publishing, 1992.
Schrecker, Ellen. *Many Are the Crimes: McCarthyism in America.* Boston: Little Brown, 1998.
Scott, Joan. 'The Evidence of Experience.' In *Questions of Evidence: Proof, Practice, and Persuasion across the Disciplines,* ed. James Chandler, Arnold Davidson, and Harry Harootunian, 363–87. Chicago: University of Chicago Press, 1994.
Sealey, D. Bruce. 'Fish Lake: A Case Study.' In *Indians without Tipis,* ed. D. Bruce Sealey and Verna Kirkness, 251–61. Manitoba: William Clare, 1973.
Shaw, David. 'Happy in Our Chains? Agency and Language in the Postmodern Age.' *History and Theory* 40 (2001): 1–9.
Sheffield, R. Scott. *The Red Man's on the Warpath: The Image of the 'Indian' and the Second World War.* Vancouver: UBC Press, 2004.
Shewell Hugh. *'Enough to Keep Them Alive': Indian Welfare in Canada 1873–1965.* Toronto: University of Toronto Press, 2004.
Shilling, Chris. *The Body in Culture, Technology and Society.* London: SAGE, 2005.
– *The Body and Social Theory.* London: SAGE, 1989.
Shohat, Ella, and Robert Stam, *Unthinking Eurocentrism: Multiculturalism and the Media.* London: Routledge, 1994.
Simonsen, Jane. *Making Home Work: Domesticity and Native American Assimilation in the American West 1860–1919.* Chapel Hill: University of North Carolina Press, 2006.
Skeggs, Beverly. 'The Toilet Paper: Femininity, Class and Mis-Recognition.' *Women's Studies International Forum* 24, no. 3–4 (2001): 295–307.

Smith, Dorothy. *Texts, Facts and Femininity: Exploring the Relations of Ruling.* London: Routledge, 1990.

Smith, Doug. *Cold Warrior: C.S. Jackson and the Electrical Workers.* St John's: Canadian Committee on Labour History, 1997.

Smith, Gavin. 'Writing for Real: Capitalist Constructions and Constructions of Capitalism.' *Critique of Anthropology* 11, no.3 (1991): 213–32.

Smith, Helen, and Pamela Wakewich. '"Beauty and the Helldivers": Representing Women's Work and Identities in a War Plant Newspaper.' *Labour/Le Travail* 44 (Fall 1999): 71–107.

Sobel, David, and Susan Meurer. *Working at Inglis: The Life and Death of a Canadian Factory.* Toronto: James Lorimer, 1994.

Solski, Mike, and John Smaller. *Mine Mill: The History of the International Union of Mine, Mill and Smelter Workers in Canada since 1895.* Ottawa: Mutual Press, 1984.

Soper, Kate. *Troubled Pleasures: Writing on Politics, Gender and Hedonism.* London: Verso, 1990.

Speers, Kimberly. 'The Royal Commission on the Status of Women: A Study of the Contradictions and Limitations of Liberal Feminism.' MA thesis, Queen's University, 1994.

Stahl, Dorinda. 'Marvelous Times: The Indian Homemaking Program and Its Effects on Extension Instructors at the Extension Division, University of Saskatchewan, 1967–72.' MA thesis, University of Saskatchewan, 2001.

Stanton, John. *Labour Arbitrations: Boon or Bust for Unions?* Vancouver: Butterworths, 1983.

Steedman, Mercedes *Angels of the Workplace: Women and the Construction of Gender Relations in the Canadian Clothing Industry, 1890–1940.* Toronto: Oxford University Press, 1997.

– 'The Promise: Communist Organizing in the Needle Trades: The Toronto Dressmakers Campaign, 1928–7.' *Labour/Le Travail* 34 (Autumn 1994): 37–74.

– 'The Red Petticoat Brigade: Mine Mill Women's Auxiliary and the Threat from Women, 1940–1970.' In *Whose National Security? Canadian State: Surveillance and the Creation of Enemies,* ed. D. Buse, G. Kinsman, and M. Steedman, 55–71. Toronto: Between the Lines, 2000.

Stepan-Norris, Judith, and Maurice Zeitlin. *Left Out: Reds and America's Industrial Unions.* Cambridge: Cambridge University Press, 2003.

Stephen, Jennifer. *Pick One Intelligent Girl: Employability, Domesticity, and the Gendering of Canada's Welfare State.* Toronto: University of Toronto Press, 2007.

Stone, Katherine Van Wezel. 'The Post-War Paradigm in American Labor Law.' *Yale Law Journal* 90, no. 7 (June 1981): 1509–80.

Storch, Randi. *Red Chicago: American Communism at Its Grassroots, 1928–35.*
   Urbana: University of Illinois Press, 2007.
Strange, Carolyn. *Toronto's Girl Problem: The Perils and Pleasures of the City,*
   1880–1930. Toronto: University of Toronto Press, 1995.
Strauss, Ernest. 'The Canadian Fur Manufacturing Industry.' MA thesis, McGill
   University, 1964.
Strong-Boag, Veronica. 'Home Dreams: Women and the Suburban Experiment
   in Canada, 1945–60.' *Canadian Historical Review* 72 (1991): 471–504.
Struthers, James. *The Limits of Affluence: Welfare in Ontario, 1920–1970.* Toronto:
   University of Toronto Press, 1994.
Stuchen, Philip. 'Canadian Newcomers: The Displaced Persons.' *Queen's*
   Quarterly, 1947: 197–30.
Sufrin, Eileen Tallman. *The Eaton Drive: The Campaign to Organize Canada's*
   Largest Department Store. Toronto: Fitzhenry and Whiteside, 1982.
Sugiman, Pamela. *Labour's Dilemma: The Gender Politics of Auto Workers in Canada,*
   1937–1979. Toronto: University of Toronto Press, 1994.
– 'Unionism and Feminism in the Canadian Auto Workers Union, 1961–1992.'
   In *Women Challenging Unions: Feminism, Democracy, Militancy,* ed. Linda Briskin
   and Patricia McDermott, 172–90. Toronto: University of Toronto Press, 1993.
Taylor, Jeff. 'The Struggle for Rights at Work: The United Electrical Workers,
   Contract Enforcement, and the Limits of Grievance Arbitration at Canadian
   General Electric and Westinghouse Canada, 1940s to 1960s.' Paper presented
   to the Canadian Historical Association, Saskatoon, 2007.
Teghtsoonian, Katherine. 'Work and/or Motherhood: The Ideological Con-
   struction of Women's Options in the Canadian Child Care Debate.' *Canadian*
   Journal of Women and the Law 8, no. 2 (1995): 411–39.
Thompson, E.P. 'The Politics of Theory.' In *People's History and Socialist Theory,*
   ed. Raphael Samuel, 396–408. London: Routledge, 1981.
– *The Poverty of Theory and Other Essays.* New York: Monthly Review Press, 1978.
– 'Time, Work-Discipline and Industrial Capitalism.' *Past and Present* 38 (1967):
   56–97.
Thorn, Brian. 'Visions of the New World Order: Women and Gender in Radical
   and Reactionary Movements in Post-World War II Canada.' PhD thesis, Trent
   University, 2006.
Tice, Karen. 'Queens of Academe: Campus Pageantry and Student Life.'
   Feminist Studies 31, no.2 (Summer 2005): 250–83.
Tillotson, Shirley. 'Human Rights Law as a Prism: Women's Organizations,
   Unions and Ontario's Female Employees Fair Remuneration Act, 1951.'
   Canadian Historical Review 72, no. 4 (1991): 532–57.

Timpson, Annis May. *Driven Apart: Women's Employment Equality and Child Care in Canadian Public Policy.* Vancouver: UBC Press, 2001.

– 'Royal Commissions as Sites of Resistance: Women's Challenges on Child Care in the Royal Commission on the Status of Women.' *International Journal of Canadian Studies* 20 (Fall 1999): 1–24.

Tomaskovic-Devey, Donald. *Gender and Racial Inequality at Work: The Sources and Consequences of Job Segregation.* Ithaca: ILR Press, 1992.

Tone, Andrea. *The Business of Benevolence: Industrial Paternalism in Progressive America.* Ithaca: Cornell University Press, 1997.

Tough, Frank. *As Their Natural Resources Fail: Native Peoples and the Economic History of Northern Manitoba, 1870–1930.* Vancouver: UBC Press, 1996.

– 'From the "Original Affluent Society" to the "Unjust Society": A Review Essay on Native Economic History in Canada.' *Journal of Aboriginal Economic Development* 4 (Fall 2005): 30–70.

Tremblay, Louis-Marie. *Le syndicalisme Québécois: Idéologies de la CSN et de la FTQ, 1940–70.* Montreal: Les Presses de l'Université de Montréal, 1972.

Trigger, Bruce. 'Early North American Responses to European Contact: Romantic versus Rationalistic Interpretations.' *Journal of American History* 77 (1991): 1195–1215.

Tulchinsky, Gerald. *Branching Out: The Transformation of the Canadian Jewish Community.* Toronto: Stoddart, 1998.

Turpel-Lafond, Mary Ellen. 'Patriarchy and Paternalism: The Legacy of the Canadian State for First Nations Women.' In *Women and the Canadian State,* ed. Caroline Andrew and Sandra Rogers, 64–78. Montreal: McGill-Queen's University Press, 1997.

Unknown. 'Pie in the Sky.' In *Women Unite,* 40–2. Toronto: Women's Educational Press, 1972.

Vadboncoeur, Pierre. 'Dupuis Frères, 1952.' In *En Grève: L'histoire de la CSN et des lutes menées par ses militants de 1937 à 1963,* ed. CSN, 99–128. Montreal: Les Éditions du Jour, 1963.

Van Kirk, Sylvia. *Many Tender Ties: Women in Fur Trade Society in Western Canada, 1670–1870.* Winnipeg: Watson and Dwyer, 1980.

Vickers, Jill. 'The Intellectual Origins of the Women's Movement in Canada.' In *Challenging Times: The Women's Movement in Canada and the United States,* ed. Constance Backhouse and David H. Flaherty, 39–60. Montreal: McGill-Queen's University Press, 1992.

Vickers, Jill, Pauline Rankin, and Christine Appelle. *Politics as if Women Mattered: A Political Analysis of the National Action Committee on the Status of Women.* Toronto: University of Toronto Press, 1993.

Vogel, Lise. *Woman Questions: Essays for a Materialist Feminism.* New York: Routledge, 1995.

Vosko, Leah. 'Gender Differentiation and the Standard/Non-Standard Employment Distinction: A Genealogy of Policy Intervention in Canada.' In *Patterns and Processes of Social Differentiation: The Construction of Gender, Age, 'Race/Ethnicity' and Locality,* ed. Danielle Juteau, 25–80. Toronto: University of Toronto Press, 2003.

– 'The Pasts (and Futures) of Feminist Political Economy in Canada: Reviving the Debate.' *Studies in Political Economy,* Summer 2002: 55–83.

– *Temporary Work: The Gendered Rise of a Precarious Employment Relationship.* Toronto: University of Toronto Press, 2000.

Walker, Mary. 'Humour and Gender Roles: The "Funny Fifties" – Feminism the Post World War II Suburbs.' In *The History of Women in the United States: Feminist Struggles for Equality,* ed. Nancy Cott. Munich: K.G. Sauer, 1994.

Warren, Wilson J. *Struggling with Iowa's Pride: Labor Relations, Unionism and Politics in the Rural Midwest since 1877.* Iowa City: University of Iowa Press, 2000.

Watkins, Mel. *Dene Nation: The Colony Within.* Toronto: University of Toronto Press, 1977.

Weigand, Kate. *Red Feminism: American Communism and the Making of Women's Liberation.* Baltimore: Johns Hopkins University Press, 2001.

– 'The Red Menace, the Feminine Mystique, and the Ohio Un-American Activities Commission: Gender and Anti-Communism in Ohio, 1951–1954,' *Journal of Women's History* 3, no 3 (Fall 1991): 70–94

Weiler, Paul. *Labour Arbitration and Industrial Change.* Study no. 6, Woods Task Force on Labour Relations. Ottawa: Privy Council, 1969.

– *Reconcilable Differences: New Directions in Canadian Labour Law.* Toronto: The Carswell Co. Ltd., 1980.

Weis, Jessica. *To Have and To Hold: Marriage, the Baby Boom and Social Change.* Chicago: University of Chicago Press, 2000.

Weisbord, Merrily. *The Strangest Dream: Canadian Communists, the Spy Trials and the Cold War.* Montreal: Véhicule Press, 1994.

Whitaker, Reginald. *Double Standard: The Secret History of Canadian Immigration.* Toronto: Lester and Orpen Dennys, 1987.

Whitaker, Reginald, and Steve Hewitt. *Canada and the Cold War.* Toronto: James Lorimer, 2003.

Whitaker, Reginald, and Gary Marcuse. *Cold War Canada: The Making of a National Insecurity State, 1945–57.* Toronto: University of Toronto Press, 1994.

White, Julie. *Sisters or Solidarity: Women and Unions in Canada.* Toronto: Thompson Educational Publishing, 1993.

White, Pamela. 'Restructuring the Domestic Sphere – Prairie Women on Reserves: Image, Ideology and State Policy, 1880–1930.' PhD dissertation, McGill University, 1987.

White, Richard. *The Roots of Dependency: Subsistence, Environment, and Social Change among the Choctaws, Pawnees, and Navajos.* Lincoln: University of Nebraska Press, 1983.

Wilkerson, William. 'Is There Something You Need to Tell Me? Coming Out and the Ambiguity of Experience.' In *Reclaiming Identity: Realist Theory and the Predicament of Postmodernism,* ed. Paula Moya and Michael Hames-Garcia, 251–78. Berkeley: University of California Press, 2000.

Wilkins, David. 'Modernization, Colonialism, Dependency: How Appropriate Are These Models for Providing an Explanation of North American Indian "Underdevelopment"?' *Ethnic and Racial Studies* 6, no. 3 (1992): 390–419.

Willett, Julie. *Permanent Waves: The Making of the American Beauty Shop.* New York: New York University Press, 2000.

Williams, Carol. 'Between Doorstep Barter Economy and Industrial Wages: Mobility and Adaptability of Coast Salish Female Laborers in Coastal British Columbia, 1885–1890.' In *Native Being? Being Native: Identity and Difference,* Proceedings of the Fifth Native American Symposium, ed. Mark Spencer and Lucretia Scoufos, 16–27. Weatherford: Southeastern Oklahoma State University, 2005.

Williams, Claire, with Bill Thorpe. *Beyond Industrial Sociology: The Work of Men and Women.* Sydney: Allen and Unwin, 1992.

Williams, Raymond. *Marxism and Literature.* London: Oxford University Press, 1977.

Willis, John. 'Cette manche au syndicat: La grève chez Dupuis Frères en 1952.' *Labour/Le Travail* 57 (2006): 43–92.

Witz, Anne, Chris Wsarhurst, and Dennis Nickson. 'The Labour of Aesthetics and the Aesthetics of Organization.' *Organization* 10, no. 1 (2003): 33–54.

Wolf, Naomi. *The Beauty Myth.* New York: Vintage Books, 1990.

Yano, Christine. *Crowning the Nice Girl: Gender, Ethnicity and Culture in Hawaii's Cherry Blossom Festival.* Honolulu: University of Hawai'i Press, 2006.

Young, Bruce. *At the Point of Discharge.* Toronto: The Canada Labour Views Co. Ltd., 1978.

Young, Shelagh. 'Feminism and the Power of Politics: Whose Gaze Is It Anyway?' In *The Female Gaze: Women as Viewers of Popular Culture,* ed. Lorraine Gamman and Margaret Marshment, 173–88. London: The Women's Press, 1988.

Zagorin, Perez. 'History, the Referent, and Narrative Reflections on Postmodernism.' *History and Theory* 38, no. 1 (Feb 1999): 1–24.

Zahavi, Gerald. 'Fighting Left-Wing Unionism: Views from the Opposition to the IFLWU in Fulton Co, NY.' In *The CIO's Left-Led Unions*, ed. Steve Rosswurm, 159–81. New Brunswick, NJ: Rutgers University Press, 1992.

– *Workers, Managers and Welfare Capitalism: The Shoeworkers and Tanners of Endicott Johnson, 1890–1950*. Urbana: University of Illinois Press, 1988.

Zay, Nicolas. 'Adaptation of the Immigrant.' *Canadian Welfare* 25, no. 7 (Feb. 1953): 25–9.

Zeiger, Robert. *The CIO, 1935–1955*. Chapel Hill: University of North Carolina Press, 1995.

Index